RMB Internationalization
& Product Innovation

www.royalcollins.com

RMB Internationalization & Product Innovation

GUANGPING ZHANG

Translated by
CHEN WEI

Books Beyond Boundaries

ROYAL COLLINS

RMB Internationalization & Product Innovation

Guangping Zhang
Translated by Chen Wei

First published in 2023 by Royal Collins Publishing Group Inc.
Groupe Publication Royal Collins Inc.
BKM Royalcollins Publishers Private Limited

Headquarters: 550-555 boul. René-Lévesque O Montréal (Québec) H2Z1B1 Canada
India office: 805 Hemkunt House, 8th Floor, Rajendra Place, New Delhi 110008

ISBN: 978-1-4878-1196-9

To find out more about our publications, please visit www.royalcollins.com.

Contents

Foreword .... *xiii*

CHAPTER ONE

Currency Internationalization 3

1.1   Major International Currencies in the International Foreign
        Exchange Market 3
1.2   Geographical Distribution of International Foreign Exchange Trade....... 6
1.3   Major International Currency Activity in Foreign Exchange
        Derivatives 12
1.4   Supporting the Continued Linked Settlement System 20
1.5   Major International Currencies in the Interest Rate Derivatives
        Market 22
1.6   Investigating the Factors for Measuring Currency
        Internationalization 28
1.7   Differentiating Daily Turnover and Nominal Turnover in Foreign
        Exchange 29
1.8   Measurement and Comparison of Major Currency
        Internationalization in 2007 33
1.9   Changes in the Internationalization of Major Currencies since the
        Global Financial Crisis... 37

1.10   Internationalization of RMB before and after the Global Financial
       Crisis..46
1.11   Measurement of Currency Internationalization in a Relative Sense........47
1.12   Alternative Method for Measuring Currency Internalization..................52
1.13   Conclusion...53
       Bibliography 56

CHAPTER TWO

PCT Patent Distribution in Main Countries and Regions............ 57

2.1   Introduction to the PCT Patent 57
2.2   Distribution of PCT Patent Applications in Main Countries and
       Regions...58
2.3   The Proportion of PCT Patent Applications in Total Patent
       Applications..60
2.4   PCT Patents Granted by Five Offices 60

CHAPTER THREE

The Export of Intellectual Property Royalties for Major Currency Issuers... 63

3.1   Top Ten Net Exporters for IP Royalties 63
3.2   Monopolistic Power to Control World IPs...67
3.3   Net Exports of Developing Countries...67
3.4   Average Exports and Net Exports for IP Royalties of Major Blocs
       and Their Implications 67

CHAPTER FOUR

Technological Autonomy and Measures of Technology Internationalization 71

4.1   Definition and Measurement of Technological Autonomy......................72
4.2   Correlation between Technological Autonomy of Major Countries
       and Regions 75
4.3   Correlation between the US and Major East Asian Economies in
       Technological Autonomy...78
4.4   Technological Autonomy Correlation between the US and the
       Asian Tigers..82

4.5   Average Annual Change of Technological Autonomy of Major
       Economies and Their Implications...83
4.6   Correlation of Technological Autonomy among Mainland China,
       Hong Kong, and Taiwan 87
4.7   Technological Autonomy of Japan 90
4.8   Analysis of Technological Autonomy in China and Related Issues.........93
4.9   Problems Related to Patent Application and Authorization in China.....94
4.10   An Appropriate Quality Measure of Family Patents.................................94
4.11   Technology Internationalization as Weighted Patent
       Internationalization...97
4.12   Conclusion..99
       Bibliography 101
       Appendix..101

CHAPTER FIVE

**Development and Current Situation of Offshore
RMB Centers** **103**

5.1   Global Distribution of Offshore RMB Centers with Clearing
       Agreements...103
5.2   The Leading Role of the Hong Kong RMB Center...................................106
5.3   Distribution and Ranking of RMB Deposits and Payments among
       Offshore RMB Centers..111
5.4   Distribution of the RQFII Quota and Authorized Quotas among
       Offshore RMB Centers..112
5.5   RMB Distribution at the Top Five Foreign Exchange Trading
       Centers 119
5.6   The Relationship between Offshore RMB Center Rankings and the
       Distribution of Approved Quotas..121
5.7   Key Problems in Offshore RMB Market Development 124
5.8   The Promotion of RMB Internationalization through Cross-Border
       Payments...125
5.9   Promoting the Cross-Border Payment System of China UnionPay 127
5.10   Conclusion..128
       Bibliography 129

CHAPTER SIX

Development of the Offshore RMB Market 131

6.1   The Development of the Offshore RMB Market in London 131
6.2   The Development of the Offshore RMB Market in Singapore.............. 133
6.3   The Development of Other RMB Centers in the Asia-Pacific Area....... 134
6.4   The Development of RMB Centers in Europe 140
6.5   The Development of RMB Centers in the US 144

CHAPTER SEVEN

Overseas Assets and Bank Internationalization of Major Currency Issuers 147

7.1   Distribution of Cross-Border Assets and Liabilities 147
7.2   Distribution of Cross-Border Banking Assets and Liabilities................ 152
7.3   Currency Distribution of All-Sector Claims, Liabilities, and Net
       Claims.. 156
7.4   Distribution of Cross-Border Assets, Liabilities, and Net Assets of
       Major Currency Issuers.. 158
7.5   Chinese and Japanese Cross-Border and Net Assets 161
7.6   Internationalization of the World's Major Banks 162
7.7   Bank Internationalization in China in Recent Years.............................. 166
7.8   Recent Internationalization of Major Chinese Banks........................... 166
7.9   Overseas Distribution and Development at the Bank of China 167
7.10   Main Challenges in the "Go Global" Strategy....................................... 171
7.11   Prospects for Internationalization in Chinese Banking 172
7.12   Conclusion... 172
       Bibliography 173

CHAPTER EIGHT

The Recent Development RMB Internationalization 175

8.1   Brief Review of RMB Internationalization 175
8.2   Basic Conditions of RMB Usage in the Offshore Market...................... 176
8.3   Offshore RMB Transactions 179
8.4   Direct Trade between RMB and Other Currencies................................ 181
8.5   Overview of Domestic RMB Spot Foreign Exchange Turnover............ 181
8.6   Development of RMB-Denominated Funds and Other Products 182
8.7   Liberalization of RMB Capital Items and Its Future Development........ 185

8.8   RMB Currency Swaps Signed 190
8.9   Average Daily Turnover of the RMB Foreign Exchange Market 193
8.10   Ranking Major World Currencies by Internationalization
       2020–2021 197
8.11   Global Rankings of Major World Currencies since 2019 200
8.12   Ranking Major World Currencies in 2020 and 2021 202
8.13   Conclusion 205

CHAPTER NINE

Relationship between National Governance and Currency Internationalization 207

9.1   Global Governance Index by the World Bank 208
9.2   What Is "National Governance"? 208
9.3   Comparison of National Governance in Major Countries or
       Regions 209
9.4   Changes and Comparisons of Key Governance Indicators in Major
       Economies 214
9.5   National Governance, GDP, and GDP per Capita 219
9.6   The Relationship between Currency Internationalization and
       Governance 220
9.7   National Governance and Other Relevant Indicators 221
9.8   National Governance Impact 221
9.9   Global Distribution of National Governance Impact 225
9.10   Promoting RMB Internationalization by Modernizing the National
       Governance System and Governance Capacity 227
9.11   Importance and Urgency of Establishing China's National
       Governance Monitoring and Evaluation System 228
9.12   Create the World Miracle of National Governance in the New Era 228
9.13   RMB Internationalization Level Compatible with National
       Governance Situation 229
9.14   Conclusion 230

CHAPTER TEN

The Role of AIIB in RMB Internationalization 231

10.1   Historical Context of the AIIB and Its Member States 231
10.2   Introduction and Distribution of AIIB's Signatories and
       Prospective Founding Members 232

10.3   Objectives, Capital Structure, and International Cooperation 235

10.4   Achievements 236

10.5   Population and Economy amongst the BRICS 236

10.6   Development and Cooperation amongst the BRICS 238

10.7   The AIIB Needs New Momentum 240

10.8   Promoting the Modernization of National Governance to the
        Successful Operation of the AIIB and the New Development Bank 241

10.9   Conclusion 242

CHAPTER ELEVEN

The Mutual Relationship between the B&R Initiative and RMB Internationalization 245

11.1   Belt and Road (B&R) Initiative 246

11.2   Distribution of Population and Economic Scale in B&R Countries 246

11.3   International Influence and Significance of the B&R Initiative 250

11.4   International Recognition of the B&R Initiative 252

11.5   Broad Cooperation Is Necessary 253

11.6   Improving Economic and Trade Cooperation along the B&R 255

11.7   The Importance of China-EU Cooperation for the B&R Initiative 255

11.8   Interaction between the B&R Initiative and RMB
        Internationalization 257

11.9   Obstacles to RMB along the B&R 258

11.10 Conclusion 259

CHAPTER TWELVE

The Role of Capital Markets in Technological Innovation 261

12.1   Market Value Distribution of Global Stock Markets 262

12.2   Distribution of Top 2,500 Companies in Research and
        Development 264

12.3   Industry Distribution and Enlightenment of R&D Investment in
        Companies Lacking Profit Data and Companies Enduring Loss 265

12.4   Research and Judgment on the Trend of Changes in the Total R&D
        Investment of Enterprises with the Most R&D in Major Countries
        and Regions 275

12.5   Research and Judgment on the Number of Companies with the
       Largest R&D of Major Currency Issuers and the Trend of Total
       R&D Investment 277
12.6   The Dependence of Major International Currency Issuers on the
       US in Terms of Technology 282
12.7   The Acceleration of Global Profitable Companies Has Led to an
       Increase in the Market Value of the Science and Technology Sector
       and the Subsequent Enlightenment of China 283
12.8   Conclusion 288

CHAPTER THIRTEEN

**The Relationship between Sci-Tech Internationalization and
Currency Internationalization 291**

13.1   Sci-Tech Internationalization of Major Currency Issuers 291
13.2   Correlation Coefficients between Sci-Tech and Currency
       Internationalization 295
13.3   Problematic Correlation Coefficients 296
13.4   Reassessing the Coefficient with Actual Foreign Exchange Turnover ... 298
13.5   The Best Measure of Currency Internationalization 302
13.6   Function of Foreign Exchange Derivatives Trading Implied in the
       Best Measure of Currency Internationalization 306
13.7   Overestimations and Underestimations 306
13.8   Conclusion 308

CHAPTER FOURTEEN

**Relationship between Monetary Autonomy and Currency
Internationalization, Technological Autonomy and
Technology Internationalization 309**

14.1   Interest Rate Determination 310
14.2   Concept of Currency Originality Capacity 312
14.3   Definition and Measurement of Currency Originality Capacity 312
14.4   Currency Originality with Better Currency Internationalization
       Measures 316
14.5   The Relationship between Currency Originality Capacity and Sci-
       Tech Originality Capacity 318

14.6   Mutual Influence between Currency Originality Capacity and Sci-
        Tech Originality Capacity 321

14.7   Relationship between Currency Originality Capacity and Currency
        Internationalization 327

14.8   Mutual Influence between Sci-Tech Originality Capacity and
        Technology Internationalization 329

14.9   Summary of Mutual Influence of Sci-Tech USD Currency
        Originality Capacity and Sci-Tech & Currency Internationalization 331

14.10   Conclusion 333

        Bibliography 334

CHAPTER FIFTEEN

The Development and Future of RMB Internationalization 335

15.1   Anticipation of Future Technological Autonomy for Major
        Currency Issuers 335

15.2   New Method to Forecast Currency Internationalization 339

15.3   Anticipation of Future Changes 342

15.4   Historical Review of Major Global Currency Shifts 344

15.5   The Future Development of the Domestic Foreign Exchange
        Market 348

15.6   Monitoring Cross-Border Capital Flows 349

15.7   IMF Monitoring of Cross-Border Capital Flows 350

15.8   The Contribution of Technology and Currency in the Global
        Surplus IP Royalties 352

15.9   Conclusion 356

        Bibliography 357

CHAPTER SIXTEEN

Future Studies 359

16.1   Introduction to Exotic Options 359

16.2   Using Exotic Options to Study Science and Technology 360

16.3   Other Applications 360

        Bibliography 360

Foreword

OVER THE PAST COUPLE OF DECADES, science and technology have, in an exponential manner, penetrated every aspect of social, business, and political arenas. We are seeing many new game-changing applications, ranging from process automation and virtualization in a high-level connected and distributed infrastructure to artificial intelligence and bio-science based health care solutions. This remarkable progress on all fronts of science and technology has spurred economic development at unprecedented levels, and now it is advancing even faster. Analytics is creating exciting new possibilities across businesses. Despite our growing capabilities to collect, analyze, and curate data, only a small fraction is collected, and an even smaller fraction is analyzed to drive meaningful outcomes. Yet, even with the limited ability to collect and analyze, more data has been collected over the past couple of years than was collected over the entire history of the world before that. We can surely anticipate further growth, considering the number of connected devices worldwide as sources for data collection has already exceeded the whole world population five times over. Given where we were 5–10 years ago and where we are today, we can, as far as our imagination can take us, think of how deeply science and technology will impact our social, economic, and geopolitical lives. Over the next decade, we can anticipate more progress than that which has occurred during the past 100 years.

Amongst a variety of indicators to substantiate the impact of technology, Gross Domestic Product (GDP) can present a clear picture at the global level. Changes in GDP per capita affected by technological investment observed over the past century, including the periods in which the First, Second, Third, and Fourth Industrial Revolutions took place, show very clear evidence: crucially, it indicates that the Fourth Industrial Revolution accelerated GDP growth ten times through technological advancements. At least 60% of the world population is predicted to be living in mostly urban settings by 2030; around 600 cities from around the world will generate 60% of global GDP growth in the next ten years.

To further substantiate the economic impact and growth potential of science and technology-based markets, the total market capitalization of the top five US technology companies recently surpassed 10 trillion dollars – about half of US GDP for 2020. Furthermore, should we extrapolate this to all US technology companies, then total market capitalization would certainly be much greater than half of the US GDP, or probably even than Chinese GDP – the world's second-largest economy – last year.

In China, one of the world's largest digital economies, e-commerce grew to USD 1.7 trillion in 2020, comprising 30% of all retail sales. This can certainly be attributed to over 1 billion internet users in China who are, in many aspects, leading the adaptation and usage of technology. Further examples can be found in diverse fields such as mobility, finance, and healthcare technology.

Over 65% of Fortune 500 company CEOs see the rapid pace of change caused by science and technology as a key challenge. Naturally, as an opportunity for business growth, it is simply not slowing down. On the contrary, we can only imagine how fast it will continue advancing in the coming years.

The impact of science and technology has been tremendous, yet we cannot conduct professional or academic studies on this without measuring or quantifying science and technology objectively by using pertinent international data. In this new version of his book, Dr. Zhang has masterfully connected the role of science and technology to the elements of global finance and investment by defining and quantifying science and technology originality capability (OC) and internationalization. He does this with the use of existing data from patents and charging for the use of intellectual property released by international organizations. Using these new quantitative measures of science and technology, its impact on trade and currency internationalization is analyzed statistically in the book.

As currency internationalization, investment, finance, and related topics have become integral to all aspects of international trade and finance, the need for scientific data-based models has become critical, especially for decision-makers in investment and trade. In this version, Dr. Zhang provides long-awaited and robust methodologies to connect various parameters in everyday trade and financial decision-making. Given that science and technology have been the backbone of international trade, economy, capital markets, international finance, foreign exchange, currency internationalization, and essentially everything in our lives, the book is rich with historical data. This has led to sophisticated models and quantitative comparative analyses of critical parameters such as originality capability and intellectual property sufficiency to GDP, etc. The contribution of science and technology to currency internationalization, currency contribution to exchange, and IP are useful for decision-makers and practitioners. As any future analysis will depend heavily on the quantifiable capability of models, Dr. Zhang's work satisfactorily defines the empirical relationship between this capability and the internationalization of science and technology.

While, naturally, the applicability range of the models is limited to the availability of current data, this book provides a fundamental base that can be further built upon. I find it to be a valuable resource in both academic and professional domains as it clearly and unambiguously connects technology and international trade parameters to other related areas.

It is also noteworthy to bring attention to Dr. Zhang's recent work using the pricing mechanism of exotic options – particularly options to exchange one asset for another, which compliments both his earlier book, *Exotic Options: A Guide to Second-Generation Options,* as well as this one. We look forward to readers embarking on this book and to the new mathematical results of his recent studies.

DR. FERIDUN HAMDULLAPHUR

Chairman of the Board of Directors, AMTD International

Professor and former President, University of Waterloo, Ontario, Canada

December 10, 2021

RMB Internationalization
& Product Innovation

CHAPTER ONE

Currency Internationalization

THE FUNCTION OF A CURRENCY IN foreign exchange and capital markets is a key performance indicator and measurement of its internationalization. It is necessary to have a basic understanding of how market liquidity and internationalization of major currencies are currently measured in order to effectively analyze the current status of Chinese renminbi (RMB) internationalization and make predictions.

1.1 Major International Currencies in the International Foreign Exchange Market

In this section, we will introduce the liquidity of the international foreign exchange market, the trading of major currency pairs, foreign exchange transactions between major countries, and other factors to discuss the status of international currencies in the market.

Foreign exchange markets are mostly over-the-counter (OTC) traded interbank markets between their clients and among banks; therefore, it is difficult to obtain accurate annual data on the turnover volume of securities in an organized worldwide exchange. The most authoritative data on global foreign exchange transactions comes from the Bank for International Settlements (BIS), which releases data every three years on the average daily turnover of currencies in April of that year.

Table 1-1 gives the proportions of average daily turnover of major currencies in international foreign exchange trading from 1998 to 2019. As each trade involves a pair of currencies, the proportion of all currency transactions adds up to 200%. Based on this data, we can calculate the proportions of the major international currencies – US dollar (USD), Euro (EUR), British pound (GBP), and Japanese yen (JPY) – in the international foreign exchange market. The results show that in 1998, transactions of the top four currencies took up 59.8% of global foreign exchange transactions (the sum of the four currencies' proportions, as shown in Table 1-1, divided by two), and the proportion reached as high as 81.2% and 81.4% in 2001 and 2004, respectively; it fell to around 77.6% from 2007 to 2013 and further dropped to 75.1% in 2019. The data reflects the monopolistic position of these four currencies in the international foreign exchange market.

Table 1-1 Proportion of Average Daily Turnover of Major Currencies in the International Foreign Exchange Market (1998–2019)

Unit: %

Currency	1998	2001	2004	2007	2010	2013	2016	2019
USD	86.8	89.9	88.0	85.6	84.9	87.0	87.6	88.3
EUR	…	37.9	37.4	37.0	39.0	33.4	31.4	32.3
JPY	21.7	23.5	20.8	17.2	19.0	23.0	21.6	16.8
GBP	11.0	13.0	16.5	14.9	12.9	11.8	12.8	12.8
AUD	3.0	4.3	6.0	6.6	7.6	8.6	6.9	6.8
CAD	3.5	4.5	4.2	4.3	5.3	4.6	5.1	5.0
CHF	7.1	6.0	6.0	6.8	6.3	5.2	4.8	5.0
RMB	0.0	0.0	0.1	0.5	0.9	2.2	4.0	4.3
HKD	1.0	2.2	1.8	2.7	2.4	1.4	1.7	3.5
NZD	0.2	0.6	1.1	1.9	1.6	2.0	2.1	2.1
SEK	0.3	2.5	2.2	2.7	2.2	1.8	2.2	2.0
KRW	0.2	0.8	1.1	1.2	1.5	1.2	1.7	2.0
SGD	1.1	1.1	0.9	1.2	1.4	1.4	1.8	1.8

(Continued)

Currency	1998	2001	2004	2007	2010	2013	2016	2019
NOK	0.2	1.5	1.4	2.1	1.3	1.4	1.7	1.8
MXN	0.5	0.8	1.1	1.3	1.3	2.5	1.9	1.7
INR	0.1	0.2	0.3	0.7	0.9	1.0	1.1	1.7
RUB	0.3	0.3	0.6	0.7	0.9	1.6	1.1	1.1
ZAR	0.4	0.9	0.7	0.9	0.7	1.1	1.0	1.1
TRY	...	0.0	0.1	0.2	0.7	1.3	1.4	1.1
BRL	0.2	0.5	0.3	0.4	0.7	1.1	1.0	1.1
TWD	0.1	0.3	0.4	0.4	0.5	0.5	0.6	0.9
DKK	0.3	1.2	0.9	0.8	0.6	0.8	0.8	0.6
PLN	0.1	0.5	0.4	0.8	0.8	0.7	0.7	0.6
THB	0.1	0.2	0.2	0.2	0.2	0.3	0.4	0.5
IDR	0.3	0.2	0.2	0.2	0.2	0.4	0.3	0.4
Others	...	7.1	7.3	8.7	6.3	3.6	4.2	2.2
RMB*	0.2	0.6	0.0	0.0	0.7	1.3	4.0	5.2

Data source: Updated data about average daily turnovers in April 2019 released by the Bank for International Settlements in December 2019 and data from previous years; RMB* refers to the proportion of RMB transactions in the international foreign exchange market; please refer to Section 11.10 for details.

As shown in Table 1-1, RMB trade only accounted for 0.5% of the total in 2007, which was disproportionate to the fact that China accounted for 6.2% of global GDP in the same year.

In 2010, the proportion of RMB trade was 0.9%, ranking 16th in the world, while China's GDP made up 9.2% of the global total, which ranked 2nd in the world.

The proportion of RMB trade in the international foreign exchange market increased to 2.2% in 2013, ranking 9th in the world, while at the same time, China's GDP was 12.7% of the global total.

RMB trade increased further to 4.0% in 2016 – 10% less than China's proportion of global GDP of 15.2%.

In 2019, RMB trade further increased to 4.3%, though it still lags far behind its GDP contribution.

By analyzing data from the Bank of International Settlements (BIS), we found that the RMB turnovers in some regions may have significant real-world differences from the statistics compiled in London and other financial centers. After some reasonable adjustments, as shown in detail in Chapter 11, the actual proportion of RMB trade in the international foreign exchange market should be 5.1% in 2019. Even so, this number is still 10% lower than China's proportion of global GDP. Having taken the BIS data into consideration, the international ranking of RMB trade rose from 16th to 8th between 2010 and 2019. However, according to the revised data in Chapter 11, the proportion of RMB trade to the global total has already surpassed that of CHF and CAD, which makes RMB the sixth most traded currency by volume.

The daily turnovers of major currency pairs, to a certain degree, reflect the internationalism of involved currencies. Table 1-2 provides the turnovers and proportions of foreign exchange trade of major currency pairs from 2001 to 2019. It shows that trade between the USD and the other three major currencies – EUR, JPY, and GBP – dominates international foreign exchange markets. In 2001 and 2004, total trade of these three currency pairs accounted for 60.6% and 58.4% of the global trade, respectively; this number fell from 51.6% to 46.8% between 2007 and 2016, showing that the proportion of trade between USD and the other three major currencies fell to below 50% for the first time. Encouragingly, Table 1-2 shows that the RMB-USD currency pair became the sixth largest pair both in the US and the world in 2016. In particular, the RMB-EUR currency pair has become the 13th largest for the EUR, and its daily turnover average reached USD 2.4 billion in 2019.

1.2 Geographical Distribution of International Foreign Exchange Trade

The geographical distribution of foreign exchange trade among countries and regions can provide important information on the global foreign exchange market. Table 1-3 identifies 36 countries and regions most actively engaged in foreign exchange trade and their share of this for the 1998–2019 period.

Table 1-2 Average Daily Turnover and Proportion of Major Currency Pairs (2001–2019)

Unit: USD billion, %

Year	2001		2004		2007		2010		2013		2016		2019	
Currency Pair	Amount	Share	Amount	Share	Amount	Share	Amount	Share	Amount	Share	Amount	Share	Amount	Share
USD/EUR	372	30	541	28	892	26.8	1099	27.7	1292	24.1	1172	23.1	1583.6	24.0
USD/JPY	250	20.2	328	17	438	13.2	567	14.3	980	18.3	901	17.8	870.7	13.2
USD/GBP	129	10.4	259	13.4	384	11.6	360	9.1	473	8.8	470	9.3	630.4	9.6
USD/AUD	51	4.1	107	5.5	185	5.6	248	6.3	364	6.8	262	5.2	357.9	5.4
USD/CAD	54	4.3	77	4	126	3.8	182	4.6	200	3.7	218	4.3	287.3	4.4
USD/RMB	...	...	...	...	...	...	31	0.8	113	2.1	192	3.8	269.4	4.1
USD/CHF	59	4.8	83	4.3	151	4.5	166	4.2	184	3.4	180	3.6	228.1	3.5
USD/MXN	...	...	...	...	...	...	...	...	128	2.4	90	1.8	219.4	3.3
USD/SGD	...	...	...	...	...	...	...	...	65	1.2	81	1.6	125.3	1.9
USD/NZD	...	...	...	...	...	...	...	...	82	1.5	78	1.5	110.1	1.7
USD/KRW	...	...	...	...	...	...	58	1.5	60	1.1	78	1.5	109.7	1.7
USD/HKD	...	...	...	...	...	...	85	2.1	69	1.3	77	1.5	106.6	1.6
USD/SEK	...	...	...	...	570	1.7	45	1.1	55	1	66	1.3	104.6	1.6
USD/TRY	...	...	...	...	...	...	...	...	63	1.2	64	1.3	86.2	1.3
USD/INR	...	...	...	...	...	...	36	0.9	50	0.9	56	1.1	73.3	1.1

(Continued)

Year	2001		2004		2007		2010		2013		2016		2019	
Currency Pair	Amount	Share	Amount	Share	Amount	Share	Amount	Share	Amount	Share	Amount	Share	Amount	Share
USD/RUB	...		...		...		...		79	1.5	53	1.1	66	1.0
USD/NOK	...		...		...		...		49	0.9	48	0.9	62.8	1.0
USD/BRL	...		...		...		25	0.6	48	0.9	45	0.9	62.3	0.9
USD/ZAR	...		...		...		24	0.6	51	1	40	0.8	62.3	0.9
USD/TWD	...		...		...		...		22	0.4	31	0.6	58.9	0.9
USD/PLN	...		...		...		...		22	0.4	19	0.4	24.7	0.4
USD/Other Currencies	199	16	307	15.9	612	18.4	446	11.2	214	4	215	4.2	319.7	4.9
EUR/GBP	27	2.1	47	2.4	69	2.1	109	2.7	102	1.9	100	2	130.7	2.0
EUR/JPY	36	2.9	61	3.2	86	2.6	111	2.8	148	2.8	79	1.6	113.5	1.7
EUR/CHF	13	1.1	30	1.6	62	1.9	71	1.8	71	1.3	44	0.9	72.7	1.1
EUR/SEK	...		...		24	0.7	35	0.9	28	0.5	36	0.7	36.2	0.5
EUR/NOK	...		...		...		...		20	0.4	28	0.6	33.5	0.5
EUR/AUD	1	0.1	4	0.2	9	0.3	12	0.3	21	0.4	16	0.3	18.4	0.3
EUR/CAD	1	0.1	2	0.1	7	0.2	14	0.3	15	0.3	14	0.3	15.1	0.2
EUR/PLN	...		...		...		...		14	0.3	13	0.3	13.2	0.2
EUR/DKK	...		...		...		...		13	0.2	13	0.2	10.7	0.2

(Continued)

Year	2001		2004		2007		2010		2013		2016		2019	
Currency Pair	Amount	Share	Amount	Share	Amount	Share	Amount	Share	Amount	Share	Amount	Share	Amount	Share
EUR/HUF	...	...	...	...	...	...	...	...	10	0.2	5	0.1	10.2	0.2
EUR/TRY	...	...	...	...	...	...	...	...	6	0.1	4	0.1	3.9	0.1
EUR/RMB	...	...	...	...	...	...	...	...	1	0	2	0	2.4	0.0
EUR/other currencies	20	1.6	38	1.9	83	2.5	102	2.6	51	0.9	65	1.3	84.6	1.3
JPY/AUD	...	...	...	...	...	...	24	0.6	46	0.9	31	0.6	35	0.5
JPY/CAD	...	...	...	...	...	...	...	...	6	0.1	7	0.1	7.2	0.1
JPY/NZD	...	...	...	...	...	...	4	0.1	5	0.1	5	0.1	6.3	0.1
JPY/TRY	...	...	...	...	...	...	...	...	1	0	3	0.1	5.7	0.1
JPY/ZAR	...	...	...	...	...	...	...	...	4	0.1	3	0.1	4.8	0.1
JPY/BRL	...	...	...	...	...	...	...	...	3	0.1	1	0	1.6	0.0
JPY/Other Currencies	15	1.2	28	1.4	66	2	50	1.3	88	1.6	45	0.9	62.9	1.0
Other Currency Pairs	13	1.1	22	1.1	74	2.2	70	1.8	44	0.8	116	2.3	102.3	1.6
All Currency Pairs	1239	100	1934	100	3324	100	3971	100	5357	100	5067	100	6590.4	100.0

Data source: Compiled based on the revised data of the average daily turnover in April 2019 and the data from previous years. Released by the Bank for International Settlements in December 2019.

Table 1-3   Countries and Regions in Global Foreign Exchange Trade (1998–2019)

Unit: %

Country/Region	1998	2001	2004	2007	2010	2013	2016	2019	Change from 2016 to 2019
UK	32.64	31.78	32.03	34.65	36.74	40.77	36.94	43.12	6.18
US	18.26	15.99	19.12	17.41	17.92	18.89	19.53	16.52	−3.01
Singapore	6.90	6.08	5.12	5.65	5.27	5.73	7.94	7.64	−0.30
Hong Kong, China	3.81	4.01	4.06	4.23	4.71	4.11	6.70	7.62	0.92
Eurozone	16.13	14.25	12.94	11.33	9.97	9.00	8.53	6.51	−2.02
Japan	6.97	8.96	7.95	5.84	6.19	5.60	6.13	4.53	−1.60
Switzerland	4.36	4.48	3.27	5.92	4.94	3.24	2.40	3.32	0.92
France	3.68	2.91	2.55	2.96	3.01	2.84	2.77	2.01	−0.76
China	0.01	0.00	0.02	0.22	0.39	0.66	1.12	1.64	0.52
Germany	4.74	5.36	4.62	2.37	2.15	1.66	1.79	1.50	−0.29
Australia	2.30	3.17	4.11	4.12	3.81	2.72	1.86	1.44	−0.42
Canada	1.81	2.60	2.27	1.50	1.23	0.97	1.31	1.32	0.01
Netherlands	2.04	1.79	2.00	0.58	0.36	1.68	1.31	0.77	−0.54
Denmark	1.34	1.40	1.61	2.06	2.39	1.76	1.55	0.76	−0.79
Luxembourg	1.08	0.77	0.56	1.02	0.66	0.77	0.57	0.69	0.12
South Korea	0.17	0.58	0.79	0.82	0.87	0.71	0.73	0.67	−0.06
Russia	0.33	0.56	1.14	1.17	0.83	0.91	0.69	0.56	−0.13
Saudi Arabia	0.11	0.12	0.08	0.10	0.15	0.10	0.12	0.55	0.43
Spain	0.95	0.48	0.53	0.40	0.58	0.64	0.50	0.49	−0.01
India	0.12	0.20	0.26	0.90	0.54	0.47	0.53	0.48	−0.05
Sweden	0.77	1.46	1.22	1.03	0.89	0.65	0.64	0.45	−0.19
Belgium	1.30	0.61	0.80	1.17	0.64	0.32	0.35	0.43	0.08
Norway	0.42	0.76	0.55	0.75	0.44	0.32	0.62	0.36	−0.26
Taiwan, China	0.23	0.28	0.36	0.36	0.36	0.39	0.41	0.36	−0.05

(Continued)

Country/ Region	1998	2001	2004	2007	2010	2013	2016	2019	Change from 2016 to 2019
South Africa	0.43	0.58	0.38	0.33	0.28	0.31	0.32	0.25	−0.07
Mexico	0.41	0.50	0.59	0.36	0.34	0.48	0.31	0.24	−0.07
Turkey	0.00	0.06	0.13	0.10	0.33	0.41	0.34	0.23	−0.11
Brazil	0.24	0.32	0.15	0.13	0.28	0.26	0.30	0.23	−0.07
Italy	1.36	1.03	0.90	0.88	0.57	0.35	0.27	0.21	−0.06
Austria	0.56	0.49	0.56	0.44	0.39	0.23	0.29	0.19	−0.10
Thailand	0.15	0.11	0.12	0.15	0.15	0.19	0.16	0.17	0.01
Malaysia	0.05	0.08	0.06	0.08	0.14	0.17	0.13	0.12	−0.01
New Zealand	0.33	0.24	0.27	0.30	0.17	0.18	0.15	0.11	−0.04
Poland	0.13	0.30	0.25	0.22	0.16	0.11	0.14	0.11	−0.03
Chile	0.06	0.14	0.09	0.09	0.11	0.18	0.11	0.10	−0.01
Israel	0.05	0.09	0.19	0.20	0.20	0.12	0.12	0.09	−0.03
Indonesia	0.08	0.23	0.09	0.07	0.07	0.07	0.07	0.08	0.01
Finland	0.21	0.10	0.07	0.19	0.62	0.22	0.21	0.08	−0.13
Colombia	0.00	0.02	0.03	0.04	0.06	0.05	0.06	0.05	−0.01
Other Countries/ Regions	1.59	1.35	1.07	1.21	1.07	0.77	0.50	0.50	0.00
Europe	56.11	54.99	53.03	57.12	56.35	56.76	51.51	54.41	2.90
Europe outside the UK	23.47	23.21	21.00	22.48	19.61	15.98	14.57	11.29	−3.28
Asia	18.60	20.65	18.91	18.42	18.84	18.20	24.04	23.86	−0.18
North America	20.50	19.10	22.00	19.30	19.50	20.30	21.20	18.08	−3.12
Other Regions	4.80	5.40	5.80	5.00	4.90	4.30	2.90	3.65	0.75
Total	100.00	100.00	100.00	100.00	100.00	100.00	100.00	100.00	0.00

Data source: Updated data released by BIS in December 2019 regarding average daily turnover in April 2019 and data from previous years; data of the Eurozone is the sum of foreign exchange transactions of 18 Eurozone countries which entered the rankings of foreign exchange transactions as published by BIS in December 2019, except for the Republic of Malta.

1.3 Major International Currency Activity in Foreign Exchange Derivatives

Despite a bad reputation following the international financial crisis, derivatives still play an important role in the international financial market. Zhang Guangping (2016) thought for over a decade that the turnover of financial derivatives was significantly larger than that of bonds, foreign exchange, shares, and other traditional financial products on the global market. As observed above, the average daily turnover of the international foreign exchange market included not only traditional foreign exchange spot goods or spot trade, but also forward trade, foreign exchange swaps, currency swaps, foreign exchange options, and other foreign exchange derivatives. In addition, foreign exchange derivatives have taken up a bigger market share than spot trades since 1992 (BIS data show that foreign exchange derivatives trading surpassed spot trading for the first time in 1992). In fact, traditional foreign exchange spot trading stopped being a key part of the foreign exchange market more than a decade ago. In other words, foreign exchange trade is mostly composed of foreign exchange derivatives. This section introduces the product composition for major international currencies on the global foreign exchange market. Table 1-4 shows the proportions of foreign exchange spot trade, foreign exchange forward trade, and foreign exchange swaps of 24 major currencies from April 2007 to April 2019.

1.3.1 Comparison of foreign exchange spot goods/spot trade and foreign exchange derivatives

Data from the Bank for International Settlements show that in 1992, spot trade in foreign exchange markets was lower than 50% for the first time. Also, the average daily turnover of foreign exchange swaps surpassed that of spot trades for the first time in 1995, making foreign exchange swaps a major product in the market. During the period of 2001–2007, the share of spot trade continued to drop to a record low – only slightly above 30%. However, as shown in Table 1-4, due to the impact of the international financial crisis, the share of foreign exchange swaps witnessed a significant slide from 2007 to 2013, while spot trading saw its share increasing noticeably, indicating a strong return to traditional products in a post-crisis era. From 2013 to 2016, foreign exchange swaps accounted for 46.9%, while spot transactions fell to 32.6%, close to the proportion seen in 2004. In 2019, the proportion of exchange rate swaps rose further to 48.6%, while that of foreign spot trade fell to 30.2%. Table 1-4 also shows that foreign exchange derivatives fell from 69.8% in 2007 to 61.7% in 2013 and rebounded to 69.8% in 2019, reaching its peak value before the financial crisis. This demonstrates the importance of derivative products in the international foreign exchange market.

1.3.2 Comparison of foreign exchange forward trade

Foreign exchange forward trade is the oldest and simplest form of derivative trading on the international foreign exchange market. As shown in Table 1-4, although the turnover of foreign exchange swaps continued to decline from 2007 to 2013, the turnover share of foreign exchange forward trade continuously increased to 12.7% and further reached 15.2% in 2019. This underscores the upward trend of forward trade over the past 21 years (from 8.4% in 1998 to 10.9% in 2007). In Table 1-4, from 2007 to 2019, the average proportion of foreign exchange forward trade of the 15 developed economies is close to the global average, while the proportion of foreign exchange forwards in the nine emerging markets is higher than the global average, thus their proportion of foreign exchange swaps are significantly lower than the global level.

1.3.3 The proportion of foreign exchange swaps in different currencies

Foreign exchange swaps are the most important product in a country's foreign exchange market. As shown in Table 1-4, the proportion of the average daily turnover of global foreign exchange swaps decreased from 51.6% to 44.3% and further to 41.7% during the 2007–2013 period. This indicates a return to traditional trade in the international foreign exchange market after the international financial crisis. However, the proportion returned to 46.8% and 48.6% in the 2016–2019 period – nearly half of the foreign exchange market – showing that adjustment after the financial crisis is over. Table 1-4 also shows that in 2019, the proportions of USD, EUR, GBP, CHF, and other major currencies' foreign exchange swaps were higher than the global average. Nevertheless, JPY, AUD, and CAD foreign exchange swaps are significantly lower than the global average, indicating that the activity levels of different major currencies in foreign exchange swaps are different. In emerging markets, only the proportion of TRY, PLN, ZAR, and RUB foreign exchange swaps is close to or higher than the global level of 48.6%. However, the proportions of other emerging countries' swaps are significantly lower than the global level. This demonstrates that there is still plenty of room for growth in those foreign exchange swap markets.

Table 1-4 Proportions of Total Average Daily Turnover of Spot Transactions, Forward Transactions, and Foreign Exchange Swaps of Major Currencies (2007–2019)

Unit: %

Year	2007			2013			2016			2019		
Currency	Spot	Forward	Swap	Spot	Forward	Swap	Spot	Forward	Swap	Spot	Forward	Swap
USD	29.7	10.9	59.4	36.4	12.6	43.6	31.2	13.5	48.7	29.0	15.2	49.9
EUR	36.9	12.1	51.1	42.2	10.0	42.9	32.7	11.2	50.7	28.9	12.0	53.6
JPY	40.4	12.1	47.5	49.7	10.0	27.0	36.0	13.8	41.8	32.5	13.1	46.5
GBP	32.5	10.0	57.4	35.9	11.0	47.8	32.5	14.2	47.1	28.4	12.9	52.6
AUD	25.7	10.0	64.3	42.4	10.8	39.6	41.0	11.7	39.6	38.2	11.9	41.8
CAD	29.7	11.8	58.6	38.3	14.8	41.3	40.1	13.2	39.6	36.7	12.9	43.9
CHF	42.2	10.1	47.7	30.6	9.8	54.1	23.5	12.3	61.5	26.2	11.1	59.4
RMB	61.4	31.3	7.4	28.4	23.5	33.4	33.4	13.8	42.6	34.1	12.5	48.1
SEK	20.7	10.0	69.3	28.7	12.5	55.9	30.0	11.9	52.6	30.7	12.5	52.8
NZD	29.4	11.3	59.3	37.0	10.9	47.6	38.8	10.7	41.7	38.6	11.7	39.4
MXN	37.4	11.7	50.9	42.0	10.2	42.8	44.3	12.4	37.1	42.4	11.2	38.2
SGD	22.5	7.9	69.6	27.4	14.3	53.6	30.4	8.7	55.4	31.2	10.1	54.3
HKD	18.4	7.0	74.6	26.9	9.6	61.3	25.3	6.9	65.5	24.4	11.3	59.7

(Continued)

Year	2007			2013			2016			2019		
Currency	Spot	Forward	Swap	Spot	Forward	Swap	Spot	Forward	Swap	Spot	Forward	Swap
NOK	18.4	9.7	71.9	27.9	13.2	55.9	34.1	9.4	51.8	35.1	12.5	47.4
KRW	44.7	29.4	25.9	30.3	37.2	24.9	34.5	41.7	16.7	23.1	54.6	14.2
TRY	61.4	11.4	27.2	22.4	13.8	55.5	27.0	8.1	54.1	33.9	7.5	49.8
RUB	70.7	5.0	24.3	42.8	10.3	43.2	40.7	10.2	45.8	46.8	13.7	36.1
INR	42.6	27.5	29.8	28.9	46.2	19.1	32.8	39.7	22.4	41.6	86.9	20.6
BRL	50.2	47.3	2.5	28.9	46.2	19.1	25.5	52.9	2.0	19.8	60.1	0.8
ZAR	19.9	12.1	68.0	32.6	11.9	52.3	32.0	8.0	48.0	38.0	9.4	43.0
DKK	21.8	10.3	67.9	17.4	12.4	69.5	16.7	11.9	71.4	16.7	11.3	70.9
PLN	20.0	10.9	69.1	28.8	14.8	52.7	34.3	11.4	51.4	29.8	12.6	53.4
TWD	47.1	40.6	12.3	23.2	45.0	25.9	29.0	41.9	25.8	21.2	57.9	17.0
HUF	34.1	15.7	50.2	33.0	15.6	45.9	26.7	13.3	53.3	32.5	11.8	46.8
Others	43.7	39.3	17.0	31.8	30.6	31.1	31.0	26.3	33.6	35.7	27.4	31.4
All Currencies	30.2	10.9	51.6	38.3	12.7	41.7	32.6	13.8	46.9	30.2	15.2	48.6

Data source: Calculated according to data on average daily turnover in April 2019 and data from previous years. Released by the BIS in December 2019.

1.3.4 Comparison of currencies on foreign exchange option markets

In addition to forward trading and swaps trading as shown in Table 1-4, two foreign exchange derivatives, namely, foreign exchange options and currency swaps, are traded on the international foreign exchange market. Foreign exchange options play a significant role in this: according to the data released by the BIS on a triennial basis, from April 1998 to April 2007, the average daily turnover of global foreign exchange option trading was only USD 87 billion, USD 60 billion, USD 119 billion and USD 212 billion, respectively. This accounted for 5.7%, 4.8%, 6.2%, and 6.4% of the total, respectively; from April 2007 to April 2010 and then April 2013, average daily turnover for option trading reached USD 207 billion and USD 337 billion, respectively, accounting for 5.2% and 6.3% of the total. This indicates that the proportion of foreign exchange option trade was around only half the proportion of foreign exchange forward trade, as shown in Table 1-1.

Table 1-5 provides the proportions of major international currency swaps and foreign exchange option trade from April 2010 to April 2019. The proportion of average daily turnover in option trade increased from 5.2% to 6.3% from 2010 to 2013, then fell back to 4.5% from 2013 to 2019, slightly exceeding a quarter of the proportion of forward trade – 15.2%. It indicates that when compared with foreign exchange swaps and foreign exchange forward trade, the scale of foreign exchange option trade is rather limited. As shown in Table 1-5, only the proportion of JPY foreign exchange option trade was significantly higher than the global average. However, the proportions of foreign exchange option trade of other major international currencies, such as USD, GBP, AUD, and CAD, are comparable to that of the global level. Among major emerging countries' currencies, the proportion of BRL foreign exchange option trade was as high as 15.7%. RMB option trade accounted for 4.7% (close to the global average of 4.5%). The proportions of TRL and INR option trade were slightly higher than the global level. The proportion of RUB foreign exchange option trade was only 2.4%, slightly over half the global average.

1.3.5 Proportions and comparisons of different currency swaps

In addition to the three foreign exchange derivatives discussed above (forwards, swaps, and options), there is another foreign exchange derivative on the market – currency swaps. Currency swaps are one of the least traded products on the foreign exchange markets, with average daily turnovers amounting to only USD 10 billion, USD 7 billion, USD 21 billion, and USD 31 billion from April 1998 to April 2007. This accounted for 0.7%, 0.6%, 1.1%, and 0.9% of the total daily

average, respectively. From April 2010 to April 2019, the average daily turnover
of currency swaps increased to USD 43 billion, 54 billion, 82 billion, and 108
billion, respectively, accounting for 1.1%, 1.0%, and 1.6% of the daily total,
respectively. Although the currency swap market is small, it has grown faster
than other foreign exchange derivatives in recent years. Table 1-5 also shows the
share of currency swaps of major currencies over this period.

**Table 1-5   Daily Turnover Proportion of Major Currency Swaps and Foreign Exchange
Options (April 2010–April 2019)**

Unit: %

Year	2010		2013		2013		2019	
Currency	Swap	Option & Others	Swap	Option & Others	Swap	Option & Others	Swap	Option & Others
USD	1.1	4.7	1.1	6.3	1.7	4.9	1.7	4.2
EUR	1.1	5.6	1.0	3.9	1.4	4.0	1.2	4.2
JPY	0.9	7.2	0.9	12.5	1.7	6.7	2.1	5.7
GBP	0.5	3.9	0.7	4.6	1.6	4.6	2.3	3.8
AUD	1.9	5.1	1.3	5.9	2.0	5.6	2.7	5.5
CAD	1.4	2.9	0.9	4.8	1.6	5.4	2.2	4.3
CHF	0.7	5.3	0.5	4.9	0.7	2.0	0.6	2.8
RMB	0.2	14.6	0.4	14.3	1.3	8.8	0.6	4.7
SEK	0.8	3.4	0.9	2.0	0.8	4.7	2.0	2.1
NZD	1.0	4.8	1.4	3.0	1.0	7.8	3.2	7.0
MXN	0.7	4.6	0.6	4.5	0.0	6.2	1.1	6.9
SGD	0.1	4.8	0.8	3.9	2.2	3.3	1.4	3.2
HKD	0.4	1.8	0.6	1.6	1.1	1.1	1.1	3.3
NOK	1.2	3.6	0.5	2.6	1.2	3.5	0.9	4.1
KRW	1.6	5.9	1.1	6.6	1.2	6.0	0.7	7.5
TRY	6.5	12.8	3.6	4.7	5.4	5.4	2.8	6.2
RUB	0.5	2.9	0.6	3.2	1.7	1.7	1.0	2.4
INR	0.1	9.9	0.6	5.2	0.0	5.2	0.3	4.9

(Continued)

BRL	1.4	17.1	4.3	18.1	3.9	15.7	2.6	16.2
ZAR	0.5	3.6	0.3	2.9	8.0	4.0	1.4	10.0
DKK	0.5	0.9	0.5	0.2	0.0	0.0	0.3	0.0
PLN	0.6	6.5	0.9	2.8	0.0	2.9	0.3	3.1
TWD	0.5	6.7	1.0	4.9	0.0	3.2	0.1	8.8
HUF	0.3	7.2	1.2	4.3	0.0	6.7	0.3	4.1
Others	0.2	0.5	0.8	5.7	2.6	6.5	0.7	4.7
All Currencies	1.1	5.2	1.0	6.3	1.6	5.0	1.6	4.5

Data source: Calculated by average daily turnover in April 2019 and data from previous years. Released by the BIS in December 2019.

1.3.6 A comparative study of the proportion of RMB foreign exchange derivatives and related issues

Table 1-2 also shows that in 2007, RMB was one of the most traditional currencies among the 24 currencies. RMB spot trade took up 61.4% of the total in 2007, second only to RUB's proportion of 70.7%. In the same year, RMB forward trade made up 31.3% of the total, behind only the corresponding proportions of BRL and TWD in the same year. RMB foreign exchange swaps accounted for 7.4% of the total – the second lowest among 24 currencies after just BZL (2.5%), indicating the inactivity of RMB foreign exchange derivatives. However, in 2010, its share of spot trade dropped significantly to 23.7%, only half the share of 2007 (61.4%). It was not only much lower than the share of spot trade (37.4%) in the global market that year, but lower than shares of 18 of the 24 currencies. This demonstrates that although there was some development in the market of RMB derivatives during the 2007–2010 period, the leap from the most "traditional" currency to a significantly "non-traditional" currency was unexpectedly impressive. Despite recovering to 28.4% in its spot trade share in 2013, the share was still 10% lower than the global average of 38.3%. The share of forward trade in total RMB trade fell to 23.5% in 2013, much closer to the global average of 12.7%, yet still 10% higher. The share of foreign exchange swaps in total RMB trade increased to 33.4%, closer to the global average of 41.7%. From 2016 to 2019, the proportions of RMB foreign exchange spots, forwards, and swaps became more similar to global levels.

The data above was issued by the Bank of International Settlements (BIS). When comparing China's foreign exchange market spot, forward, and swap trade data from recent years with the data above, errors can easily be found in RMB foreign exchange market's data in 2007–2019 published by IMF.

1.3.7 Foreign exchange derivatives from global exchange

The main contents of the global foreign exchange market were introduced above, including liquidity in the inter-bank OTC market. In addition to this, the inter-bank market, exchange products traded in global exchange markets, and foreign exchange futures and foreign exchange options also have certain market shares.

1.3.7.1 Brief introduction to foreign exchange futures and options traded at global exchanges

According to data published by the BIS, every three years from 1998 to 2013, the global foreign exchange futures and options transactions amounted to 3.1 trillion, 3.5 trillion, 8 trillion, 24.6 trillion, 38.7 trillion, and 35.6 trillion dollars, respectively. The average daily turnover amounted to 12.4 billion, 14 billion, 32 billion, 98.4 billion, 154.8 billion, and 142.6 billion dollars, accounting for 0.8%, 1.1%, 1.7%, 3%, 3.9%, and 2.7%, respectively, of the daily turnover of the OTC Foreign Exchange Market, as shown in Table 1-2. According to data published on the BIS website, daily average turnovers of foreign exchange futures and options trade were 115 billion and 294 billion in the 2016–2019 period, accounting for 2.3% and 4.5% of the turnover of global inter-bank foreign exchange trade, respectively. This underlines how the proportion of turnovers of foreign exchange products trades at global exchanges and between banks rose during this period.

1.3.7.2 Currency distribution of developed countries' foreign exchange futures and options

The Bank for International Settlements has released its currency distribution of the transaction value of foreign exchange futures and options in global exchange since 2014. The BIS announced that the average daily turnover of futures and options in 2014 and 2015 was 125 billion and 122 billion dollars, respectively. The corresponding average daily turnover of USD foreign exchange futures and options was up to 118 billion and 114 billion dollars, accounting for as high as 94.4% and 93.4% of the total. In April 2019, the proportion of USD dropped to 82.7% (bilateral calculations as per Table 1-1, the same as below). In April

2019, the average daily turnover of foreign exchange futures and options of EUR, JPY, GBP, AUD, CAD, CHF, and KRW accounted for only 30.6%, 21.5%, 10.1%, 8.3%, 4.8%, 3.1%, and 3.3%, respectively. The rankings are similar to those shown in Table 1-1 for inter-bank foreign exchange market turnover. Ultimately, USD assumed an even greater monopoly position.

1.3.7.3 *Currency distribution of emerging market foreign exchange futures and options*

Compared to the currency distribution of developed nations in foreign exchange futures and options in recent years, the liquidity of foreign exchange futures and options of BRL, INR, RUB, and MXN in four major emerging countries is lower but still impressive. In April 2019, the average daily turnovers of futures and options traded in the four currencies were as high as 11 billion, 6 billion, 8 billion, and 2 billion dollars, respectively, accounting for 3.9%, 1.9%, 2.7% and 0.6% of the global market. The proportions of BRl, INR, and MXN were significantly larger than the proportions of their inter-bank foreign exchange trade (as shown in Table 1-1). This demonstrates that the development of foreign exchange derivatives traded was impressive, and their liquidity was better than RMB futures and options.

1.4 Supporting the Continued Linked Settlement System

As shown above, the global foreign exchange market is open 24 hours a day, with an average daily turnover of trillions of dollars. In this market, American dollars hold a leading position that is absolute: the USD has the world's highest liquidity for many reasons, yet its continued linked settlement system plays the most important role – this is a good reference for the internationalization of RMB. This section will simply introduce the continued linked settlement system and its function on the global stage.

1.4.1 Foreign exchange settlement risk and the Bank of Herstatt

In 1974, the Bank of Herstatt in West Germany received a payment of Deutsch marks from the Bank of America. Due to the time difference between Germany and the US, the Bank of Herstatt issued a receipt before they received the appropriate dollar amount, which eventually led to its bankruptcy. With the volume of foreign exchange markets increasing substantially, the risk of settlement in the global foreign exchange market increased. In order to reduce this settlement risk, the Continuous Linked Settlement (CLS) was incorporated in New York in 2002. CLS, supervised by the Federal Reserve, was designated by the US Financial Stability Oversight Council as a systemically important financial market function in 2012. CLS has played an important role in the settlement of the global foreign exchange market for more than ten years. (CLS Group, www.en.wikipedia.org)

1.4.2 Members and settlement currency of the CLS institution

In 2002, CLS was established with only 39 members and seven major international currencies for settlement. By November 2015, CLS had become the world's largest foreign exchange settlement institution, with 64 settlement members, 18 settlement currencies, and 74 shareholders. There are more than 9,000 active participants from third markets. At present, there are 18 currency settlements of CLS (AUD, CAD, DKK, EUR, HKD, HUF, ILS, JPY, MXN, NZD, NOK, NZD, ZAR, KRW, SEK, CHF, GBP, USD). As shown in Table 1-1, except for HUF and ILS, 16 currencies entered the world's 20 most active currencies in 2019. The total turnover of these 18 currencies accounted for 93.2% of the total in the global foreign exchange market.

1.4.3 Estimation of time of RMB being one of CLS currencies and influence

When observing the aforementioned 18 CLS currencies, we found that RMB, INR, RUB, and BRL – the four currencies of the BRIC nations – are not CLS currencies. All currencies must obtain written approval from the Federal Reserve to join the CLS system. The monetary policy direction of the monetary authorities in the US may also have a potential impact on this process. The accession of RMB to the CLS is ongoing. However, with the signed Sino-US memorandum of cooperation arrangements in RMB clearing banks, it is believed that Sino-US financial cooperation will reach new heights; the process for RMB to become a CLS currency will be accelerated. In turn, this will benefit the exchange of RMB against USD and other major currencies. Nevertheless, the Central Counterparties, used in RMB foreign exchange trading since November 3, 2014, need to be constantly improved to better guard against Herstatt risk (Xu Qiyuan, 2016) and properly prepare for the gradual improvement of the international status of RMB.

1.5 Major International Currencies in the Interest Rate Derivatives Market

The interest rate is the most important market factor affecting the whole financial market or even the whole economy. Interest rate risk, therefore, is the most important market risk in the financial market; in turn, this makes interest rate derivatives the most active risk management instruments in the financial market. On the other hand, interest rates are the foundation of foreign exchange rates, whose trends are determined by interest rate changes. Therefore, a currency's trading activity in interest rate derivatives reflects, to a great extent, the international status of that currency. Similar to the bonds market – especially for government bonds issued by developed countries – it will continue to be an important component of the global financial market in the future, with internationally traded interest rate derivatives also set to play an increasingly significant role.

1.5.1 Monetary distribution of global inter-bank interest rate derivatives

Interest rate derivatives make up the world's largest derivatives market. It mainly includes forward rate agreements, interest rate swaps, interest rate options, and other interest rate derivatives. Interested readers may refer to Guangping (Peter G.) Zhang (2015) for details. Table 1-6 shows the monetary distribution of the average daily turnover of global inter-bank interest rate derivatives from April 1998 to April 2019. As shown in the table, between 2001 and 2013, the average daily turnover of EUR interest rate derivatives is more than that of USD, indicating that EUR is the most important currency in global inter-bank interest rate derivatives. However, from 2013 to 2019, EUR turnover increased by 40%, but its proportion to the global total decreased from 49.03% to 24.42%. Meanwhile, USD inter-bank interest rate derivatives have long averaged a daily turnover of 511.7%, accounting for an increase from 27.65% to 50.30%. Essentially, the US dollar has replaced the Euro as the main currency of global inter-bank interest rate derivatives. More than that, its proportion of the global total was more than 50%, significantly exceeding its turnover proportion in the global foreign exchange market (44.2%). This shows that the international status of USD has further strengthened in recent years.

As shown in Table 1-1, from April 2013 to 2019, in addition to the daily average turnover of USD increasing substantially, AUD and CAD daily turnover also increased by more than 30%. GBP and JPY had daily average turnovers increase by more than 20%. BRL's average daily turnover fell by 11.2%, which reflected the significant drop in the Brazilian economy in the financial market. The SEK average daily turnover fell by 6.2%, and the magnitude of its drop was smaller than that of BRL during the same period.

Table 1-6   Proportion of Average Daily Turnovers of on and Off-Exchange Trade of Interest Rate Derivatives of Different Currencies in April (1998–2019)

Unit: %, USD trillion

Currency	1998	2001	2004	2007	2010	2013	2016	2019	Ranking in 2019
USD	26.68	31.02	33.88	31.59	31.83	27.65	50.88	50.30	1
EUR	…	47.38	44.96	38.91	40.60	49.03	24.03	24.42	2
GBP	6.26	7.52	8.77	10.20	10.39	8.08	8.89	8.27	3
AUD	1.14	1.71	1.16	1.11	1.78	3.29	4.05	6.17	4
JPY	10.29	5.58	4.50	8.11	6.04	2.99	3.11	3.28	5
CAD	2.71	1.17	0.74	0.92	2.35	1.29	1.46	1.39	6
SEK	0.66	1.06	1.28	1.95	0.98	1.56	0.71	0.94	7
NZD	0.11	0.09	0.19	0.39	0.18	0.21	0.97	0.86	8
RMB	0.00	0.00	0.00	0.01	0.09	0.61	0.37	0.51	9
NOK	0.66	0.62	0.81	0.47	0.73	0.40	0.56	0.47	10
KRW	0.00	0.01	0.03	0.28	0.80	0.52	0.49	0.41	11
CHF	3.51	1.32	0.96	1.10	0.99	0.62	0.52	0.40	12
ZAR	0.19	0.08	0.15	0.19	0.26	0.68	0.60	0.39	13
MXN	0.06	0.05	0.17	0.32	0.22	0.42	0.97	0.36	14
HKD	0.20	0.30	0.42	0.55	0.15	0.09	0.19	0.27	15
INR	0.00	0.01	0.04	0.21	0.11	0.28	0.22	0.25	16
SGD	0.00	0.07	0.26	0.22	0.21	0.16	0.45	0.23	17
PLN	0.00	0.05	0.06	0.11	0.07	0.32	0.22	0.13	18
BRL	0.00	0.04	0.08	0.10	0.14	0.71	0.26	0.12	19
HUF	0.00	0.00	0.01	0.07	0.01	0.11	0.30	0.12	20
MYR	0.00	0.00	0.00	0.02	0.01	0.08	0.11	0.03	21

(Continued)

Currency	1998	2001	2004	2007	2010	2013	2016	2019	Ranking in 2019
CLP	0.00	0.00	0.00	0.00	0.01	0.05	0.15	0.02	22
RMB*	0	0	0	0.01	0.03	0.1	0.07	0.20	18
Global Takeover	0.265	0.489	1.025	1.686	2.054	2.311	2.667	6.501	…

Data source: Calculated based on the average daily turnover of inter-bank interest rate derivatives released by the Bank for International Settlements in September 2019; RMB* ratio is calculated on the basis of domestic and overseas inter-bank data.

1.5.2 The monetary distribution of futures and options for daily transactions on global exchanges

Table 1-6 only shows the currency distributions of global inter-bank interest rate derivatives. In fact, unlike the global foreign exchange market, which is dominated by the inter-bank market, the global inter-bank interest rate derivatives market has much less liquidity than interest rate derivative products traded at exchanges. Therefore, if we do not consider the currency distribution of interest rate derivatives traded at exchanges, we can't fully understand the currency distribution of global interest rate derivatives. Table 1-7 shows the monetary distribution of average daily turnover of interest rate derivatives traded at global exchanges during 2014–2019.

Table 1-7 shows that the proportion of interest rate derivatives of USD traded in global exchanges was 73.86%, which was 23.56% higher than the inter-bank interest rate derivatives (50.30%). This indicates that USD is more popular in the global trading derivatives market. However, the proportion of EUR interest rate derivatives traded in global exchanges was 11.17% lower than the inter-bank interest rate derivatives, suggesting that EUR is less active in comparison with inter-bank interest rate derivatives. The difference between GBP, AUD, and CAD is rather small. On the other hand, the proportion of JPY exchange rate derivatives traded was only 0.48%, 2.80% lower than the inter-bank interest rate derivatives (3.28%). Its rank was even behind BRL, showing that JPY interest rate derivatives traded were less compared with other inter-bank products. We can see a very interesting currency from Table 1-7. It shows the proportion of average daily turnover of BRL interest rate derivatives traded was 0.57% of the global total. It ranked 6th in April 2019, second only to the CAD of 1.04% but slightly higher than the JPY of 0.48%. The development of BRL interest rate derivatives is not only higher than all other developing countries, but also higher than many developed countries. This is worth learning and drawing lessons from.

Table 1-7   Money Distribution and Ranking of Interest Rate Derivatives, Average Daily Turnover of Global Exchange Transactions (2014–2019)

Unit: %, USD trillion

Currency	2014	2015	2016	2017	2018	2019	Ranking in 2019
USD	59.87	69.28	71.83	72.60	72.16	73.86	1
EUR	22.99	12.91	13.19	16.68	14.35	13.25	2
GBP	10.92	9.52	7.78	6.03	8.79	7.52	3
AUD	2.17	3.65	3.16	1.70	1.69	2.61	4
CAD	1.41	1.66	1.72	1.02	1.07	1.04	5
BRL	0.90	1.22	0.79	0.84	0.61	0.57	6
JPY	0.65	0.71	0.67	0.38	0.54	0.48	7
CHF	0.65	0.53	0.30	0.39	0.41	0.26	8
KRW	0.16	0.31	0.26	0.14	0.15	0.17	9
RMB	0.00	0.04	0.10	0.11	0.11	0.09	10
NZD	0.05	0.11	0.08	0.04	0.07	0.08	11
SEK	0.18	0.07	0.08	0.05	0.05	0.06	12
ZAR	0.00	0.00	0.02	0.01	0.01	0.01	13
NOK	0.02	0.00	0.02	0.00	0.00	0.00	14
RMB*	0.0035	0.0513	0.0972	0.1094	0.1001	0.0917	10

Source: www.bis.org – Bank for International Settlement website. To better compare the data of trade taking place in the inter-bank market and in exchanges, the average daily turnover in April of every year is chosen, and the proportion-related data is calculated based on the average daily data. RMB* refers to the turnover of China's domestic government bond futures. Due to rounding off, it is possible that the proportion of China's RMB interest rate derivatives is larger than the proportion of RMB interest rate derivatives in the world.

1.5.3 Currency distribution of the average daily transactions of interest rate derivatives inside and outside the global market

The above introduces the currency distribution of the average daily transaction amount of interest rate derivatives traded in over-the-counter (interbank) and floor (exchange) respectively. Using the results presented in Tables 1-6 and Table 1-7, we can calculate the currencies distribution of the average daily turnover of interest rate derivatives around the world in April 2016, and the results are shown in Table 1-8.

Table 1-8   Currencies Distribution of the Average Daily Turnover of Interest Rate Derivatives around the World

Currency	Proportion in 2016	Ranking in 2016	Proportion in 2019	Ranking in 2019
USD	64.52	1	63.13	1
EUR	16.91	2	18.33	2
GBP	8.15	3	7.86	3
AUD	3.46	4	4.23	4
JPY	1.51	6	1.75	5
CAD	1.63	5	1.20	6
SEK	0.30	12	0.46	7
NZD	0.39	8	0.43	8
BRL	0.61	7	0.36	9
CHF	0.37	9	0.32	10
KRW	0.34	10	0.28	11
RMB	0.19	15	0.28	12

As shown in Table 1-8, the average daily transaction amount of interest rate derivatives inside and outside the US dollar market accounted for 63.13% of the world, 25.17% lower than 88. 3% of the dollar's proportion in the global foreign exchange market in April 2019, given in Table 1-1. It shows that the US dollar's position in the global foreign exchange derivatives market is much higher than that in the global interest rate market. The average daily transaction value of EUR and GBP in the global market was 18.33% and 7.86%, 13.97% and 4.94% lower than the 32.3% and 13.97% and 12.8% in April 2019 given in the Table 1-1; The average daily turnover of interest rate derivatives inside and outside the JPY market accounted for only 1.75% of the world, 15.05% lower than the 16.8% of JPY's share in the global foreign exchange market in April 2019 given in Table

1-1. It shows that the world's major currencies have a lower monopoly in interest rate markets than foreign exchange markets.

1.5.4 Comparison of the turnover ratio of RMB interest rate derivatives and related problems

Table 1-6 shows that from April 2010 to April 2013, the proportion of inter-bank RMB interest rate derivatives to the global total increased from 0.09% to 0.61%, and its ranking rose from 18th to 10th. However, in 2016, the proportion dropped to 0.38%, and its ranking fell to the 15th. In 2019, its proportion was 0.51% of the total, ranking in 9th place. Accordingly, this underlines the rapid progress made by RMB in this area in the past ten years.

Since 2007, the quarterly monetary policy report released by the People's Bank of China (PBOC) has provided domestic RMB interest rate swap trans-actions. Using this data and the RMB exchange rate against the dollar from April 2007 to 2019, we can calculate the domestic inter-bank RMB interest rate derivatives figures. These were 117 million, 595 million, 2.25 billion, 5.5 billion, and 13.4 billion dollars, respectively.

In the first half of 2015, the City of London announced that the average daily turnover of RMB interest rate swaps in London was only a few million dollars; thus, the whole overseas inter-bank RMB interest rate swap as compared to the average daily turnover of the domestic market can be ignored. Therefore, using the domestic inter-bank RMB interest rate swap average as mentioned above, the proportion of RMB interest rate swaps in the world from 2010 to 2019 can be calculated. The results are shown in Table 1-6. The BIS indicates that the proportions of RMB inter-bank interest rate derivatives were 0.09% in 2010, 0.61% in 2013, 0.38% in 2016, and 0.51% in 2019, which is 0.03%, 0.10%, 0.21%, and 0.20% higher than the RMB's proportions according to the BIS data. This shows the data provided by BIS has a lot of problems, especially concerning RMB in 2013. We will list other serious problems of the agency's data, which will enable us to have a clearer understanding of the positions and international rankings of the RMB market inside and outside of China.

As shown in Table 1-7 and Table 1-8, there are some differences regarding the data and rankings of RMB interest rate derivatives traded in exchanges inside and outside of China and RMB derivatives products traded in exchanges and the inter-bank market. These differences will not be further detailed here.

As shown in Table 1-8, the average daily turnover of RMB in the global exchange and OTC interest rate derivatives market ranked 12th in 2019. This ranking would be 16th if China's domestic data were considered. Compared to three years ago, China's rankings have moved up by 3 and 5, respectively.

1.6 Investigating the Factors for Measuring Currency Internationalization

Factors to determine the extent of a currency's internationalization discussed above include the share of special drawing rights in the International Monetary Fund (IMF), weight of an international reserve currency, turnover proportions in the international foreign exchange market, status in the international foreign exchange and interest rate derivatives market, size of the international bond market, and bond circulation. In fact, there are also other indicators to this end, such as the status of a currency in offshore markets, the international trade system, the international credit market, the direct investment system, and international aids, which will not be explained here. This demonstrates the complicated process of determining currency internationalization.

In "Non-International Currencies, Currency Internationalization and Capital Account Convertibility" (Yao Li, *Financial Studies*, no. 8, 2003), Li Yao proposes a model for measuring currency internationalization and concludes that RMB was 1.85% as internationalized as USD in 2000. Many domestic and overseas financial institutions, as well as research institutions, have compiled and issued some related indexes about RMB internationalization in recent years. These indices measure the internationalization of the RMB from different perspectives, yet the vast majority have difficulty in accurately measuring the overall degree of internationalization of RMB.

In "The Reality, Approaches, and Strategies of RMB Internationalization," Li Yao uses a similar model and concludes that RMB was 2.0% as internationalized as USD in 2002. Although the use of a currency in different markets or fields does reflect how internationalized the currency is, the measurement for different fields may vary, and it is difficult to determine the weight that should be given to a specific field. Therefore, using this model to determine currency internationalization is relatively complicated, and a lot of data needed is hard to obtain. If currency internationalization can be measured by a simple parameter, with the use of simple data periodically released by international institutions, it will be much easier to determine how internationalized a currency is and have a rough idea of its changes. An example of such a method is introduced below.

Although international demand for a currency is composed of demand for settlements, transactions, and risk management, these must all be realized through foreign exchange trade eventually. For this reason, how active a currency is in the international foreign exchange market greatly reflects how internationalized the currency is. However, as countries vary in the size of their economies, this should be considered when a currency's trading volume is used to determine currency internationalization.

Specifically, the share of a currency's foreign exchange turnover as a total of the global foreign exchange turnover divided by the share of its GDP compared to global GDP can serve as a simple and easy parameter to measure currency internationalization. For instance, according to Table 1-1, the share of USD on the international foreign exchange market in 2007 was 42.8% (half of 85.6%), and the US made up 25.02% of the global GDP that year. Therefore, USD internationalization is measured at 42.8% divided by 25.02%, namely, 171.1%. Using the same method, we find that RMB internationalization in 2007 was 3.7% (0.23% divided by 6.17%, which is China's GDP contribution to the world). This is equivalent to 2.2% of the USD figure and slightly higher than what was estimated by Li Yao for RMB internationalization in 2000 and 2002. In 2007, the RMB internationalization level was only 2.2% of that of USD.

1.7 Differentiating Daily Turnover and Nominal Turnover in Foreign Exchange

1.7.1 Actual turnover of foreign exchange derivatives

Since the international application of all currencies is reflected by international foreign exchange trade, the proportion of a currency's foreign exchange trade in the global market is the optimal measurement of this currency's internationalization. A variety of methods can be used to measure foreign exchange trade: as shown in Table 1-1, the average daily turnover of global foreign exchange trade includes traditional spot trade, foreign exchange forward trade, foreign exchange swap trade, currency swap trade, foreign exchange currency options trade, and the trade of other foreign exchange derivatives. Additionally, the turnover of these foreign exchange derivatives has made up more than 2/3 of the daily average turnover of foreign exchange in the world, making the major products in global foreign exchange trade. In fact, the daily average turnover of foreign exchange derivatives trade, as shown in Table 1-1 and Table 1-6, is not the actual turnover

– which has already changed hands between buyers and sellers; it is the nominal turnover of all foreign exchange derivatives traded.

As a matter of fact, the trading of foreign exchange forwards and swaps, currency swaps, and foreign exchange options are not transacted with a nominal amount directly. They are traded on the basis of a nominal amount by buyers paying deposits in ways approved by sellers, and the settlement is completed with the difference between the agreed spot exchange rate and due exchange rate at the agreed payment time. In most cases, the amount to be paid is smaller than the deposit, which is usually about 5%. As for the foreign exchange options trade, buyers of options pay an option premium to sellers, which is usually lower than 5% of the nominal amount. In other words, the actual turnover of most foreign exchange derivatives is much lower than their nominal amount in foreign exchange. As shown in Table 1-1, the daily average turnover in the global foreign exchange trade is much larger than the actual trade; thus, it is inaccurate to measure the currency internationalization based on this. Some reasonable adjustments must be made.

1.7.2 A reasonable estimation for the daily average turnover

With rapid technological development, it is feasible to complete the statistics for the global daily average turnover of foreign exchange trade from a technological perspective. However, most foreign exchange derivatives can be used for risk management or for speculation. Some financial institutions and enterprises, due to their trading and risk management strategies, decide not to publish their trading positions, which makes it hard to compile statistics on global foreign exchange trade. Particularly, for foreign exchange forwards, swaps, and options, the prices locked in by different contracts are different, and the ratios of trade amount to the nominal amount can be different. This makes compiling statistics on foreign exchange derivatives more complicated. In Table 1-1, the statistics based on the nominal amount of foreign exchange derivatives are expedient, and the actual trade amount is exaggerated. In fact, the actual daily average turnover of foreign exchange trade in the world, as shown in Table 1-1, cannot be easily calculated. However, we can use some simple methods. By setting 5% of each foreign exchange forward and swap as the upper limit of the deposit and 5% of each foreign exchange option premium as the upper limit, the nominal amount of foreign exchange derivatives in Table 1-4 and Table 1-5 are used to estimate the upper limit of the actual turnover of foreign exchange derivatives. Including the daily average turnover of foreign exchange spot trade in Table 1-4, the actual daily turnover of different currencies' foreign exchange trade can be calculated. Results from 2007–2019 are displayed in Table 1-8.

Table 1-8 Actual Average Daily Turnover of the Top Eight Currencies in the Global Foreign Exchange Market and Proportions (2007–2019)

Unit: USD billion, %

Currency	2007	2010	2013	2016	2019	Annual Average Change
USD	892.99	1,296.09	1,839.29	1,540.10	1,894.02	6.47
EUR	460.60	733.17	805.85	573.68	691.19	3.44
JPY	224.33	322.70	643.29	430.53	397.64	4.89
GBP	167.13	227.71	246.96	233.73	269.96	4.08
AUD	61.13	120.53	209.26	154.22	183.84	9.61
CAD	43.70	84.37	93.92	112.44	132.30	9.67
CHF	94.97	99.65	101.02	66.66	97.75	0.24
RMB	9.28	9.43	38.23	74.29	106.30	22.53
Others	287.57	332.88	444.34	465.50	662.67	7.20
Global	1,120.85	1,613.26	2,211.08	1,825.58	2,217.84	5.85
Currency	2007	2010	2013	2016	2019	Annual Average Change
USD	7.97	8.03	8.32	8.44	8.54	0.48
EUR	4.11	4.55	3.65	3.14	3.12	−0.83
JPY	2.00	2.00	2.91	2.36	1.79	−0.17
GBP	1.49	1.41	1.12	1.28	1.22	−0.23
AUD	0.55	0.75	0.95	0.85	0.83	0.24
CAD	0.39	0.52	0.43	0.62	0.60	0.17
CHF	0.85	0.62	0.46	0.37	0.44	−0.34
RMB	0.08	0.06	0.17	0.41	0.48	0.33
Others	2.57	2.06	2.01	2.55	2.99	0.35
Global	100.00	100.00	100.00	100.00	100.00	0.00

Note: Assuming that the actual turnover of foreign exchange derivatives is only 5% of nominal turnover.

Data source: Calculated by using data from Table 1-4 and Table 1-5.

1.7.3 A comparison of actual average daily turnover and nominal turnover

As shown in Table 1-8, the actual daily average turnovers of foreign exchange trade in the globe were 1.12 trillion, 1.61 trillion, 2.21 trillion, 1.83 trillion, and 2.22 trillion dollars from 2007 to 2019. This only amounts to 33.73%, 40.55%, 41.28%, 36.03%, and 33.63%, respectively, of the nominal daily average turnover of foreign exchange trade, as shown in Table 1-1. This demonstrates that the actual daily average turnover in the global foreign exchange market is much smaller than the nominal turnover. Thus, it is more reasonable to compare the actual daily average turnover with turnover in the stock and bond market. Besides, the proportions of actual daily average turnovers of the global top eight currencies, as shown in Table 1-9, are close to the proportions of average daily nominal turnovers, as shown in Table 1-1. However, the proportions of nominal turnovers in Table 1-1 overestimate the proportion of USD in the world, underestimate the proportion of EUR from 2007 to 2013, overestimate the proportion of EUR in 2019, underestimate the proportion of JPY from 2007 to 2016, overestimate the proportion of JPY in 2019, underestimate the proportions of GBP in 2010 and 2016, and overestimate the proportions of GBP in 2013 and 2019. Although the proportions of different currencies do not differ significantly, it makes a big difference to the global rankings of different currencies. The proportions of actual turnovers of RMB foreign exchange trade in 2016 and 2019 are 4.07% and 4.79%, which means RMB should rank 7th in the world. However, according to the nominal turnovers as shown in Table 1-1, the rankings of RMB (i.e., the 8th) are lower than that of CHF (in 7th place).

Since the average daily nominal turnovers shown in Table 1-1 significantly exaggerate the actual foreign exchange trade, it is safe to say that the actual daily average turnovers are more reasonable than the nominal turnovers in Table 1-1; the exaggerated nominal turnover can't reflect the actual internationalization level of a currency. In the following chapters of this book, the nominal turnover in Table 1-1 will also be used as the basis for the measurement of a currency's internationalization level. Meanwhile, the actual average daily turnover, as shown in Table 1-9, will be regarded as the benchmark when measuring a currency's internationalization level. In this way, a more accurate relationship between currency internationalization and technological internationalization can be found.

1.8 Measurement and Comparison of Major Currency Internationalization in 2007

As observed above, the importance of an international currency in the international foreign exchange market greatly reflects how internationalized it is; however,
the economy of its issuer is not considered. Currency internationalization can
be better measured if the share of a country's economy of the world's economy
is considered alongside a currency's share of the international foreign exchange
market. Table 1-9 shows the share of the world's major currencies in global
foreign exchange trade and their contributions to global GDP in 2007. We
chose 2007 to measure currency internationalization because it was only one
year before the global financial crisis. It was also the year when the Bank for
International Settlements was set to release its triennial data on the international
foreign exchange market.

In Table 1-9, the excess of a foreign exchange share of a currency over the
GDP share of its issuer can reflect how internationalized the currency is. However, the excess may be a positive or a negative number, which makes it hard to
compare. The ratio of foreign exchange share to GDP share will always be positive; thus, it better reflects the extent of currency internationalization.

Table 1-9   Measurement and Comparison of Major Countries and Regions by Currency
in 2007

Unit: %

Currency	Foreign Exchange Share in 2007	GDP Share in 2007	Excess of Foreign Exchange Share over GDP Share	Foreign Exchange Share / GDP Share
USD	42.80	25.66	17.14	166.82
EUR	18.52	21.93	−3.41	84.44
JPY	8.62	7.72	0.91	111.74
GBP	7.43	5.06	2.37	146.79
AUD	3.31	1.68	1.63	196.79
CHF	3.41	0.80	2.61	427.39
CAD	2.14	2.58	−0.44	83.04
Total of 7 Currencies	86.24	65.43	20.81	131.80

(Continued)

Currency	Foreign Exchange Share in 2007	GDP Share in 2007	Excess of Foreign Exchange Share over GDP Share	Foreign Exchange Share / GDP Share
NZD	0.95	0.24	0.71	402.53
SEK	1.35	0.82	0.53	164.76
HKD	1.35	0.37	0.98	360.74
NOK	1.05	0.70	0.35	150.89
SGD	0.58	0.32	0.27	184.79
Total of 5 Currencies	5.29	2.44	2.84	216.39
MXN	0.66	1.85	−1.19	35.47
TRY	0.09	1.15	−1.06	7.80
KRW	0.58	1.86	−1.28	31.09
DKK	0.42	0.55	−0.13	76.29
PLN	0.38	0.75	−0.37	50.61
TWD	0.18	0.70	−0.51	26.09
HUF	0.03	0.24	−0.21	11.77
MYR	0.11	0.34	−0.24	31.21
CZK	0.08	0.32	−0.24	24.14
THB	0.10	0.44	−0.34	22.34
CLP	0.06	0.37	−0.31	15.01
ILS	0.03	0.31	−0.28	8.40
IDR	0.05	0.77	−0.71	6.89
Total of 13 Currencies	2.75	9.64	−6.89	28.54
Total of 9 Currencies	1.54	6.22	−4.68	24.82
ZAR	0.46	0.51	−0.05	89.98
RUB	0.37	2.30	−1.93	16.27
INR	0.36	2.19	−1.84	16.19
BRL	0.20	2.42	−2.22	8.14

(Continued)

Currency	Foreign Exchange Share in 2007	GDP Share in 2007	Excess of Foreign Exchange Share over GDP Share	Foreign Exchange Share / GDP Share
RMB	0.23	6.19	−5.97	3.65
Total of BRICS	1.61	13.62	−12.01	11.81
Total of BRICS Excluding RMB	1.38	7.43	−6.04	18.62

Data source: Data on shares of foreign exchange trade are from Table 1-1; data on GDP shares are calculated based on the data on each country and region's GDP released by the IMF in April 2018.

1.8.1 Measurement and comparison of major international currency internationalization in 2007

As shown in Table 1-9, the foreign exchange shares of the five major international reserve currencies all exceeded their GDP shares, with two other international reserve currencies – EUR and CAD – failing to show this positive excess. The total foreign exchange share of the seven international reserve currencies was as high as 86.2% – 21.1% higher than their combined GDP share of 65.1%; the ratio of the former to the latter reached as high as 132.4%, indicating the importance of these seven currencies in the international foreign exchange market.

The Share of CHF foreign exchange trade in the world was 3.4%, significantly higher than Switzerland's GDP share of 0.8%. To be precise, the former was 413% larger than the latter. This shows that despite a small economy, CHF is highly internationalized. Table 1-10 shows that with a high ratio of 203.1%, AUD came second after CHF in terms of currency internationalization. In addition, USD and GBP also witnessed high ratios of 171.8% and 140.5%, respectively, with JPY's ratio standing at 111.0%. The EUR and CAD were the least internationalized currencies among the seven reserve currencies, with their ratios at 83.5% and 85.1%, respectively.

1.8.2 Measurement and comparison of currency internationalization of other major developed countries and regions in 2007

Table 1-9 shows that currencies of the five major developed countries and regions, including NZD, all saw their foreign exchange shares exceed their economies' GDP shares (with ratios above 100%). Among them, NZD had the highest ratio amounting to 408.2%, followed by HKD's ratio of 371.5%, indicating the important role of Hong Kong, China as a regional financial center. The ratio of those five currencies' combined share to their economies' combined GDP's share reached as high as 217.0%, higher than the same ratio of the seven reserve currencies of 132.4%. This indicates that despite the smaller influence of those five currencies in the international foreign exchange market, they were highly internationalized relative to their economic size. The ratios of foreign exchange shares of SGD and SEK to GDP shares of Singapore and Sweden were 188.5% and 160.9%, respectively, slightly lower than the combined ratio of the five currencies of 217.0%.

1.8.3 Measurement and comparison of internationalization of currencies of other developed countries and regions in 2007

The third group of currencies in Table 1-9 contains KAW, DKK, TWD, CZK, and ILS – currencies of five developed economies. Since the Czech Republic was admitted to the developed economies in 2016, CZK has been listed as such. The proportions of those five currencies trade in the global foreign exchange market are low, and their proportions in the market are also lower than the proportions of their GDPs to the global total. The combined proportion of those five currencies is only 1.4%, while their combined GDP accounts for 3.8% of the global total. The former proportion is smaller by 2.5% than the latter proportion, and the proportion of the former to the latter is only 35.8%. This underlines how the internationalization of these currencies is generally low.

1.8.4 Measurement and comparison of internationalization of currencies of developing countries in 2007

In Table 1-9, the 13 currencies starting from the MXN are those of developing countries. The reason why we categorize them together is that the shares of these currencies' foreign exchange trade are lower than their GDP contribution to the world. As shown in Table 1-10, of these 13 currencies, ZAR is the most internationalized, with a foreign exchange share at 88.6% of its economy's GDP share. This is followed by HUF and PLN – the ratios of their foreign exchange shares to their GDP share are 55.9% and 51.6%, respectively. The ratio of MXN trade share to Mexico's GDP share is 36.2%. In the group of 13 currencies, the degrees of internationalization of BRL, TRY, INR and RMB were the last four, and ratios of their foreign exchange trade to their GDP shares are only 8.2%, 7.7%, 6.8%, and 3.7%, respectively.

1.9 Changes in the Internationalization of Major Currencies since the Global Financial Crisis

As shown above, we used the ratio of a currency's foreign exchange trade share to its country's GDP share to measure how internationalized a currency was in April 2007. In this section, we will leverage global foreign exchange data released by the BIS in 2010 and 2016 to analyze and determine changes in internationalization of major currencies. Table 1-10, Table 1-11, Table 1-12, and Table 1-13 give results that are comparable to those from 2010–2016, as shown in Table 1-9.

Table 1-10   Comparison of Internationalization of Major Currencies in 2010

Unit: %

Currency	Foreign Exchange Share in 2010	GDP Share in 2010	Excess of foreign Exchange Share over GDP Share	Foreign Exchange Share/GDP Share
USD	42.4	22.7	19.7	187.0
EUR	19.5	19.2	0.3	101.6
JPY	9.5	8.6	0.9	109.9
GBP	6.4	3.7	2.7	173.8
AUD	3.8	1.9	1.9	200.2
CAD	2.6	2.4	0.2	108.0
CHF	3.2	0.9	2.3	356.5
Total of 7 Currencies	87.5	59.5	28.0	147.1
NZD	0.8	0.2	0.6	361.3
SEK	1.1	0.7	0.4	147.9
HKD	1.2	0.3	0.8	341.3
NOK	0.7	0.7	0.0	101.5
SGD	0.7	0.4	0.4	197.7
Total of 5 Currencies	4.4	2.3	2.1	191.8
KRW	0.8	1.7	−0.9	45.7
DKK	0.3	0.5	−0.2	58.1

(Continued)

Currency	Foreign Exchange Share in 2010	GDP Share in 2010	Excess of foreign Exchange Share over GDP Share	Foreign Exchange Share/GDP Share
TWD	0.2	0.7	−0.4	35.4
CZK	0.1	0.3	−0.2	30.4
ILS	0.1	0.4	−0.3	21.2
Total of 5 Currencies	1.5	3.5	−2.0	41.6
MXN	0.6	1.6	−1.0	39.2
ZAR	0.4	0.6	−0.2	63.4
RUB	0.5	2.5	−2.0	18.2
INR	0.5	2.6	−2.1	18.3
PLN	0.4	0.7	−0.3	55.4
BRL	0.3	3.3	−3.0	10.2
TRY	0.4	1.2	−0.8	31.5
HUF	0.2	0.2	0.0	108.8
MYR	0.1	0.4	−0.2	35.6
THB	0.1	0.5	−0.4	18.6
CLP	0.1	0.3	−0.2	24.8
IDR	0.1	1.1	−1.1	6.6
RMB	0.4	9.2	−8.8	4.7
Total of 13 Currencies	4.1	24.3	−20.2	16.8
Total of BRIC	1.7	17.6	−15.9	9.6
Total of BRICS	2.1	18.2	−16.1	11.3

Data source: Same as Table 1-9.

Table 1-11   Comparison of Internationalization of Major Currencies in 2013

Unit: %

Currency	Foreign Exchange Share in 2013	GDP Share in 2013	Excess of Foreign Exchange Share over GDP Share	Foreign Exchange Share/GDP Share
USD	43.5	21.8	21.7	199.7
EUR	16.7	17.2	−0.5	97.0
JPY	11.5	6.7	4.8	171.2
GBP	5.9	3.6	2.3	165.1
AUD	4.3	2.0	2.3	218.2
CAD	2.3	2.4	−0.1	94.8
CHF	2.6	0.9	1.7	287.0
Total of 7 Currencies	86.8	54.6	32.2	159.0
NZD	1.0	0.2	0.7	402.2
SEK	0.9	0.8	0.1	116.7
HKD	0.7	0.4	0.4	200.9
NOK	0.7	0.7	0.0	105.4
SGD	0.7	0.4	0.3	175.5
Total of 5 Currencies	4.1.0	2.4	1.6	164.1
KRW	0.6	1.7	−1.1	35.2
DKK	0.4	0.4	−0.1	87.5
TWD	0.2	0.7	−0.4	34.1
CZK	0.2	0.3	−0.1	65.1
ILS	0.1	0.4	−0.3	24.0
Total of 5 Currencies	1.5	3.5	−2.0	42.8
MXN	1.3	1.7	−0.4	75.9
ZAR	0.6	0.5	0.1	116.4
RUB	0.8	3.0	−2.2	26.6
INR	0.5	2.4	−1.9	20.3

(Continued)

Currency	Foreign Exchange Share in 2013	GDP Share in 2013	Excess of Foreign Exchange Share over GDP Share	Foreign Exchange Share/GDP Share
PLN	0.4	0.7	−0.3	51.2
BRL	0.6	3.2	−2.7	17.1
TRY	0.7	1.2	−0.6	53.2
HUF	0.2	0.2	0.0	120.0
MYR	0.2	0.4	−0.2	47.1
THB	0.2	0.5	−0.4	29.1
CLP	0.1	0.4	−0.2	40.8
IDR	0.1	1.2	−1.1	7.1
RMB	1.1	12.6	−11.5	8.9
Total of 13 Currencies	6.6	28.0	−21.4	23.5
Total of BRIC	3.0	21.2	−18.3	13.9
Total of BRICS	3.5	21.7	−18.2	16.2

Source: Same as Table 1-9.

Table 1-12   Comparison of Internationalization of Major Currencies in 2016

Unit: %

Currency	Foreign Exchange Share in 2016	GDP Share in 2016	Excess of Foreign Exchange Share over GDP Share	Foreign Exchange Share/ GDP Share
USD	43.8	24.7	19.1	177.5
EUR	15.7	15.8	−0.1	99.2
JPY	10.8	6.6	4.3	164.9
GBP	6.4	3.5	2.9	181.6
AUD	3.4	1.7	1.8	205.1
CAD	2.6	2.0	0.5	126.3
CHF	2.4	0.9	1.5	271.1

(Continued)

Currency	Foreign Exchange Share in 2016	GDP Share in 2016	Excess of Foreign Exchange Share over GDP Share	Foreign Exchange Share/ GDP Share
Total of 7 Currencies	85.1	55.2	29.9	154.3
NZD	1.0	0.2	0.8	417.9
SEK	1.1	0.7	0.4	162.6
HKD	0.9	0.4	0.4	203.6
NOK	0.8	0.5	0.3	170.1
SGD	0.9	0.4	0.5	220.0
Total of 5 currencies	4.7	2.3	2.5	210.2
KRW	0.8	1.9	−1.0	44.3
DKK	0.4	0.4	0.0	102.9
TWD	0.3	0.7	−0.4	45.1
CZK	0.1	0.3	−0.1	54.3
ILS	0.1	0.4	−0.3	32.8
Total of 5 Currencies	1.8	3.7	−1.8	50.3
MXN	1.0	1.4	−0.5	67.1
ZAR	0.5	0.4	0.1	124.2
RUB	0.6	1.7	−1.1	33.8
INR	0.6	3.0	−2.4	19.0
PLN	0.3	0.6	−0.3	55.8
BRL	0.5	2.4	−1.9	21.1
TRY	0.7	1.1	−0.4	62.8
HUF	0.2	0.2	0.0	88.2
MYR	0.2	0.4	−0.2	45.4
THB	0.2	0.5	−0.4	33.0
CLP	0.1	0.3	−0.2	37.1
IDR	0.1	1.2	−1.1	8.1

(Continued)

Currency	Foreign Exchange Share in 2016	GDP Share in 2016	Excess of Foreign Exchange Share over GDP Share	Foreign Exchange Share/ GDP Share
RMB	2.0	14.9	−12.9	13.4
Total of 13 Currencies	6.9	28.2	−21.3	24.4
Total of BRIC	3.6	22.0	−18.3	16.6
Total of BRICS	4.1	22.3	−18.2	18.5

Source: Same as Table 1-9.

Table 1-13   Comparison of Internationalization of Major Currencies in 2019

Unit: %

Currency	Foreign Exchange Share in 2019	GDP Share in 2019	Excess of Foreign Exchange Share over GDP Share	Foreign Exchange Share/GDP Share
USD	44.2	24.5	19.7	180.5
EUR	16.2	15.6	0.6	103.7
JPY	8.4	5.9	2.5	141.7
GBP	6.4	3.2	3.2	197.4
AUD	3.4	1.6	1.8	208.1
CHF	2.5	0.8	1.7	310.7
CAD	2.5	2.0	0.5	124.5
Total of 7 Currencies	83.5	53.6	29.8	155.6
HKD	1.8	0.4	1.3	403.7
NZD	1.0	0.2	0.8	428.1
SEK	1.0	0.6	0.4	162.3
KRW	1.0	1.9	−0.9	52.4
SGD	0.9	0.4	0.5	211.6
Total of 5 Currencies	4.8	3.2	1.6	150.2

(Continued)

Currency	Foreign Exchange Share in 2019	GDP Share in 2019	Excess of Foreign Exchange Share over GDP Share	Foreign Exchange Share/GDP Share
NOK	0.9	0.5	0.4	184.0
MXN	0.9	1.4	−0.6	60.6
INR	0.9	3.4	−2.5	25.3
RUB	0.5	1.8	−1.3	29.7
ZAR	0.5	0.4	0.1	128.6
Total of 5 Currencies	3.7	7.6	−3.9	49.0
TRY	0.5	0.8	−0.3	66.8
BRL	0.5	2.2	−1.7	23.9
TWD	0.5	0.7	−0.2	66.4
DKK	0.3	0.4	−0.1	79.0
PLN	0.3	0.7	−0.4	45.4
THB	0.2	0.6	−0.4	40.5
MYR	0.2	0.4	−0.2	47.8
HUF	0.2	0.2	0.0	104.3
CZK	0.2	0.3	−0.1	68.9
ILS	0.2	0.4	−0.3	35.1
CLP	0.1	0.3	−0.2	43.5
IDR	0.1	1.3	−1.1	11.2
RMB	2.2	16.3	−14.1	13.2
RMB*	2.6	16.3	−13.7	16.0
Total of 13 Currencies	5.6	24.6	−19.1	22.7
Total of BRIC	4.1	23.8	−19.7	17.2
Total of BRICS	4.6	24.2	−19.6	19.2

Data source: Same as Table 1-9. RMB* is calculated by using data from Table 1-1.

1.9.1 Changes in the internationalization of currencies of developed countries from 2010 to 2019

Comparing the results of Table 1-9 and Table 1-10, we found that from 2007 to 2010, the internationalization of CAD and EUR increased significantly. The difference between the two currencies' foreign exchange trade shares and their GDP shares in the world changes from negative to positive, and the ratio of their foreign exchange share to their GDP share increased to 101.6% and 108.0%, respectively. Therefore, the seven international reserve currencies had foreign exchange shares larger than the corresponding GDP shares in 2010. Simultaneously, the degree of the dollar's internationalization has not declined, but has actually increased to 187.0%; the proportion of GBP foreign exchange share to its GDP rose by 33.4% to 173.8%, demonstrating the largest increase among the seven currencies. However, the degree of internationalization of CHF, AUD, and JPY has declined to varying degrees. The decline of CHF was 56.4%, the largest drop among seven currencies, and underlining the more severe impact of the financial crisis on CHF. The proportion of foreign exchange trade of seven international reserve currencies rose from 86.2% in 2007 to 87.6% in 2010, while the proportion of their GDP fell by 5.6%. The ratio of their trade share compared to their GDP share rose from 132.4% to 147.2%. Therefore, these main currencies slightly increased in internationalization during the three years after the financial crisis.

Comparing the results of Table 1-10 and Table 1-11, we found that USD's international status strengthened slightly from 2010 to 2013, while the international positions of EUR and CAD weakened slightly; CHF's international position declined further, because the proportion of CHF foreign exchange trade share to its country's GDP share dropped by 69.5% in comparison with 2010. Meanwhile, the ratio of JPY increased by 61.4% to 171.2% (mainly due to its devaluation, resulting in a significant decline of Japanese GDP to the global total, which was USD-denominated and a significant rise in the proportion of JPY foreign exchange trade). In 2013, the ratio of total foreign exchange trade of the seven major currencies compared to their GDP share further increased to 159%.

As shown in Table 1-11 and Table 1-13, from 2013 to 2019, the internationalization of CAD increased significantly, and USD internationalization weakened a bit (the ratio of CAD foreign exchange trade share to Canada's GDP share increased by 29.7%, the largest among the seven major currencies; meanwhile, the ratio for USD dropped by 19.2% to 180.5%), while the internationalization of the other six major currencies did not change significantly from 2013. The combined ratio of these seven major currencies' trade share to their GDP share dropped 15.9% from 2013, but was still high at 155.6%.

1.9.2 Changes in the internationalization of currencies of other developed economies from 2010 to 2019

By comparing Table 1-9, Table 1-10, and Table 1-11, we find that NZD, SEK, HKD, NOK, and SGD – five developed economies' currencies – have maintained their currency trade shares higher than their GDP shares from 2010 to 2013. The combined ratio of these five currencies' foreign exchange trade shares, compared to their GDP shares, dropped slightly by 25.2% to 191.8% from 2007 to 2010 and further dropped by 27.7% to 164.1% from 2010 to 2013. However, this ratio rose by 46.1% to 210.2% from 2013 to 2016 and reached close to 217.0% in 2007. It is noteworthy that the ratio of SGD foreign exchange trade share to Singapore's GDP share increased by 44.5% to 220.0% from 2013 to 2016, exceeding HKD's ratio of 203.6%. This suggests that the internationalization of SGD is higher than that of HKD.

By comparing Table 1-9, Table 1-10, and Table 1-11, we find that KRW, DKK, TWD CZK, and ILS – another five currencies of developed economies – have maintained currency trade shares lower than their economies' GDP shares between 2010 and 2013. The ratios of these five in-trade shares compared to their GDP shares increased slightly to 41.6% and 42.8%, respectively, in the 2007–2010 period and in 2013. However, from 2013 to 2016, only DKK's foreign exchange trade ratio improved, and the total combined ratio increased very marginally to 50.3%, indicating that little change occurred in this regard after the global financial crisis.

1.9.3 Changes in currency internationalization of developing countries since the global financial crisis

We can conclude from Table 1-10 that during 2010–2013, HUF's foreign exchange trade shares were higher by 8.8% and 20.0% than Hungary's GDP share on two occasions. In 2013, ZAR's foreign exchange trade share was higher than South Africa's GDP share by 16.4%. Yet, except for these two currencies, the other 13 currencies' foreign exchange trade shares were lower than their GDP shares. Although the trade share of these 13 currencies increased from 3.1% to 6.9% from 2007 to 2013, the total share of their economies also increased from 19.5% to 28.0%; therefore, the ratio between them increased slightly from 16.1% in 2007 to 23.5%. From 2013 to 2016, only ZAR's foreign exchange trade share was larger than South Africa's GDP share among these 13 currencies. The total combined share of foreign exchange trade rose from 6.6% to 6.9%, while the total share of their economies increased slightly to 28.2%, which allowed their ratio to rise from 23.5% to 24.4%. From 2016 to 2019, in addition to RMB, only the difference between BRL's foreign exchange trade share and its economy's GDP share was larger than 1%, while the others were within 0.5%, showing small overall changes.

1.9.4 Changes of major developed economies in currency internalization since the global financial crisis

By comparing Table 1-10 with Table 1-13, we find that the foreign exchange trade share of 7 major international currencies dropped by 2.7% to 83.5% during the 11 years after the global financial crisis, while their GDP share dropped by 11.5% to 53.6%; the latter's drop was 8.8% higher than the former. The ratio between the two shares increased by 23.2% to 155.6%. This means that the internalization level of these major international currencies improved.

The total share of foreign exchange trade (including NZD) dropped by 0.5% to 4.8%, while the total share of their GDPs dropped by 0.2% to 3.2%, for which their ratio between those two shares increased by 19.8% to 211.6%. This means that the growth of the former was slower than that of the latter.

1.9.5 Changes of major developing economies in currency internalization since the global financial crisis

The total share of foreign exchange trade of the 13 emerging economies' currencies (including MXN) increased by 3.9% to 6.9%, while the total share of those 13 emerging economies' GDP increased by 8.5% to 24.4%. Both these shares did not increase a lot because the growth of those 13 emerging economies' GDP share was larger than the foreign exchange trade share. In 2019, the figures showed some changes, but the shares showed almost no change.

1.10 Internationalization of RMB before and after the Global Financial Crisis

According to GDP statistics released by the International Monetary Fund in October 2016, China's GDP share amongst the five BRICS countries exceeded 50% for the first time (52.4%) in 2009, and exceeded 60% for the first time in 2014 (60.7%). Following the measurement and comparison of internationalization levels of major currencies, this section focuses on changes in RMB internationalization from 2007 to 2016 and provides a comparative study of RMB and currencies of other developing countries.

According to Table 1-9 to Table 1-12, in 2007, there was a huge gap between RMB's foreign exchange trade share of 0.23% and China's GDP share of 6.2%. In 2010, while RMB's foreign exchange trade share was 0.43%, China's GDP share was 9.2%, with the former registering −8.8% compared to the latter. In 2013, RMB's foreign exchange trade share rose significantly to 1.11%, and China's GDP share was 12.7% of the global total, which enlarged their difference to −11.5%. In 2016, the RMB share rose significantly to 1.99%, and China's GDP share was 15.3%, which enlarged their difference to −13.3%. Although the share of RMB foreign exchange trade rose significantly from 2007 to 2013, the magnitude of this rise was smaller than its GDP share. The ratio of RMB's foreign exchange trade share to China's GDP share increased from 3.7% in 2007 to 4.7% in 2010 – the lowest ranking not only among five BRICS currencies, but also among 30 currencies shown in Table 1-10. Table 1-11 shows that although this ratio increased to 8.8% in 2013, it was still the lowest among the five BRICS currencies and the second lowest in the rankings in Table 1-12. Yet, some progress was made: This ratio for RMB increased to 13.0% in 2016 and 13.2% in 2019. However, RMB was still the second lowest amongst the BRICS, and its gap with other currencies was still large.

1.11 Measurement of Currency Internationalization in a Relative Sense

Using data from Tables 1-10 to Table 1-13 on the internationalization of 30 currencies, we can easily produce the internationalization level of any currency relative to all other currencies. This section addresses the relativity of currency internationalization.

1.11.1 Currency internationalization relative to USD

Internationalization of any currency relative to USD can be easily shown by a fraction of USD as the denominator and the currency in question as the numerator. This section introduces currency internationalization in a relative way. Table 1-14 shows such relativity for different currencies from 2007 to 2019.

Table 1-14   Internationalization of Currencies of Major Countries and Regions Relative to USD (2007–2019)

Unit: %

Currency	2007	2010	2013	2016	2019
USD	100	100	100	100	100
EUR	48.6	54.3	48.6	55.9	57.4
JPY	64.6	58.7	85.7	92.9	78.5
GBP	81.8	92.9	82.6	102.3	109.4
AUD	118.2	107.0	109.3	115.6	115.3
CHF	240.3	190.6	143.7	152.8	172.1
CAD	49.5	57.7	47.5	71.2	69.0
Total of 7 Currencies	77.1	78.7	79.6	86.9	86.2
HKD	216.2	182.5	100.6	114.7	223.6
NZD	237.6	193.2	201.4	235.5	237.1
SEK	93.6	79.1	58.4	91.6	89.9
KRW	17.4	24.4	17.6	24.9	29.1
SGD	109.7	105.7	87.9	124.0	117.2
Total of 5 Currencies	126.3	102.6	82.2	118.5	83.2
NOK	88.7	54.3	52.8	95.8	101.9
MXN	21.1	21.0	38.0	37.8	33.6
INR	9.7	9.8	10.2	10.7	14.0
RUB	9.1	9.7	13.3	19.0	16.4
ZAR	51.5	33.9	58.3	70.0	71.3
Total of 5 Currencies	20.8	22.2	21.5	28.4	27.1
TRY	4.5	16.8	26.6	35.4	37.0
BRL	4.8	5.5	8.6	11.9	13.2
TWD	15.1	18.9	17.1	25.4	36.8
DKK	44.6	31.1	43.8	58.0	43.8
PLN	30.0	29.6	25.6	31.5	25.1

(Continued)

Currency	2007	2010	2013	2016	2019
THB	12.6	10.0	14.6	18.6	22.4
MYR	11.3	19.0	23.6	25.6	26.5
HUF	32.5	58.2	60.1	49.7	57.8
CZK	19.2	16.3	32.6	30.6	38.2
ILS	14.6	11.3	12.0	18.5	19.5
CLP	10.4	13.2	20.5	20.9	24.1
IDR	4.0	3.5	3.5	4.5	6.2
RMB	2.1	2.5	4.4	7.6	7.3
RMB*	2.1	2.5	4.4	7.6	9.0
Total of 13 Currencies	9.4	9.0	11.8	13.7	12.6
Total of BRIC	5.1	5.2	7.0	9.3	9.6
Total of BRICS	6.9	6.1	8.1	10.4	10.6

Data source: Calculation is based on data from Table 1-9 to Table 1-10. RMB* data is calculated based on data from Table 1-1 and Table 1-10.

Table 1-14 shows that the overall internationalization of the seven international reserve currencies relative to USD slightly improved from 77.1% in 2007 to 78.7% in 2010 before increasing to 79.6% in 2013, 86.9% in 2016, and 86.2% in 2019. Relative internationalization of these five developed currencies, including New Zealand, dropped significantly from 126.3% in 2007 to 82.2% in 2013, and rose very slightly to 83.2% in 2019, 3% lower than the relative internationalization level of seven reserve currencies (86.2%) in the same year. The internationalization level of the five BRICS currencies relative to USD dropped slightly from 6.9% in 2007 to 6.1% in 2010 before continuously rising to 10.6% in the 2010–2019 period. The internationalization level of RMB to USD rose from 2.1% in 2007 to 7.3% in 2019. If the adjusted RMB (RMB*) were put into consideration, its internationalization level would have risen to 9.0% in 2019. The internationalization of RMB relative to USD in 2007 and 2010 shown here is close to the results of the internationalization of RMB relative to USD in 2000 and 2002 produced by Li Yao (2003) and the research team on RMB internationalization.

1.11.2 Internationalization of RMB relative to other currencies

Using the same methodology, we can put RMB internationalization data in Table 1.10 to Table 1-12 as the numerator to effectively calculate its rate relative to other currencies from 2007 to 2019. The details are shown in Table 1-15.

Table 1-15   Internationalization of RMB Relative to Other Currencies (2007–2019)

Unit: %

Currency	2007	2010	2013	2016	2019
USD	2.1	2.5	4.4	7.6	9.0
EUR	4.3	4.6	9.1	13.6	15.7
JPY	3.3	4.3	5.1	8.2	11.5
GBP	2.6	2.7	5.3	7.4	8.2
AUD	1.8	2.3	4.0	6.6	7.8
CHF	0.9	1.3	3.1	5.0	5.2
CAD	4.2	4.3	9.3	10.7	13.0
Total of 7 Currencies	2.7	3.2	5.5	8.7	10.4
HKD	1.0	1.4	4.4	6.6	4.0
NZD	0.9	1.3	2.2	3.2	3.8
SEK	2.2	3.2	7.5	8.3	10.0
KRW	12.1	10.2	25.0	30.5	30.9
SGD	1.9	2.4	5.0	6.1	7.7
Total of 5 Currencies	1.7	2.4	5.4	6.4	10.8
NOK	2.4	4.6	8.3	7.9	8.8
MXN	10.0	11.9	11.6	20.1	26.8
INR	21.6	25.5	43.1	71.0	64.3
RUB	23.1	25.8	33.1	40.0	54.9
ZAR	4.1	7.4	7.5	10.9	12.6
Total of 5 Currencies	10.1	11.3	20.5	26.8	33.2

(Continued)

Currency	2007	2010	2013	2016	2019
TRY	46.7	14.9	16.5	21.5	24.3
BRL	43.8	45.5	51.2	63.9	68.2
TWD	13.9	13.2	25.7	29.9	24.5
DKK	4.7	8.0	10.0	13.1	20.5
PLN	7.0	8.4	17.2	24.1	35.9
THB	16.7	25.0	30.1	40.9	40.2
MYR	18.6	13.2	18.6	29.7	34.0
HUF	6.5	4.3	7.3	15.3	15.6
CZK	10.9	15.3	13.5	24.8	23.6
ILS	14.4	22.1	36.7	41.1	46.2
CLP	20.2	18.9	21.5	36.4	37.3
IDR	52.5	71.4	125.7	168.9	145.2
RMB	100.0	100.0	100.0	100.0	123.3
RMB*	100.0	100.0	100.0	100.0	100.0
Total of 13 Currencies	22.3	27.8	37.3	55.5	71.4
Total of BRIC	41.2	48.1	62.9	81.7	93.8
Total of BRICS	30.4	41.0	54.3	73.1	84.9

Data source: Calculated based on data from Table 1-10 to Table 1-12.

Table 1-15 shows the internationalization level of adjusted RMB (RMB*) relative to the seven international reserve currencies increased from 2.7% in 2007 to 10.4% in 2019. Meanwhile, its internationalization level relative to NZD and the other four developed economies' currencies increased from 1.7% in 2007 to 10.8% in 2019; RMB's internationalization level relative to the five developed economies' currencies, including NOK, increased from 10.1% to 33.0% in 2019; RMB's internationalization level relative to 12 emerging economies' currencies increased from 22.3% to 71.3%, and its level relative to the BRICS currencies increased from 30.4% to 84.9% in 2019. All these are remarkable achievements.

1.12 Alternative Method for Measuring Currency Internalization

Tables 1-1 and Tables 1-3 show the proportions of foreign exchange trade by currency and by country/region in the global foreign exchange market from 1992 to 2019. For any country or region, foreign exchange trade between its currency and other currencies usually takes up the largest share, supplemented by trade between other currencies. This section starts by introducing the ratio of foreign exchange trade between a currency and other currencies in offshore markets to the currency's total onshore foreign exchange trade. It then moves to introduce the share of a currency's offshore and onshore foreign exchange trade in the international foreign exchange market, followed by calculating its ratio of offshore foreign exchange turnover to its onshore foreign exchange turnover. In general, the higher the ratio, the higher the level of internationalization. As such, this can be an alternative method for measuring currency internationalization.

1.12.1 Proportion of foreign exchange between major currencies and other currencies

Table 1-16 shows the global distribution of foreign exchange trade in major countries and regions. However, without any information on the amount of foreign exchange trade transacted between their own currencies and other currencies, it is difficult to determine the level of activity of their own currencies in their domestic and offshore foreign exchange markets. Table 1-16 shows the ratios of offshore foreign exchange trade to domestic foreign exchange trade in major currencies from 2007 to 2019.

1.12.2 Changes in the RMB domestic/offshore foreign exchange trade ratio and related problems

As shown in Table 1-15, based on data from BIS, the ratio of RMB offshore foreign exchange trade to domestic foreign exchange trade was as high as 14.01 in April 2007. The offshore RMB market just started in August 2010, so the offshore RMB foreign exchange trade should have been zero in April 2007, which made the ratio of 14.1 an impossible number. The ratios of offshore foreign exchange trade to domestic foreign exchange trade from April 2010 to April 2019, as shown in Table 1-16, suggest rapid development of the offshore RMB market from 2010 to 2019; analysis will be made in the following chapters regarding the progress of the domestic and offshore RMB foreign exchange market over the past two years.

Table 1-16   **Ratios of Major Currencies' Offshore/ Domestic Foreign Exchange Trade in Daily Average Turnover (2007–2019)**

Currency	2007	2010	2013	2016	2019
USD	4.23	3.30	3.15	3.03	3.78
EUR	5.10	4.16	3.96	3.93	4.92
JPY	2.23	2.03	3.36	2.47	2.79
GBP	0.68	0.55	0.49	0.62	0.42
AUD	1.63	2.52	4.05	5.21	6.57
CAD	2.45	3.92	5.19	4.10	4.44
CHF	2.26	2.23	3.40	3.19	2.55
RMB	14.01	1.83	2.57	2.65	1.81
SGD	0.60	0.78	1.27	1.27	1.09
HKD	0.22	0.30	0.55	0.57	0.60
RMB	15.4	0.25	1.45	1.68	1.11
RMB*	15.4	0.25	1.45	1.68	1.56

Data source: The calculation is based on global foreign exchange data released in April every three years released by the BIS from 2007 to 2019. The Eurozone's data is calculated based on data from Austria, Belgium, Estonia, Finland, France, Germany, Greece, Ireland, Italy, Latvia, Lithuania, Luxembourg, the Netherlands, Portugal, Slovakia, and Spain, while data from Cyprus and Malta were missing. RMB* was calculated based on the results shown in Table 4-1.

1.13 Conclusion

This chapter provides an overall introduction to the composition of major international currencies, foreign exchange products and liquidity in those currencies, and their internationalization. In addition, we have also touched on currencies of other major developed and developing countries and regions, foreign exchange products in those currencies and liquidity, and their internationalization. Our analysis shows that the international status of international reserve currencies is best reflected by their functions as trading and reserve currencies, with their spot trading, forward trading, and swap trading all playing a significant role in the international foreign exchange market. International currencies with USD at the center have increasing, rather than decreasing, influence in the international market after the global financial crisis. Other than major international currencies, those of developed countries and regions also play an important role in the international market, despite a drop in internationalization. The status of almost all currencies of developing countries and regions in the international market is disproportionately related to their economic status; in other words, the proportions of foreign exchange trade in almost all those currencies are lower than their countries' and regions' GDP shares in the world.

The measurement of currency internationalization is a complicated concept. To objectively understand the changes in the level of internationalization of different currencies over time is impossible without an unbiased and scientific measuring methodology. In the course of on-going RMB internationalization in the years to come, measurement of RMB internationalization, especially one that enables comparison with other currencies, is of great significance. If the level of internationalization of RMB relative to that of other currencies achieves our target set for a certain time period, we will feel motivated to carry on the work. If it fails to do so, we can easily find the causes to adjust and improve our strategies and methods for an orderly and sound progression of RMB internationalization.

As the international functions of a currency often manifest in various areas and involve numerous data and parameters, an accurate and comprehensive measurement of currency internationalization is difficult. However, no matter how many areas the international functions of a currency involved, improved performance in each area will certainly translate into the higher activity of the currency in foreign exchange trading. Therefore, we measure the internationalization level of a currency indirectly by assessing how active the currency is on the international foreign exchange market. This chapter, with this methodology in mind, builds a simple and practical approach, which allows for the calculation of a currency or currency pair's internationalization, relative to other currencies or currency pairs.

With over a decade of development, especially after 2005, when a RMB exchange rate formation mechanism was implemented, tremendous progress has been made in areas such as domestic foreign exchange trading mechanisms and product innovation and launch. This has increased liquidity for foreign exchange forwards, swaps, forward rate agreements, interest rate swaps, forward options, and other products. However, further growth of China's financial market necessitates a need for comparison not only with the past, but also with the financial markets of other countries and regions so that the gap can be bridged. From these discussions, it is clear that significant gaps still exist between China and major developed countries and even between China and most major developing countries in foreign exchange and interest rate markets. China still faces issues such as low product liquidity, ineffective market roles, and insufficient supply of on-exchange financial derivatives, which urgently need resolving. Using a simple measuring method, we calculated the extent of RMB internationalization relative to other currencies from 2007 to 2019. Our results show that despite an increase in the RMB internationalization level from 2007 to 2010, this level runs counter to China's economic achievements in recent years. Although RMB internationalization significantly grew from 2013 to 2019, it has a long way to go before it matches China's economic and trade status in the world, and even reaches the level of other BRICS currencies.

Ever since 2009, China has been promoting RMB cross-border settlements, offshore issuance of RMB bonds, and direct offshore investment using RMB and other businesses, with enormous progress made in those aspects. Despite such efforts, however, foreign exchange trade in China failed to register any growth during the same period, which makes it clear that while promoting RMB businesses internationally, we need to place importance on the sound development of RMB foreign exchange markets as well, as new RMB businesses in the international market will lose strong market support and miss the steady and continuous growth target if a sound development of RMB foreign exchange markets is lacking. In other words, any measure promoting RMB internationalization should be accompanied in a coordinated fashion by efforts to achieve sound RMB growth in foreign exchange markets. We are confident that RMB will become far more internationalized in the years to come; Rome was not built in one day. Earnest studies on the success of, and lessons from, developed and developing countries should be carried out to produce proper roadmaps and timetables for short-term (three to five years), mid-term (five to eight years), and long-term (10 to 20 years) development of China's financial markets and regulatory mechanisms. Only by doing this can the financial sector better serve the real economy and lay a solid foundation for RMB internationalization. Such trends will be discussed further in later chapters.

Currency internationalization levels are reflected in areas where the currencies are applied globally. However, it is hard to acquire accurate data on the international application of currencies in all areas. Even when data is available, ratios will be inconsistent in different areas. Thus, it will be difficult to accurately measure the internationalization level. Although currencies are applied in a variety of areas, the international application of currencies can be reflected by data on the foreign exchange trade between a currency and other currencies.

Therefore, the share of a currency's average daily turnover in the global foreign exchange market is the best method to measure its internationalization level.

In the past two decades, 60% of the average daily turnover of the global foreign exchange market has come from the nominal turnover of foreign exchange derivatives rather than the foreign exchange spot trade. Thus, as shown in Table 1-1, most of the daily average turnover, including the average daily nominal turnover of foreign exchange derivatives, is from foreign exchange derivatives trade. The nominal turnover is not the turnover of trade which actually changes hand, but the exaggerated turnover. Thus, currency internationalization, as measured by the average daily nominal turnover in the global foreign exchange market, has many limitations; related problems will be analyzed and discussed below. The best ways to accurately measure real currency internationalization will be presented and proved.

Bibliography

International Monetary Fund. 2020. *Review of the Method of Valuation of the SDR.* Prepared by the Finance Department. In consultation with the Legal and Other Departments. Approved by Andrew Tweedie, October 26.

Li, Yao. 2003. "Non-International Currencies, Currency Internationalization and Capital Account Convertibility." *Financial Studies*, no. 8.

Mihaljek, Dubravko, and Frank Packer. 2010. "Derivatives in Emerging Markets." *BIS Quarterly Review*, December 2010.

Monetary and Economic Department. 2010. "Triennial Central Bank Survey, Foreign Exchange and Derivatives Market Activity in April 2010." Preliminary results, September.

———. 2010. "Triennial Central Bank Survey, Report on Global Foreign Exchange Market Activity in 2010." December.

Xu, Qiyuan. 2016. "How Does China Face Herstatt Rsk." Research Center for International Finance Institute of Institute of World Economics and Politics Chinese Academy of Social Sciences, August 1.

Zhang, Guangping, and Yang Jian. 2008. "Indian Financial Reforms and Experiences for China to Learn." Research sponsored by Asian Development Bank.

Zhang, Guangping. 2016. *RMB Derivatives.* 4th ed. China Finance Press, February.

Zhang, Peter G., and Thomas Chan. 2011. *Chinese Yuan Internationalization and Financial Products in China.* John Wiley & Sons.

Zhou, Xiaochuan. n.d. "Thoughts on Reform of the International Monetary System." People's Bank of China website.

CHAPTER TWO

PCT Patent Distribution in Main Countries and Regions

2.1 Introduction to the PCT Patent

Although most of the valid patents granted and maintained by the top five offices are resident files (in 2017, valid patents filed in Europe, Japan, the Republic of Korea, China, and the US accounted for 60%, 83%, 75%, 68%, and 50%, respectively; those in other countries and regions accounted for 35%, global resident patents accounted for 66.4%), abroad patent globally accounted for only 33.6%. However, these abroad patents or international patents in global trade and other business activities play a more important role. The globalization of markets and production remains a major business trend. The PCT patent is the patent coordinated by general international standards, and cross-border patent application is an important connotation of economic and trade globalization trends.

The universal international patent standard follows the Patent Cooperation on Treaty (PCT) signed in Washington, US, in 1970, which was later amended in 1979 and 2001. As of October 2, 2019, 153 countries and regions in the world had signed the treaty – a significant sign of progress in the field of international patents. The treaty provided detailed regulations and constraints on international cooperation among signatory countries and played an important role in promoting international patent cooperation. China entered the treaty in January 1994.

The PCT patent was actually met by the provisions of the patent cooperation treaty first by patent applicants to its in-charge receiving office, by the WIPO's International Bureau for international disclosure, and by the international search unit for international retrieval. This chapter introduces, compares, and analyzes the PCT patents of the top five offices and other countries and regions by using the relevant international patent data from these top five offices and WIPO.

2.2 Distribution of PCT Patent Applications in Main Countries and Regions

Table 2-1 shows the number of PCT patent applications in the top five offices from 2007 to 2019 and the annual compound growth rate in relevant periods. This table indicates that from 2007 to 2019, the number of global PCT patent applications maintained a relatively stable growth rate of slightly more than 4%; China had the biggest increase, with applications rising nearly tenfold to 58,990, surpassing South Korea, Europe, Japan, and the US for the first time in 2010, 2016, 2017, and 2019, respectively. It has become the world's largest PCT patent applicant country, demonstrating China's impressive achievements in this area over the past decade. From 2007 to 2019, the number of PCT patent applications in South Korea doubled the global average annual growth rate at 8.6%, while the average annual growth rate in Japan also slightly exceeded the global growth rate. Europe's annual growth rate was relatively stable, but it was 1% lower than the global average. The average annual growth rate of the US was only 0.5%, slightly more than 10% of the global growth rate, while the number of patent applications from other countries and regions outside of the top five offices did not increase but declined slightly.

According to the data in Table 2-1, from 2007 to 2019, the proportion of PCT international filings accepted by the top five offices increased from 75.1% to 85.1% in the world, indicating the importance of the top five offices in global international patent management.

Table 2-1   PCT International Filings by Receiving Offices and Annual Compound
Growth Rates of Filings by Receiving Offices (2007–2019)

Unit: %

Year	EPC	Japan	Korea	China	USA	Other	Global
2007	26,061	26,935	7,060	5,400	54,595	39,876	159,927
2008	29,494	28,027	7,911	6,081	52,054	39,674	163,241
2009	27,360	29,291	8,025	8,000	46,055	36,671	155,402
2010	28,900	31,523	9,639	12,917	45,228	36,133	164,340
2011	30,893	37,972	10,413	17,471	49,366	36,322	182,437
2012	32,430	42,787	11,787	19,924	52,009	36,315	195,252
2013	32,036	43,075	12,439	22,927	57,678	37,125	205,280
2014	32,902	41,292	13,138	27,088	61,963	37,897	214,280
2015	34,151	43,097	14,593	31,044	57,419	36,551	216,855
2016	35,288	44,495	15,595	44,463	56,665	36,347	232,853
2017	36,619	47,425	15,789	50,657	56,256	36,599	243,345
2018	37,937	48,630	16,990	55,204	55,230	38,539	252,530
2019	37,999	51,652	18,885	60,997	56,230	39,594	265,357
2007–2011 Average Growth	4.34	8.96	10.20	34.12	−2.49	−2.31	3.35
2011–2015 Average Growth	2.54	3.22	8.80	15.46	3.85	0.16	4.42
2012–2019 Average Growth	2.71	4.63	6.66	18.39	−0.52	2.02	5.18
2007–2019 Average Growth	3.19	5.58	8.54	22.39	0.25	−0.06	4.31

Data source: Data from 2007 to 2019 is from the IP5 statistical report 2019.

2.3 The Proportion of PCT Patent Applications in Total Patent Applications

Data from the 2011–2019 Patent Report of the top five offices shows that from 2008 to 2016, the share of PCT patent applications accounted for 2.98% to 3.41% of total patent applications in China, and increased by 0.30% to 3.71% in 2017, yet decreased slightly to 3.61% in 2018; while the corresponding percentages in EPC states, US, Japan, South Korea, and other countries and regions averaged 20%, 15%, 10%, 6%, and 8%, respectively, over the same period. This implied that the proportion of PCT patent applications in China was the lowest. However, most of the Chinese patents were only applied domestically, and it was difficult for such patents to enter the international market or even to replace foreign patents in China.

2.4 PCT Patents Granted by Five Offices

Table 2-2 gives the total PCT patents granted by each patent office from 2009 to 2019. It shows that, despite the low annual growth rates of PCT patents granted, the EPO granted the largest number of PCT patents over the past decade by far, followed by JPO and USPTO; although the number of PCT patents granted by CNIPA has been smaller than the above three offices, the average growth rate of 22.06% was the highest from 2009 to 2014. Despite the lower average annual growth rate of 6.20% between 2014 and 2019, the number of PCT patents granted by CNIPA is expected to surpass USPTO in the next decade or so.

The number of PCT patents granted by each office in Table 2-2 includes the PCT patents granted to overseas patent applicants within its jurisdiction as well as to domestic applicants. As such, from the number of PCT patents in Table 2-2, it is still difficult to see the number of PCT patents originating from the office or the international competitiveness of science and technology, which cannot be represented by PCT patents of each office.

Table 2-2   PCT-Patents Granted and Average Annual Growth Rates in Five Offices (2009–2019)

Unit: %

Year	EPO	JPO	KIPO	CNIPA	USPTO
2009	14,501	3,515	1,364	2,000	5,066
2010	16,184	4,413	1,639	2,842	5,880
2011	17,609	6,076	1,770	3,494	6,911
2012	18,161	7,702	2,255	3,985	8,321
2013	18,581	8,615	2,363	4,585	9,805
2014	19,741	9,084	2,496	5,418	11,153
2015	21,174	10,343	2,919	5,277	10,910
2016	22,584	10,234	2,963	7,559	10,766
2017	23,541	11,198	3,118	7,105	11,253
2018	24,659	11,671	3,398	6,624	11,046
2019	24,699	12,945	3,777	7,320	11,584
2009–2014	6.36	20.91	12.84	22.05	17.10
2014–2019	4.58	7.34	8.64	6.20	0.76

Source data: www.fiveipoffices.org.

CHAPTER THREE

The Export of Intellectual Property Royalties for Major Currency Issuers

Exports for intellectual property (ip) royalties of economies represent the science and technology capacity of these economies; meanwhile, imports of IP royalties represent a reliance on science and technology from other economies. Thus, net exports for IP royalties of one economy represent its own net capacity. Table 3-1 shows the net exports for IP royalties of major economies.

3.1 Top Ten Net Exporters for IP Royalties

Table 3-1 shows that the US is by far the largest net exporter of charges for IP royalties, with average net exports of over 60% of total global net exporters from 2008 to 2019, indicating American monopolistic power in global science and technology. The next largest net exporter of charges for IP royalties is Japan, with over 10% of the total from 2008 to 2019, underlining its importance in this field.

The second tier of net exporters for IP royalties are Switzerland, Germany, and the UK, with average annual net exports for IP royalties around USD 10 billion in recent years; total net exports for IP royalty charges of these three nations had an average annual share of about 16% of the global total; the third tier of net exporters are Finland, France, Denmark, Israel, and Sweden, with averages between USD 0.5 billion and USD 2.5 billion from 2008 to 2019, and total net exports from these five combined had an average annual global share of less than 10%.

Unit: %

Table 3-1 Net Exports for IP Royalties of Major Countries and Regions (2005 to 2019)

Country/Region	2008	2010	2012	2014	2016	2018	2019	Average Annual Growth Rate
US	61.91	63.85	72.81	78.82	71.01	74.94	74.67	1.72
Japan	7.40	7.91	11.99	16.52	19.03	23.75	20.88	9.89
Switzerland	4.13	5.33	6.27	4.63	9.78	12.21	11.99	10.18
Germany	−1.30	1.16	3.89	4.71	7.50	8.80	8.62	18.79
UK	4.10	4.03	3.72	7.70	7.34	11.82	8.34	6.66
Finland	−0.76	0.81	1.55	1.46	2.16	2.40	2.43	11.08
France	5.04	3.61	3.97	1.82	0.73	0.88	1.79	−9.00
Denmark	1.17	0.70	0.87	0.83	0.81	1.78	1.84	4.17
Israel*	0.05	−0.07	0.65	0.82	1.17	1.61	1.83	38.97
Sweden	2.64	4.28	5.07	5.27	4.31	2.58	1.02	−8.32
UAE	0.00	0.00	0.00	1.09	1.01	0.93	0.95	−2.65
Belgium	−0.51	0.59	−0.17	−0.09	1.03	0.66	0.76	3.72
Netherlands*	0.00	0.00	0.00	−10.72	−3.55	−7.56	0.21	54.42
Hungary	−0.89	0.24	0.34	0.38	0.35	0.27	0.04	164.20

(Continued)

Country/Region	2008	2010	2012	2014	2016	2018	2019	Average Annual Growth Rate
Austria	−0.93	−0.69	−0.86	−0.50	−0.30	−0.60	−0.65	3.11
Italy	−3.27	−2.89	−1.48	−1.83	−1.25	−0.19	−0.72	12.85
Taiwan, China	−2.82	−4.48	−4.75	−4.41	−4.06	−2.07	−1.86	3.73
Korea	−3.39	−6.00	−4.71	−5.00	−2.49	−2.13	−2.28	3.55
Australia	−2.23	−2.44	−3.31	−3.11	−2.50	−2.67	−2.55	1.22
Poland	−1.57	−2.01	−2.10	−2.61	−2.25	−3.04	−3.10	6.40
Spain*	0.00	0.00	−4.11	−3.04	−3.07	−4.11	−3.45	−2.47
Luxembourg	−0.36	−0.18	−1.26	−2.83	−1.91	−2.58	−3.67	23.57
Brazil	−2.23	−3.04	−3.92	−5.55	−4.49	−4.30	−4.70	7.01
Thailand	−2.47	−3.05	−3.51	−3.91	−3.91	−5.11	−5.12	3.56
Russian Federation	−4.08	−4.46	−6.97	−7.36	−4.45	−5.41	−5.85	3.34
Canada	−4.82	−6.92	−6.97	−6.94	−7.05	−6.30	−6.01	2.03
India	−1.38	−2.31	−3.67	−4.19	−4.94	−7.12	−7.02	15.93
Singapore	−12.39	−15.10	−20.29	−16.97	−8.43	−8.45	−7.68	−4.26
China	−9.75	−12.21	−13.41	−21.94	−22.81	−30.04	−27.68	9.95

(Continued)

Country/Region	2008	2010	2012	2014	2016	2018	2019	Average Annual Growth Rate
Ireland	-33.98	-34.54	-33.21	-50.52	-67.69	-71.33	-84.01	8.58
Sum	-2.67	-7.87	-3.55	-27.47	-22.21	-20.39	-31.00	24.96
Rest of World	-33.49	-41.64	-39.99	-53.24	-47.53	-48.03	-57.72	4.18
World	-35.26	-39.93	-37.77	-51.14	-45.42	-45.94	-55.97	4.29
Top 10	84.37	91.60	110.80	122.58	123.83	140.76	133.39	4.25
Top 11–20	-15.60	-17.67	-17.04	-23.52	-17.30	-16.40	-9.19	4.69
Top 21–30	-71.45	-81.80	-100.60	-123.24	-128.74	-144.75	-155.19	7.31
Sum/World	7.58	19.70	18.12	53.72	48.90	44.37	55.38	
EPC States	-71.42	-42.68	-44.62	-78.97	-61.46	-97.12	-91.50	2.28
Eurozone	-54.11	-48.22	-43.57	-63.67	-71.74	-76.08	-80.97	3.73
Euro/EPC	75.8	113.0	97.7	80.6	113.4	78.3	88.5	
Developed Economies*	19.69	18.96	29.68	16.62	19.29	33.44	21.48	0.80
Other Developed Economies	-64.69	-72.64	-81.12	-105.97	-104.54	-107.32	-111.91	5.11
Developing Economies*	-22.36	-23.53	-36.53	-44.09	-41.50	-53.82	-52.48	8.06

Data source: Calculated using data from the Chinese version of this book; other developed economies discount the ten net positive exporters in Table 3-1.

3.2 Monopolistic Power to Control World IPs

The top 10 net exporters of charges for IP royalties in Table 3-1 are all developed countries, and only the US, Japan, Switzerland, Germany, the UK, and France are among the largest 20 economies of the world. This suggests that most major developed economies are actually net exporters of IP royalties, yet many developed economies are actually net importers, and all developing countries are also net importers of IP royalties. In other words, the major developed countries have the monopolistic power to control global Ips with their resources in research and development.

3.3 Net Exports of Developing Countries

Table 3-1 shows that the net exports of 8 developing countries dropped from USD −22.36 billion in 2008 to USD −52.48 billion in 2019. Overall, the technological dependence of major developing countries in the past decade or so has worsened, according to these figures. It is noticeable that net imports (of charges for IP royalties) for China as a share of the total from the eight major developing countries grew steadily from 43.60% in 2008 to 55.82% in 2018, yet dropped to 52.76% in 2019. This implies that recent technological progress in China has not clearly reflected IP royalty exports, since the average annual compound growth rate was 9.95% from 2008 to 2019, higher than the corresponding figure of most developed countries in the same period.

3.4 Average Exports and Net Exports for IP Royalties of Major Blocs and Their Implications

3.4.1 Average exports per family patent of major blocs
Table 3-2 shows the total exports for IP royalties of major countries and regions; we can find average export charges for IP royalties per family patent of major blocs.

3.4.2 Average net exports of IP family patents of major blocs
Table 3-3 gives the total net exports for IP royalties of major countries and regions; we can find the average net export IP royalty charges per family patent of major blocs.

Table 3-2   Export Charges for IP Family Patents of Major Blocs (2000 to 2019)

Unit: USD million

Year	EPC States	Japan	Korea	US	China	Others	World
2000	14.73	1.63	0.57	8.75	2.50	18.58	6.98
2001	10.98	1.20	0.64	5.53	1.41	13.52	5.01
2002	10.07	1.08	0.43	5.14	1.06	14.77	4.62
2003	9.96	1.23	0.47	4.81	0.72	15.17	4.51
2004	10.81	1.61	0.61	5.23	1.54	15.40	4.98
2005	11.30	1.81	0.65	5.24	0.67	15.09	5.19
2006	12.90	2.11	0.73	6.17	0.76	18.72	5.93
2007	16.10	2.81	0.77	7.74	0.93	24.03	7.63
2008	16.05	3.30	1.18	7.06	1.45	24.16	7.85
2009	14.86	2.56	1.39	6.32	0.61	19.24	6.92
2010	17.01	2.93	1.13	7.15	1.03	18.73	7.46
2011	19.14	3.32	1.38	7.62	0.77	18.59	8.18
2012	18.74	3.83	1.23	7.71	0.88	22.92	8.34
2013	20.49	4.21	1.51	7.54	0.57	31.92	8.89
2014	21.53	4.95	2.02	8.42	0.34	34.08	9.82
2015	21.37	5.19	2.42	8.44	0.53	45.09	10.10
2016*	22.37	5.90	2.67	8.71	0.48	45.93	10.60
2017*	24.74	6.63	2.93	9.26	1.68	54.36	11.70
2018*	27.62	7.63	3.25	9.47	1.66	62.13	12.69
2019*	27.65	8.28	3.38	9.50	1.69	66.56	12.80

Data source: Data for Japan, US, Korea, and China from 2000–2004 was from their official websites; data for the EPC and others for this period were estimated using 2005 data as a base and average annual compound rates.

Table 3-3   Export Charges for IP Royalties of Major Blocs (2000 to 2019)

Unit: USD million

Year	EPC States	Japan	Korea	US	China	Others	World
2000	−3.69	−0.13	−2.11	5.50	−35.83	−113.73	−1.41
2001	−2.77	−0.08	−1.47	3.34	−23.46	−77.49	−1.14
2002	−2.56	−0.06	−1.09	2.96	−23.84	−79.22	−1.02
2003	−2.55	0.13	−0.81	2.91	−23.24	−76.06	−0.82
2004	−2.79	0.21	−0.86	3.14	−27.84	−72.18	−0.66
2005	−2.94	0.31	−0.86	3.28	−22.16	−66.02	−0.47
2006	−5.06	0.48	−0.92	4.16	−23.81	−83.05	−0.71
2007	−6.15	0.79	−1.48	5.49	−21.39	−101.66	−0.68
2008	−6.99	0.95	−1.65	4.87	−24.81	−106.40	−1.17
2009	−5.57	0.57	−1.75	4.15	−15.07	−87.92	−1.15
2010	−5.77	0.87	−2.13	4.81	−15.15	−112.89	−1.21
2011	−5.85	1.13	−0.95	5.28	−14.38	−93.50	−0.99
2012	−4.82	1.44	−1.48	5.21	−14.14	−118.88	−1.11
2013	−5.15	1.83	−1.90	5.20	−13.01	−150.61	−1.14
2014	−7.37	2.19	−1.82	5.70	−11.10	−119.44	−1.52
2015	−8.83	2.76	−1.30	5.77	−10.21	−108.46	−1.47
2016*	−7.89	2.86	−0.96	5.48	−9.45	−108.75	−1.41
2017*	−7.40	3.23	−0.97	5.78	−8.38	−114.86	−1.24
2018*	−7.69	3.98	−0.89	5.97	−8.98	−125.51	−1.44
2019*	−9.04	3.70	−0.99	6.04	−7.03	−128.68	−1.75

Data source: Same as Table 3-2.

CHAPTER FOUR

Technological Autonomy and Measures of Technology Internationalization

THE HIGHER THE INTERNATIONAL LEVEL OF family patents, the more competitive exports of both goods and services will naturally be. Based on the results in Chapter 3, this chapter discusses another important concept closely related to patent internationalization – technological independence or autonomy. That is the proportion of export charges used for the intellectual property of a country or region to its import and export charges used for intellectual property. The lower the degree of technological autonomy, the higher the degree of external dependence on technology, and vice versa. Of course, the higher the degree of technology internationalization of a country or region, the higher the degree of technological autonomy; the two are closely related. With the results of the technological independence or autonomy of major countries and regions in the past two decades, the status of different countries and regions in the global technological chain is further assessed by using IP export and import data. Such results will help prepare us for the interaction analysis between technology internationalization and currency internationalization hereinafter.

4.1 Definition and Measurement of Technological Autonomy

4.1.1 Definition of technological autonomy

Since patent families are only one part of international patents, the number of patent families in each country or region and their global share cannot represent the technological autonomy level. All family patents of each country or region have the same influence domestically and abroad. At the same time, each country or region benefits from family patents of its own and accepts foreign family patents. Therefore, the proportion of "the number of patent families in each country or region in the world," to "its own patent families plus the total number of foreign family patents within its jurisdiction," only reflects the patent autonomy of that country or region.

As export and import IP charges of any country or region contain the most information about their relative technological competitiveness – including all information on the relative competitiveness of all family patents – the proportion of export IP charges for the use of IPs to the total used by said country or region can better reflect its technological independence or autonomy. This is a broader concept than patent autonomy.

4.1.2 Top ten countries with the highest technological autonomy

Table 4-1 shows an average annual technological independence or autonomy of over 60% from 2008 to 2019; the average annual change of technological autonomy growth was highest (2.69%) from 2008 to 2019 in Israel, posting an autonomy figure of 80.93% in 2019; technological autonomy was also over 70% in Finland and the US; technological autonomy in Denmark, Switzerland, Japan, and Germany was over 60% in 2019, indicating their relative sci-tech competitiveness. It is noticeable that the average annual change of technological autonomy in Sweden, France, and the US was −1.46%, −0.60%, and −0.28%, respectively, while Finland, Germany, and Japan were 3.28%, 1.35%, and 0.54%, respectively, indicating the relative decline and progress of technological independence in these countries. Total technological autonomy remained around 66.36% of the top ten countries, without much change from 2008 to 2019.

Table 4-1   Technological Independence or Autonomy of Major Countries and Regions
(2000 to 2019)

Unit: %

Country/ Region	2008	2010	2012	2014	2016	2018	2019	Average Annual Change
Israel	51.31	45.95	73.76	73.91	78.48	78.90	80.93	2.69
Finland	39.79	60.58	65.22	69.22	77.58	76.44	75.86	3.28
US	76.36	75.32	75.47	75.60	72.91	73.02	73.31	−0.28
Denmark	66.47	60.45	61.94	59.82	59.97	68.10	67.89	0.13
Switzerland	64.65	62.47	60.72	57.06	64.27	65.45	66.73	0.19
Japan	58.41	58.70	61.58	64.18	65.98	67.66	64.38	0.54
Germany	45.94	53.76	61.68	58.99	62.45	60.99	60.76	1.35
UK	58.36	58.27	58.02	62.01	61.83	64.49	59.88	0.14
Sweden	69.52	79.43	75.30	70.14	69.57	60.47	53.42	−1.46
France	59.72	57.62	59.24	53.33	51.21	51.34	53.08	−0.60
UAE	...	...	...	60.01	58.44	57.15	57.09	−0.97
Belgium	42.84	56.72	48.48	49.31	57.86	54.09	55.27	1.13
Hungary	39.66	53.11	54.50	54.98	55.34	54.08	50.71	1.01
Netherlands*	0.00	0.00	0.00	44.80	46.36	46.90	50.08	1.76
Italy	35.43	35.81	42.34	39.28	42.34	49.07	46.32	0.99
Korea	29.48	25.77	31.17	34.45	42.38	43.96	43.59	1.28
Austria	35.80	36.50	35.92	41.83	44.41	41.15	41.15	0.49
Singapore	8.19	10.19	10.85	15.77	31.27	33.23	34.41	2.38
Spain	...	...	19.95	24.34	27.84	27.61	33.24	1.90
Thailand	11.67	15.15	27.07	35.45	36.37	31.60	32.50	1.89
Canada	31.51	22.43	26.51	28.90	28.07	31.81	32.08	0.05
Taiwan, China	5.96	8.51	14.09	14.10	18.93	29.92	30.09	2.19
Luxembourg	32.72	42.83	34.03	30.33	35.21	32.71	29.10	−0.33
Australia	19.71	22.18	17.08	17.72	19.80	21.00	21.43	0.16

(Continued)

Country/ Region	2008	2010	2012	2014	2016	2018	2019	Average Annual Change
China	5.24	5.98	5.56	2.90	4.64	13.51	16.22	1.00
Poland	10.50	9.49	8.97	10.47	14.20	14.44	14.92	0.40
Russian Federation	8.31	7.38	8.01	7.67	9.88	12.23	12.87	0.41
Brazil	14.71	5.56	6.17	5.95	11.24	13.87	10.71	−0.36
Ireland	3.99	7.23	11.54	10.81	10.42	14.03	10.45	0.59
India	8.83	4.95	7.45	11.96	8.76	9.03	9.95	0.10
Top 10	66.36	66.87	68.14	67.34	67.14	67.26	66.37	0.00
World	46.53	46.26	46.87	46.42	46.88	47.32	46.80	0.02
EPC States	41.06	42.75	44.30	42.70	42.50	43.89	42.98	0.17
Euro Zone	36.69	37.67	39.36	37.74	37.09	38.86	38.66	0.18
Euro/EPC	89.3	88.1	88.9	88.4	87.3	88.5	89.9	0.00
12 Other Developed Economies	17.32	17.70	20.41	30.17	31.05	33.70	33.87	1.50
8 Major Developing Economies	12.19	11.12	10.19	13.46	14.75	17.35	18.43	0.57

4.1.3 Technological autonomy of other developed economies

Table 4-1 also shows that the technological autonomy of the other 12 developed economies as a group grew from 17.32% in 2008 to 33.87% in 2019, with an average annual growth rate of 1.50%. This was slightly higher than the corresponding average annual growth rate of Germany (1.35%) over the same period, indicating significant progress in this area compared to the relatively stagnant status of the top ten countries. It is noticeable that technological autonomy was the lowest in Australia among the top 20 advanced economies.

4.1.4 Technological autonomy of the Eurozone and EPC States

Table 4-1 also shows that the technological autonomy of the Eurozone 19 countries as a group grew from 36.69% in 2008 to 38.66% in 2019, with an average annual growth rate of 0.18%. This was much lower than the corresponding figure of the eight major developing countries and 12 other developed economies in Table 4-1, indicating relatively slow growth in this area; the technological autonomy of EPC States as a group grew from 41.06% in 2008 to 42.98% in 2019 with an average annual growth rate of 0.17%. This was almost the same rate as the Eurozone (unsurprisingly, since most of the countries are part of both groups), further indicating the sluggish progress of technological independence of EPC states.

4.1.5 Technological autonomy of the eight major developing countries

Table 4-1 also shows that the technological autonomy of the eight major developing countries combined grew from 12.19% in 2008 to 18.43% in 2019, with an average annual growth rate of 0.57%. This was slightly higher than the corresponding figure (0.43%) of the 38 EPC States, suggesting the relatively slow growth of technological independence; the technological autonomy of these eight major developing countries as a group was lower than the autonomy of Australia, the lowest of all major developed countries in the top 20 economies.

4.1.6 Technological autonomy of China

Table 4-1 shows that technological autonomy remained almost unchanged from 2008 to 2016 and then increased from 4.64% in 2016 to 16.22% in 2019. New data from the State Administration of Foreign Exchange showed that technological autonomy grew further to 18.75% in 2020 – probably higher than the corresponding autonomy of the eight major developing countries combined in 2020 for the first time, demonstrating significant technological progress in China in recent years; yet there is much to be done to catch up with the other 12 developed economies and Eurozone. We will forecast technological progress in China in relation to the Eurozone, Japan, and US when we forecast currency internationalization of the top eight currencies.

4.2 Correlation between Technological Autonomy of Major Countries and Regions

Technological independence or autonomy is defined above by using market data on the IP of major countries and regions. This is not only more accurate than all kinds of patent data, but also includes all IP information, including patents. The higher the level of technological autonomy of any country or region, the greater its IP export revenue and the lower its IP import costs. Thus, we can conclude that if patents can neither generate export revenue nor replace foreign patents to reduce IP import charges, they are of no actual use to the economy. The relationship between the technological autonomy of major countries and regions given in this section is an important reference point; with this, the correlation of the technological autonomy among the top ten net IP exporters can be calculated. Table 4-2 shows the results.

4.2.1 Relationship between the US and other major net IP exporters

Table 4-2 shows that the US, the country with the highest net IP export charges, has the highest correlation of 61.43% with Sweden, underlining US technological support for Sweden. In addition, the correlation between the technological autonomy of the US and that of France was also 42.01%; the correlation coefficients between the US and that of Switzerland, Finland, Israel, Japan, Germany, Denmark, and the UK were −62.36%, −39.95%, −35.66%, −25.17%, −22.56%, −21.74%, and −21.14%, respectively, indicating various degrees of competition between US technological autonomy and these countries.

It is noticeable that besides the positive correlation coefficients between US technological autonomy and Sweden and France, all other correlation coefficients between the US and the other seven nations were negative to various degrees. This data indicates that top IP exporters are usually in competition with most other major net exporters.

4.2.2 Relationship between Japan and other major net IP exporters

Table 4-2 also shows that the correlation of technological autonomy between Japan and Israel, Finland, Germany, and the UK were 90.43%, 89.22%, 85.65%, and 53.24%, respectively, indicating close cooperation or complementarity relationships between Japan and these four countries; the correlation of technological autonomy between Japan and France, Sweden, US and Switzerland, however, were −92.47%, −47.83%, −25.17%, and −19.37%, respectively, indicating various degrees of competition. Overall, there were four negative correlation coefficients between Japanese technological autonomy and other countries, and seven positive coefficients.

Unit: %

Table 4-2   Correlation of Technological Autonomy among Top Ten Net IP Exporters (2005–2019)

Exporter	Israel	Finland	US	Denmark	Switzerland	Japan	Germany	UK	Sweden	France
Israel	100.00	87.67	−35.66	−4.16	−11.92	90.43	89.32	37.08	−49.43	−80.10
Finland	87.67	100.00	−39.95	−0.36	−16.13	89.22	94.23	32.65	−39.35	−82.08
US	−35.66	−39.95	100.00	−21.74	−62.36	−25.17	−22.56	−21.14	61.43	42.01
Denmark	−4.16	−0.36	−21.74	100.00	56.68	1.16	−10.28	19.08	−55.75	8.51
Switzerland	−11.92	−16.13	−62.36	56.68	100.00	−19.37	−28.26	4.98	−52.36	8.93
Japan	90.43	89.22	−25.17	1.16	−19.37	100.00	85.65	53.24	−47.83	−92.47
Germany	89.32	94.23	−22.56	−10.28	−28.26	85.65	100.00	17.83	−21.49	−69.75
UK	37.08	32.65	−21.14	19.08	4.98	53.24	17.83	100.00	−47.66	−62.21
Sweden	−49.43	−39.35	61.43	−55.75	−52.36	−47.83	−21.49	−47.66	100.00	57.22
France	−80.10	−82.08	42.01	8.51	8.93	−92.47	−69.75	−62.21	57.22	100.00

4.2.3 Relationship between Switzerland, Germany, and the UK with other major net IP exporters

Table 4-2 shows that Switzerland, Germany, and the UK have the highest net IP export charges behind the US and Japan. Table 4-2 shows that Swiss technological autonomy had the highest correlation with Denmark 56.68%; a correlation with France and the UK of less than 10%; and its correlation with the other six major net exporters were all negative, indicating competition with these six countries; German technological autonomy has a correlation with Israel, Finland and Japan (89.32%, 94.23%, and 85.65%, respectively), indicating high cooperation with these three countries in sci-tech. German technological autonomy had negative correlation coefficients with the five other major net IP exporters, however, particularly its correlation with France (−69.76%); and British technological autonomy had the highest correlation (53.24%) with Japan, and a negative correlation with other three countries, especially with France (−62.11%). These correlation coefficients show competition and cooperation between these nations in IP exports.

4.3 Correlation between the US and Major East Asian Economies in Technological Autonomy

The correlation between the US and major East Asian economies gives us a very good indication of the technological dependence of these economies on US technology. This section concentrates on this relationship.

4.3.1 Reconsidering the correlation between Japanese and US technological autonomy

Statistics from the Japan External Trade Organization (JETRO) show that Japanese IP net export charges grew from USD −0.78 billion in 1977 to USD 1.28 billion in 2003, and its technological autonomy grew from 17.50% to 52.75% over the same period. Table 4-2 also shows the correlation of technological autonomy between the two nations was −25.17% between 2000 to 2019, giving evidence of mild competition between them; however, more data is needed to analyze the relationship further. Meanwhile, Figure 4-1 gives their rolling correlation coefficients from 2003 to 2020.

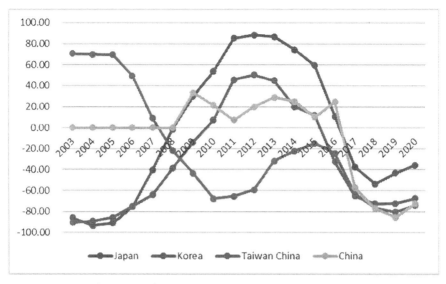

Figure 4-1   Correlation Coefficients between the US and Major East Asian Economies (2003–2020) (Unit: %)

Data source: The US Bureau of Economic Analysis: www.bea.gov and the Japan External Trade Organization: www.jetro.go.jp; correlation coefficients between the US and Mainland China were zero from 2003 to 2008 because both export and import IP charges were not released by the China Administration of Foreign Exchange over this period.

Figure 4-1 clearly shows that shortly after Japan became a net IP exporter in 2003, correlation coefficients between the US and Japan reached an all-time low of −93.51% in 2004, indicating intense rivalry; yet this subsided from 2004 to 2008 as the correlation coefficient increased to −1.34%. The relationship became one of cooperation from 2009 to 2016, peaking at 88.22% in 2012, and Japanese technological autonomy increased from 56.25% to a historic high of 68.14% in 2015; however, the relationship switched to competition again from 2017 to 2020 as the gap in technological autonomy closed to a historic low of 6.55%. Japanese technological autonomy declined by 5.44% from 2017 to 2020 as a result of competition between the countries, registering the only consecutive 3-year period with a continuous annual decrease since 1977.

These results show the relationship between major technology originators may switch between competition and cooperation depending upon the relative levels of technological autonomy; cooperation and competition may also yield significant progress or decline of technological autonomy.

4.3.2 Correlation between the US and the other three major East Asian economies

Figure 4-2 shows that the relationship between US technology and South Korea, Mainland China was similar to that with Japan, though cooperation was not as strong as with Japan from 2009 to 2015, and competition was not as severe from 2016 to 2020; the only exception was Taiwan, China, with steady US cooperation before 2008, and steady squeezing from 2009 to 2015. The relationships between US technological autonomy and the four major East Asian economies given in Figure 4-1 also revealed both US technology and USD influences on East Asian economies after the 2008 world financial crisis. We will further analyze related effects in later chapters.

4.3.3 Correlation between Japanese technological autonomy and the other major East Asian economies

Table 4-3 gives the correlation coefficients between US technological autonomy and those of the four major East Asian economies. It shows that the correlation coefficients were all negative, with Taiwan, China and South Korea all above 60% in absolute terms, and correlation coefficients with Mainland China and Japan at −55.60% and −25.17%, indicating competition to various degrees; correlation coefficients between Japanese technological autonomy and Korea, Taiwan, China, and Mainland China were 78.66%, 77.87%, and 52.56%, respectively indicating cooperation here.

It is noticeable that correlation coefficients between Japanese technological autonomy and those of South Korea and Taiwan, China were above 77%, indicating close cooperation. The relationships between Japanese technological autonomy and the other three major East Asian economies are better revealed in Figure 4-2, which contains much more information than Table 4-3. Figure 4-2 shows that cooperation between Japanese and Korean technology was much higher before the 2008 world financial crisis, yet was squeezed after 2008, before recovering after 2014 to some extent. However, the relationship between Japan and Taiwan, China improved dramatically from 2008 to 2016 when US and Japanese cooperation shifted to competition; thus, cooperation among major East Asian economies became necessary. Japan-Taiwan, China technological cooperation remained at a similar level to Japan-Korea cooperation.

Table 4-3   Correlation Coefficients between the US and the Six Major East Asian Economies and Asian Tigers (2005 to 2019)

Country/ Region	US	Japan	Mainland China	Korea	Taiwan, China	Singapore	Hong Kong, China
US	100.00	−25.17	−55.60	−61.76	−64.08	−57.83	−43.18
Japan	−25.17	100.00	52.56	78.66	77.87	87.52	93.42
Mainland China	−55.60	52.56	100.00	68.80	86.48	74.45	66.59
Korea	−61.76	78.66	68.80	100.00	87.75	92.11	85.72
Taiwan, China	−64.08	77.87	86.48	87.75	100.00	89.71	85.89
Singapore	−57.83	87.52	74.45	92.11	89.71	100.00	93.91
Hong Kong, China	−43.18	93.42	66.59	85.72	85.89	93.91	100.00

Data source: Same as Table 4-1.

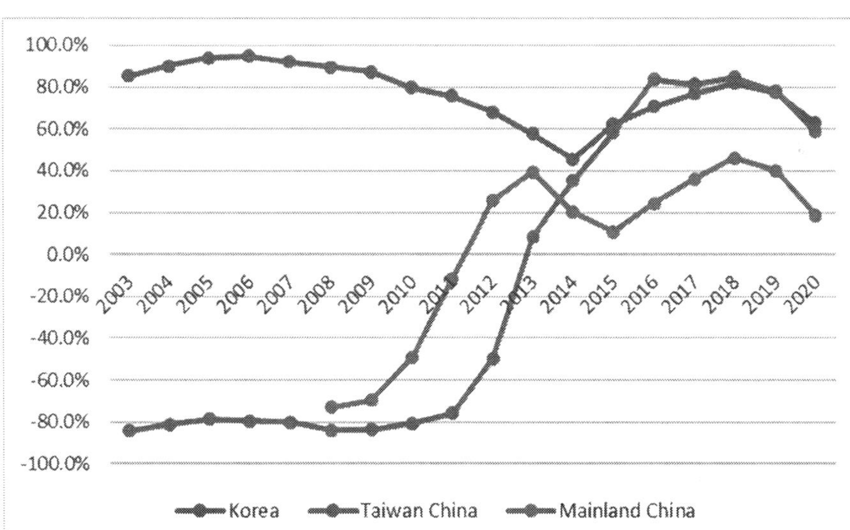

Figure 4-2 Correlation Coefficients between Japanese Technological Autonomy and the Other Three Major East Asian Economies (1992–2020) (Unit: %)

Data source: Same as Figure 4-1.

Figure 4-2 also shows that Japan and Mainland China had a relationship from 2008 to 2011 based on technological squeezing to various degrees; Japan and Mainland China entered a relationship of mild cooperation from 2012 to 2016, with an average correlation coefficient of about 20%, similar to that between the US and China, as shown in Figure 4-1; although the US-China relationship entered a tighter squeeze with more negative correlation coefficients, cooperation continued and even strengthened between Japan and Mainland China from 2017 to 2020.

4.3.4 Close cooperation between Mainland China and Taiwan, China in technology

Table 4-3 also shows the correlation coefficient between Mainland China and Taiwan, China was as high as 86.56% from 2005 to 2019, second only to the correlation coefficient of 87.75% between Taiwan, China and Korea during the same period. Historical data shows the correlation increased to 86.98% from 2006 to 2020, and similar data shows that correlation coefficients between the technological autonomy of China and that of Japan, Switzerland, Germany, UK, Denmark, Israel, Finland, Korea, as well as Canada, Australia, and New Zealand were all positive. However, they were all lower than the China – Taiwan coefficient, indicating the special technological relationship enjoyed by these two.

4.4 Technological Autonomy Correlation between the US and the Asian Tigers

South Korea, Taiwan, China, Hong Kong, China, and Singapore – the "Asian Tigers" – are well known for their rapid economic growth from the 1970s to the 1990s. Their export-oriented development model of leveraging US technology was of great interest to Mainland China in the initial stages of its reform and opening up policy. Thus, these Asian tigers somewhat stimulated China's economic reform through their economic miracles, and the technological progress of these tigers should give a clear indication of technological progress in China.

Table 4-3 shows that the correlation pattern of the Asian Tigers with US is the natural extension of that with the four major East Asian economies: Japanese technology was more positively correlated with Hong Kong, China and Singapore than with South Korea and Taiwan, China, indicating higher cooperation between Japan and these two Asian financial centers; Korean correlation with Singapore, Taiwan, China, and Hong Kong, China was higher than with Japan; Taiwan correlation (89.71%) with Singapore was also higher than with Korea (87.75%) and with Japan (77.87%); and Singapore's correlation with Hong Kong, China (93.91%) was higher than with Korea (92.11%) and with Taiwan, China (89.71%); Hong Kong, China's correlations with Singapore and Japan were both over 93%, close to the highest correlation between Germany and Finland 94.23% in Table 4-3; Hong Kong, China's correlation with Mainland China (66.59%) was higher than most correlations among the top ten net IP exporters in Table 4-3, yet the lowest of Hong Kong, China's correlations with other major East Asian economies or Tigers. These high correlations underline the high level of cooperation among such countries.

It is noticeable that the correlation between US technology and Singapore and Hong Kong, China was somewhat higher or less negative than between US technology and South Korea and Taiwan, China, indicating less of a squeezing influence of US technology on these two Asian financial centers.

4.5 Average Annual Change of Technological Autonomy of Major Economies and Their Implications

This gives us a clear indication of the speed of progress or backwardness in technology. We discuss the annual changes in this section.

4.5.1 Annual change of technological autonomy of major economies

Table 4-1 shows that of the 30 major economies, only 6 posted a negative average annual change in technological autonomy, notably −1.46%, −0.97%, and −0.60% from 2008 to 2019 in Sweden, UAE, and France, respectively; of the 24 economies with a positive average annual change, (notably a 3.28% average annual increase in Finland, and 2.69%, 2.38%, 2.19% in Israel, Singapore and Taiwan, China, respectively, showing significant technological progress in these countries; the average annual increase of technological autonomy in Spain, Thailand, Netherlands, Germany, Korea, Belgium, Hungary, and China was 1.90%, 1.89%, 1.76%, 1.35%, 1.28%, 1.13%, 1.01%, and 1.00%, respectively, indicating steady progress; the average annual increase of technological autonomy of other 12 major economies was lower than 1.00%.

4.5.2 Average annual change of technological autonomy in major East Asian economies

Because export and import IP charges in Hong Kong, China were relatively low, Hong Kong, China was not included in Table 4-1, yet the corresponding average annual increase of technological autonomy in Hong Kong, China was 0.75% from 2008 to 2019, lower than the corresponding averages of 2.38%, 2.19%, 1.28%, and 1.00% in Singapore, Taiwan, China, South Korea, and Mainland China over the same period, respectively, yet higher than Japan (0.54%). This is because from 2008 to 2019, Japan had already passed its fast-growing period before 2008. (Historical data show that the average annual growth of technological autonomy was 1.39% from 1997 to 2008, and 1.53% from 1984 to 1997.)

South Korea's technological autonomy increased from 5.91% to 23.17% (exceeding one-fifth for the first time) from 1992 to 2001, with an average annual growth rate of 1.92%. From 2001 to 2018, the growth rate continued to increase to 43.96%, and the annual average growth rate dropped to 1.22%. The continuous improvement of South Korea's technological autonomy in the past 20 years also provides some reference for the improvement of China's technological autonomy over the next ten years.

Although the technological autonomy of Taiwan, China over the past 30 years or so was a phenomenon rarely seen in other economies, the changing rhythm of its technological autonomy over different periods should also be of certain reference significance to Mainland China. According to the relevant data above, Taiwan, China's technological autonomy increased from 1.63% to 24.07% (exceeding one-fifth for the first time) with an average annual growth rate of 2.80% from 1984 to 1992. However, the average annual growth rate was only 0.18% from 1992 to 2020, showing sluggish progress in the past 18 years.

4.5.3 Technological progress in Singapore

Table 4-1 shows that the average annual growth of technological autonomy was 2.38%, the third highest of the top 30 economies from 2008 to 2019 and the highest of all Asian economies.

According to WIPO data, from 2000 to 2003, Singapore's technological autonomy was only slightly over 1%, and more than half its import IP revenue was from the US; from 2004 to 2005, Singapore's technological autonomy increased from 3.7% to 5.2%, but more than half was also from the US; and from 2005 to 2009, it remained 5%–6%, but still with more than half of IP revenue from the US; Singapore's technological autonomy exceeded 10% for the first time in 2010, and its proportion of IP revenue from the US dropped to 26.6% in 2010; Singapore's technological autonomy increased to 15.77% in 2014, with about 30% from the US; Singapore's technological autonomy exceeded 30% for the first time in 2015, with its IP revenue from the US accounting for 33.9%. Its technological autonomy increased to 34.41%, and the proportion of Singapore imports for charges when using IPs from the US remained around 30% of Singapore's total IP imports in the same year.

With steady help from the US, Singapore has made significant technological progress in the past two decades. Singapore's IP per unit charge of GDP, or IP sufficiency to GDP, has reached the fourth highest in the world and highest in Asia, indicating high technological competitiveness.

4.5.4 Technological progress in the Asian Tigers

Figure 4-3 gives the technological autonomy of the Asian Tigers: it shows that technological autonomy remained highest from 2005 to 2019, while Singapore jumped from being the lowest to the second highest – behind only South Korea. Taiwan, China remained third over the same period, and Hong Kong, China dropped from second to lowest.

Figure 4-3   Technological Progress of the Asian Tigers (2005 to 2019) (Unit: %)

Data source: Same as Figure 4-1.

Results from Figure 4-3 indicate that although the Asian tigers were in the middle stage of economic and trade development – before reform and opening up of Mainland China – they had effectively been developed economies for many years; yet the overall technological autonomy of the Asian tigers was not only much less than major net IP exporters as shown in Table 4-1, but also than the other 12 developed economies in Table 4-1. These results indicate that the export-oriented development model supported by technology-dependent policies of the Asian tigers suffered from severe dependence on US technology from the 1970s to the middle of 2010s. Additionally, overall technological autonomy was still rather low compared to other developed economies, despite rapid progress.

4.5.5 Long-term average annual growth of major East Asian economies and their implications

The average annual change of technological autonomy of major economies from 2008 to 2019 has good implications for China in the next decade or so, yet this time frame was relatively short of forecasting technological autonomy progress in China over the next two to three decades. For this, we need broader data parameters.

Using data from the Japan External Trade Organization (JETRO), we can find that Japanese technological autonomy increased from 32.14% in 1991 to 60.59% in 2020, with an average annual growth of 0.98% in 29 years. Although Japanese technological autonomy (32.14%) was significantly higher than Chinese technological autonomy (18.75%) in 2020, its most recent average annual growth rate of 0.98% in the past 29 years is too low, and its average annual growth rate of 1.34% from 19.31% in 1978 to 58.27% in 2007 is useful for Chinese technological autonomy.

Similarly, we can find that Korean technological autonomy increased from 5.91% in 1992 to 43.43% in 2020, with an average annual growth of 1.34% (almost the same as Japan from 1978 to 2007); and Korean technological autonomy increased from 17.53% in 2001, most comparable to China's increase from 18.76% to 43.43% in 2020 with a 20-year average annual growth rate of 1.30%, and the corresponding Korean 29-year annual growth rate from 2001 to 2030 is very likely to be lower than this. The average annual growth rate of technological autonomy in Taiwan, China was only 0.33% from 1991 to 2020 – too low to be of any reference value.

Thus, the average annual growth rates of Japan and Korea in the past 29 years should have some implications for China, yet these historical average annual growth rates are likely to be too low for Chinese technological autonomy in the coming 29 years.

4.6 Correlation of Technological Autonomy among Mainland China, Hong Kong, and Taiwan

We will introduce the relationship of technological autonomy among Mainland China, Hong Kong, and Taiwan, as well as the reasons for the "abnormality" of technological autonomy, which had not increased but decreased in the decade or so before 2008.

4.6.1 Technological autonomy and related issues in Hong Kong

For many years, Hong Kong has played a special role in the financial and trade sectors of Asia and the world at large. However, Hong Kong's position in the technological sector has been less prominent. According to the import and export charges for IP use of the Hong Kong government from 1995 to 2018 – published on its website – Hong Kong's IP trade deficit continued to increase from HKD 640 million to HKD 12.26 billion, and its corresponding technological autonomy dropped from 38.0% to 16.8% from 1995 to 2010; the deficit fell to HKD 9.60 billion, and technological autonomy rose to 27.59% in 2019.

Figure 4-4 gives the technological autonomy in Mainland China, Hong Kong, Taiwan, and China from 1997 to 2020; here, China stands for the technological autonomy calculated using the total IP export and import charges of the three regions together.

Figure 4-4 shows that from 1997 to 2005, Hong Kong's technological autonomy decreased from a historical peak of 39.40% to a historical low of 15.99%; Hong Kong's technological autonomy barely changed from its historic low between 2004 to 2006; it rose to 19.2% in 2007, but continued to fall to the low of 16.83% from 2007 to 2010; it rose steadily to 27.59% in 2019, still 12% below its peak in 1997. These results show that in the 22 years from 1997 to 2019, the average of Hong Kong's technological autonomy was just over 20% annually – still a big gap from the relative autonomy of 50%. And in 2019, its technological autonomy was 27.59%, 22.41% lower than its relative autonomy of 50%. These results indicate that Hong Kong, an international financial center, has been dependent on external technology for many years. Enhancing Hong Kong's independent innovation capability is one of the most important tasks for it to ensure future development by virtue of its geographical advantages and talent accumulation, which is in line with Mainland China's goal of continuously improving its independent innovation capability in the future.

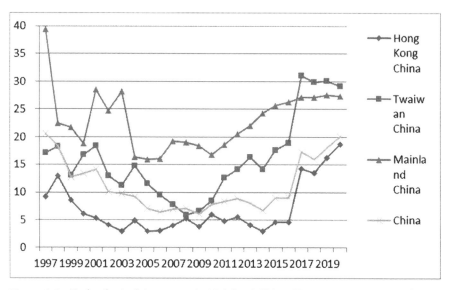

Figure 4-4   Technological Autonomy in Mainland China, Hong Kong, Taiwan, and Greater China (1997–2020) (Unit: %)

Data source: Data of Mainland China from SAFE website: www.safe.gov.cn; Hong Kong, China data from the website of the Census and Statistics Department of the Hong Kong Government: www.censtatd. gov.hk; Taiwan, China data source same as Figure 4-1; data for Hong Kong 2020 was estimated with CAGR from 2016 to 2019.

4.6.2 Correlation of technological autonomy among Mainland China, Hong Kong, and Taiwan

By using the results of technological autonomy in Hong Kong from 1997 to 2019, given in Figure 4-4, and the corresponding results in Mainland China and Taiwan in Table 4-1, we can calculate the correlation between Hong Kong's technological autonomy and that of the mainland and Taiwan over the same period. The results are 43.42% and 55.43%, respectively, indicating obvious mutual assistance and interaction between Hong Kong and Mainland China and Taiwan; yet these were significantly lower between Mainland China and Taiwan, which is 83.00%, indicating much closer cooperation between these two.

4.6.3 The necessity of Mainland China, Hong Kong, and Taiwan considered as a whole

Due to the "one country, two systems" principle, although more than 20 years have passed since Hong Kong's return to the motherland, statistics such as domestic output, foreign exchange reserves, and foreign trade in the Hong Kong Special Administration Region (HKSAR) are still calculated separately; this is an internationally acceptable practice. Taiwan shall follow the same statistical rules nevertheless, given the high correlation between Mainland China and Taiwan in technological autonomy as shown above, and also the similar patterns of technological autonomy of the three regions, it is necessary to calculate Mainland China, Hong Kong SAR, and Taiwan together in this field in order to assess the overall characteristics of Chinese technology.

4.6.4 Technological autonomy in Mainland China, Hong Kong, and Taiwan 10 years before 2008

Figure 4-4 clearly shows that in the decade before the global financial crisis from 1998 to 2008, technological autonomy in Mainland China, Hong Kong SAR, and Taiwan all declined. Mainland China, Taiwan, and Hong Kong SAR posted cumulative declines of 3.93%, 11.15%, and 20.31%, respectively, and China's total had a cumulative decline of 13.49% compared to cumulative growth of 15.27% and 20.56% in Japan and Korea, respectively. Thus, it is clear that while the technological autonomy in Japan and Korea continued to improve, Mainland China, Hong Kong, and Taiwan all suffered huge losses in this regard. But why? This question deserves further thought, and the conclusion will be of great significance to technological autonomy improvement in the future.

4.6.5 Reasons for the simultaneous decline of technological autonomy in Mainland China, Hong Kong SAR, and Taiwan

Answers to the above questions would require considerable length, which would be beyond the scope of this book. However, the course of economic and trade development in these three regions over the past three decades should provide answers. The return of Hong Kong to the mainland in 1997 brought them closer together economically. Mainland China and Hong Kong SAR signed the Mainland and Hong Kong Closer Economic Partnership Arrangement (CEPA) in 2003, with supplementary agreements signed in 2004, 2005, and 2006. The signing and implementation of these agreements have facilitated economic and trade cooperation between Hong Kong SAR and Mainland China. In addition, the Asian financial crisis that affected the whole of East Asia broke out in 1997. From 1998 to 2002, Mainland China issued more than RMB 100 billion of long-term Treasury bonds each year for several consecutive years, directly driving more than trillions of yuan of investment. In the meantime, the loosening of monetary conditions, including the reduction of interest rates and reserve ratios and the easing of lending policies, have further expanded the opportunities for domestic investment and development and created greater room for Hong Kong SAR and Taiwanese investment to explore business opportunities on the mainland.

In addition, with the encouragement and support of a series of policies adopted by the Central Government to promote cross-straits cooperation, especially from 1992 to 1996, the political dialogue was strengthened, and cross-straits economic and trade cooperation was rapidly deepened. Mainland China's accession to the World Trade Organization (WTO) in 2001 has also created better conditions for investment from Taiwan. From 2002 to 2008, globalization accelerated, the RMB continued to appreciate, and foreign capital flowed into Mainland China. With the special relationship based on common language and culture ties between Mainland China, Hong Kong SAR, and Taiwan, helped with special policy arrangements, it is more convenient for Hong Kong SAR and Taiwan to conduct trade and investment on the mainland than any other "foreign" region or government. In this way, the development space of the Mainland China market was vast, and there was massive profit potential for businesses and products without much technological content compared to the US, Europe, and Japan. Who would take the effort and resources to improve technological autonomy? Broad market profit space squeezed or weakened some independent scientific and technological innovation that needs vast amounts of capital and energy, which to some extent provides a partial answer to the "abnormal" phenomenon that technological autonomy in Mainland China, Taiwan, and particularly Hong Kong declined instead of increasing in the decade before 2008. The average annual IP export charges of USD 0.190 billion, compared to imports of USD 4.196 billion in Mainland China from 1998 to 2008, showed a steady reliance on foreign IP.

4.7 Technological Autonomy of Japan

Steady Japanese technological progress in the past three to four decades has created a great model for the whole world, especially for China to learn from.

Analysis in previous chapters and earlier in this chapter have given us a lot of information on Japanese improvement in technology, yet the time span was not long enough. We will analyze technological progress over the past four decades to find useful information for Chinese progress going forward. Figure 4-5 gives the technological autonomy of Japan and China from 1997 to 2020, which shows steady progress in Japanese technological autonomy from 1977 to 2015 – a miracle in world history.

Figure 4-5   Technological Autonomy of Japan and China (1977 to 2020) (Unit: %)

Data source: Dada of China from SAFE website: www.safe.gov.cn, both exports and imports of charges for the use of IPs in China were zero before 1997; and data of Japan from the Japan External Trade Organization (JETRO) website: www.jetro.go.jp.

4.7.1 Progress from 1977 to 1985

Figure 4-5 shows that Japanese technological autonomy grew from 17.50% in 1977 to 23.44% in 1985, with a moderate average annual growth of 0.74%. This reflects the average annual growth rate of exports and imports for IP usage of 17.30% and 11.77% over the same period, indicating moderate Japanese improvement in this area before the Plaza Agreement was signed.

4.7.2 The Plaza Agreement and its impact

The famous "Plaza Agreement" was signed between Japan and the US at the Plaza Hotel in New York City in 1985; the implementation of this over the next three years had a large impact on the Japanese economy and financial markets, resulting from significant yen appreciation against the USD. The appreciation of the yen, coupled with big rises in the Japanese stock and real estate markets, naturally made IP import charges less for Japan from 1985 to 1990, with the average annual growth of IP import charges rising to 21.20%, the highest of all five-year periods from 1977 to 2020. The average annual growth of export IP charges in Japan rose to 28.15%, also the highest in the same period, leading to Japanese technological autonomy growth from 23.44% in 1985 to 29.10% in 1990. This is shown in Figure 4-5, with an average annual growth rate of 1.13%, much higher than the average annual growth rate of 0.74% from 1977 to 1985, indicating the implementation of the Plaza Agreement somewhat accelerated technological progress in Japan.

4.7.3 Bubble broke, yet continued technological progress

The stock market crash in December 1989 marked the beginning of the Japanese bubble bursting, with the stock and real estate markets breaking up. This had a monumental impact on the Japanese economy and financial markets in the following decades. Yet, statistics show that the break of the Japanese bubble did interrupt the rising trend of Japanese technological progress. Data relating to Figure 4-5 shows it did reduce the Japanese average annual growth rate of IP import charges to a single digit from 1990 to 1995, and it has mostly remained a single-digit growth since then. However, the average annual growth rate for IP export charges mostly maintained a two-digit level from 1990 to 2008; Japanese technological autonomy grew from 29.10% in 1990 to 52.75% in 2003 with an average annual rate of 1.82%, more than double the rate from 1977 to 1990. This suggests that the bubble bursting did not interrupt technological progress in Japan, but also accelerated the process.

It is noticeable that Japan achieved a USD 1.28 billion trade surplus in IP charges for the first time in 2003, with technological autonomy (52.75%) surpassing 50% for the first time after 27 years of deficits from 1977.

4.7.4 Growth from 2003 to 2015

Data from Figure 4-5 shows that Japanese IP export revenue continued double-digit annual growth from 2003 to 2008, yet the 2008 global financial crisis caused big declines in both IP exports and imports: they were −15.58% and −7.74%, respectively, from 2008 to 2009 – both the largest annual decrease from 1977 to 2009; technological autonomy rose to a historical high of 68.14% in 2015, as shown in Figure 4-5, yet average annual growth fell to 1.28% from 2003 to 2015.

4.7.5 First decline

Figure 4-5 shows that Japan faced its first decrease over a 5-year period in technological autonomy from 2015 to 2020, with an average annual decrease of 1.55%; the annual decline of 3.39% from 2019 to 2020 also marked the historical record of annual decline since 1977. The rare steady decline in autonomy from 2015 to 2020 may have been the result of severe competition with the US, following a narrowing in technological autonomy between the two nations.

4.8 Analysis of Technological Autonomy in China and Related Issues

4.8.1 Changes in Chinese technological autonomy from 1997 to 2020

Using data from China's service trade from 1997 to 2020 (updated by the State Administration of Foreign Exchange on May 28, 2021), we can calculate China's technological autonomy over this period. Figure 4-5 shows the results.

Technological autonomy increased rapidly from 9.17% to 13.0% from 1997 to 1998. However, it declined steadily to 2.93% in 2003, and a low of 2.87% in 2005; although it increased to 5.99% in 2010, it fell to 2.90% in 2014 – almost back to the low between 2003 and 2005; it grew slightly to 4.69% and 4.62% in 2015 and 2016. Average annual autonomy was merely 4.64%, without much change from 1999 to 2016, indicating almost two decades of stagnant technological autonomy.

Figure 4-5 also shows that technological autonomy increased from 9.67% to 14.28% between 2016 and 2017 – the highest annual growth since 1997; it grew from 14.28% in 2017 to 18.75% in 2020, with an average annual growth rate of 1.49%, and registered an average annual growth rate of 3.53% from 2016 to 2020, showing significant technological progress in recent years.

4.8.2 Chinese technological autonomy and the role of foreign enterprise

Despite the improvement in China's technological autonomy in recent years, the level of its scientific and technological independence has only just increased to 18.75% in 2020, indicating that more than 80% of China's economic and trade development relied on foreign technology over the past decades. These results are consistent with the fact that of 2018, about 70% of China's commodity exports were still dominated by foreign investment; US-funded enterprises accounted for slightly more than a third of China's imports and exports during this same period. These results also explain why China's IP deficit maintained steady growth until 2018, when its service trade deficit was also significant. China has a complete supply chain, but most of the technology or patents that the supply chains rely on depend on foreign technology. If steps are not taken to improve independent Chinese technology, its economy and trade will remain dependent, to some degree, on foreign technology.

4.8.3 Indication of Japanese technological autonomy for China

The similarity between the technological autonomy (18.75%) of China in 2020 and that of Japan (19.31%) in 1978 indicates that Japan may be a precursor to some extent for changes in Chinese technological autonomy in the coming decades, despite different international environments.

4.9 Problems Related to Patent Application and Authorization in China

According to World Intellectual Property Organization (WIPO) updated data in October 2019, the number of patent applications in China increased from 19.6% to 24.4% from 2010 to 2011, surpassing Europe, Japan, and the US for two consecutive years and largest reaching the highest number of patent applications in the world. From 2010 to 2015, China's cumulative patent application increment accounted for 77.0% of the global total and further increased to 98.3% from 2016 to 2018 – providing almost all new patent applications in the world during these three years.

However, according to the data in Figure 4-5, China's IP charges deficit continued growing to reach a record high of USD 30.03 billion in 2018; despite a slight decrease of USD 2.35 billion to USD 27.72 billion, it went up slightly to USD 28.95 billion in 2020, indicating a large number of domestic patent applications did not really reduce IP import costs, nor China's reliance of foreign IP.

4.10 An Appropriate Quality Measure of Family Patents

The average IP export charges per family patents of any bloc are a good quality measure as they reflect the relative capacity of family patents to generate export fees. However, it is not good enough, since the charge per IP in other countries and regions outside the top five blocks was higher due to fewer family patents, i.e., marginal cost theory. It can rank the relative quality of family patents between the US, Japan, South Korea, and China, yet it cannot rank between EPC States and Korea easily, since average net export IP charges in EPC States were much lower than in Korea. The purpose of this section is to find an appropriate quality measure of family patents among all five blocks as well as the others.

4.10.1 Quality measures for family patents

Because IP export and import charges contain information on technological qualities or usefulness, technological independence or autonomy given in Table 4-1 is broader than patent internationalization defined in Table 4-6. Therefore, the ratio of the former over the latter should be a good quality measure of family patents.

Using this definition, we can find the ratios of technological autonomy/ patent autonomy. Table 4-4 gives the results.

Table 4-4   Quality Measures of Family Patents (2000 to 2020)

Year	EPC States	Japan	Korea	US	China	Others
2000	77.5%	68.6%	49.1%	114.7%	330.2%	191.6%
2001	78.2%	69.3%	75.4%	111.6%	264.7%	177.2%
2002	75.6%	70.1%	62.3%	107.5%	140.8%	252.4%
2003	77.9%	78.0%	67.4%	110.7%	107.1%	233.7%
2004	79.7%	80.9%	72.2%	107.4%	197.3%	232.6%
2005	80.4%	84.4%	77.0%	106.4%	80.2%	241.4%
2006	77.0%	85.4%	80.1%	110.8%	69.0%	264.9%
2007	76.1%	89.3%	71.6%	112.2%	64.1%	274.9%
2008	73.2%	94.1%	95.7%	106.7%	85.2%	247.9%
2009	75.9%	90.0%	96.6%	104.5%	38.3%	218.3%
2010	80.1%	91.0%	72.0%	107.0%	55.6%	182.6%
2011	82.5%	95.8%	97.5%	107.8%	38.2%	162.0%
2012	84.1%	99.2%	81.2%	106.3%	37.0%	175.2%
2013	84.4%	108.1%	86.2%	105.2%	21.7%	231.4%
2014	78.8%	107.3%	99.1%	107.0%	12.6%	227.6%

(Continued)

Year	EPC States	Japan	Korea	US	China	Others
2015	74.9%	115.3%	108.6%	108.8%	18.0%	296.1%
2016	76.1%	113.6%	117.8%	104.7%	16.5%	303.9%
2017	77.1%	116.0%	117.4%	104.6%	47.0%	328.8%
2018	77.1%	120.9%	125.7%	105.4%	41.4%	343.1%
2019	74.9%	117.4%	127.1%	106.2%	46.3%	358.0%
2020	75.6%	113.1%	129.8%	107.3%	49.4%	389.7%

Data source: Calculated using results of technological autonomy in Table 4-1.

4.10.2 Conditions for quality measures to be lower or higher than 100%

We can prove that the quality measure in Table 4-4 is greater (lower) than 100% if average IP export charges per patent family is greater (lower) than the average IP import charges per foreign patent. For those interested further, please read the appendix of this chapter for the proof.

4.10.3 Extreme results from Table 4-4

The extremely high values of quality measures of family patents from 2000 to 2004 in China and other results from 2000 to 2020 are due to the relatively low number of family patents; high values from 2015 to 2020 in Korea and from 2013 to 2020 in Japan also resulted from decreasing numbers of family patents of these two countries.

4.10.4 Leading roles of the US and Japan

Table 4-4 shows that besides these extreme results in China, the quality measures in the US remained above 100% despite a general declining pattern. Also, US results were higher than any other blocs from 2000 to 2012, indicating that US family patents were of the highest quality in this time span.

Table 4-4 shows that the Japanese quality measure from 2000 to 2002 was lower than those of US and of EPC States, yet it increased steadily from 2002 to 2012 – improving its quality so much to become second only to the US; the Japanese quality measure continued to rise from 2012 to 2018, surpassing the US over the same period.

4.10.5 Quality measures of EPC states and South Korea

Table 4-4 shows that quality measures of EPC States remained third from 2003 to 2012, lower than both the US and Japan; and the quality measure of EPC states fell below South Korea from 2013 to 2020, resulting from lower and decreasing family patents

4.10.6 Quality measures of China

Table 4-4 shows that quality measures in China decreased dramatically from 2000 to 2014, as a consequence of increasing family patents and stagnant technological autonomy simultaneously, as shown in Table 4-1; yet it almost quadrupled from 12.6% in 2014 to 49.4% in 2020, indicating significant progress in this area in China from 2014.

4.11 Technology Internationalization as Weighted Patent Internationalization

4.11.1 Weighted family patents using quality measures as weights

We can prove that the quality measure defined in Section 4.10 is proportional to average IP export charges (see the appendix). We can also prove the quality measure defined in Section 4.10 is proportional to average IP export charges. Therefore, these quality measures can be used as "weights" to find average family patents, as given in Table 4-5.

Table 4-5 Distribution of "Weighted" Family Patents of Various Blocs and Others (2000–2020)

Year	EPC States	Japan	Korea	US	China	Others	Global
2000	26,077	35,829	5,277	54,811	1,312	4,206	127,512
2001	36,406	50,666	9,540	77,375	1,706	5,617	181,310
2002	43,798	58,007	11,300	90,531	1,613	7,700	212,949
2003	46,119	66,157	16,503	99,586	1,307	7,272	236,945
2004	46,282	66,259	18,918	105,710	2,334	7,545	247,048
2005	48,252	68,523	20,040	118,762	2,807	8,448	266,830
2006	42,182	67,893	18,908	115,567	1,432	7,893	253,875
2007	39,231	61,321	13,653	110,409	1,805	7,496	233,916

(Continued)

Year	EPC States	Japan	Korea	US	China	Others	Global
2008	41,741	60,473	15,714	122,654	2,554	7,797	250,933
2009	46,245	63,746	18,199	128,830	2,105	8,323	267,448
2010	45,142	69,652	16,303	128,295	3,507	6,780	269,680
2011	46,771	70,466	25,176	136,132	2,997	7,962	289,504
2012	47,391	69,238	20,893	133,060	3,527	7,750	281,859
2013	48,410	67,694	19,893	141,914	2,698	8,285	288,892
2014	46,797	67,568	21,656	131,499	1,997	9,863	279,380
2015	44,372	67,735	23,479	123,743	3,266	11,964	274,558
2016*	44,762	62,168	24,064	114,993	3,235	11,697	260,919
2017*	45,083	59,120	23,677	111,064	9,996	12,052	260,992
2018*	44,792	57,458	22,954	108,186	9,532	11,975	254,897
2019*	43,214	51,987	21,952	105,414	11,566	11,900	246,034
2020*	43,362	46,652	21,193	103,047	13,360	12,341	239,954

4.11.2 Technology internationalization

Using the results from Table 4-5, we can obtain technology internationalization as patent internationalization of weighted family patents. Table 4-6 gives the results.

Table 4-6 Technology Internalization as "Weighted" Patent Internationalization (2007–2019)

Unit: %

Year	EPC States	Japan	Korea	US	China	Others
2000	20.45	28.10	4.14	42.98	1.03	3.30
2001	20.08	27.94	5.26	42.68	0.94	3.10
2002	20.57	27.24	5.31	42.51	0.76	3.62
2003	19.46	27.92	6.96	42.03	0.55	3.07
2004	18.73	26.82	7.66	42.79	0.94	3.05
2005	18.08	25.68	7.51	44.51	1.05	3.17
2006	16.62	26.74	7.45	45.52	0.56	3.11

(Continued)

Year	EPC States	Japan	Korea	US	China	Others
2007	16.77	26.21	5.84	47.20	0.77	3.20
2008	16.63	24.10	6.26	48.88	1.02	3.11
2009	17.29	23.83	6.80	48.17	0.79	3.11
2010	16.74	25.83	6.05	47.57	1.30	2.51
2011	16.16	24.34	8.70	47.02	1.04	2.75
2012	16.81	24.56	7.41	47.21	1.25	2.75
2013	16.76	23.43	6.89	49.12	0.93	2.87
2014	16.75	24.19	7.75	47.07	0.71	3.53
2015	16.16	24.67	8.55	45.07	1.19	4.36
2016*	17.16	23.83	9.22	44.07	1.24	4.48
2017*	17.27	22.65	9.07	42.55	3.83	4.62
2018*	17.57	22.54	9.01	42.44	3.74	4.70
2019*	17.56	21.13	8.92	42.85	4.70	4.84
2020*	18.07	19.44	8.83	42.94	5.57	5.14

Table 4-6 shows that although Japan's technological autonomy continued to decline slightly from 2000 to 2020, the average annual level in Japan of 24.83% was significantly higher than the European average of 17.70% over the same period. This is consistent with the results above – Japan is at the high end of the global technological chain. South Korea's technology internationalization averaged 7.73% a year, second only to Europe and ranking fourth in the top five blocks.

It is worth noting that Table 4-6 also shows that the average annual growth rate of technology internationalization in China from 2014 to 2020 was the highest of all five blocks (0.81%), indicating rapid technological progress in recent years.

4.12 Conclusion

Patents are important carriers and indicators of technology, and technology is the pillar of the economy and trade. Reports from the top five blocks above provide us with the most detailed data and regional distribution regarding patent families; the data related to patent families are published according to the residence or block of origin of first fillings and patent families. Therefore, the data makes it possible to determine the location of these highly international patents, and then the level of patent internationalization and technological independence or autonomy in different regions. This chapter uses the patent data from the top five blocks, especially patent family data, to calculate and estimate the level of technological independence or autonomy of major countries and regions in the world from 2000.

Because IP export and import data essentially contain all information of all types about IP, including patents, the ratio of IP export charges over IP export and import charges is a more accurate measure of technological independence or autonomy. The ratios, as defined in Chapter Three, can be taken as the quality measures of patent families, and such measures are further taken as "weights" of patent families. Therefore, technology internationalization can be calculated from this.

Despite China having one of the complete supply chains in the world, most of the technology these supply chains rely on is foreign (more than 80% before 2020). Consequently, up to 70% of Chinese exports are actually the exports of foreign-funded enterprises. Therefore, it is imperative to improve China's technological internationalization level of China's technological, especially to attain real technological independence.

In addition, the positive correlation of technological autonomy among some countries or regions underlines the mutual technological assistance or complementary relationship among these countries or regions to some extent. At the same time, the negative correlation between some countries and regions underlines the trend of squeezing technology among these countries or regions. Such results reveal a deep relationship between scientific and technological development among countries or regions, providing new evidence on the economic and trade activities of corresponding economies. What is particularly noteworthy is that from 1998 to 2008, the technological autonomy in major global countries increased significantly and continuously, while a significant gap existed in the technological autonomy of Mainland China, Hong Kong, and Taiwan. Technological autonomy in Mainland China, Hong Kong, and Taiwan shows a unique phenomenon of decreasing instead of increasing simultaneously; extensive analysis is required on the market, capital, and other factors that influence technological independence.

Bibliography

CNIPA website: http://www.cnipa.gov.cn/tjxx/index.htm.

KIPO ed. 2019. *IP5 Statistics Report 2018 Edition*. October, https://www.fiveipoffies. org/statistics/statisticsreport.

Liu, Zunyi. 2019. *The Sky Won't Fall—The Trade War between China and the US and Future Economic Relations*. Hong Kong: The Chinese University of Hong Kong Press.

Website of the top five offices: https://www.fiveipoffies.org/statistics/statisticsreport.

Zhou, Qiuju, and Leng Fuhai. 2018. "Research and Demonstration of Research Frontier Identification Method Based on the Perspective of Technology Media." *Journal of Modern Information*, no. 2: 62–67.

Appendix

Let x stand for average IP export charges. Then, the quality measure in Table 4-2 can be rewritten as the following:

$$\mathbf{QM} = \mathbf{x}\,(1+\mathbf{b})/(\mathbf{x}+\mathbf{a})$$

Where a = IP import charges of one bloc/family patents, and b = foreign family patents in one bloc/family patents of the bloc. Thus, the first order derivative of QM with respect to $x = a(1+b)/(x+a)^2 > 0$, and the second order derivative of QM with respect to $x = -2a(1+b)/(x+a)^3 < 0$; and the first order derivative of QM with respect to x-a is the same as the first order derivative of QM with respect to $x = a\,(1+b)/(x+a)^2 > 0$.

$QM = x\,(1+b)/(x+a) > 1$ implies that xb > a, or x > a/b = IP import charges/ number of foreign patent families in the bloc; a similar procedure yields that when x < a/b, QM < 1.

CHAPTER FIVE

Development and Current Situation of Offshore RMB Centers

HONG KONG, CHINA IS THE FIRST and most important offshore RMB center. Besides Hong Kong, China, the number of other offshore RMB centers has increased rapidly in the past few years. These offshore centers have become a major driving force of RMB internationalization. The main purpose of this chapter is to introduce the recent developments and future trends of over 20 offshore RMB centers around the world, which will provide evidence to help us forecast future trends in the development of RMB internationalization.

5.1 Global Distribution of Offshore RMB Centers with Clearing Agreements

RMB clearing is the basis of the offshore RMB business. In July 2010, the People's Bank of China (PBC), for the first time, signed the Settlement Agreement on the Clearing of RMB Businesses with the Hong Kong branch of the Bank of China (BOC). After that, the PBC signed similar clearing agreements with more than 30 countries or regions, which lay the basis for the construction and development of RMB centers in these countries.

Table 5-1 shows that the Bank of China has 13 offshore RMB clearing banks, while the Industrial and Commercial Bank of China (ICBC) has seven; China Construction Bank (CCB) has three, the Bank of Communications (BOCOM)

Table 5-1   List of Offshore RMB Clearing Banks

Country/Region	Clearing Center	Clearing Bank	Date
Hong Kong, China	Clearing bank of RMB business in Hong Kong, China	Bank of China (Hong Kong) Limited	19/07/2010
Macao, China	Clearing bank of RMB business in Macao, China	Bank of China Macao Branch	24/09/2012
Taiwan, China	Clearing bank of RMB business in Taiwan, China	Bank of China Taipei Branch	11/12/2012
Singapore	Clearing bank of RMB business in Singapore	ICBC Singapore Branch	08/02/2013
Britain	Clearing bank for RMB business in London	China Construction Bank (London) Limited	18/06/2014
Germany	Clearing bank of RMB business in Frankfurt	Bank of China branch in Frankfurt	19/06/2014
South Korea	Clearing bank of RMB business in Seoul	Bank of Communications Seoul branch	04/07/2014
France	Clearing bank of RMB business in Paris	Bank of China Paris Branch	15/09/2014
Luxembourg	Clearing bank of RMB business in Luxemburg	ICBC Luxemburg Branch	16/09/2014
Qatar	Clearing bank of RMB business in Doha	ICBC Doha Branch	04/11/2014
Canada	Clearing bank of RMB business in Toronto	ICBC (Canada) Ltd.	09/11/2014
Australia	Clearing bank of RMB business in Sydney	Bank of China Sydney Branch	18/11/2014
Malaysia	Clearing bank of RMB business in Kuala Lumpur	Bank of China (Malaysia) Limited	05/01/2015
Thailand	Clearing bank of RMB business in Bangkok	ICBC (Thailand) Co., Ltd.	06/01/2015
Chile	Clearing bank of RMB business in Chile	China Construction Bank Chile Branch	25/05/2015

(Continued)

Country/Region	Clearing Center	Clearing Bank	Date
Hungary	Clearing bank of RMB business in Hungary	Bank of Hungary	28/06/2015
South Africa	Clearing bank for RMB business in South Africa	Bank of China Johannesburg Branch	07/07/2015
Argentina	Clearing bank of RMB business in Argentina	ICBC (Argentina) Limited by Share Ltd	18/09/2015
Zambia	Clearing bank of RMB business in Zambia	Bank of China Zambia	30/09/2015
Switzerland	Clearing bank of RMB business in Switzerland	China Construction Bank Zurich Branch	30/11/2015
New Zealand	Clearing bank of RMB business in New Zealand	Bank of China New Zealand Branch	21/09/2016
Russia	Clearing bank of RMB business in Russia	ICBC (Moscow) Branch	23/09/2016
The United Arab Emirates	Clearing bank of RMB business in the United Arab Emirates	Agricultural Bank of China Dubai Branch	09/12/2016
America	Clearing bank of RMB business in the US	J.P. Morgan	13/02/2018
Japan	Clearing bank of RMB business in Japan	Bank of China Tokyo Branch	17/04/2019
Japan	Clearing bank of RMB business in Japan RMB	MUFG Bank	27/06/2019
Philippines	Clearing bank of RMB business in Philippines	Bank of China Manila Branch	17/09/2019

Data source: http://www.xinhua08.com.

and the Agricultural Bank of China (ABC) have one each, respectively. The other two foreign RMB clearing banks are J.P. Morgan Chase and MUFG Bank. With the prospective need for offshore RMB, the number of offshore clearing banks will increase in the next few years. These centers will play an important role in promoting the development of offshore RMB. Except for the offshore deposit and clearing business offshore RMB bonds are the main activity of such centers. The PBC issued a notice on June 3, 2015, that permitted clearing banks and overseas participating banks to enter the inter-bank bond market and the offshore RMB business, and to conduct bond repurchase transactions, including bond collateral repo and outright bond repurchase transactions.

5.2 The Leading Role of the Hong Kong RMB Center

Hong Kong, China is home to the oldest and largest offshore RMB center. Deposits are the most basic and simple financial service, as well as being the foundation of other financial services. Prior to 2004, the amount of RMB flowing into Hong Kong, China had already reached tens of billions and even hundreds of billions. However, due to the lack of accurate statistics from authorities, different scholars hold different opinions on the amount of inflow. The publication titled "RMB Exchange Rate System and RMB Internationalization" (Li Jing, *Shanghai University of Finance and Economics Journal,* no. 2, 2009) as a reference.

With the approval of the State Council, the PBC started to provide clearing arrangements for banks in Hong Kong, China engaged in personal RMB business, including deposits, exchanges, RMB cards, and remittances. This was done to facilitate economic, trade, and personnel exchanges between the mainland and Hong Kong, and to channel the RMB in Hong Kong back to the mainland in an orderly manner. On November 18, 2003, the PBC released an announcement on providing clearing arrangements for the Individual RMB Business of Hong Kong Bank – laying a solid foundation for RMB business development in Hong Kong.

5.2.1 Changes in RMB deposit scale

Table 5-2 shows both quarterly RMB deposit amounts and quarter-on-quarter growth rates after the banking industry in Hong Kong, China incorporated RMB deposit services in February 2004. The Figure indicates a continuous increase in RMB deposit since 2004, and reached a hike of RMB 77.64 billion in June 2008 before the financial crisis. However, during the post-crisis period from 2008 till March 2009, the deposit went through a decrease to RMB 53.11 billion; From

2009 to 2014, the total RMB deposit in Hong Kong, China regained an increasing momentum, and reached a record high over one trillion to RMB 1.00356 trillion by the end of 2014, with a 5-year average compound growth rate of 74.1%. This was mainly due to the substantial growth of RMB deposits in Hong Kong, China, after the trial practice of domestic RMB cross-border trade, and also the increasing confidence in holding RMB on the RMB appreciation, as the US dollar fell against major global currencies after the launch of the quantitative easing policy in the US.

Table 5-2　RMB Deposits and Allocation in the Hong Kong Banking Industry

Unit: RMB billion

Time	Current Deposit	Term Deposit	Total	Current Deposit Share	Term Deposit Share	Change of Total	Banks
02/2004	0.70	0.19	0.90	78.7%	21.3%	...	32
03/2004	2.10	2.30	4.39	47.7%	52.3%	...	36
06/2004	2.85	3.95	6.80	41.9%	58.1%	...	39
12/2004	5.42	6.71	12.13	44.7%	55.3%	...	38
06/2005	9.36	11.54	20.90	44.8%	55.2%	207.2%	39
12/2005	10.62	11.97	22.59	47.0%	53.0%	86.2%	38
06/2006	11.29	11.43	22.71	49.7%	50.3%	8.7%	39
12/2006	12.23	11.18	23.40	52.2%	47.8%	3.6%	38
06/2007	17.23	10.39	27.62	62.4%	37.6%	21.6%	38
12/2007	22.54	10.86	33.40	67.5%	32.5%	42.7%	37
06/2008	51.24	26.40	77.64	66.0%	34.0%	181.1%	40
12/2008	38.12	17.94	56.06	68.0%	32.0%	67.8%	39
06/2009	35.92	18.46	54.38	66.1%	33.9%	−30.0%	40
12/2009	40.66	22.06	62.72	64.8%	35.2%	11.9%	60
06/2010	52.43	37.28	89.70	58.4%	41.6%	65.0%	77
12/2010	117.57	197.37	314.94	37.3%	62.7%	402.1%	111
06/2011	180.35	373.26	553.60	32.6%	67.4%	517.2%	128
12/2011	176.40	412.13	588.53	30.0%	70.0%	86.9%	133

(Continued)

Time	Current Deposit	Term Deposit	Total	Current Deposit Share	Term Deposit Share	Change of Total	Banks
06/2012	136.62	421.09	557.71	24.5%	75.5%	0.7%	133
12/2012	123.54	479.45	603.00	20.5%	79.5%	2.5%	139
06/2013	127.51	570.45	697.96	18.3%	81.7%	25.1%	140
12/2013	151.06	709.42	860.47	17.6%	82.4%	42.7%	146
06/2014	150.70	775.22	925.91	16.3%	83.7%	32.7%	148
12/2014	176.97	826.59	1003.56	17.6%	82.4%	16.6%	149
06/2015	180.45	812.48	992.92	18.2%	81.8%	7.2%	146
12/2015	160.91	690.20	851.11	18.9%	81.1%	−15.2%	145
06/2016	204.28	507.27	711.55	28.7%	71.3%	−28.3%	146
12/2016	135.52	411.19	546.71	24.8%	75.2%	−35.8%	144
06/2017	142.52	383.56	526.08	27.1%	72.9%	−26.1%	140
12/2017	159.70	399.44	559.14	28.6%	71.4%	2.3%	137
06/2018	167.02	417.50	584.52	28.6%	71.4%	11.1%	137
12/2018	194.43	420.59	615.02	31.6%	68.4%	10.0%	136
06/2019	214.54	389.70	604.24	35.5%	64.5%	3.4%	136
12/2019	223.98	408.22	632.21	35.4%	64.6%	2.8%	138
06/2020	241.11	398.80	639.91	37.7%	62.3%	5.9%	140
12/2020	260.02	461.63	721.65	36.0%	64.0%	14.1%	141
03/2021	265.40	507.08	772.48	34.4%	65.6%	16.3%	143

Data source: Hong Kong Monetary Authority: www.hkma.gov.hk; the change rate of March 2021 was the change with respect to March 2020.

With RMB exchange rate reform in 2015 and the US ceasing its quantitative easing policy, RMB depreciation against the American dollar accelerated. At the same time, China's regulatory authorities stepped up efforts to combat false trade and cross-border arbitrage, leading to a sharp decrease in offshore RMB settlements, and thus a downward trend in Hong Kong's RMB deposits. By March 2017, it dropped to a historical low of 507.27 billion since March 2008 – barely over half its 2014 peak. Table 5-2 shows that RMB deposits in Hong Kong began rebounding in March 2017, with period-to-period annual growth increasing to a peak of 16.3% in March 2021. The average compound annual growth rate was 11.09% from March 2017 to March 2021, reflecting both trade and economic growth in China during this time. With steady trade growth and RMB appreciation pressure, its deposits in Hong Kong are expected to peak in the next couple of years.

5.2.2 The relationship between RMB deposit movement in Hong Kong, China and offshore appreciation/depreciation

The RMB deposits from 2004 to Q1 of 2021 in Table 5-2 indicate offshore RMB expectations in appreciation and depreciation. When there was a high expectation of appreciation, the ratio of deposit increase was high; when the expectation of depreciation was high, the deposit ratio dropped. This relationship showed its strongest symbiosis during the financial crisis – from September 2008 to March 2009 – and during the reform of the RMB exchange rate – from June 2015 to March 2017 – during which RMB depreciation significantly reduced Hong Kong, China's RMB deposit; however, from March 2009 to the end of 2014, RMB appreciation and cross-border RMB settlement jointly promoted rapid growth in RMB deposits.

5.2.3 Comparison between current and term deposits

The amount of RMB current deposits in Hong Kong, China largely exceeded that of term deposits from September 2006 to the second quarter of 2010. (During this period, the total current deposit made up over 60% of total deposits.) Since the end of the third quarter of 2010, the increasing rate of current deposits was significantly lower than term deposits. The balance of current deposits reached a historical low of 15.3% in September 2014, and then increased back to 37.7% in June 2020 – still lower than term deposits.

5.2.4 Certified Institutions that hold licenses for RMB services in Hong Kong, China

The number of certified institutions that held licenses for RMB services in Hong Kong, China remained within the interval of 30 to 40, with little variety from February 2004 to June 2009. However, the amount accelerated rapidly afterwards, reaching a record high of 149 in December 2014. This is consistent with the historical high of RMB deposits in Hong Kong, China during the same period. From the second half of 2015 till the second quarter of 2019, with the decline of RMB deposits in Hong Kong, China, the number of certified institutions that held licenses for RMB services declined accordingly – dropping to 136 – yet it rebounded steadily to 143 by March 2021.

5.2.5 The proportion of RMB deposits in Hong Kong, China

As indicated in Table 5-2, RMB deposits in Hong Kong, China only amounted to 12.13 billion at the end of 2004, which was 0.57%, 0.62%, and 0.29% of HKD, foreign currency, and total deposits, respectively, in Hong Kong, China. These proportions increased to 19.40%, 18.83%, and 9.56% in 2011 and further increased to 26.09%, 23.75%, and 12.43% (respectively) by the end of 2014. However, from 2014 to 2017, these proportions decreased to 10.34%, 10.69%, and 5.26%, falling back to less than half the previous peak, and slightly lower than in January 2011. The corresponding proportions rose slightly to 10.55%, 10.51%, and 5.26% at the end of March 2020, though they remained relatively low. It shows that in the environment of RMB depreciation since 2014, RMB deposits in Hong Kong, China have dropped significantly compared to the Hong Kong dollar and other foreign currencies.

5.2.6 The ratio of RMB deposits in Hong Kong compared to Mainland China

We can easily calculate the ratio of total RMB deposits in Hong Kong, China to that of Mainland China on any particular date, based on the data in Table 5-2 and the data from the PBC website. The results show that from 2006 to 2009, the ratio was limited from 0.07% to 0.10%. However, from 2010 to 2014, this rate grew sharply to 0.86%. However, it decreased to 0.33% in 2015–2019. Ultimately, the ratio of Hong Kong, China's total RMB deposits to the mainland's has continuously dropped to less than 40% of the level at the end of 2014.

5.2.7 Development of RMB certificate of deposits

With the rising of RMB deposits and offshore RMB loans in Hong Kong, China, the certificate of deposit (CD) was initiated in the second half year of 2010. CITIC International, a subsidiary of CITIC Bank in Hong Kong, issued the first offshore RMB deposit certificate in Hong Kong, China. According to the Hong Kong Monetary Authority (HKMA), from 2010 to 2012, the total amount of RMB deposit certificates reached 6.8 to 117.3 billion, respectively (Chan 2013). By the end of 2013, the accumulated amount had risen to a historical high of RMB 192.5 billion. One year later, it dropped to RMB 154.7 billion. The amount increased slightly to 159.3 billion by the end of 2015, but decreased to 59.3 billion at the end of 2017 (HKMA annual report 2017) – less than one-third of its peak at the end of 2013; by the end of 2019, this number had dropped to RMB 25.8 billion – only 14% of the peak value. By January 2021, it had further increased to RMB 28.6 billion.

5.2.8 The scale of RMB loans in Hong Kong, China

In accordance with the statistics provided by the HKMA, RMB loans in Hong Kong, China continuously increased from 30.8 billion to 297.4 billion from 2011 to 2015 (refer to the 2015 Annual Report of HKMA), and the corresponding RMB loan-to-deposit ratio increased from 5.2% to 34.9%. RMB loans decreased to 294.8 billion and 144.5 billion in 2016 and 2017; the correspondent loan-to-deposit ratios were 53.92% and 25.8%. By the end of 2018, RMB loans in Hong Kong, China were only RMB 105.6 billion, a decrease of 64.5% from the peak in 2015, and the ratio of loans to deposits was only 17.17%. In 2019, the balance of RMB loans in Hong Kong, China rebounded to 153.7 billion yuan. In recent years, its loan and deposit business has shown a different trend of change (RMB loans only started to decline significantly since 2016; and in 2017 alone, it declined more than half compared with the previous year.). By the end of January 2021, the balance of RMB loans had slightly increased to 159.2 billion.

5.2.9 Changes in the proportion of RMB cross-border settlements

Hong Kong, China is the earliest established RMB center as well as the first offshore RMB clearing center. The RMB cross-border payment ratio in Hong Kong, China reached as high as 86% in 2011. Nevertheless, with the arrival of other offshore RMB centers, it decreased to about 80% in 2012. This rate further dropped below 70% several times during 2013 and October 2016. After that, the rate increased and reached 75.07% in June 2020. Hong Kong has maintained its position as the largest offshore RMB payment center.

5.3 Distribution and Ranking of RMB Deposits and Payments among Offshore RMB Centers

5.3.1 The distribution of RMB deposits among major offshore RMB centers

Hong Kong, China, Taiwan China, and Singapore are the three large offshore RMB deposit centers. The RMB deposit amounts of other offshore RMB centers are relatively low compared to the three regions; thus, we will not discuss them herein.

5.3.2 Comparisons on the proportion of RMB cross-border payments in overseas RMB centers

According to data from SWIFT, the proportion of RMB centers other than Hong Kong, China in overseas RMB payments remained at 14% from January to August 2012; from August 2012 to August 2016, it continued to rise to 29.7%. However, from August 2016 to April 2018, the proportion of offshore RMB payments (excluding Hong Kong) dropped to 25.0% in April 2018; as of April 2021, the proportion was 24.7%, showing that the proportion from 2012 to 2016 has gradually increased, though in recent years its has registered a slight decline. Table 5-3 shows the proportions of offshore RMB payments (excluding Hong Kong) from January 2012 to March 2021.

5.3.3 Ranking of major RMB payment centers outside Hong Kong, China

Although more than one hundred countries and regions have RMB payment services with Mainland China and Hong Kong, China, most countries and regions have relatively small RMB payments. Hong Kong, China and dozens of major overseas RMB centers accounted for more than 90% of these: Table 5-3 shows that in December 2012, the UK ranked first in RMB payments outside Hong Kong, China. From March 2014 to June 2015, Singapore regained this first position. And from June 2014 to June 2015, the proportion of Singapore's RMB payment to its overall amount, excluding Hong Kong, China, exceeded that of London, making it the largest RMB payment center outside Hong Kong, China; however, in November 2015, London regained the first place till July 2016. This underlines how London and Singapore have competed fiercely as offshore RMB centers in recent years. The rankings of these centers have stabilized in recent years. It should be noticed that the US remained in the fourth position, following Singapore, since the second half of 2019; the Korean ranking fell significantly from 2020, and the Eurozone as a whole came close to Singapore in total share.

5.4 Distribution of the RQFII Quota and Authorized Quotas among Offshore RMB Centers

The quota of different RQFIIs is the foundation for opening up offshore RMB services and also one of the most important indicators for measuring offshore RMB centers. In previous chapters, we introduced the quota for some RQFIIs in offshore RMB centers. In this section, we will systematically introduce and

Table 5-3　Shares and Ranking of RMB Payments in RMB Centers outside Hong Kong, China (January 2012 to March 2021)

Country/Region	012012	122012	062013	062014	122015	122016	122017	122018	122019	122020	032021
UK	23.7%	28.3%	30.9%	22.5%	20.8%	25.4%	23.0%	24.7%	25.9%	24.5%	24.5%
Singapore	32.7%	22.7%	16.5%	28.4%	20.8%	17.0%	18.1%	18.7%	12.7%	16.8%	16.1%
US	5.6%	4.1%	8.5%	10.8%	10.8%	13.2%	10.6%	10.5%	10.3%	12.2%	11.5%
Taiwan, China	...	...	10.3%	9.3%	13.2%	11.8%	9.0%	8.9%	8.9%	9.3%	9.1%
France	5.0%	7.2%	8.1%	5.4%	4.8%	5.8%	6.4%	6.8%	5.5%	7.1%	7.3%
Korea	...	...	1.0%	2.4%	8.8%	6.8%	12.3%	5.7%	10.6%	4.7%	5.4%
Australia	...	8.2%	3.4%	4.8%	4.0%	4.0%	4.2%	5.6%	4.8%	3.6%	3.6%
Japan	...	...	...	...	2.4%	3.3%	...	3.3%	3.9%	2.7%	2.7%
Germany	...	...	3.4%	2.5%	2.0%	2.1%	2.8%	4.2%	3.2%	3.0%	2.6%
Luxembourg	3.9%	4.3%	3.8%	2.3%	2.4%	1.7%	1.4%	2.0%	1.8%	1.8%	1.5%
Canada	...	...	...	...	1.6%	1.3%	0.9%	1.4%	1.6%	2.0%	2.6%
Belgium	...	...	...	...	2.4%	1.6%	...	1.1%	1.7%	2.0%	2.6%
Netherlands	...	...	...	...	1.2%	1.2%	...	...	1.5%	1.3%	1.2%
Russia	...	...	...	...	...	...	0.5%	0.8%	...	...	...
Euro Zone	8.9%	11.5%	15.3%	10.2%	12.8%	12.3%	10.6%	14.1%	13.7%	14.9%	16.1%

Data source: Calculated using data released by RMB Tracker Monthly, reporting and statistics on RMB progress towards becoming an international currency.

compare the total quota and approved quota of RQFII for different offshore RMB
centers. Table 5-4 shows the total and approved quotas as of May 31, 2020.

Table 5-4   Comparison of Total RQFII Quotas Obtained by Offshore RMB Centers and the Approved Quota

Unit: RMB billion, %

Country/Region	Total Approved Quota	Accumulated Obtained Quota	Obtained Quota/ Approved Quota Ratio
Hong Kong, China	500	365.16	73.03%
US	250	39.17	15.67%
Japan	200	9	4.50%
ROK	120	73.19	60.99%
Singapore	100	78.26	78.26%
UK	80	48.49	60.61%
France	80	24	30.00%
Germany	80	10.54	13.18%
Australia	50	32.01	64.02%
Luxembourg	50	15.19	30.38%
Switzerland	50	9.6	19.20%
Canada	50	8.65	17.30%
Thailand	50	2.1	4.20%
Ireland	50	1.85	3.70%
Malaysia	50	1.6	3.20%
Holland	50	0	0.00%
Hungary	50	0	0.00%
Chile	50	0	0.00%
UAE	50	0	0.00%
Qatar	30	0	0.00%
IMF	...	4.2	...
Total	1,990	722.99	36.33%
Euro Zone	310	51.58	16.64%

Data source: http://www.the PBC.gov.cn/; http://www.safe.gov.cn/en/index.html.

5.4.1 RQFII data based on the registration agency

Table 5-4 shows that the total amount of RQFII obtained by Hong Kong, China is up to RMB 500 billion, and 73.03% of this quota has been used in these years; the quota obtained by the US was second to Hong Kong, China (RMB 250 billion), but as of May 31, 2020, only RMB 39.17 billion of quota was approved, accounting for 15.67% of its total quota; South Korea's quota than Hong Kong, China, the US, and Japan, reaching as high as RMB 120 billion. Its approved quota reached 73.187 billion, ranking third after Hong Kong, China and Singapore, with a start-up rate of 60.99%; Singapore's accumulative approved quota was as high as RMB 78.255 billion, ranking second only to Hong Kong, China; whilst, the UK, France, and Germany all had a quota of RMB 80 billion, yet their accumulated approved quotas were 48.484 billion, 24 billion, and RMB 10.543 billion, respectively; the start-up rates were 60.61%, 30%, and 13.18%, respectively. Luxembourg, Canada, Switzerland, Malaysia, and Thailand all obtained quotas for RMB 50 billion, and the accumulative approved quotas were 15.187 billion, 8.653 billion, 9.60 billion, 1.6 billion, and 2.1 billion, respectively, with the start-up rates being 30.37%, 17.31%, 19.20%, 3.20%, and 4.20%, respectively.

The five Eurozone centers in France, Germany, Luxembourg, the Netherlands, and Ireland had a total quota of RMB 310 billion, second only to Hong Kong, China and the US. However, the cumulative approved quota was only 51.58 billion, and the start-up rate was only 16.64%; Chile, Hungary, and the United Arab Emirates all received RMB 50 billion for their quota, and Qatar received 30 billion, but all four RMB centers have not yet obtained the approved quota. The RQFII quota or utilization rate of different centers given in Table 5-4 reflects their enthusiasm for promoting RMB business to a large extent and also reflects the activity of their RMB business, which corresponds to the RMB payment given in Table 5-3.

5.4.2 RQFII quota distribution based on country and region

The distribution of RQFII quotas in different countries and regions given in Table 5-4 is actually based on the investor's registration place. To a large extent, it shows the degree of support for RMB internationalization in these countries or regions. However, this classification has certain limitations: for example, in Table 5-4, Australia's 32.006 billion yuan RQFII are given respectively to Vanguard Investment Australia Ltd., VanEck Investment Limited, and Russell Investment Management Limited. These three companies are actually from the US. Using Australia's RQFII quota, it may seem like this is Australian support for RMB

internationalization, yet it in fact comes from American funds. According to the
country and region where the investors are located, we will get a new RQFII
distribution. This will be combined with China's foreign securities investment
data, and the results are shown in Table 5-5.

The results in Table 5-5 are significantly different from those in Table 5-4:
most RQFIIs in Hong Kong, China is mainland investors. Regarding investment
activities, the approved amount of mainland RQFII investment in Hong Kong,
China exceeds 70% of the total approved amount in Hong Kong, China, and the
total RQFII amount on the mainland accounts for more than 40% of the total
approved amount of RQFII globally. The result shows that mainland institutional
investors are the main promoters of RMB internationalization. At the same time,
the mainland's securities investment in Hong Kong, China also accounted for
more than 30% of the total, showing the close relationship between the mainland
and Hong Kong, China's financial markets.

5.4.3 US funds promote RMB internationalization

From the beginning of the RQFII pilot program in 2011 to the end of 2016,
RQFII-approved quotas were mainly distributed in these major overseas RMB
centers: Hong Kong, China, South Korea, Singapore, the Eurozone, the UK, and
Australia. In early June 2016, Yi Gang, deputy governor of the PBC, stated at
the China-US Strategic Economic Dialogue briefing that China had decided to
give the US an RQFII investment quota of 250 billion yuan. However, it was
not until February 2017 that the first investor in the US – BlackRock Fund
Advisors – applied for an RQFII quota of 11 billion yuan; in September and
November 2017, the American Acadian Asset Management LLC and BlackRock
Institutional Trust were approved for RQFII 1.6 billion and 4 billion yuan
respectively. In the second quarter of 2018, the US Wisdom Tree Management
Limited was approved for an RQFII quota of 1.22 billion yuan. The data shows
that by the end of the second quarter of 2018, US funds had limited enthusiasm
for RQFII. However, in the third quarter of 2018, Bridgewater Associates and
the State Street Global Advisors Trust Company were approved for 2.6 billion
yuan, 4.4 billion yuan, and 5 billion yuan, respectively – totaling 12 billion
yuan. The RQFII quota accounted for 66.3% of the total global RQFII increase of
18.1 billion yuan that quarter, which significantly exceeded the total increase of
8.6 billion in the three RMB centers in the UK, Hong Kong, China, and Ireland
during the same period.

Table 5-5 Distribution of RQFII Quotas in Different Countries and Regions, and the Statistics of Security Investment from China in Corresponding Countries and Regions

	RQFII Quota by Country/Region (Unit: RMB billion)			China's Foreign Securities Investment Assets (Unit: USD billion)				
Country/Region	Cumulative Approved Quota	Percentage of Quota	Total	Equity Securities	Debt Securities	Long-Term	Short-Term	Percentage of Total
Mainland China	331.25	45.80%	...	...	...	...	...	...
US	142.68	19.70%	162.83	110.87	67.56	61.54	6.02	19.83%
ROK	74.99	10.40%	7.3	2.87	2.6	0.66	1.94	0.61%
UK	37.07	5.10%	21.8	11.3	10.23	9.21	1.03	2.39%
France	31.3	4.30%	8.61	4.74	4.6	4.59	0.01	1.04%
Switzerland	21.4	3.00%	4.45	3.84	0.51	0.5	0.01	0.48%
Japan	18.74	2.60%	13.67	9.97	6.54	3.02	3.52	1.83%
Singapore	18.37	2.50%	7.49	1.1	5.45	4.17	1.27	0.73%
Germany	12	1.70%	12.57	4.47	9.93	9.41	0.53	1.60%
Canada	10.15	1.40%	4.7	3.08	2.46	2.46	0	0.62%
Hong Kong, China	6.4	0.90%	226.43	341.62	67.48	57.05	10.43	45.46%

(Continued)

	RQFII Quota by Country/Region (Unit: RMB billion)		China's Foreign Securities Investment Assets (Unit: USD billion)					
Country/Region	Cumulative Approved Quota	Percentage of Quota	Total	Equity Securities	Debt Securities	Long-Term	Short-Term	Percentage of Total
Italy	5	0.70%	2.41	2.33	1.73	0.61	0.61	0.26%
International Organizations	4.2	0.60%	2.92	0	4.25	4.18	0.08	0.47%
Holland	3	0.40%	3.96	2.43	1.43	1.34	0.09	0.43%
Thailand	2.1	0.30%	0.69	0.27	0.11	0.07	0.03	0.04%
Luxemburg	1.69	0.20%	12.7	9.65	3.8	2.69	1.11	1.49%
Australia	1.5	0.20%	7.66	4.87	5.07	3.63	1.44	1.10%
Taiwan, China	1.16	0.20%	1.15	1.05	0.24	0.24	0	0.14%
Total	722.99	100.00%	Total is USD 899.9 billion					
Eurozone	52.99	7.30%	40.25	6	5.23	5.07	0.16	12.48%

Data source: RQFII quotas are calculated according to the statistics of the approved quota and the country and region where the investors are located as announced by the State Administration of Foreign Exchange as of May 31, 2020; the approved quota of Sino-foreign joint venture funds is calculated based on the country where the holding company is located; for some investors, especially those registered in Hong Kong, China, it is difficult to classify their countries or regions, which may result in some deviations. The data on China's foreign securities investment are taken from the data at the end of 2020 published on the SAFE website.

In the third quarter of 2018, RMB depreciated 3.6% against the US Dollar. US funds significantly increased their holdings of the RQFII quota, however, clearly underlining their support for RMB. By June 2020, US investors had accumulated approved quotas of nearly 20%, showing their significant support for this. Also, 25.2% of China's foreign securities investment went to the US, and the high proportion reflected the close connection and tacit relationship between the financial economies of both countries. It's worth noting as well that by July 2019, 425 US institutional investors had entered China's bond market, accounting for 23% and ranking in the first place, followed by Hong Kong, China and Singapore.

5.4.4 A brief analysis of RQFII quotas approved from other countries and regions

Table 5-5 shows that the total amount of RQFII approved to South Korea is second only to China and the US, accounting for over 10% of the total, indicating that South Korean investors have a high degree of support for RMB internationalization. Meanwhile, investors in the UK, France, Switzerland, Japan, and Singapore accounted for 2% to 5% of the approved RMB quota. Table 5-5 shows the Swiss investors were approved an RQFII amount as high as 21.4 billion yuan at the end of May 2020 – more than twice the 9.6 billion yuan given in Table 5-4; the approved amounts in Germany and Canada also exceed the total amount given in the table. As a regional financial center, Luxembourg is similar to Singapore and Hong Kong, China, with the majority of its financial institutions being foreign. The total approved RQFII amount given in Table 5-5 is significantly lower than the total amount given in Table 5-4 (It is worth noting that Taiwan, China does not have the approved amount in Table 5-4, and the approved amount in Table 5-5 is obtained through institutions registered in other RMB centers).

5.5 RMB Distribution at the Top Five Foreign Exchange Trading Centers

We have introduced RMB development at major centers globally over the past few years, and RMB rankings will now be compared across the top five global exchange centers.

5.5.1 Hong Kong, China

Hong Kong, China has been the most important offshore RMB center, averaging about three quarters of offshore RMB payments in the past few years. Data from the Hong Kong Treasury Markets Association (HKTMA, www.hktma.org.hk) show that the average daily turnover of RMB made up 16.8% of the average daily turnover in Hong Kong, China, lower than shares of USD and Japanese yen, which were 95.4% and 23.9%, respectively; and it surpassed both HKD and Japanese yen to become the second most traded currency in April 2020. Yet, the daily turnover of RMB 93.6 billion was 22.9% of the corresponding US daily turnover of USD 408.3 in April; the share of RMB daily turnover in Hong Kong, China grew from 18.0% to 20.2% from April to October 2020, and the RMB/USD turnover ratio also increased to 26.2%, consolidating RMB's position as the second most traded currency in Hong Kong, China.

5.5.2 Singapore

According to data released by the Monetary Authority of Singapore, the RMB daily average turnover was USD 23.86 billion in April 2013. This was lower than the corresponding daily average turnover of the USD, Japanese yen, Euro, Australian dollar, British pound, and Singapore dollar; it increased significantly to USD 42.54 billion in April 2016 but remained lower than all aforementioned currencies except the Singapore dollar.

5.5.3 London

Data from the Bank of England (www.bankofengland.co.uk) shows that the daily average turnover of RMB ranked 8th in London in April 2016, and the average ranking remained in this position until October 2020.

5.5.4 Tokyo

Data from the Tokyo Foreign Exchange Market Committee (www.fxcomtky.com) shows that the RMB (including CNH) daily average turnover was USD 1.88 billion, ranking 11th in April 2017; it increased significantly to USD 3.08 billion in April 2020 and moved up to 10th; it increased further to USD 5 billion in October 2020 and ranked 8th, indicating steady growth over the past few years.

5.5.5 New York

According to data released by the New York Fed (www.newyorkfed.org), the RMB daily average turnover of USD 7.08 billion ranked 14th in April 2016; it increased to USD 8.23 billion in April 2020, ranking 13th; it increased significantly to USD 13.95 billion in October 2020 to reach 12th place. The tremendous growth rate of 633% from April to October 2020 indicated higher market acceptance of RMB in New York in 2020, despite trade friction and other tensions between the world's two largest economies.

5.6 The Relationship between Offshore RMB Center Rankings and the Distribution of Approved Quotas

The number of applications for China Qualified Foreign Institutional Investors (QFII) from different countries and regions can largely reflect their interest in the development of China's capital market. Table 5-6 shows the distribution of QFII-approved quotas in different countries and regions as of May 31, 2020.

Table 5-6   Distribution of Approved Quotas of QFII among Different Offshore RMB Centers

Country/Region	Number of Approved Organizations	Percentage of Approved Organizations to Total	Accumulated Approved Quota	Percentage of Accumulated Approved Quota
Hong Kong, China	72	24.41%	26.06	22.41%
UK	25	8.47%	11.56	9.94%
Taiwan, China	37	12.54%	10.86	9.34%
US	43	14.58%	10.14	8.72%
Singapore	22	7.46%	7.92	6.81%
South Korea	16	5.42%	7.75	6.66%
Macau, China	1	0.34%	5.00	4.30%
UAE	1	0.34%	5.00	4.30%
Canada	9	3.05%	4.16	3.58%
Switzerland	9	3.05%	3.83	3.29%
France	7	2.37%	3.68	3.16%

(Continued)

Country/Region	Number of Approved Organizations	Percentage of Approved Organizations to Total	Accumulated Approved Quota	Percentage of Accumulated Approved Quota
Japan	15	5.08%	3.50	3.01%
Australia	5	1.69%	3.32	2.85%
Norway	1	0.34%	2.50	2.15%
Malaysia	3	1.02%	2.06	1.77%
Kuwait	1	0.34%	2.00	1.72%
Germany	4	1.36%	1.42	1.22%
Portugal	2	0.68%	1.20	1.03%
Qatar	1	0.34%	1.00	0.86%
Holland	4	1.36%	0.83	0.71%
Luxemburg	4	1.36%	0.40	0.34%
Thailand	2	0.68%	0.40	0.34%
International Organizations	1	0.34%	0.28	0.24%
Sweden	3	1.02%	0.23	0.20%
Lithuania	1	0.34%	0.23	0.20%
Belgium	1	0.34%	0.21	0.18%
Brunei	1	0.34%	0.20	0.17%
Ireland	1	0.34%	0.20	0.17%
South Africa	1	0.34%	0.15	0.13%
Spain	1	0.34%	0.10	0.09%
Italy	1	0.34%	0.08	0.07%
Eurozone	26	8.81%	8.35	7.18%
Total	295	100.00%	116.30	100.00%

Data source: Calculated based on the statistics of the approved quota and the place of registration of the institution as of May 31, 2020, announced by the State Administration of Foreign Exchange.

5.6.1 The distribution of QFII in different RMB centers

Table 5-6 shows the level of approved foreign institutional investors in Hong Kong, China ranks among the top, accounting for close to one-quarter. The amount of QFII approved in the UK is second only to Hong Kong, China, accounting for slightly less than 10%. The total amount of QFII approved for Taiwan, China is slightly lower than this. The total QFII quotas applied to the US, South Korea, and Singapore ranked 4–6th place, accounting for around 7%; Macau, China, United Arab Emirates, Canada, Switzerland, France, Japan, Australia, and Norway rank 7th to 14th, respectively, accounting for 2% to 5%; France and Germany and 10 other Eurozone countries account for 8.81% of the total approved QFII quota, slightly surpassing the US, showing a growing trend in this region. In addition, the total amount approved in Japan is less than USD 3.5 billion, less than one-third of the UK, which is not commensurate with Japan's global economic and trade clout. This shows that China-Japan financial cooperation still has huge potential.

5.6.2 Comparison of QFII and RQFII quotas in different countries and regions

Table 5-6 shows that, except for the Taiwan, China region, the QFII proportion and ranking of other RMB centers are basically the same as the proportion and ranking of the RQFII given in Table 5-5. This underlines how the interest of different overseas RMB centers in the domestic capital market is basically the same as their interest in RMB.

5.6.3 Enlightenment of QFII Custodian Bank Related Information

The information of QFII's corresponding custodian bank given in Table 5-6 also has an important meaning. It shows that among the 295 QFII institutions, HSBC, ICBC, Citibank, China Construction Bank, and the Bank of China, as custodian banks, managed 99, 51, 42, 32, and 25 institutions, respectively; in addition, Standard Chartered Bank and Deutsche Bank have 11 custodians each; Agricultural Bank of China and the Bank of Communications have ten respectively, and Industrial Bank, China Minsheng Bank, and China CITIC Bank have two, one and one, respectively; the four foreign banks: HSBC, Citibank, Standard Chartered Bank, and Deutsche Bank, managed 163 institutions, accounting for 55.3% of the total, further underlining their influence in the domestic capital market.

In addition, among these 295 QFII institutions, HSBC, Citibank, ICBC, China Construction Bank, and Bank of China have custodian amounts of 42.906 billion, 19.193 billion, 14.881 billion, 11.973 billion, and 10.278 billion dollars, respectively. In addition, the three banks of Bank of Communications, Standard Chartered Bank, and Deutsche Bank have custodial amounts of 3.425 billion, 5.168 billion, and 2.802 billion dollars, respectively. ABC, ICBC, and China CITIC Bank have custodian amounts of 4.814 billion, 700 million, and 100 million dollars, respectively; HSBC, Citibank, Standard Chartered, and Deutsche Bank have total custodian amounts of 70.069 billion dollars – accounting for as much as 60.3% of the total. Considering that the total of the four foreign banks exceeded that of the five largest domestic banks combined with the two joint-stock banks, their relationship with foreign institutional investors appears robust.

5.7 Key Problems in Offshore RMB Market Development

There are some major issues in the development of the offshore RMB market. In this paragraph, we will briefly introduce some of these in offshore RMB centers.

5.7.1 Improving offshore RMB centers
Offshore RMB centers prospered from scratch and after only a few years can now be found all over the world. Such rapid development cannot, however, be devoid of problems: the only data source reflecting the business scale in RMB centers is the payment amount and trade financing data from SWIFT, while the deposits and transactions, etc., are difficult to obtain; a different degree of errors still existed even if published by some centers themselves. It is believed that with further development and maturity of these offshore RMB centers, the data will gradually become comprehensive and disclosed in a timely fashion.

5.7.2 Offshore RMB progress is not synchronized with international trade development
In previous chapters, trade and financial cooperation between China and some other major developing countries (the BRICS) was briefly discussed. Although trade and finance cooperation began early between Russia and China, RMB trade in Russia has shown slow progress. Secondly, although China and Brazil signed an exchange swap deal of RMB 190 billion as early as March 2013, and Brazil was China's largest trade partner in South America, its RMB progress in Brazil was also relatively slow. Thirdly, India, the main initiator of the BRICS and

the New Development Bank, has not yet signed a swap deal with China, and the RMB business grows slowly in India.

In addition, RMB centers have not yet been established in Italy or Spain, despite these two Eurozone countries providing an important degree of cooperation between China and the Eurozone as a whole.

5.7.3 Basic business starts up

Major RMB businesses in offshore RMB centers, including Hong Kong, China, are only RMB payments and deposits. The RMB loan amount in Hong Kong, China – the most important RMB center – only accounted for 25%–33% of total deposits from 2015–17. In 2018, this dropped below 20%, though it rose back to 25% in 2019. The breadth and strength of the offshore RMB market must improve urgently.

With the approval of the PBC, offshore RMB clearing banks and participant banks are allowed to deal with offshore repurchases of the China onshore interbank bond, which connects the two interbank bond markets; Sovereigns and multilateral institutions may also issue RMB bonds in London. Along with the development of the offshore RMB business, enterprises and products in these centers will be gradually enriched; further details will be discussed in a later chapter.

5.8 The Promotion of RMB Internationalization through Cross-Border Payments

On October 8, 2015, the Cross-Border Interbank Payment System (CIPS) Phase 1 was officially launched. CIPS is a significant financial infrastructure providing clearing and settlement of RMB cross-border business and offshore RMB business for both onshore and offshore institutions. The project was planned into two phases: firstly, to facilitate cross-border RMB business; support settlement of cross-border trade in goods and services; cross-border direct investment; financing, personal remittances, and other services. Its main features: firstly, CIPS (Phase 1) utilizes real-time gross settlement, handling both personal remittance and institutional remittance. Secondly, all direct participants are able to access via a single point, and they are allowed to be part of central clearing to simplify operations and improve efficiency. Thirdly, CIPS uses ISO20022 standard message to enable the convenient processing of cross-border participants. Fourthly, its operating time covers main time zones, including those in Europe, Asia, Africa,

Oceania, etc. Fifthly, onshore direct participants are able to connect to CIPS via dedicated lease lines.

To cultivate a fair competition environment, the PBC issued the "Interim Rules for Business Conducted through the Cross-Border Interbank Payment System," ruling on eligible participants, account management requirements, and business processing requirements. At the same time, the Cross-Border Interbank Payment System (Shanghai) Co., Ltd. was established and made responsible for the independent operation of CIPS. The company is supervised and managed by the PBC.

The first batch of direct CIPS participants were the top five banks in China (ICBC, ABC, BOC, China Construction Bank, Bank of Communications), six joint-stock banks (China Merchants Bank, Shanghai Pudong Development Bank, China Minsheng Bank, Industrial Bank, Ping An Bank, Hua Xia Bank), and eight foreign banks with legal entities in China (HSBC, Citibank, Standard Chartered Bank, DBS Bank, Deutsche Bank, BNP Paribas, ANZ and Bank of East Asia). In addition, other indirect participants included 38 domestic banks and 138 foreign banks in Asia, Europe, Oceania, Africa, and other regions.

After much research, as well as the cooperation and support of domestic commercial banks, the PBC established the CIPS in 2012. This was another milestone in China's financial market infrastructure, marking important progress for the modern payment system in both domestic and international RMB payments. As an important financial instrument, CIPS meets international regulatory requirements such as the "Principles for Financial Market." It plays a key supporting role in promoting RMB internationalization.

On March 26, 2018, the second CIPS phase was put into trial operation. 10 Chinese and foreign banks were simultaneously launched on a trial basis to further improve the clearing and settlement efficiency of RMB cross-border funds (Xinhuanet March 26, 2018); by the end of 2019, there had been 33 direct onshore and offshore CIPS participants and 903 indirect participants. The business scope extended to 167 countries and regions. The "Overall Operation of Payment System in 2019" published on the PBC website shows that in 2019, CIPS processed a total of 1.8843 million transactions with a total value of 33.93 trillion yuan – a year-on-year increase of 30.64% and 28.28%, respectively. The continuous CIPS updates promote RMB usage internationally and pave the way for it to become a global currency.

On January 16, 2019, SWIFT signed a letter of intent with the CIPS operating agency to further deepen cooperation between the two parties in the development of cross-border payment services. SWIFT will set up a wholly foreign-owned enterprise in Beijing to provide localized services to Chinese users. After the establishment of a wholly owned institution in China, SWIFT will join the Payment and Clearing Association of China and will be supervised and managed by the PBC. SWIFT is jointly owned by around 2,400 banks globally and serves more than 11,000 banks and financial institutions around the world; by January 16, 2019, 141 Chinese banks had joined the SWIFT Global Payment Initiative (SWIFT GPI). Their cross-border payments accounted for more than 97% of all Chinese banks' cross-border payments.

5.9 Promoting the Cross-Border Payment System of China UnionPay

China UnionPay, an association of Chinese bank cards, realizes the communication and information shared among commercial bank systems through the UnionPay interbank transaction clearing system, ensuring the cross-bank, region, and border use of bank cards. China UnionPay has had extensive cooperation with hundreds of domestic and overseas institutions, and the UnionPay network has spread throughout China's urban and rural areas. It has been extended to 160 countries and regions in Asia, Europe, America, Oceania, and Africa. When China UnionPay expands cross-border business, it takes advantage of networks, products, and technology to participate in the financial infrastructure of overseas markets. Thus, it can innovate business models and accelerate the localization of the UnionPay card business. For example, Thailand banking refers to the standards of UnionPay chip cards. The local transit network – Thai Payment Network (TPN) – built cooperatively by UnionPay and major banks in Thailand, was launched; UnionPay also took part in the construction of the national bank card payment system in Laos (*Financial Times*, October 13, 2016).

On October 12, 2016, China UnionPay signed a cooperation agreement with six international institutions: National Interbank Transaction Management and Exchange (NITMX); Network for Electronic Transfers (NETS); Rintis (an ATM switch network in Indonesia); BancNet (a Philippine-based interbank network); Malaysian Electronic Payment System (MEPS), and the Korea Financial Telecommunications & Clearings Institute (KFTC). This agreement was of great significance for market parties. Firstly, it was a form of upgraded cooperation between UnionPay and the overseas payment industry. Second, it satisfied the upgrade requirements from magnetic to chip cards in the payment industry, which laid the foundation for the overseas extension of UnionPay innovative products, such as contactless and mobile payments, and e-wallets. Third, it made full use of Sino-foreign cooperation, such as the Belt and Road Initiative, and it raised the international competitiveness of the Chinese payment industry by promoting payment and clearing infrastructure, and technical standards. These processes involve the five founding members and other members of ASEAN, indicating that China UnionPay has been especially relevant in the Southeast Asian region.

5.10 Conclusion

This chapter introduced the development of more than 20 offshore RMB centers, including Hong Kong, China, in the past seven years. Data from various sources shows that the offshore RMB payment business has developed rapidly in recent years: more than 20 RMB centers across the four continents of Asia, Europe, America, and Africa display this rapid development. Considering the depreciation of RMB against USD in August 2015 (with an expectation to depreciate significantly), the global cross-border RMB payment ratio still accounted for an impressive 2.79%. For the first time, it exceeded JPY, which was 2.76%, to become the world's 4th largest payment currency.

The offshore RMB payment service still shows pleasing development momentum, with strong faith remaining for the development of RMB and China's economy in the future. However, since August 2015, the percentage of RMB offshore payments has fallen below that of Canadian dollars in 6th place; RMB depreciation has affected its offshore payments. As of June 2020, its global share of cross-border payments reached 1.76%, making it the 5th largest payment currency.

The uneven distribution between offshore RMB centers and China's international trade should also be recognized. There are some countries and regions to take note of: India, the third largest economy in Asia and the largest in South Asia; Brazil, the ninth largest economy globally and the largest in Latin America; as well as Italy and Spain, two of the main Eurozone countries. As to the main developing nations – Mexico, Turkey, and Saudi Arabia, for example – RMB centers have not yet been established, despite the huge growth potential for RMB cross-border payments. It is believed that over the next few years, RMB internationalization will increase, and RMB payments will be distributed to more countries and regions.

Bibliography

Chan, Norman T. L. 2013. "Development of Offshore RMB Business in Hong Kong, China: Review and Outlook." February 21.

———. 2014. "Hong Kong, China as Offshore RMB Centre: Past and Prospects."

Hong Kong Monetary Authority. 2014. "Briefing to the Legislative Council, Panel on Financial Affairs." Accessed May 5, 2014. www.hkma.gov.

Li, Jing. 2009. *The Impact and Strategies for Chinese Economy of RMB Regionalization*. China Financial Publishing House, 57–58.

Lu, Ting. 2014. "The Current Situation, Problems and Prospects of Offshore RMB Market in Taiwan, China" International Financial Research Center, Institute of International Economics and Politics, Chinese Academy of Social Sciences.

Mikeni, Robert, and Liu Jianheng. 2013. *The Rising of RMB: International Status and Impacts*. China CITIC Press.

Yue, Eddie. 2012. "Hong Kong, China: Challenges and Opportunities Ahead." Speech at the Hong Kong Institute of Bankers Annual Conference 2012, September 13.

———. 2013. "The Development and Future of the Offshore RMB Market." Keynote address at Euromoney Global Offshore RMB Funding Forum 2013, May 8.

Zhang, Guangping. 2017. *RMB Internationalization & Products Innovation*. 7th ed. China Financial Publishing House.

CHAPTER SIX

Development of the Offshore RMB Market

6.1 The Development of the Offshore RMB Market in London

Due to its position as the largest foreign exchange center in the world and its positive attitude toward offshore RMB business, London has become the second largest RMB settlement center behind Hong Kong, China.

6.1.1 Intercommunication and cooperation between China and the UK

The UK-China economic and financial dialogue was based on the mutual perspectives of the Chinese premier and British prime minister in 2008. It is a bilateral dialogue mechanism based on economy, fiscal policies, and finance. Ten dialogues were held about this mechanism were held in April 2008, May 2009, November 2010, September 2011, October 2013, September 2014, September 20f15, November 2016, December 2017, and June 2019; such mechanisms are very rare in China's bilateral relationships with other countries. It later proved a good driver of this bilateral relationship, promoting economic and financial development between the two nations. Since August 2015, the 7th round of strategic dialogue between China and the UK, the 3rd high-level cultural exchange conference, and the 7th China-UK economic and financial dialogue have been held in quick succession. During the 7th economic and financial dialogue in Beijing, George Osborne, the UK Chancellor, claimed Britain was

China's best partner in the Western world (CCTV 2015). The following dialogue, held in November 2016, led to both sides agreeing to the "Establishment of Sino-UK Comprehensive Strategic Partnership in the 21st Century," and developed cooperation on trade and investment, financial services, infrastructure, energy, and industry strategy fields. With respect to financial services, both parties point to the success of the 3 billion offshore RMB sovereign bond and 5 billion short-term central bank bonds. These achievements underline deepening cooperation on finance and economy between China and the UK; both countries have welcomed the active issuance of RMB bonds in London and improved RMB liquidity, products, and service, so as to promote the development of offshore RMB markets. (The 8th Sino-UK Economic and Financial Dialogue, Xinhua News Agency, London, November 11).

Early in June 2013, both countries signed a foreign exchange swap deal worth RMB 200 billion. In October 2015, the contract amount of this swap deal increased to RMB 350 billion. The UK has also become the first Western country to sign such an agreement with China. During Osborne's visit to China in October 2013, London was granted a quota of RMB 80 billion as an RMB Qualified Foreign Institutional Investors (RQFII). Before this, Hong Kong, China was the only place to be granted an RQFII quota. By the end of May 2020, the UK had received a total of RMB 48.484 billion of RQFII quotas – the largest amount approved amongst Western countries. The successful offering of the first RMB government bond in the UK on October 14, 2014, was a further highlight for the London RMB Center. This first issuance of the RMB government bond for major developed countries will drive the development of RMB business in other offshore centers. In March 2015, the UK was also the first Western nation to join the Asian Infrastructure Investment Bank.

6.1.2 The establishment and development of the RMB center in London

London has been closely monitoring the rise of the renminbi as a new international currency. Early in April 2012, the City of London announced the establishment of an offshore RMB center. To become a truly international currency, RMB must first be used internationally. London, as the most important foreign exchange center in the world, can contribute significantly to this. On March 31, 2014, People's Bank of China and the Bank of England signed a collaboration memo on the establishment of an RMB clearing center in London. On June 18 of the same year, the PBC authorized China Construction Bank's London branch to be the clearing bank for RMB in London. It became the world's 5th and Europe's

1st offshore RMB clearing center authorized by the PBC. This has brought vitality and motivation to the development of the London RMB center.

Even though the RMB business started later in London than in Singapore, statistics show that its offshore center is growing at a fast pace. Data from the Society for Worldwide Interbank Financial Telecommunication (SWIFT) indicates that RMB payments in the UK exceeded Singapore for the first time since December 2012. However, it didn't last long. Singapore regained the top position in 2013. Yet, since the beginning of 2016, London has maintained its position as the largest RMB payment center besides Hong Kong, China. We will compare the daily turnover of RMB foreign exchange of major offshore centers in Chapter 10.

In August 2014, China Construction Bank and London Securities Exchange signed a cooperative agreement to actively seek opportunities in product innovation. On March 25, 2015, the first money market exchange fund of RQFII was officially listed on the London Securities Exchange; this was another big breakthrough for offshore RMB services in Europe.

On June 17, 2019, the Shanghai-London Stock Connect officially launched. This will not only promote the development of the cross-border securities industry by domestic securities companies, but also the two-way opening of the capital market as well as broadening the level of internationalization.

6.2 The Development of the Offshore RMB Market in Singapore

Many years ago, Singapore had already started to prepare and actively push offshore RMB services. As a major driving strategy, the Monetary Authority of Singapore (MAS) signed an RMB swap deal of 150 billion with the PBC back in July 2010. Both governments increased this amount to 300 billion in March 2013; on February 8, 2013, the PBC announced the ICBC Singapore branch as the RMB clearing bank, making Singapore the 4th RMB center to have such a clearing bank. On May 27, 2013, the offshore RMB clearing service was initiated in Singapore, and RMB services in the city's bank also began.

In recent years, the Singapore RMB Center has also experienced sustained and rapid growth in RMB deposits. Figure 6-1 gives the RMB deposit volume in Singapore from June 2003 to March 2021, as released by MAS. Figure 6-1 shows that from June 2012 to December 2014, Singapore's RMB deposit continued to grow. However, since June 2015, Singapore's RMB deposits showed an overall downward trend till June 2020; it has maintained a clear recovery trend since June

2020 and returned to the level of 152 billion in December 2017. Still, Singapore has remained second only to Hong Kong, China and Taiwan, China as the third largest RMB deposit center.

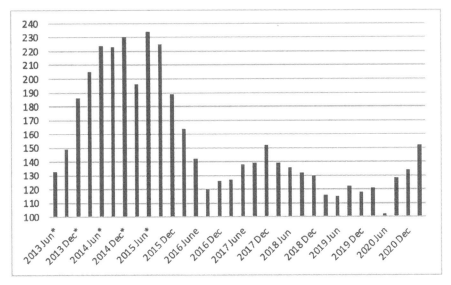

Figure 6-1   RMB Deposit Volume in Singapore (Unit: RMB billion)

*Data source: Singapore Monetary Authority, www.mas.gov.sg; *deposit data adjusted in December 2015 to reflect data re-submission by the financial institution.*

It is expected that RMB deposits in Singapore may surpass their historical high of June 2015 in the summer of 2022 if its recent recovery trend is maintained.

Singapore surpassed Japan for the first time in 2013, becoming the 3rd largest offshore RMB payment center, following Hong Kong, China and the UK. Singapore's RMB payment business has maintained its position as the third largest overseas RMB payment center after Hong Kong, China and the UK. As the third largest foreign exchange trading center in the Asia Pacific, and the largest trading and financial center in Southeast Asia, Singapore will play an important role in the promotion of RMB internationalization in this region.

6.3 The Development of Other RMB Centers in the Asia-Pacific Area

The Asia-Pacific region is the most important region for China's trade, and it has naturally become the most active region for the overseas use of RMB in recent years. After introducing two major offshore RMB centers in Hong Kong, China and Singapore, this section will introduce the business development of other major RMB centers in the Asia-Pacific region.

6.3.1 South Korea

South Korea signed an RMB 180 billion foreign exchange swap with the Bank of China in December 2008, being one of the first countries to sign a foreign exchange swap after the global financial crisis. In October 2011, the deal was doubled to RMB 360 billion, indicating very active cooperation between China and South Korea. According to SWIFT statistics in July 2014, RMB payments increased by 563% from June 2013 to June 2014, accounting for 2.5% of all RMB offshore payments in offshore RMB centers other than Hong Kong, China; South Korea became the 8th largest RMB center outside Hong Kong, China. Even though the swap deal between China and South Korea was the earliest, the center grew relatively slower than other Asia-Pacific RMB centers several years ago. In October 2015, the PBC increased the RQFII quota for South Korean institutions to RMB 120 billion. As of May 31, 2020, the total amount of RQFII approved for South Korean institutions had reached RMB 73.187 billion.

In April 2017, South Korea accounted for 12.82% of offshore RMB payments (aside from Hong Kong, China), surpassing the US and Taiwan, China to become the fourth largest offshore RMB payment center. However, the proportion of South Korea's RMB payments has been on a downward trend since June 2019. By the end of 2020, its corresponding proportion declined to 4.7%. Under the influence of the Terminal High Altitude Area Defense (THAAD) in recent years, RMB payments in South Korea have increased significantly, underlining the potential for future cooperation between the two countries. Due to close economic and trade relations, it is believed that the proportion of Korean RMB payments may soon return to the levels from a few years ago.

6.3.2 Taiwan, China

Although financial cooperation between Taiwan, China and Mainland China started later than Hong Kong, China, it's still much earlier than other countries and areas. Early in June 2008, 14 financial institutions were officially authorized for cash trading in RMB; the Monetary Authority in Taiwan, China gradually canceled the limitations on RMB services to banks and other financial institutions in Taiwan, China. RMB businesses were further expanded to offshore banking units (OBU) and offshore banks in July 2011. Since the signing of the "Memorandum of Cooperation on Currency Clearing between

Mainland China and Taiwan, China" in August 2012, financial cooperation has increased. With the deregulation of RMB services, the innovation of RMB financial products is encouraged. This facilitates Taiwan, China's offshore RMB market to develop rapidly. On February 6, 2013, the PBC announced the Bank of China Taipei Branch would be Taiwan, China's RMB clearing bank, making it the third offshore RMB center to have such a clearing bank. In February 2013, Taiwan, China initiated RMB services in domestic banking units (DBU). After that, the government further deregulated RMB financial derivatives. In this way, RMB services have been expanded, providing a good foundation for the rapid development of RMB services in Taiwan, China. On May 24, 2013, after the Money Authority of Taiwan and the Bank of China Taipei Branch signed the currency clearing deal, RMB services in Taiwan, China were officially initiated. By February 2014, total RMB deposits in Taiwan, China were 247.051 billion, with an increasing year-on-year rate of 533%.

Figure 6-2 gives the RMB deposit amount in Taiwan, China since January 2012: the Figure shows a steady increase to 338.22 billion from January 2012 to June 2015; it declined slightly and then increased again to a lower peak of 322.25 billion by the end of 2017; it then decreased steadily to 244.49 billion in December 2020, and fell below RMB 244 billion in April 2021. The changing pattern of RMB deposits in Taiwan, China in Figure 6-2 is similar to the downward trend of RMB deposits in Hong Kong, China and Singapore. Nevertheless, total RMB deposits in Taiwan picked up to RMB 241.173 billion by June 2020. Taiwan's RMB center has maintained its position as the second largest offshore center behind Hong Kong, China.

The RMB tracker report published by SWIFT in March 2013 indicated that over the past six months, RMB payments had increased by 120%, exceeding America and Australia to become the 4th RMB offshore center from 136 centers globally. An RMB report published by SWIFT in August 2015 shows that Taiwan, China remained in 4th place after Singapore, the UK, and America. It was briefly surpassed by South Korea at the end of 2015, yet by August of the following year Taiwan, China moved ahead of Korea once more. Taiwan's RMB payments accounted for 9.08% to 9.28% from September 2020 to December 2020 outside of Hong Kong, China; from December 2020 to April 2021, Taiwan, China maintained its position as the fourth largest RMB payment center after the UK, Singapore and the US (excluding Hong Kong, China). This has shown the clear advantages of cross-strait financial cooperation.

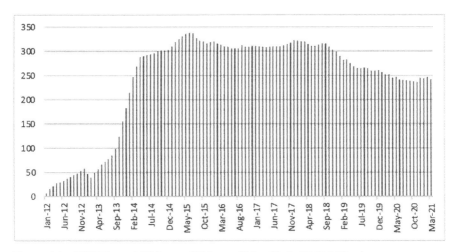

Figure 6-2   RMB Deposit Volume of Taiwan, China (Unit: RMB billion)

Data source: Taiwan Monetary website: www.cbc.gov.tw.

6.3.3 Australia

Australia has maintained its position as the 8th largest trading partner of China. In recent years, bilateral trade has increased. To enhance economic and financial cooperation, both countries signed an RMB swap deal of 200 billion back in March 2012. Australia was one of the first developed countries to sign such a deal with China. After some initial preparation time, the RMB service in Australia grew quickly. According to SWIFT statistics, after an inactive period, the RMB payment amount increased a lot from August to November 2012, rising from 12th to 4th place in the rankings (except Hong Kong, China). By the end of April 2014, RMB payments had increased 2.5 times compared to the year before. In June 2014, Australia's RMB payments accounted for 4.8% of total offshore RMB payments (not including Hong Kong, China), to become the 6th largest RMB center (after Singapore, UK, US, Taiwan, China, and France). This proportion decreased from 4.0% in July 2015 to 3.4% in November, dropping to 8th in the rankings. Furthermore, by the end of June 2020, its RMB clearing proportion remained the 7th largest overall.

6.3.4 Malaysia

Malaysia's trade with China has grown rapidly in recent years. In addition, cooperation in other areas has also been close. In 2013, the trading volume between the two countries exceeded USD 100 billion for the first time. Malaysia has been the 9th largest trading partner with China (following Australia) since then. Early in February 2009, Malaysia signed an RMB foreign currency swap deal with China for 80 billion – a solid foundation for driving this service. Aside from the big four currencies and the HKD, the Malaysian ringgit (MYR) was the first currency to be traded with the RMB in this way.

According to SWIFT data in September 2012, Malaysia's RMB payments in August were behind only London and Singapore, indicating an active RMB center at the time. In June 2014, RMB payments accounted for 2.1% of all RMB centers outside Hong Kong, China. Until July 2015, Malaysia retained its position as the 10th largest RMB center. However, since August 2016, its proportion of RMB clearing fell out of the top 14, underlining that the development of Malaysia's RMB business has been relatively slow in recent years; there is still tremendous room for growth.

6.3.5 Macau, China and Mongolia

Although the economic scale of Macau, China is relatively small, and its trading volume with Mainland China is not large, its RMB center has developed at a fast pace. Early in December 2009, the Bank of China Macau Branch was chosen as the RMB clearing bank. According to SWIFT data from September 2012, RMB payments ranked 5th (except Hong Kong, China) for August of that year – higher than Taiwan, China. In July 2015, RMB payments accounted for 1.3%, ranking 10th alongside Malaysia and Japan. In November of that year, RMB payments slightly increased to 1.4%, and the offshore RMB business ranked 11th after Japan (9th) and Luxemburg (10th), but dropped to 12th in January 2017. Since January 2018, Macau, China's RMB center has fallen behind 12th place. However, by July 2020, Macau, China returned to 10th place in this ranking; in September and October 2020, its RMB clearing rankings rose to 8th and 7th, respectively.

Like Macau, China, the development of Mongolia's RMB center was relatively fast compared to its economic scale. Mongolia signed an RMB foreign exchange swap deal of RMB 5 billion with China on May 6, 2011, and increased to RMB 10 billion in March 2012. According to SWIFT data from August 2012, RMB payments in Mongolia ranked 7th (except Hong Kong, China), indicating rapid business growth in the early stage. Due to the fact that this growth slowed considerably over the next few years, its ranking fell outside the top ten in June 2014 and by 2016 was in 14th place.

6.3.6 Japan

The governments of Japan and China made an agreement of cooperation to strengthen financial ties between the two countries back in December 2011 (the PBC, December 25, 2011). Yet there were neither official currency swap deals signed, nor RMB clearing arrangements in Japan. Eventually, on October 26, 2018, the People's Bank of China and the Bank of Japan signed a bilateral domestic currency swap agreement for 200 billion yuan – valid for three years. At the same time, the PBC authorized the Bank of China Tokyo Branch to act as Japan's RMB clearing bank; on June 27, 2019, the PBC authorized Japan's Mitsubishi UFJ Bank to act as the clearing bank for Japan's RMB business. RMB payments in Japan ranked 9th amongst offshore RMB centers (SWIFT, October 2012); in July 2015, its ratio reached as high as 1.3%, ranking 10th alongside Macau, China and Malaysia. In November 2015, the ratio doubled to 2.7%, and it became the 9th largest offshore RMB center again. From June to October 2020, it ranked 8th amongst all offshore centers, excluding Hong Kong, China.

It should be noticed that the average RMB daily turnover in Tokyo increased from USD 4.06 billion in September 2019 to USD 5 billion in September 2020 (www.fxcomtky.com), jumping from the 10th to the 8th highest trading currency in Tokyo over the same period. This signified the measurable growth of RMB trading in Japan. Since Mainland China surpassed the US to become Japan's largest trading partner for the first time in 2007, China has maintained this position. The trade volume between China and Japan far surpasses that of China and Australia, and Japan's RMB payment is expected to increase significantly with the implementation of the Regional Comprehensive Economic Partnership Agreement (RCEP).

6.3.7 Qatar and the United Arab Emirates (UAE)

Early on November 3, 2014, the PBC signed a RMB 35 billion bilateral currency swap agreement with the Qatar Central Bank. At the same time, the two sides signed a cooperation memorandum for establishing RMB clearing arrangements in Doha and agreed to expand the RMB Qualified Foreign Institutional Investors (RQFII) pilot areas with an initial investment of RMB 30 billion). The following day, a clearing agreement with Qatar was signed. The Qatar RMB Center held a launch ceremony on April 14, 2015, becoming the first such center in the Middle East. According to SWIFT data from January 2016, 60% of payments between Qatar, Mainland China, and Hong Kong, China in 2015 were in RMB

– an increase of 247% over 2014. The Qatar RMB Center will play an important leading role in promoting this business in the Middle East.

The United Arab Emirates (UAE) signed an RMB 35 billion bilateral currency swap agreement with the PBC before January 2012; however, the UAE's RMB center was established later than Qatar's. The PBC renewed the bilateral currency swap agreement with the UAE on December 14, 2015 – maintaining an agreement of the RMB 35 billion scale and valid for three years. Simultaneously, the two sides signed a cooperation memorandum for establishing RMB clearing arrangements in UAE and agreed to expand the RMB Qualified Foreign Institutional Investors (RQFII) pilot areas. On December 9, 2016, the Dubai branch of ABC was designated as the UAE's RMB Clearing Bank. According to SWIFT data from January 2016, 74% of payments made between UAE and Mainland China as well as Hong Kong, China used RMB – a 52% increase compared with 2014 and elevating the UAE to the second largest RMB payment country in the region. From August 2014–15 and August 2015–16, RMB payments increased by 210.8% and 44.6%, respectively, indicating rapid growth. These are good indicators for the future development of the RMB business in the Middle East.

6.3.8 Other RMB centers in the Asia-Pacific

In addition to RMB centers in the Asia Pacific mentioned earlier, RMB centers in Thailand, the Philippines, Indonesia, and Vietnam have also developed to different levels in recent years. In particular, the Philippines's RMB payment to both Mainland China and Hong Kong, China increased from 53% to 73% from April 2012 to April 2015. During the same period, the rate in Indonesia, Thailand, and Vietnam went from 7%, 13%, and 6% to 26%, 25%, and 14%, respectively, indicating rapid growth in these three countries. However, the overall proportion of RMB settlements in these countries to the whole is relatively low, which indicates tremendous room for further growth.

6.4 The Development of RMB Centers in Europe

Other than the UK RMB center discussed previously, the European region has added the most RMB centers in addition to the Asia-Pacific area in recent years. Central Bank of Europe signed an RMB swap agreement with the PBC in October 2013 for up to RMB 350 billion. This amount was second only to the swap amount signed with Hong Kong, China and South Korea. This swap deal suggests an attitude of encouraging the Eurozone to push forward the development of RMB services.

6.4.1 France

France has been the first and most prevalent RMB center in the Eurozone for more than eight years. According to SWIFT statistics, from March 13, 2012, RMB payments in France increased by 249%, making it the 4th largest offshore RMB center behind the UK, Singapore, and Taiwan, China by March 2013. Later statistics from SWIFT showed that in July 2015, France dropped to 7th place in offshore RMB centers, accounting for 1.1% of payments. It kept this status from June 2015 to December 2016, and then became the 6th largest after January 2017. On March 26, 2014, a joint declaration from the People's Republic of China and the French Republic announced a distribution quota of RMB 80 billion RQFII to France (Xinhuanet Paris March 27, 2014). As of May 31, 2020, seven financial institutions in France have received an accumulative RQFII quota of RMB 24 billion, the second largest in Europe. On June 28, 2014, the PBC and the Bank of France signed a memorandum of RMB clearing.

For many years, France has had a lower GDP than Germany, and from 1998 to 2004, France's FX trading ratio was also 1% lower than Germany's. However, since 2007, its FX trading ratio has started to surpass Germany. Furthermore, the ratio exceeded Germany by 1.18% in 2013 and 0.98% in 2016. From 2001 to 2013, the FX trading ratio of France remained around 2.8%. At the same time, Germany's ratio decreased by 3.7%, indicating a clear difference in the international FX trading market of the two countries after the international financial crisis. In the meantime, to a great extent, the ratio displayed a very active attitude in France's RMB foreign exchange market. It is believed that France will continuously lead the RMB business in Europe.

6.4.2 Germany

Although Germany is Europe's largest economy, the transaction ratio of its global foreign exchange market in Germany dropped from 5.4% in 2001 to 1.7% in 2013. Though that ratio rose to 1.8% in 2016, the overall trend was still downwards. According to SWIFT data from June 2013, RMB payments increased by 71% on a year-on-year basis in April and May 2013, making Germany the 8th largest offshore RMB center outside Hong Kong, China. Germany also moved up to the 8th place in RMB payments in July 2015, and that proportion doubled to 4.1%

from then to November of that year, surpassing France (3.7%) for the first time to become the 6th largest offshore RMB center. However, its ranking declined to 9th in September 2016, falling even further down the rankings until regaining 9th position in June 2020.

For many years, Germany has been regarded as the largest trading partner of China in Europe. On March 28, 2014, the PBC and Deutsche Bundesbank signed a cooperation memorandum to establish an RMB clearing center in Frankfurt. Later, the PBC assigned its Frankfurt branch as the RMB clearing bank. As of May 31, 2020, only three institutions in Germany have received an RQFII quota, totaling only RMB 10.543 billion – less than half of that of France; financial cooperation between China and Germany can be significantly strengthened.

6.4.3 Luxemburg

As an important financial center in Europe, financial cooperation between it and China is relatively high in spite of its small size. Table 5-1 shows that Banque Centrale du Luxembourg signed the RMB clearing agreement with the PBC in early September 2014 and appointed the ICBC Luxemburg branch as its clearing bank. According to SWIFT data from August 2013, as of July 2013, the RMB payments ratio increased by 86%, making it the 2nd largest RMB center in the Eurozone after France. In July 2013, over 58% of payments between Luxemburg and Mainland China or Hong Kong, China was in RMB, while the ratio was only 42% a year before. In July 2015, Luxemburg's RMB payment ranked 8th, the same as Germany's. In August 2016, its ranking dropped to 11th, and then in June 2019, it dropped to 12th. Although Luxembourg's population is very small, it received a total of RMB 15.187 billion in RQFII, which exceeded the corresponding total quota of Germany. The total quota also exceeded that of RQFII in Canada and Switzerland. All this underlines Luxembourg's important position as an offshore RMB center.

6.4.4 Other Eurozone RMB centers

Belgium was one of the earlier RMB centers, and it made reasonable progress in this RMB business. In January 2012, RMB payments in Belgium ranked 3rd largest in the Eurozone and 6th largest of all. Due to recent rapid developments of other RMB centers, however, by July 2015, the cross-border RMB payment ratio in Belgium only ranked 12th place. In August 2016, its ranking fell further to 14th, where it has mostly remained (rising and falling the odd place). Given that there is no RMB clearing arrangement between China and Belgium, and

Belgium is neither an RQFII pilot country nor a founding member of the Asian Infrastructure Investment Bank, its ranking is impressively high.

Although the Netherlands' GDP is only around one-third of the UK's, it kept its position as the 2nd or 3rd largest trading partner with China in Europe. Although the RMB center in the Netherlands started up late, the cross-border RMB payment ratio accounted for 0.3% in July 2015, ranking 13th and exceeding that of Belgium. In November 2015, the RMB cross-border settlement ratio increased to 1.4%, with its ranking increasing accordingly. As of June 2020, its ranking has remained in 14th place. Due to the considerable trade volume between China and the Netherlands, the proportion of RMB center payments will increase significantly in the future, and its ranking will further improve.

6.4.5 Comparing the Eurozone with other major RMB centers

The five major RMB centers in the Eurozone were briefly introduced earlier. By adding the amounts of respective Eurozone nations, it is possible to calculate total RMB payments from the Eurozone. As shown in Figure 5-3, the number of Eurozone RMB centers grew from 2 in January 2012 to 5 in June 2013, and the relevant proportion of RMB payments increased from 8.9% to 15.3%. The Eurozone can be regarded as the 3rd largest RMB center, following the UK and Singapore. In June 2014, total RMB payments decreased to 10.2%, lower than the US. In June 2016, its proportion rebounded back to 12.8%, exceeding both the US and Taiwan, China; its ranking returned to 3rd. In June 2017, the total share of the Eurozone remained behind London, Singapore, and South Korea, ranking the 4th; however, from February 2018 to April 2021, its total share surpassed Singapore and the US, ranking as the 2nd largest offshore RMB center behind London.

6.4.6 Russia

China is Russia's 2nd largest trading partner after the Eurozone. Since November 22, 2010, the China State Administration of Foreign Exchange began to publish the exchange rate between the Chinese renminbi and the Russian ruble. The China branch of Vneshtorgbank (VTB) has already started providing loans in RUB and RMB – a pillar of Sino-Russian bilateral trade. On October 13, 2014, the PBC and the Central Bank of the Russian Federation signed a bilateral currency swap agreement of up to RMB 150 billion aimed at facilitating bilateral trade and direct investment and promoting economic development (www.pbc.gov.cn). Although there have been many reports on the economic and trade cooperation between China and Russia in recent years, Russia's RMB clearing arrangement was launched relatively late. In September 2016, it was finalized, with the Industrial and Commercial Bank of China acting as Russia's RMB clearing bank. In December 2016, Russia's RMB cross-border payments accounted for 0.35%, ranking 17th (outside Hong Kong, China). Over the next two years, this ranking rose to 11th place, showing that Russia's RMB center developed rapidly over this period. However, as of June 2020, its ranking had dropped to 14th place.

6.4.7 Switzerland

On July 21, 2014, the Swiss central bank signed a currency swap deal of RMB 150 billion with the PBC. In January 2015, the PBC announced an RQFII test region expansion to Switzerland, with a quota of RMB 50 billion. This expansion benefited foreign investors investing products in China's capital market in Switzerland. In the meantime, it also enlarged the channels of RMB investment. China Construction Bank was authorized to establish a clearing center at its Zurich branch for RMB clearing (www.gov.cn). In December 2016, Swiss RMB payments accounted for 0.35% of the total, ranking in 16th place.

6.5 The Development of RMB Centers in the US

Despite being the world's largest economy, America has not signed an RMB currency swap agreement with China, and RMB clearing was only launched in September 2016. In January 2012, RMB payments in the US only accounted for 5.6% of the total, after Singapore and London. By November 2012, this had risen to 6.6%. However, one month later, the ratio dropped to 4.1%, and its ranking dropped accordingly to 6th.

An article titled "US Enterprises Prefer Settlement in RMB" was published in the *Wall Street Journal* on July 10, 2014. It stated that RMB transactions for US enterprises had reached a record-breaking level. Data from SWIFT showed that from April 2013–14, RMB payments increased by 327%, becoming the 3rd largest RMB center after Singapore and London. This ranking remained until December 2014. By June 2020, the US had once again fallen behind South Korea into 4th place (excluding Hong Kong, China).

On June 8, 2016, the PBC announced that it had recently signed a memorandum of cooperation to establish an RMB clearing arrangement with the Federal Reserve Board of the US (China News Network June 8, 2016). In September 2016, the PBC designated the Bank of China's New York branch as the RMB clearing bank. The implementation of this will play an important role in promoting the development of US RMB cross-border payments and other RMB businesses; on February 13, 2018, JP Morgan Chase & Co was approved by the PBC and US regulatory authorities to become the second RMB clearing bank in the US. (It was also one of the only two non-Chinese RMB clearing banks among a total of 27 overseas). With the promotion of RMB internationalization in the Asia-Pacific region and Europe, RMB payments in the US and its proportion of global RMB cross-border payments will increase significantly; the US is expected to become one of the main RMB centers overseas.

It should be noticed that the average RMB daily turnover in New York increased 63.3% from USD 8.54 billion in September 2019 to USD 13.95 billion in September 2020 (website: www.newyorkfed.org), signifying the significant growth of RMB trading in New York and closer the financial cooperation between the world's two largest economies.

CHAPTER SEVEN

Overseas Assets and Bank Internationalization of Major Currency Issuers

THE INTERNATIONAL FOREIGN EXCHANGE MARKET IS essentially an inter-bank market; thus, banks play a crucial role in currency internationalization. This chapter will firstly compare the sizes of cross-border assets of major currency issuers and of cross-border holdings of the bank sectors of major currency issuers, and finally compare the international holdings of top multinational firms and the internationalization of banks of major currency issuers.

7.1 Distribution of Cross-Border Assets and Liabilities

The size of the cross-border assets and liabilities of major world currency issuers gives us an indication of their underlying strength as currency issuers. There are different definitions of cross-border assets and corresponding liabilities. We follow the definition and data of cross-border positions from the Bank for International Settlements (BIS) or holdings of foreign institutions in residence of major currency issuers. Table 7-1 gives us the assets, liabilities, and net assets of major world currency issuers from 2007 to 2020.

Table 7-1   Distribution of Cross-Border Assets, Liabilities, and Net Assets of Major World Currency Issuers (2007 to 2020)

Unit: Trillion US Dollars %

Currency Issuer	2007	2009	2011	2013	2015	2017	2019	2020	CAGR
Cross-Border Assets of Major Currency Issuers									
US	5.59	5.01	5.43	4.92	4.74	4.99	5.28	6.13	0.7
Eurozone	11.57	10.68	9.03	8.38	7.26	7.77	8.14	9.48	−1.5
Japan	0.66	0.68	0.90	1.00	1.18	1.33	1.47	1.75	7.8
UK	5.72	4.70	4.91	4.17	3.61	3.65	3.90	5.23	−0.7
Australia	0.35	0.37	0.40	0.38	0.40	0.44	0.47	0.55	3.6
Canada	0.36	0.39	0.39	0.42	0.47	0.48	0.58	0.72	5.6
Switzerland	1.05	0.61	0.65	0.63	0.61	0.65	0.62	0.66	−3.5
China	0.19	0.18	0.48	0.90	0.76	0.96	0.94	1.00	13.7
Other	7.42	6.89	7.62	7.67	8.11	8.96	9.64	10.19	2.5
World	32.91	29.52	29.80	28.48	27.12	29.22	31.05	35.71	0.6

(Continued)

| Cross-Border Liabilities of Major Currency Issuers | | | | | | | | | |
Currency Issuer	2007	2009	2011	2013	2015	2017	2019	2020	CAGR
US	4.16	4.31	4.45	3.84	3.34	3.54	3.71	4.41	0.4
Eurozone	7.86	6.93	6.85	6.74	5.78	6.22	6.82	8.10	0.2
Japan	0.76	0.56	0.76	0.76	0.77	0.84	0.86	0.93	1.6
UK	5.21	4.44	4.86	4.34	3.86	4.15	4.11	5.40	0.3
Australia	0.11	0.13	0.18	0.19	0.24	0.23	0.24	0.32	8.6
Canada	0.15	0.20	0.26	0.26	0.29	0.33	0.38	0.49	9.3
Switzerland	1.68	1.00	0.92	0.83	0.66	0.68	0.71	0.70	−6.5
China	0.28	0.20	0.30	0.36	0.59	0.68	0.78	0.96	9.9
Other	8.85	7.67	7.79	8.11	9.12	9.75	9.86	10.37	1.2
World	29.07	25.45	26.38	25.43	24.69	26.41	27.48	31.68	0.7

(Continued)

Cross-Border Net Assets of Major Currency Issuers

Currency Issuer	2007	2009	2011	2013	2015	2017	2019	2020	CAGR
US	1.42	0.71	0.97	1.08	1.40	1.45	1.57	1.72	1.5
Eurozone	3.70	3.75	2.18	1.64	1.48	1.55	1.32	1.38	−7.3
Japan	−0.10	0.12	0.14	0.24	0.41	0.49	0.61	0.82	17.7
UK	0.51	0.26	0.05	−0.17	−0.26	−0.50	−0.21	−0.17	−192.0
Australia	0.24	0.24	0.21	0.20	0.16	0.20	0.23	0.23	−0.3
Canada	0.20	0.19	0.13	0.16	0.18	0.15	0.20	0.24	1.2
Switzerland	−0.62	−0.39	−0.27	−0.19	−0.05	−0.03	−0.09	−0.04	−19.8
China	−0.09	−0.02	0.17	0.53	0.16	0.28	0.17	0.05	5.4
Other	−1.43	−0.79	−0.17	−0.44	−1.05	−0.79	−0.22	−0.18	14.6
World	3.84	4.07	3.42	3.05	2.43	2.81	3.58	4.04	0.4

Data source: Cross-border positions by residence and counterparty, BIS website: www.bis.org.

7.1.1 Changes in world cross-border assets and liabilities and their implications

Changes in world cross-border assets and liabilities reflect changes in globalization and currency internationalization. Table 7-1 shows the cumulative average annual growth rates (CAGR) of total world cross-border assets, liabilities, and net assets, which were merely 0.6%, 0.7%, and 0.4%, respectively, from 2007–20. This implies cross-border business only just returned to the pre-2008 global financial crisis level after 13 years.

7.1.2 Size of cross-border assets and world financial centers

Table 7-1 shows that the Eurozone, US, and UK were by far the largest holders of cross-border assets from 2007–20. As more than half of the cross-border assets in the Eurozone are within these countries themselves, actual Eurozone cross-border assets should be less than half the figure given in Table 7-1.

The biggest decrease in cross-border assets occurred in Switzerland from 2007-19, which is consistent with its decline in ranking as an international foreign exchange trading center – dropping from 3rd place in 2007 to 6th in 2019. The magnitude of cross-border assets in Japan, Singapore, Hong Kong, China, and Luxembourg are largely comparable to the international rankings of these economies in international foreign exchange trading.

7.1.3 Changes in cross-border assets and liabilities of major currency issuers

Table 7-1 shows that cross-border assets in Switzerland, the Eurozone, and the UK decreased with CARGs of 3.5%, 1.5%, and 0.7%, respectively, from 2007–20, indicating a relative decline in these three areas as world foreign exchange centers. Meanwhile, the increase in assets in China, Japan, Canada, and Australia, with CARGs greater than 3% over this same time scale, indicates their relative rise in the global foreign exchange market.

7.1.4 Cross-border net assets and international financial centers

Besides the magnitude of cross-border assets being representational of global foreign exchange centers, to some extent, net assets are also a good reference point. For example, Table 7-1 shows that net cross-border assets in the UK were negative from 2013–20, consistent with its global foreign exchange over this period. The negative cross-border assets of Hong Kong, China, Singapore, and Belgium are also consistent with their lofty positions in global foreign exchange markets.

7.2 Distribution of Cross-Border Banking Assets and Liabilities

Banks play an important role in global foreign exchange markets; the magnitudes of cross-border bank sector assets and liabilities of major world currency issuers are useful indicators.

Table 7-2   Distribution of Bank Sector Cross-Border Assets, Liabilities, and Net Assets of Major World Currency Issuers (2007–2020)

Unit: Trillion US dollars and %

Cross-Border Assets of Major Currency Issuers									
Currency Issuer	2007	2009	2011	2013	2015	2017	2019	2020	CAGR
US	2.60	2.62	2.90	2.44	2.15	2.02	2.01	2.21	−1.24
Eurozone	7.58	6.79	5.63	4.65	3.91	4.37	4.39	4.95	−3.23
Japan	0.39	0.50	0.60	0.71	0.80	0.90	0.95	1.07	8.05
UK	4.59	3.69	3.84	2.90	2.47	2.30	2.23	2.70	−3.99
Australia	0.21	0.24	0.25	0.25	0.27	0.27	0.29	0.32	3.38
Canada	0.24	0.26	0.25	0.28	0.30	0.28	0.37	0.45	4.85
Switzerland	0.86	0.44	0.47	0.46	0.46	0.48	0.44	0.46	−4.70
China	0.12	0.12	0.33	0.61	0.45	0.62	0.55	0.57	12.57
Other	4.37	4.05	4.54	4.11	3.88	4.21	4.19	4.27	−0.17
World	20.97	18.69	18.82	16.41	14.68	15.45	15.42	17.01	−1.60
Cross-Border Liabilities of Major Currency Issuers									
Currency Issuer	2007	2009	2011	2013	2015	2017	2019	2020	CAGR
US	2.27	2.51	2.68	2.01	1.88	1.69	1.80	2.00	−0.97
Eurozone	7.58	4.92	4.59	4.02	3.41	3.59	4.02	4.44	−4.03
Japan	0.55	0.40	0.56	0.59	0.55	0.61	0.59	0.62	0.92
UK	3.85	3.42	3.48	2.95	2.59	2.68	2.48	2.89	−2.18
Australia	0.06	0.08	0.12	0.12	0.18	0.17	0.18	0.22	10.40
Canada	0.10	0.13	0.18	0.16	0.19	0.21	0.27	0.34	9.97
Switzerland	1.37	0.77	0.70	0.61	0.48	0.47	0.51	0.45	−8.19

(Continued)

| China | 0.20 | 0.13 | 0.20 | 0.23 | 0.39 | 0.45 | 0.52 | 0.65 | 9.25 |

Cross-Border Liabilities of Major Currency Issuers

Currency Issuer	2007	2009	2011	2013	2015	2017	2019	2020	CAGR
Other	4.03	4.92	4.93	4.28	4.27	4.47	4.26	4.44	0.76
World	20.01	17.29	17.44	14.98	13.95	14.34	14.64	16.05	−1.68

Cross-Border Net Assets of Major Currency Issuers

Currency Issuer	2007	2009	2011	2013	2015	2017	2019	2020	CAGR
US	0.34	0.11	0.23	0.43	0.27	0.33	0.21	0.22	−3.34
Eurozone	7.58	1.87	1.04	0.63	0.49	0.78	0.37	0.51	−18.77
Japan	−0.16	0.09	0.04	0.12	0.25	0.29	0.36	0.45	8.43
UK	0.74	0.27	0.36	−0.04	−0.12	−0.37	−0.25	−0.19	−10.09
Australia	0.15	0.16	0.12	0.13	0.08	0.10	0.12	0.10	−3.06
Canada	0.15	0.12	0.07	0.11	0.11	0.07	0.10	0.11	−1.99
Switzerland	−0.51	−0.33	−0.23	−0.15	−0.01	0.01	−0.07	0.01	27.09
China	−0.08	−0.01	0.13	0.37	0.06	0.17	0.03	−0.08	−0.21
Other	0.34	−0.88	−0.38	−0.17	−0.38	−0.26	−0.07	−0.17	−5.31
World	0.96	1.40	1.38	1.44	0.74	1.11	0.79	0.96	−0.03

Data source: Same as Table 7-1.

7.2.1 Distribution of banking sector cross border assets and liabilities

Table 7-2 shows that bank sector cross-border asset holdings deceased by a CARG rate of 1.6%, compared to a corresponding CARG rate of 0.6% of total cross-border assets, suggesting a decreased role for the world banking sector following the 2008 global financial crisis.

Table 7-2 also shows that a similar pattern is followed for cross-border assets: in the US, Eurozone, UK, and Switzerland, the rate decreased, but in China, Japan, Canada, and Australia, it increased.

Although the overall rate has dropped by more than 10%, cross-border assets as a pillar of global banking remain strong. In the meantime, the proportion of cross-border liabilities has been higher than assets proportions, and cross-border equity in global banking was less than 1/3 on average.

7.2.2 Bank sector cross-border net assets

Table 7-2 shows that although bank sector cross-border net assets of all major currency issuers decreased from 2007–20, net assets of the Eurozone and UK decreased with a CARG of 18.77% and 10.09%, respectively – higher than the rest.

7.2.3 The bank sector compared to major currency issuers

We cannot see the relative importance of the banking sector directly from Tables 7-1 and 7-2. However, Table 7-3 gives us the shares of banking sector cross-border assets, liabilities, and net assets from their total shares of major currency issuers.

Table 7-3 Distributional Share of Banking Sector Cross-Border Assets, Liabilities, and Net Assets

Cross-Border Assets of Major Currency Issuers								
Currency Issuer	2007	2009	2011	2013	2015	2017	2019	2020	Change from 2007 to 2020
US	46.6%	52.3%	53.5%	49.6%	45.3%	40.5%	38.2%	36.1%	−10.5%
Eurozone	65.5%	63.5%	62.3%	55.5%	53.9%	56.2%	53.9%	52.2%	−13.3%
Japan	59.1%	72.6%	66.4%	71.0%	67.9%	67.6%	64.7%	61.2%	2.1%
UK	80.3%	78.5%	78.2%	69.6%	68.5%	63.1%	57.1%	51.7%	−28.5%
Australia	60.0%	64.1%	62.1%	65.4%	66.4%	61.9%	62.4%	58.7%	−1.4%
Canada	68.6%	65.1%	65.3%	65.6%	63.9%	58.0%	63.3%	62.4%	−6.2%
Switzerland	81.8%	72.1%	72.3%	73.1%	76.0%	73.8%	70.5%	69.4%	−12.4%
China	64.2%	66.9%	69.8%	67.5%	59.4%	64.6%	58.6%	56.3%	−7.9%
Other	58.9%	58.8%	59.7%	53.6%	47.9%	47.0%	43.5%	42.0%	−16.9%
World	63.7%	63.3%	63.2%	57.6%	54.1%	52.9%	49.7%	47.6%	−16.1%

(Continued)

Cross-Border Liabilities of Major Currency Issuers									
Currency Issuer	2007	2009	2011	2013	2015	2017	2019	2020	Change from 2007 to 2020
US	54.5%	58.3%	60.1%	52.3%	56.3%	47.7%	48.7%	45.3%	−9.2%
Eurozone	96.3%	70.9%	67.0%	59.6%	59.1%	57.7%	58.9%	54.8%	−41.5%
Japan	72.3%	71.4%	73.8%	77.5%	71.5%	72.8%	68.5%	66.3%	−6.0%
UK	73.9%	77.1%	71.6%	67.9%	67.2%	64.5%	60.3%	53.5%	−20.3%
Australia	57.2%	60.7%	67.1%	66.6%	76.8%	72.3%	72.7%	70.6%	13.4%
Canada	64.3%	64.9%	70.4%	61.7%	65.5%	64.2%	70.1%	69.8%	5.5%
Switzerland	81.8%	77.3%	75.7%	73.7%	72.9%	69.2%	71.8%	64.7%	−17.1%
China	72.6%	65.2%	65.8%	64.2%	66.4%	66.4%	67.2%	67.5%	−5.2%
Other	45.5%	64.2%	63.3%	52.8%	46.6%	45.9%	43.3%	42.9%	−2.7%
World	68.8%	67.9%	66.1%	58.9%	56.5%	54.3%	53.3%	50.7%	−18.1%
Cross-Border Net Assets of Major Currency Issuers									
Currency Issuer	2007	2009	2011	2013	2015	2017	2019	2020	Change from 2007 to 2020
US	23.7%	15.7%	23.2%	40.1%	19.0%	23.0%	13.4%	12.6%	−11.1%
Eurozone	204.6%	49.8%	47.5%	38.6%	33.4%	50.1%	28.0%	36.9%	−167.7%
Japan	161.8%	78.4%	26.4%	50.3%	61.2%	58.7%	59.2%	55.4%	−106.3%
UK	145.6%	103.8%	678.8%	25.4%	48.4%	75.3%	119.6%	107.7%	−37.9%
Australia	61.3%	66.1%	57.9%	64.2%	50.7%	49.8%	51.2%	42.3%	−19.0%
Canada	71.8%	65.3%	55.3%	71.9%	61.2%	44.8%	50.1%	47.2%	−24.6%
Switzerland	81.7%	85.6%	84.0%	75.9%	30.9%	−34.4%	81.2%	−23.7%	−105.4%
China	89.7%	52.8%	76.7%	69.8%	33.9%	60.1%	18.1%	−179.2%	−268.9%
Other	−24.0%	111.4%	224.8%	39.4%	36.3%	32.6%	34.2%	92.4%	116.4%
World	25.1%	34.5%	40.3%	47.1%	30.2%	39.6%	22.0%	23.8%	−1.3%

Data source: Calculated from data in Table 7-1 and Table 7-2.

Table 7-3 shows that cross-border bank assets as a share of the total for all major currency issuers declined other than Japan, which registered a slight increase of 2.1% from 2007–20. In total, such assets declined 16.1% over this period. As for bank sector liabilities, all major currency issuers posted declines, except for Australia and Canada, which posted increases of 13.4% and 5.5%, respectively.

The share of total liabilities dropped 18.1% from 2007–20, and the share of total net assets also declined over this period. It is noticeable that the US had the smallest shares in all these areas, implying that the non-banking sector is large there. The tremendous growth of the global equity market, particularly in the US, may provide some explanation for the decline in recent years: the world securitization ratio (year-end equity market capitalization/global GDP) more than doubled from 56% in 2008 to 125.2% in 2020.

7.3 Currency Distribution of All-Sector Claims, Liabilities, and Net Claims

Corresponding to Table 7-1, the Bank of International Settlements periodically publishes all sector claims and liabilities of the world's top five currencies.

Table 7-4 shows that claims and liabilities in all sectors of major currencies decreased, while all sectors' claims of other currencies increased with a CAGR of 9.50% and 2.71%. The contrast indicates that the dominance of the top five world currencies has decreased. Using data from the table, calculations show that claims in all sectors can be considered as "substitutes" for currency internationalization, as more claims reflect more international trading volume and risk management.

Table 7-4   All-Sector Net Claims and Liabilities of Major International Currencies (2007–2020)

Unit: %

All-Sector Claims of Major Currencies								
Currency	2007	2010	2011	2013	2015	2016	2019	2020	Change 2006–7
USD	8.23	8.37	8.62	7.37	7.25	7.37	7.33	7.53	−0.68
EUR	8.40	6.90	6.81	5.59	4.28	4.10	4.74	5.56	−3.12

(Continued)

JPY	0.99	0.96	0.96	0.69	0.56	0.62	0.63	0.73	−2.32
GBP	1.81	1.02	0.81	0.81	0.74	0.61	0.64	0.75	−6.57
CHF	0.37	0.32	0.36	0.40	0.32	0.27	0.35	0.32	−1.07
Other Currencies	0.26	0.28	0.30	0.46	0.57	0.56	0.64	0.83	9.50
Unallocated	0.91	0.94	0.94	1.09	0.96	0.93	1.08	1.29	2.71
World	20.97	18.79	18.82	16.41	14.69	14.46	15.42	17.01	−1.60

All Sectors Liabilities of Major Currencies

Currency	2007	2009	2011	2013	2015	2017	2019	2020	Change from 2007 to 2020
USD	8.99	8.45	8.82	7.67	7.52	7.47	7.57	7.86	−1.03
EUR	7.11	5.94	5.70	4.56	3.56	3.53	4.08	4.69	−3.16
JPY	0.76	0.76	0.71	0.48	0.46	0.51	0.57	0.61	−1.76
GBP	1.85	1.05	0.81	0.84	0.83	0.67	0.66	0.77	−6.53
CHF	0.29	0.24	0.32	0.29	0.24	0.21	0.27	0.27	−0.34
Other Currencies	0.33	0.44	0.44	0.55	0.78	0.71	0.92	1.17	10.31
Unallocated	0.69	0.61	0.64	0.59	0.55	0.57	0.56	0.69	0.09
World	20.01	17.48	17.44	14.98	13.95	13.67	14.64	16.05	−1.68

All-Sector Net Claims of Major Currencies

Currency	2007	2009	2011	2013	2015	2017	2019	2020	Change from 2007 to 2020
USD	−0.76	−0.07	−0.19	−0.30	−0.27	−0.10	−0.24	−0.33	−6.22
EUR	1.29	0.96	1.11	1.03	0.72	0.57	0.66	0.88	−2.92
JPY	0.22	0.20	0.26	0.21	0.10	0.11	0.06	0.12	−4.61
GBP	−0.03	−0.04	0.00	−0.03	−0.09	−0.07	−0.02	−0.02	−4.38
CHF	0.08	0.09	0.04	0.11	0.08	0.06	0.07	0.04	−4.44
Other Currencies	−0.07	−0.16	−0.14	−0.09	−0.21	−0.15	−0.28	−0.33	12.78
Unallocated	0.23	0.33	0.30	0.50	0.41	0.36	0.52	0.60	7.77
World	0.96	1.31	1.38	1.44	0.74	0.79	0.79	0.96	−0.03

Data source: Summary of locational statistics by currency, BIS website: www.bis.org.

7.4 Distribution of Cross-Border Assets, Liabilities, and Net Assets of Major Currency Issuers

7.4.1 Distribution of cross-border assets, liabilities, and net assets by country

Table 7-5 shows cross-border assets, liabilities, and net assets by country from 2007–21 released by the BIS. By 2020, global cross-border assets had only just returned to the pre-crisis level in 2007. Of the eight major world currency issuers, only the Eurozone and Switzerland experienced decreases in both cross-border assets and liabilities, and only China registered double-digit growth in both of these.

Table 7-5   Cross-Border Assets, Liabilities, and Net Assets by Country (2007–2021)

Unit: billion USD, %

Cross-Border Assets by Nationality of Reporting Bank										
Country	2007	2008	2010	2011	2013	2015	2016	2019	2020	2020 Q1	Change from 2007 to 2020
US	3.10	3.62	3.80	4.13	2.95	2.87	2.93	3.42	4.12	4.44	2.21
Eurozone	16.61	15.07	12.70	11.38	10.75	9.19	8.95	9.93	11.76	10.72	−2.62
Japan	2.67	2.89	3.41	3.66	4.09	4.14	4.44	4.93	5.44	5.49	5.62
UK	3.40	3.24	3.86	4.02	3.15	2.63	2.44	3.09	3.86	3.82	0.96
Australia	0.24	0.29	0.37	0.48	0.48	0.57	0.57	0.66	0.77	0.64	9.45
Canada	0.69	0.68	0.84	0.90	0.95	0.99	1.02	1.55	1.89	1.73	8.09
Switzerland	3.70	2.50	2.12	2.13	2.25	1.92	1.78	2.06	2.05	2.11	−4.41
China	...	...	...	...	...	1.45	1.73	2.26	2.47	2.60	11.18
Other	2.50	2.35	2.66	3.10	3.86	3.36	3.22	3.16	3.36	4.08	2.30
World	32.91	30.64	29.76	29.80	28.48	27.12	27.08	31.05	35.71	35.63	0.63

(Continued)

Cross-Border Liabilities by Nationality of Reporting Bank										
	2007	2008	2010	2011	2013	2015	2016	2019	2020	2020 Q1	Change from 2007 to 2020
US	3.94	4.43	4.43	4.72	3.68	3.51	3.43	3.85	4.65	5.01	1.27
Eurozone	14.66	13.16	11.66	10.47	9.67	8.20	8.09	8.96	10.45	10.40	−2.57
Japan	1.13	1.41	1.60	1.86	2.14	1.97	2.08	2.16	2.38	2.24	5.91
UK	3.31	3.05	3.48	3.74	2.84	2.58	2.46	3.07	3.97	3.98	1.41
Australia	0.47	0.47	0.68	0.79	0.81	0.85	0.83	0.86	0.92	0.80	5.41
Canada	0.54	0.52	0.63	0.71	0.72	0.80	0.84	1.15	1.53	1.42	8.30
Switzerland	3.52	2.65	2.20	2.18	2.05	1.83	1.74	1.89	1.93	1.99	−4.52
China	...	...	...	...	...	1.40	1.57	2.08	2.27	2.41	10.14
Other	1.50	1.14	1.49	1.91	3.52	3.54	3.45	3.46	3.56	3.67	6.89
World	29.07	26.83	26.17	26.38	25.43	24.69	24.48	27.48	31.68	31.91	0.66

Cross-Border Net Assets by Nationality of Reporting Bank										
Country	2007	2008	2010	2011	2013	2015	2016	2019	2020	2020 Q1	Change from 2007 to 2020
US	−0.84	−0.81	−0.63	−0.59	−0.73	−0.64	−0.51	−0.43	−0.52	−0.58	−3.56
Eurozone	1.95	1.91	1.04	0.90	1.07	1.00	0.86	0.97	1.30	0.32	−3.06
Japan	1.54	1.48	1.82	1.80	1.95	2.16	2.36	2.77	3.05	3.26	5.40
UK	0.09	0.19	0.38	0.28	0.31	0.05	−0.02	0.01	−0.12	−0.16	−201.67
Australia	−0.23	−0.19	−0.32	−0.31	−0.32	−0.28	−0.26	−0.20	−0.16	−0.17	−2.89
Canada	0.14	0.16	0.21	0.19	0.22	0.19	0.18	0.40	0.36	0.31	7.27
Switzerland	0.17	−0.14	−0.08	−0.05	0.19	0.09	0.04	0.18	0.12	0.12	−2.54
China	...	...	...	...	...	0.05	0.16	0.18	0.20	0.20	30.53
Other	1.00	1.21	1.17	1.19	0.34	−0.19	−0.23	−0.30	−0.21	0.41	−188.54
World	3.84	3.81	3.59	3.42	3.05	2.43	2.60	3.58	4.04	3.72	0.39

Data source: Cross-border position by the summary of locational statistics by currency. BIS website: www.bis.org.

It is noticeable in Table 7-5 that the net cross-border assets of Japan as a percentage of total world cross-border net assets increased from 40.14% in 2007 to the highest level of 91.08% in 2016 and declined slightly to 87.64% in the first quarter of 2021. The high share of Japanese cross-border net assets indicated the strength of the Japanese banking industry worldwide to support the Japanese yen.

7.4.2 Bank Internationalization of Major Currency Issuers

Using cross-border assets of major currency issuers and the corresponding GDP data released by the IMF in April 2021, we are able to calculate bank internationalization; Table 7-6 shows the results. Despite Switzerland registering the biggest decline from 2007–20, its bank internationalization was still 274.9% at the end of this period – higher than any other major currency. However, the severe impact of the 2008 financial crisis on Switzerland and the Swiss franc is still clear. Meanwhile, the Eurozone fell from 2nd position in 2007 to 5th in 2020; Japan remained in 4th position despite the internationalization rate increasing from 58.3% in 2007 to 107.7% in 2020; bank internationalization in the UK rose from 3rd to 5th over this period; whilst Canada experienced the biggest accumulated increase (68.24%), moving from 5th to 3rd place.

It is somewhat surprising that bank internationalization in the US has remained lower than that of every other major global currency from 2007–20, with the exception of China.

Table 7-6   Bank Internationalization of Major Currency Issuers (2007–2020)

Unit: %

Currency Issuer	2007	2008	2010	2011	2013	2015	2016	2019	2020	Change from 2007 to 2020
US	21.5	24.6	25.3	26.6	17.6	15.7	15.6	15.9	19.7	−1.79
Eurozone	129.1	106.5	100.4	83.5	81.5	78.8	74.8	74.3	91.0	−38.04
Japan	58.3	56.6	59.3	58.8	78.5	93.0	88.7	95.7	107.7	49.38
UK	110.0	109.6	155.3	151.2	113.1	89.7	90.4	109.0	142.2	32.22
Australia	25.0	27.1	29.3	31.6	31.9	45.8	45.1	47.2	56.5	31.47

(Continued)

Currency Issuer	2007	2008	2010	2011	2013	2015	2016	2019	2020	Change from 2007 to 2020
Canada	46.8	44.1	51.7	50.1	51.2	63.9	66.7	89.0	115.1	68.24
Switzerland	748.3	439.3	352.4	294.5	314.8	273.0	255.3	281.9	274.9	−473.32
China	...	...	...	...	...	13.1	15.4	15.8	16.8	3.69
Other	14.8	12.2	12.8	13.0	15.2	14.6	14.0	12.0	13.7	−1.12
World	56.5	47.9	44.9	40.5	36.9	36.2	35.6	35.6	42.2	−14.21

Data source: Calculated using data in Table 7-5 and corresponding GDP data from the IMF (www. imf.org) in April 2021.

7.5 Chinese and Japanese Cross-Border and Net Assets

Although China's economy and trade volume surpassed Japan's over a decade ago, China's foreign exchange reserves have also been significantly larger. There is still a significant gap between Chinese international investment positions (IIP) and net IIPs from Japan, and an even wider gap in cross-border net assets. Because of the great comparability between China and Japan in many aspects, the internationalization process of the Japanese is seen as a useful reference point for the Chinese renminbi. In this section, total cross-border assets, bank assets, and bank internationalization between the two nations will be compared.

7.5.1 Bank internationalization of China and Japan

Table 7-5 shows that despite a high CAGR of 11.18% for cross-border assets in China from 2015–20, its cross-border assets of USD 2.6 trillion and net assets of USD 0.2 trillion in Q1 of 2021 were merely 47.4% and 6%, respectively, of Japan's corresponding figures. China's bank internationalization was merely 16.8% in 2020 – 90.9% lower than Japan's rate of 107.7%. All this data indicated a significant gap between Chinese bank internationalization and that of Japan, in spite of China's larger GDP and its recent rapid growth in this area.

7.5.2 Chinese and Japanese assets in the US, UK, and Hong Kong, China

BIS data shows that total Japanese assets and liabilities in the US were USD 494.6 billion and USD 221.27 billion, respectively, at the end of Q1 2021 – much higher than China's corresponding figures. Total Japanese assets and liabilities in the

UK were USD 363.26 billion and USD 139.31 billion, respectively, for Q1 2021, compared to USD 83.67 and USD 117.64 billion for China's corresponding figures. The significant gap between Japan and China in this regard is consistent with the ranking gaps between the yen and renminbi, as discussed in later chapters.

For Hong Kong, China, total Japanese assets and liabilities were USD 194.53 billion and USD 118.62 billion, respectively, for Q1 2021. The corresponding Chinese assets were much higher at USD 411.84 billion and USD 380.37 billion, respectively. Thus, a currency's total assets in a particular country or region are the underlying force behind its foreign exchange market in that country or region. Since it takes many years for China to catch up with Japan's total assets in the US and UK, it will take a similar time for RMB to catch up with the yen in these foreign exchange markets.

7.6 Internationalization of the World's Major Banks

Global trade internationalization is the foundation of global financial inter-nationalization. More specifically, international banks support international financial centers and international currencies. The bank internationalization results in Table 7-6 are the aggregate bank internationalization of major currency issuers; They should be the aggregate results or weighted results of all banks of each currency issuer. We have focused on the internationalization of major global banks in recent years to better understand bank internationalization of major currency issuers.

7.6.1 Overseas Assets of Major International Banks

According to Ben Shenglin et al. (2020), the top 10 banks in 2019 in terms of overseas assets in the world were HSBC, Banco Santander, MUFG, Citigroup, Bank of China, Deutsch Bank, ING Bank, Mizuho FG, JP Morgan Chase, and Barclays – five of these are European banks. Measured by share of overseas assets, the top 10 banks were Ahli United Bank, Banco Santander, Nordea Bank, HSBC Holdings, ING Bank, Standard Chartered Bank, Credit Suisse, Arab Bank, UniCredit Group, and Citi Group. The top seven were all European, with overseas assets accounting for 69.59% of total assets on average. The share for the Bank of China accounted for 27.58%, ranking below the top 20. These results indicate that the degree of internationalization in European banks is not only significantly higher than China's, but also significantly higher than those from the US and Japan.

7.6.2 Share and ranking of overseas revenue and profits of major international banks

For a bank, overseas revenue and its share of total revenue is a better measurement of its internationalization. Ben et al. (2020) showed the top 10 banks by global overseas revenue in 2019 were Banco Santander, Citigroup, HSBC, MUFG, BNP Paribas, JP Morgan Chase, UBS, Bank of China, ICBC, and Mizuho FG; four of these banks are European. Measured by overseas revenue share, the top 10 global banks were Standard Chartered Bank, Banco Santander, UBS, HSBC, Nordea Bank, MUFG, Arab Bank, ING Bank, BNP Paribas, and Credit Suisse – eight of these are European, and their average overseas revenue share was 74.28%. It is noticeable that the Bank of China ranked outside the top 30 for this criterion. Overall, the bank internationalization rate in Europe is much higher than in most other regions; Chinese banks have much work to do to achieve similar levels of internationalization.

7.6.3 Ranking of internationalization indexes

As well as using overseas assets and shares to measure internationalization, overseas profit share, deposit and loan shares, and business outlet numbers are also important indicators for a bank's internationalization level. Ben et al. (2020) proposed an index for this based on eight sub-measures – the proportion of overseas assets, customer deposits, customer loans, overseas revenues, overseas profits, the number of operating locations, overseas branches, and overseas employees. Such an index can measure internationalization more comprehensively. According to Ben et al. (2020), nine of the top 12 banks were European (the other three were Citibank, Mitsubishi UFJ, and Scotiabank). The highest-ranking Chinese bank was the Bank of China in 23rd place, followed by ICBC and BOC in 30th and 37th place, respectively. The results indicate that China's banking industry was not only significantly lower in internationalization than much of Europe and the US, but also in places like Singapore and Canada.

7.6.4 Changes in bank internationalization indexes from 2016 to 2019

Comparing the bank internationalization indexes from Ben et al., 2018 and 2020, we can find changes between 2016 and 2019, with the results given in Table 7-7. It shows that despite the decrease of BII of Standard Chartered Bank from 67.46 to 62.71 from 2016–19, it remained the highest-ranking bank. Besides Standard Chartered, only BIIs from Deutsch Bank and UBS Group decreased among the top 12 banks. Most American banks improved their level, with the exception of JP

Morgan and Bank of America, whilst Mitsubishi UFJ and Mizuho improved their BIIs significantly. Bank of China, ICBC, and Bank of Communications slightly improved their BIIs, but China Construction Bank had a very slight decrease.

Table 7-7   Rankings of Major Global Banks in Bank Internationalization Index (BII) 2016 and 2019

BII Index Ranking	Bank Name	Country	Index in 2019	Index in 2016	Index Change from 2016 to 2019
1	Standard Chartered	UK	62.71	67.46	−4.75
2	HSBC Holdings	UK	59.12	55.37	3.79
3	Banco Santander	Spain	57.92	56.36	1.56
4	Citigroup	US	54.92	51.77	3.15
5	ING Bank	Netherlands	53.23	49.97	3.26
6	Credit Suisse	Switzerland	51.83	51.38	0.45
7	Deutsche Bank	Germany	46.28	54.47	−8.19
8	Mitsubishi UFJ FG	Japan	45.1	36.69	8.41
9	UBS Group	Switzerland	43.43	54.71	−11.28
10	UniCredit Group	Italy	42.04	39.92	2.12
11	BNP Paribas	France	41.66	40.18	1.48
12	Bank of Bova Scotia	Canada	39.45	39.01	0.44
13	Société Générale	France	39.19	42.93	−3.74
14	Barclays Bank	UK	36.73	…	…
15	Mizuho FG	Japan	35.2	27.79	7.41
16	Royal Bank of Canada	Canada	34.6	…	…
17	Rabobank Group	Netherlands	33.41	…	…
18	Goldman Sachs	US	32.33	31.59	0.74
19	TD Canada Trust	Canada	30.58	…	…
20	Groupe Crédit Agricole	France	30.53	31.07	−0.54

(Continued)

BII Index Ranking	Bank Name	Country	Index in 2019	Index in 2016	Index Change from 2016 to 2019
21	State Street Corp	US	30.48	…	…
22	ANZ Group	Australia	28.66	…	…
23	Bank of China	China	27.68	26.62	1.06
24	Bank of New York Mellon	US	27.44	20.63	6.81
25	SMBC	Japan	26.61	…	…
26	Morgan Stanley	US	25.07	23.00	2.07
27	Groupe BPCE	France	21.73	…	…
28	JP Morgan Chase	US	21.15	25.95	−4.80
29	Intesa Sanpaolo	Italy	19.74	…	…
30	ICBC	China	17.79	15.96	1.83
31	Credit Mutuel	France	14.12	…	…
32	Bank of America	US	13.84	15.08	−1.24
33	Commonwealth Bank of Australia	Australia	12.13	14.25	−2.12
34	Westpac Banking Corporation	Australia	12.08	…	…
35	Wells Fargo	US	10.8	…	…
36	Banco Bilbao Vizcaya Argentaria	Argentina	10.44	…	…
37	Bank of Communications	China	8.83	8.12	0.71
38	Royal Bank of Scotland	UK	8.55	8.51	0.04
39	Sberbank	Russia	8.39	…	…
40	China Construction Bank	China	7.92	8.25	−0.33
41	Agricultural Bank of China	China	6.33	…	…
42	Capital One Financial Corp	US	5.51	…	…

(Continued)

BII Index Ranking	Bank Name	Country	Index in 2019	Index in 2016	Index Change from 2016 to 2019
43	China Citic Bank	China	4.28	…	…
44	China Minsheng Bank	China	4.23	…	…
45	Shanghai Pudong Development Bank	China	4.21	…	…
46	China Everbright Bank	China	2.89	…	…
47	China Merchants Bank	China	2.89	…	…
48	The Norinchukin Bank	Japan	2.71	…	…
49	Industrial Bank	China	2.12	…	…

Data source: Ben et al. (2018, 2020).

7.7 Bank Internationalization in China in Recent Years

Table 7-5 shows that the CAGR of cross-border assets was 11.18% from 2015–20 – much higher than the corresponding CAGR of commodity trade and nominal GDP in China (3.28% and 5.78%), yet only slightly higher than the CAGR of banking assets at 9.9%. This implies that bank internationalization increased marginally over this period.

Table 7-6 shows that bank internationalization in China increased from 13.1% in 2015 to 16.8% in 2020, with an accumulated growth of 3.7%. To compare better with the proportion of overseas assets of a particular bank, we can find China's bank internationalization using total cross-border assets in Table 7-5 and total assets in China. Results show that the rate increased slightly from 4.9 to 5.2% from 2015–20.

7.8 Recent Internationalization of Major Chinese Banks

Table 7-8 presents total overseas assets, overseas loan balance, overseas pretax profit, and the ratio of overseas pretax profit to overseas assets in China from 2015 to 2020.

7.8.1 Overseas assets of major banks

Table 7-8 indicates that the Bank of China had the largest overseas assets as well as the most overseas settlement functions of all Chinese banks. The proportion of overseas assets remained around half, though it has kept declining. In recent years, ICBC's growth rate of overseas assets has exceeded that of the Bank of China. In 2019, overseas assets from CCB and ABC ranked 3rd and 4th, respectively, with the Bank of Communications in 5th place.

7.8.2 The proportion of overseas assets

Table 7-8 shows that this proportion has steadily grown from 4.9% to 5.1% between 2013 and 2019, underlining China's "go global" banking strategy.

7.8.3 Overseas profitability

The table shows that the ratio of pretax profits to overseas assets (return on assets, ROA) was kept around 1% – not only lower than most domestic ROAs, but also lower than many international banks.

7.8.4 Brief introduction to "Go Global"

The total compound growth rate of overseas assets of ICBC, CCB, ABC, BOCOM, and CMB from 2013–19 were 13.8%, 12.8%, 19.6%, 11.8%, and 13.1%, respectively – all double-digit growth. For CITIC Bank and Bank of China, the compound growth rates were 9.6% and 7.5%, also reflecting the positive momentum in overseas development.

7.9 Overseas Distribution and Development at the Bank of China

The Bank of China is the leader of the "go global" strategy; both its overseas assets and profits rank far ahead of all other Chinese banks. This section will introduce overseas operations and international rankings for the bank.

7.9.1 Overseas distribution and development

The number of overseas entities of the Bank of China has grown from 20 in 1978 to 559 in 2020, with total overseas assets of USD 155.1 billion – accounting for 42% of total assets. By the end of 2019, there were 557 overseas identities distributed in 61 countries and regions, with total overseas assets of USD 0.9 trillion (27.6% of total assets).

Table 7-8   Total Overseas Assets, Loans, Pretax Profits, and the Proportion of Pretax Profits to Assets of Major Chinese Banks (2013–2019)

Unit: USD billion, %

Bank	2013	2014	2015	2016	2017	2018	2019
Total Overseas Assets							
Industrial and Commercial Bank of China (ICBC)	262.33	313.69	377.38	451.18	517.59	538.48	569.26
China Construction Bank (CCB)	120.04	152.89	177.03	240.22	264.16	246.90	246.97
Total Overseas Assets							
Agricultural Bank of China (ABC)	58.08	85.37	109.79	109.31	122.27	132.97	170.16
Bank of China (BOC)	630.80	683.18	699.14	730.73	833.33	904.35	900.16
Bank of Communications (BOC)	85.27	100.92	107.99	123.38	147.63	155.79	166.86
CITIC Bank	28.06	32.60	36.97	41.15	47.11	49.33	48.52
China Merchants Bank (CMB)	16.33	20.74	21.90	25.55	30.58	34.98	34.26
China Guangfa Bank	3.67	3.63	3.51	2.96	2.90	3.23	4.00
Total	1,204.58	1,393.02	1,533.75	1,724.48	1,965.57	2,066.03	2,140.17
Total bank assets	24,824.86	28,164.00	30,698.75	33,480.35	38,628.14	38,088.08	41,570.27
Proportion in the banking industry	0.49	0.49	0.50	0.52	0.51	0.54	0.51
Balance of Overseas Loans							
Industrial and Commercial Bank of China (ICBC)	108.12	130.98	144.06	175.87	216.36	207.59	
China Construction Bank (CCB)	88.26	92.16	105.53	129.41	153.27	1,292.90	

(Continued)

Agricultural Bank of China (ABC)	50.80	64.83	68.78	63.51	58.96	56.74	
Bank of China (BOC)	306.81	303.66	295.77	308.59	351.29	365.28	
Bank of Communications (BOC)	45.80	45.27	50.26	55.41	64.57	51.82	
CITIC Bank	15.28	19.06	21.46	24.42	25.43	26.08	
China Merchants Bank (CMB)	8.37	11.36	8.90	14.29	16.76	17.97	
China Guangfa Bank	2.52	1.97	2.27	1.80	2.06	1.83	
Total	625.96	669.29	697.03	773.30	888.70	856.60	
Overseas Pretax Profits							
Industrial and Commercial Bank of China (ICBC)	2.23	3.02	3.17	3.25	3.92	4.12	4.98
China Construction Bank (CCB)	0.64	1.04	0.82	0.98	1.86	1.50	0.82
Agricultural Bank of China (ABC)	0.36	0.52	0.60	0.28	0.50	0.66	1.48
Bank of China (BOC)	6.66	8.66	8.78	12.23	10.19	9.95	10.53
Bank of Communications (BOC)	0.63	0.85	0.93	0.88	1.06	1.15	1.30
CITIC Bank	0.34	0.46	0.34	0.40	0.57	0.48	0.48
China Merchants Bank (CMB)	0.15	0.34	0.28	0.22	0.32	0.44	0.39
China Guangfa Bank	0.03	0.04	0.04	0.02	−0.01	0.04	0.03
Total	11.04	14.93	14.96	18.26	18.41	18.34	20.00

(Continued)

Overseas Pretax Profit/Overseas Assets							
Industrial and Commercial Bank of China (ICBC)	0.09	0.10	0.08	0.07	0.08	0.08	0.09
China Construction Bank (CCB)	0.05	0.07	0.05	0.04	0.07	0.06	0.03
Agricultural Bank of China (ABC)	0.06	0.06	0.06	0.03	0.04	0.05	0.09
Bank of China (BOC)	0.11	0.13	0.13	0.17	0.12	0.11	0.12
Bank of Communications (BOC)	0.07	0.08	0.09	0.07	0.07	0.07	0.08
CITIC Bank	0.12	0.14	0.09	0.10	0.12	0.10	0.10
China Merchants Bank (CMB)	0.09	0.16	0.13	0.09	0.11	0.13	0.11
China Guangfa Bank	0.08	0.11	0.11	0.07	−0.03	0.12	0.08
Total	0.09	0.11	0.10	0.11	0.09	0.09	0.09

Data source: Sorted from the annual reports of each bank.

7.9.2 Bank of China overseas operations

Pretax profits of overseas entities (including Hong Kong, Macau, and Taiwan) accounted for 37.72% in 2006 and 42.25% in 2007 of total profits. However, due to the severe impact of the global financial crisis in 2008, overseas profits fell sharply to 8.09% in 2009 before gradually rebounding. Since 2013, growth has accelerated significantly – from RMB 3.1 trillion in 2012 to over 5 trillion in 2016. Overseas pretax profits increased from 6.65 billion to 12.2 billion dollars over this period, jumping up from 19.37% to 36.3% of total profits. However, in 2016/17, overseas profits decreased to 10.2 billion, and in 2018–19, they were 9.95 billion and 10.53 billion, respectively.

7.9.3 Rankings of overseas assets and profits

According to Ben et al. (2018), overseas assets, deposits, and loans from the Bank of China ranked 5th, 6th, and 6th in the world in 2016, respectively. As for ranking by the proportion of these indexes, the results were 23rd, 24th, and 27th, respectively.

Overseas operating income and profit ranked 9th and 2nd, respectively, while its proportionally rankings were only 30th and 20th, respectively. This underlines that despite the Bank of China being a top ten bank globally in terms of asset and profit volume, its overseas assets and profits form a relatively small proportion of its total compared to more internationalized banks.

Ben et al. (2020) measured the overall degree of internationalization by using weighted proportions of eight sub-indexes: overseas deposits, loans, revenues, profits, outlets, and employees. Bank of China was ranked 23rd according to these criteria.

7.9.4 Internationalization ranking of other major banks

According to Ben et al. (2020), ICBC, BOCOM, CCB, and ABC ranked 30th, 37th, 40th, and 41st, respectively, in bank indexes for 2019. China CITIC Bank, Minsheng Bank, Shanghai Pudong Development Bank, China Everbright Bank, China Merchants Bank, and China Industrial Bank ranked 43rd, 44th, 45th, 46th, 47th, and 49th, respectively. Although the rankings for Chinese banks were generally low, they have been rising faster than most foreign banks in recent years, though a significant gap still remains.

7.10 Main Challenges in the "Go Global" Strategy

Ben Shenglin and Yu Jiefang (2020) effectively summarized the achievements of China's "Go Global" strategy in recent years. However, some challenges have also risen too, which will be introduced here.

7.10.1 Bridging the internationalization gap

According to Ben et al. (2020), the average BII index of China's big five banks was only 13.71 in 2019, with joint-stock at 3.43. In contrast, the average BII index of the top 20 global banks was 43.52 – 3.17 times higher than China's big five and 12.69 times higher than its joint-stock figure. These results show that a large gap remains between China's biggest banks and the biggest foreign banks.

7.10.2 Improving risk management

Ben Shenglin and Yu Jiefang (2016) listed and analyzed risks in China's go global strategy since 2000. This included events such as the failure of the Minsheng Bank merger and the loan fraud case of Bank of China's New York branch, which was fined 10 million dollars.

7.10.3 Strengthening legal compliance and awareness overseas

In addition to the market and operational risks, legal and compliance risks should not be ignored. The lawsuit case at ICBC's Madrid branch arose from political and cultural differences between Spain and China. Similarly, ABC's New York branch was fined over 200 million dollars (about 1/3 of its overseas profits) for violating an American anti-money laundering statute.

In addition to these risks and problems, China's banking industry also faces other issues. After the global financial crisis in 2008, US regulatory authorities punished several US-funded financial institutions with a cumulative amount of more than 100 billion dollars, as well as many foreign financial institutions with a cumulative amount of more than 40 billion dollars. Several Chinese banks were on this list. To fully realize the potential of the "go global" strategy, risk management and other areas need to be improved, and care must be taken to train overseas executives in local laws and regulations.

7.11 Prospects for Internationalization in Chinese Banking

As the renminbi was enlisted in the SDR (special drawing rights) of the IMF, there will be greater demand for RMB in the future. The proportion of global RMB reserves has already surpassed that of the British pound and Japanese yen, helping the internationalization level of Chinese banks.

The RMB share of the SDR is 10.92%, 2.59% more than the yen. However, its international reserves of 1.86% were merely a third of the Japanese yen's corresponding figure, and its 2.16% share of the global foreign exchange market was only one quarter. For the renminbi to catch up with the yen, there is more work to be done.

7.12 Conclusion

The amount of cross-border assets in a certain country or region reflects its position as a financial or foreign exchanger center. From the criteria and data shown in this chapter, the impact of the 2008 global financial crisis on international markets cannot be understated.

With the steady growth of cross-border assets in China – from USD 0.19 trillion in 2007 to 1.06 trillion in 2021, its ranking went from 8th to 5th among major currency issuers. However, there is still a sizeable gap between the Chinese renminbi and the Japanese yen when it comes to currency internationalization, as backed up by the data.

Bibliography

Ben, Shenglin, and Yu Jiefang. 2016. *Report in Internationlization of China's Banks.* Beijing: China Financial Publishing House.

Ben, Shenglin, Yu Jiefang, Gu Yue, et al. 2018. *Racing: Chinese and Foreign Banks Galloping in International Market.* Hangzhou: Zhejiang University Press.

———. 2020. *Will De-globalization Disrupt Banks' International Expansion? Report on Internationalization of China's Banks.* Hangzhou: Zhejiang University Press.

CHAPTER EIGHT

The Recent Development RMB Internationalization

Rᴍʙ ɪɴᴛᴇʀɴᴀᴛɪᴏɴᴀʟɪᴢᴀᴛɪᴏɴ ɪs ᴀ ɴᴀᴛᴜʀᴀʟ ᴘʀᴏᴄᴇss within the internationalization of the Chinese economy and international trade development. Only through steady RMB internationalization can China reduce the influence of other major currencies and constraints on its monetary policies. China can then assert economic influence commensurate with its economic size in international finance, for example, by implementing the Belt and Road initiatives. Having introduced offshore RMB centers and their development in previous chapters, this chapter will use domestic and foreign data to account for data bias from the Bank for International Settlements. This will allow us to measure the progress of RMB internationalization since 2016 more effectively.

8.1 Brief Review of RMB Internationalization

Before 2004, RMB had never been used or circulated outside of Mainland China. Early in November 2001, the Hong Kong Monetary Authority (HKMA) proposed an idea to conduct personal RMB business in Hong Kong, China to the PBC, with discussions beginning in early February 2002. However, the outbreak of SARS in March 2003 delayed discussions somewhat. In June 2003, the HKMA and the PBC reached an agreement on the application of RMB in Hong Kong, China; in November, the State Council approved the proposal. After around three months of preparation, banks in Hong Kong, China began to provide retail RMB deposits, foreign exchange, debit cards, and credit card services on February 25, 2004 (Chan 2014).

Since the 1990s, China has increasingly converged with the global economy – its proportion of trade imports and exports compared to GDP soared from around 30% to a record high of 63.5% in 2006. Influenced by the global financial crisis, China's trade dependence declined to 43.1% in 2009. Although there was a slight increase to 49.0% in 2010, the country's trade dependence had declined to 32.8% by 2016 – the lowest level since 1998. However, it slightly increased to 34.2% in 2017. In addition, as part of its foreign exchange management reform, China undertook obligations under Articles 2, 3, and 4 of Section 8 of an IMF accord, with a view to free convertibility of the RMB. In the wake of the 1997 Asian financial crisis, prominent economics scholars have studied in great detail the risk arising from global capital flows. When emerging markets come under speculative raids, capital restrictions can temporarily play the role of a firewall; thus, China has been discreet in the free convertibility of the RMB. Since the outbreak of the international financial crisis, particularly after America abandoned its quantitative easing strategy, cross-border capital flows caused a serious shock to many developing nations' economies and finances.

8.2 Basic Conditions of RMB Usage in the Offshore Market

Following China's reform and opening up, Hong Kong, China has become China's bond to the world, the most important source of its foreign direct investment, and one of its most important trading partners. According to foreign investment statistics from the Ministry of Commerce, 65% of direct foreign investment in Mainland China came from Hong Kong, China in 2016. Thanks to its unique status and particularly the implementation of the Mainland and Hong Kong Closer Economic Partnership Arrangement (CEPA) on January 1, 2004, Hong Kong, China has become the most active offshore RMB market. Leveraging its close relationship with Mainland China, Hong Kong, China, one of the major financial centers in East Asia, will play a pivotal role in RMB internationalization.

8.2.1 Implementation and changes of related policies

At the end of 2003, as approved by the State Council, the PBC agreed to arrange a settlement for retail RMB business in Hong Kong, China. Following the official launch of RMB business on January 18, 2004, local shops and automatic teller machines started to accept debit cards and credit cards issued by mainland banks. Furthermore, banks in Hong Kong, China have been able to provide RMB deposits, exchange, and remittance services since February 25, 2004, and to issue RMB debit and credit cards for Hong Kong residents' use in Mainland China since April 30, 2004.

On November 1, 2005, the PBC announced its intention to widen the scope of closing positions and settlements for Hong Kong banks involved in RMB business, and to further improve and expand local RMB business by following the five-pronged approach: (1) allowing the PBC Shenzhen Central Sub-Branch to accept deposits from clearing banks for RMB business in Hong Kong, China; (2) relaxing requirements for closing positions between the RMB and the HKD by increasing the limit on personal RMB exchanges per person each time from the equivalent of no more than RMB 6,000 to the equivalent of no more than RMB 20,000, expanding the list of designated local RMB exchange operators to cover those engaged in transportations, communications, medical and education industries, and allowing designated shops to convert their RMB deposits maintained in participating banks into HKD; (3) increasing the maximum amount of Hong Kong residents' RMB remittance accepted by eligible mainland banks per person per day from RMB 50,000 to RMB 80,000; (4) clearing Hong Kong residents' personal RMB checks issued by clearing banks, these non-transferable personal checks can be used to draw up to RMB 80,000 from each account per day to pay for consumer expenditures in the Guangdong province; and (5) cancelling the credit limit of RMB 100,000 for each RMB card issued by Hong Kong banks.

On July 19, 2010, the PBC and Bank of China (Hong Kong) Limited, as the RMB clearing bank, signed a newly revised settlement agreement. On the same day, a supplementary cooperation memorandum on the expansion of the RMB trade settlement scheme was also signed by the PBC and the HKMA. The revised agreement loosened restrictions on RMB exchange and opening institution accounts not involving cross-border capital flows, thereby stimulating the need for offshore RMB markets, promoting the self-cycling of market supply and demand, and creating a necessary foundation for the start of the Hong Kong offshore RMB market. The HKMA announced that effective November 2014, the RMB 20,000 per person per day conversion limit was no longer applicable for Hong Kong residents.

8.2.2 Remittance

Since customers usually prefer remittance over carrying cash to Mainland China, remittance services have expanded steadily. From information published by the HKMA in 2010, the maximum remittance amount available for Hong Kong residents would be RMB 80,000 per day in 2010. Since July 2009, enterprises have been able to use RMB checks to transfer funds from accounts opened in different banks and collect money for trade settlement. However, remittance is limited between overseas enterprises and pilot enterprises in Mainland China. Participant banks can transfer funds in Hong Kong, China, but only among accounts of the same enterprise opened in different banks. In 2011, the maximum remittance amount for Hong Kong residents was still RMB 80,000 per day. For check payments, RMB checks drawn by account holders from participating banks could be used in Hong Kong, China and Mainland China. Since November 2014, individuals and enterprises can freely make RMB payments and transfers through Hong Kong banks.

With the rapid growth of the cross-border RMB trade settlement business, the volume of receipts and payments between Hong Kong, China and outside has also increased rapidly. According to data from the HKMA, the account of receipts and payments from Hong Kong banks' offshore RMB business has increased from RMB 19.6 billion and 10.9 billion (net balance 8.7 billion) in 2010 to 164.5 billion and 166.0 billion (net balance –1.5 billion) in 2013. This increased to 193.3 billion and 145.2 billion (net balance 48.1 billion) in 2014.

Following the "8.11" RMB Exchange Rate Regime Reform, the data above dropped to RMB 105.7 billion and RMB 132.1 billion in 2015, with a net balance of –27.4 billion. During 2016, receipts and payments declined further to 91.6 billion and 69 billion, respectively, with a net balance of 22.6 billion. In 2017, due to the stable RMB exchange rate, these figures increased to 132.8 billion and 87.8 billion, respectively, with a net balance of 45 billion.

8.2.3 The rapid growth of overseas credit card consumption

The usage of UnionPay cards overseas also reflects the internationalization of RMB to a certain extent. The overseas transactions of China UnionPay cards increased from 363.4 billion in 2012 to 520.3 billion in 2014, with annual growth rates of 25.5% and 14.1%, respectively. In addition, overseas transactions from UnionPay cards grew from 5.08 billion to 6.42 billion, with an annual growth rate of 26.4%. In 2015, Chinese residents spent USD 133 billion overseas by credit card (SAFE March 31, 2016), equivalent to RMB 828.2 billion (estimated according to the average exchange rate of RMB against the USD in 2015, 6.2269). In 2016, the amount of overseas consumption conducted by domestic individuals using credit cards decreased to USD 109.1 billion. However, in 2017, the consumption amount increased to USD 114.6 billion. Although SAFE no longer publishes detailed data regarding residents' overseas credit card expenditures, overseas consumption amounted to nearly 200 million dollars in 2019. As the acceptance of RMB overseas further improves, the usage of Union Pay cards overseas will continuously increase, which will also enhance RMB internationalization.

8.2.4 The Hong Kong RMB RTGS system

A Hong Kong RMB settlement system was launched in March 2006 to improve the efficiency of settlements for inter-bank transactions. In June 2007, the HKMA upgraded the system to become a general RMB Real Time Gross Settlement system (RTGS). The Bank of China (Hong Kong) Limited was designated as the clearing bank, and Hong Kong Interbank Clearing Limited (HKICL) was responsible for operating the system. Since June 2007, this has transferred to the open SWIFT platform from the original dedicated operational platform. In recent years, RMB RTGS's average daily transactions have increased continuously. The average amount of RMB transactions conducted daily through Hong Kong's RTGS system was RMB 5 billion in 2010. The total amount increased from 213.7 billion in 2012 to 395.4 billion in 2013, a growth rate of 85%. Between 2014 and 2015, the amount grew from RMB 734.1 billion to 947 billion before declining to 863.6 billion in 2016. In 2017, the amount rose to 903.6 billion. In 2018, the amount increased further to 1,010 billion before reaching USD 1,134 billion in 2019 (HKMA Annual Report 2015). These figures indicate that the level of activity in the overseas RMB market has generally been trending upwards in recent years.

8.3 Offshore RMB Transactions

8.3.1 Introduction to RMB overseas transactions

In August 2015, RMB surpassed JPY for the first time to become the world's fourth-largest payment currency. In September 2020, RMB accounted for 1.97% of the world's cross-border payments, ranking 5th globally; meanwhile, JPY notched a proportion of 3.43%, and GBP accounted for 7.04%, ranking 4th and 3rd during the corresponding time period (data from SWIFT).

8.3.2 Overseas RMB securities products

On April 29, 2011, the first RMB-denominated security, Hui Xian Real Estate Investment Trust, began trading in Hong Kong, China. As the first RMB-denominated security, Hui Xian was the touchstone of the RMB business, which will promote the development of RMB securities in Hong Kong, China.

The Hong Kong Stock Exchange's (HKEx) first RMB-traded equity securities, the RMB-traded shares of Hopewell Highway Infrastructure Limited, were listed for trading on October 29, 2012. These were the first RMB-traded equity shares to be listed in an overseas market and the first dual counter equity securities. Xiaojia Li, the CEO of HKEx, said that both were important milestones for developing RMB products, which further strengthened the leading position of Hong Kong as a RMB offshore center. Li expressed that RMB equity securities would be another important product besides RMB bonds, Exchange Traded Funds (ETFs), Real Estate Investment Trusts (REITs), and RMB currency futures. He also predicted investors would have more interest in RMB products due to RMB internationalization. It is believed that more and more RMB-denominated security products will be launched in Hong Kong, China in the future.

CSOP Asset Management Limited and Source, the provider of the London Exchange's Exchange Traded Fund (ETF), announced on January 9, 2014, that the ETF launched by both would officially begin trading that day on the London Exchange. It is the first RMB Qualified Foreign Institutional Investors (RQFII) ETF in European markets, providing a new channel for European investors to enter China's A-share market. On March 25, 2015, the first European RQFII ETF officially began trading on the London Exchange, with CCB International Asset Management Limited acting as the fund manager.

8.3.3 General introduction of the Eurodollar market

The offshore RMB business has only been in existence for a relatively short amount of time; however, it has quite a lot of similarities with the Eurodollar market, which has existed for half a century and is already quite mature. The Eurodollar market can be a useful reference point for RMB.

The Eurodollar boomed in the early 1960s thanks to control of the American capital account and tax restrictions. Not subject to the regulation of the Federal Reserve Bank and American Taxation authorities, the Eurodollar market, based in London, could not only provide lower interest rates than the US domestic market, but also offer higher rates for saving dollars overseas. Despite the further spread of regulation on American capital accounts and tax restrictions in the

1980s and 1990s, the Eurodollar market quietly progressed. By the end of 2008, dollar bonds in offshore markets amounted to USD 8,396 billion, covering 30.6% of all dollar bonds inside and outside of the US (Standard Chartered, Special Report 2010).

At the end of 2017, US treasury bonds had a scale of USD 10.78 trillion, more than 70% higher than the USD 6.28 trillion of global dollar reserves over the same period. There are many factors to the success of the Eurodollar market, but one of the main reasons is that the American government never interfered with the Eurodollar settlement in America (He and McCauley 2010). In other words, institutions in the offshore Eurodollar market can conduct business settlements freely with domestic institutions in America. This has played an important role in developing US dollars harmoniously inside and outside the foreign exchange market (Standard Chartered, Special Report 2010).

8.4 Direct Trade between RMB and Other Currencies

The higher the level of direct trading between currencies, the lower the transaction costs will be, which directly reflects a higher degree of currency internationalization. Since January 4, 2006, the PBC has authorized the China Foreign Exchange Trade System (CFETS) to publish the central parity rate of the RMB compared to USD, EUR, JPY, and HKD at 9:15 a.m. every weekday. (The figure taken is the middle rate of the interbank foreign exchange market, including OTC and deal-making, and the over-the-counter transaction rate.) From 2010 onwards, RMB trading directly with the Malaysian Ringgit (MYR), Russian Ruble (RUB), Australian Dollar (AUD), and Canadian Dollar (CAD) began respectively, in addition to the USD, EUR, JPY, and GBP.

8.5 Overview of Domestic RMB Spot Foreign Exchange Turnover

8.5.1 Distribution of foreign exchange transaction volume since 2014
Table 8-1 provides the turnover of RMB spot foreign exchange in Mainland China since 2014. It shows that the USD maintained its top position as RMB's largest currency pairing domestically from 2014 to the first quarter of 2021. USD-RMB turnover accounted for over 94% of the entire market from 2014 to 2021 Q1, with its highest share of 96.81% in 2018. The RMB's second largest currency pairing, the EUR, increased its share steadily from 1.24% in 2014 to 3.11% in the first quarter of 2021, yet still much lower than shares of EUR in the world foreign

exchange market; the Japanese yen remained the third largest foreign currency in Mainland China since 2015, yet its share declined from 1.77% in 2014 to 0.56% in the first quarter of 2021, much lower than the corresponding share of yen in the world foreign exchange market from 2014 to 2019. Shares of other currencies, particularly the British pound, the fourth world currency, are relatively low compared to the top three foreign currencies in Table 8-1.

8.6 Development of RMB-Denominated Funds and Other Products

8.6.1 Development of RMB-denominated funds in the offshore market

With the rapid promotion of RMB cross-border trade settlement, overseas offshore RMB funds drew more and more attention in the second half of 2010. On August 31, 2010, Haitong Securities in Hong Kong, China issued the first RMB-denominated fund overseas – Haitong Global RMB Income Fund, with an upper limit of RMB 5 billion. By February 28, 2017, the fund's total assets amounted to about RMB 526 million. Besides Haitong Global Fund, other funds already launched include Hang Seng RMB bond, ICBC Asia Global RMB Fixed-income Fund, and CCB International Income Fund. Aside from these public bond funds, Guoxin Securities (Hong Kong), Schroder, and UBS plan to issue an offshore RMB-denominated Private Equity Fund and other PE. Pharo Management, with total assets of about USD 4 billion, plans to issue the first RMB-denominated hedge fund. HSBC Global Asset Management, Alliance Bernstein, Amundi, Barclays, BNP Paribas, Manulife, and Allianz Global Investors have also launched RMB bond funds.

On February 15, 2012, the first global RMB golden ETF (Exchange Traded Fund) began trading in Hong Kong, China. This fund was issued by Hang Seng Bank, and its return was denominated in RMB; it aimed to offer new investment choices for RMB in Hong Kong, China. The Taiwan RMB-denominated fund has also developed very fast, with the Funhua Umbrella Fund, the first issued in Taiwan, China back in April 2013, now worth RMB 28 billion.

Citadel LLC, under hedge fund manager Kenneth C. Griffin, became the first foreign company based on a pilot plan to achieve RMB fund raising. According to the statement released by the Shanghai Government on May 21, Citadel, based in Chicago, could use all raised RMB to convert into USD for investment. In September 2013, China's foreign exchange regulation institution granted Citadel and another five offshore hedge funds the "Qualified Domestic Limited Partner Program (QDLP), with each one able to raise up to USD 50 million. This trial

Table 8-1 Turnover of RMB Spot Foreign Exchange Trading against Other Countries (2014 to 2021 Q1)

Unit: RMB billion, %

Currency	2014	Share	2016	Share	2018	Share	2020	Share	2021 Q1	Share	2018 to 2020
USD	23,994.2	94.17	38,261.5	96.77	49,190.7	96.81	55,320.5	96.20	14,484.6	95.20	−0.07
EUR	315.5	1.24	459.8	1.16	754.7	1.49	1419.4	2.47	473.8	3.11	0.14
JPY	451.1	1.77	327.5	0.83	278.4	0.55	273.4	0.48	85.7	0.56	−0.13
CAD	1.4	0.01	25.2	0.06	58.1	0.11	33.7	0.06	34.2	0.22	0.04
HKD	293.1	1.15	149.3	0.38	192.0	0.38	145.7	0.25	27.0	0.18	0.12
AUD	148.6	0.58	79.3	0.20	87.9	0.17	58.9	0.10	22.0	0.14	0.00
SGD	83.8	0.33	108.8	0.28	55.4	0.11	84.0	0.15	20.5	0.13	−0.28
GBP	137.7	0.54	49.0	0.12	51.6	0.10	58.7	0.10	14.5	0.10	−0.02
CHF	...	...	18.0	0.05	29.6	0.06	13.5	0.02	13.9	0.09	−0.05
NZD	28.1	0.11	13.8	0.03	19.6	0.04	21.4	0.04	11.8	0.08	0.07
THB	...	...	......	0.00	18.1	0.04	35.9	0.06	11.7	0.08	0.00

(Continued)

Currency	2014	Share	2016	Share	2018	Share	2020	Share	2021 Q1	Share	2018 to 2020
RUB	25.5	0.10	11.8	0.03	14.8	0.03	14.4	0.02	5.2	0.03	-0.03
DKK	...	...	...	0.00	4.7	0.01	5.5	0.01	3.2	0.02	0.00
SKW	...	0.00	31.3	0.08	21.8	0.04	6.2	0.01	1.9	0.01	0.02
ZAR	...	...	0.9	0.00	0.6	0.00	1.1	0.00	1.8	0.01	0.00
SEK	0.0	0.00	0.0	0.00	10.0	0.02	2.8	0.00	1.7	0.01	0.00
MYR	1.2	0.00	3.4	0.01	3.5	0.01	0.5	0.00	0.1	0.00	-0.01
NOK	...	...	...	0.00	2.1	0.00	1.6	0.00	0.0	0.00	0.00
Others	...	0.00	0.3	0.00	17.9	0.04	6.7	0.01	0.9	0.01	0.00
Total	25,480.2	100.00	39,539.9	100.00	50,811.4	100.00	57,503.7	100.00	15,214.5	100.00	0.00

Data source: China Monetary Policy Reports for 2014 Q4 to 2020 Q1.

plan allowed China's high net-worth individuals to invest in overseas markets through offshore hedge funds.

On May 22, 2015, the spokesman of the China Securities Regulatory Commission (CSRC), Deng Ge, announced that the CSRC and the Hong Kong Securities and Futures Commission had signed the Memorandum of Regulatory Co-operation on Mutual Recognition of Mainland and Hong Kong funds between CRSC and HKSFC. This was implemented on July 1, 2015. CRSC said mutual recognition would help to attract foreign capital and broaden cross-border investment channels to improve the competitiveness of the two markets. It would lay a foundation for regulators to build fund supervision standards and provide more diversified investment products.

8.6.2 Breakthrough of RMB-denominated commodities

On November 19, 2012, the Hong Kong Exchange and Clearing Limited's (HKEx) acquisition of the London Metal Exchange (LME) was approved by the Financial Service Authority (FSA). It issued the first Aluminum, Zinc, and Copper small-sized futures contract, denominated by RMB, in December 2014. On July 28, 2015, London Metal Exchange (LME) began accepting RMB as collateral – a milestone event for China entering the London Commodities market and for future development.

On March 26, 2018, RMB-denominated crude oil futures were listed for trading on the Shanghai International Energy Exchange, a subsidiary of the Shanghai Futures Exchange. The experience gained in the oil futures market in various areas, including open paths, tax management, foreign exchange management, bonded delivery, and cross-border regulatory cooperation, can gradually be applied to the trading of other mature commodity futures, such as iron ore and non-ferrous metals, thereby promoting the opening-up of China's RMB-denominated commodity futures market.

8.7 Liberalization of RMB Capital Items and Its Future Development

The Chinese government's RMB internationalization initiatives can be traced back to 2003 when the following measures were proposed at the 3rd session of the 16th Central Committee of the CCP. This legislation broadened the limits on cross-border capital transactions selectively and incrementally, gradually realizing capital account convertibility and expediting trial trade settlements in RMB for Hong Kong and Macao. Over the decades, China has made a series of important steps in capital account liberalization and convertibility. This section will focus mostly on the progress of the liberalization of RMB capital items.

8.7.1 Two-way opening orderly of capital items

During the 11th Five-Year Plan, the liberalization of RMB capital items made significant progress. Firstly, the financial channels of foreign investments were broadened. In April 2006, the Qualified Domestic Institutional Investor (QDII) was implemented to achieve this goal.

Secondly, the domestic securities market was widened. After introducing the Qualified Foreign Institutional Investor (QFII) in 2002, successively increased total QFII quotas and single QFII quotas helped encourage foreign investors to invest in the domestic market from 2007 (Yi Gang 2011). According to SAFE data from its website, as of July 31, 2020, 152 QDIIs have been approved with a quota of USD 116.26 billion; by May 28, 2020, there were 295 such QFIIs. In order to broaden the investment channels of RMB flowing into Hong Kong, China, the China Securities Regulatory Commission, the PBC and SAFE jointly published "Trial Measures of domestic securities investment for RQFIIs of Fund Management Companies and Securities Companies" on December 16, 2011. By May 28, 2020, 230 RQFIIs had been approved, amounting to a cumulative quota of RMB 722.99 billion (equivalent to USD 104.79 billion); this accounted for almost 90% of the total authorized QFII amount. On September 18, 2019, the SAFE officially abolished investment quota restrictions for QFII/RQFII, including total investment quota restrictions for QFII and RQFII, the filing and approval requirements for single foreign institutional investors, and the restrictions on RQFII pilot countries and regions. These changes marked an advancement in RMB internationalization.

Thirdly, domestic and foreign capital markets have been further integrated, and a trading interconnection mechanism for Mainland China, Hong Kong, China, and the London stock market has been implemented. On November 17, 2014, the stock trading mechanism that connects the Shanghai and Hong Kong stock exchanges (herein referred to as the Shanghai-Hong Kong Stock Connect) was officially launched. This mechanism represents a major institutional innovation in the opening-up of the capital market and a new model for cross-border securities investment. Through specific technology and cross-border settlement arrangements, investors from Mainland China and Hong Kong, China can directly buy and sell stocks listed on each other's exchanges.

On December 5, 2016, the Shenzhen-Hong Kong Stock Connect was officially opened, and bilateral control over the total quota was canceled. In April 2018, the daily quotas of the Shanghai-Hong Kong Stock Connect and Shenzhen-Hong Kong Stock Connect were expanded four times to RMB 52 billion and 42 billion, respectively. On August 31, 2018, the China Securities Regulatory Commission publicly solicited opinions on the *Shanghai-London Stock Connect Depository Receipt Business Regulatory Rules* and clarified the Shanghai-London Stock Connect China Depository Receipt (CDR) issuance review system and the CDR cross-border conversion system arrangements, among other matters. The Regulatory Rules provide important principled provisions on matters such as the issuance of public offerings, cross-border conversion, continuous regulatory requirements, regulatory enforcement, and investor protection for the Shanghai-London Stock Connect's east-bound and west-bound business. On October 12, 2018, the Regulatory Rules were officially released. Compared with the draft for comments, the final version clarified multiple issues. For example, the final version details the limit on the withdrawal period for domestic listed companies that issue CDRs overseas, and clarifies the allotment of shares for issuers of overseas underlying securities that issue domestic CDRs. On June 17, 2019, the Shanghai-London Stock Connect officially launched trading. It promotes the development of domestic securities firms' cross-border securities business while also promoting the two-way opening-up and internationalization of China's capital market.

Fourthly, the inter-bank bond market has been fully liberalized, attracting overseas institutions to participate in domestic financial transactions. Since 2010, foreign central banks and monetary authorities, RMB clearing banks in Hong Kong and Macau, banks participating in overseas cross-border RMB trade settlement, and other "Tier 3 institutions" have been able to invest in the interbank bond market within the approved (later changed to record) quota; this change marked the opening-up of the domestic bond market. In May 2016, the inter-bank bond market was fully opened to foreign investors; and investment was not subject to administrative licenses, single institution limits, or total limits. Foreign institutional investors do not need to receive approval for remittances or inflows of funds. Furthermore, investments in the inter-bank bond market are not subject to lock-up periods, remittance ratios, or quota restrictions. Only the filing and foreign exchange registration requirements have been retained, which greatly facilitates foreign institutional investors' investment in the inter-bank bond market. The Bond Connect officially launched in July 2017, and this mechanism has effectively promoted the integration of capital markets in Mainland China and Hong Kong, China. The Bond Connect also provides more convenient investment channels for foreign investors. As of June 2020, the scale of RMB bonds held by foreign institutions in the inter-bank bond market amounted to RMB 2,196.011 billion.

8.7.2 RMB cross-border settlement and direct investment business

In 2007, the PBC, as well as the National Development and Reform Commission, decided to allow qualified domestic financial institutions to issue RMB bonds in Hong Kong. The pilot for the cross-border capital items business, including RMB offshore direct investment, foreign lending, and guarantees, was carried out in 2010. The PBC published "trial measures on RMB settlement of offshore direct investment" on January 13, 2011. According to the measures, banks and enterprises in the pilot area of cross-border trading RMB settlement could develop pilot settlements of offshore direct investment. It meant that the offshore direct investment settlement trialed in Hong Kong at the end of October 2010 was extended.

In 2010, the pilot area dealt with 386 RMB cross-border investment and financing businesses, amounting to RMB 70.17 billion. From 2011–16, banks cumulatively handled offshore direct investment settlements worth RMB 20.15 billion, 29.2 billion, 85.61 billion, 186.56 billion, 736.2 billion, and 1,061.9 billion, respectively. For foreign direct investment settlements, the figures were RMB 90.72 billion, 251 billion, 448.13 billion, 862.02 billion, 1,587.1 billion, and 1,398.8 billion, respectively. With the continuous growth of RMB cross-border direct investment, RMB foreign direct investment also increased in 2016. In 2017, total RMB transactions under the capital account amounted to RMB 4,830 billion. In 2018, this figure reached RMB 10,740 billion – an increase of 122.4% from 2017. In 2019, the figure was 1,360 billion, which represented an annual increase of 26.7%.

8.7.3 Liberalization of IMF categories

By early 2011, there were seven categories and 40 capital items referred to the IMF. China maintains strict controls mainly in cross-border financial derivatives trading; the convertibility of RMB capital items has clearly improved. With the continuous opening-up of the domestic inter-bank bond market, foreign exchange risk hedging tools for investment in the bond market are being fully liberalized. Foreign investors can flexibly use foreign exchange derivatives to avoid risk, which has greatly promoted the opening-up of the capital account (Yigang 2011).

It needs many requirements to realize capital item convertibility: whether the macro-economy is stable; whether the financial system is comprehensive; whether enterprises and financial institutions have an awareness of risk management and management skills; whether the balance of international payments is stable; whether the path and means of domestic macro-control are mature; and whether the cross-border capital flow can be monitored effectively, and so on.

8.7.4 Cancellation of the obligatory foreign exchange-selling system

In December 1996, China made current items convertible: there was no limit on foreign payments and transferring of current items, but foreign exchange earnings like firms export, in principle, should still be sold to designated banks. In 2002, the quota was 20% of the previous year's foreign exchange earnings of current items. In 2004, this was raised to 30% or 50%, and further to 50% or 80% in 2005. In 2006, the method of verifying the quota by earnings was changed. Then, in 2007, the quota management was canceled, and enterprises could retain foreign exchange independently based on operational needs. In 2008, the revised "Regulations on Foreign Exchange Control" specified that enterprises and individuals could retain foreign exchange or sell to banks. Since 2009, in order to further facilitate trade and investment and improve policy transparency, foreign exchange regulation authorities vigorously cleared regulations, and many normative documents related to the obligatory foreign exchange-selling systems were abolished, revised, or expired. Now, this system is not executed in practice anymore.

8.7.5 Liberalization of capital items and currency internationalization

The IMF and the American government repeatedly emphasized free capital flows as a necessary condition for RMB to join the SDR basket of currencies. However, Japan's capital account liberalization started in December 1998 after the implementation of "Programs of Financial System Reform." In 1975, JPY only covered 0.5% of internationally recognized foreign currency reserve assets. It increased to 2.5% and 3.3% from 1977 to 1978 and exceeded 4% in 1980. In fact, early in July 1974, JPY became one of the currencies of the SDR basket, making up 7.5% of the total. In other words, the JPY was included in the SDR basket of currencies 24 years before the liberalization of Japan's capital account.

8.7.6 China's capital account liberalization

For years, the process and timescale of RMB capital account liberalization have drawn much attention inside and outside China. On February 27, 2012, the *People's Daily Online* published an article titled, "The PBC outlines the path to capital account liberalization for the first time, indicating that the time is ripe." This article referred to a report introduced in *Economic Information Daily*, written by a research group led by Sheng Songcheng, director of the Financial Survey and Statistics Department of the PBC. It specified that the conditions for China's capital account liberalization had been met, and it had short-term, mid-term, and long-term phases: "short-term arrangement (1–3 years): relaxing controls on direct investments with real transaction background and encouraging enterprises to 'go out.' Direct investment itself is stable and less affected by the economy; mid-term arrangement (3–5 years): relaxing the control of commercial credit and improving RMB internationalization; long-term arrangement (5–10 years): enhancing the construction of the financial market and first opening inflows and then outflows. Real estate and stocks and bonds transactions will be opened successively and prudently, and price-oriented management replaces quantity-oriented management." This was the first time the PBC described such a specific path for capital account liberation in an official report.

8.8 RMB Currency Swaps Signed

Before the full liberalization of the RMB capital account, signing RMB currency swap agreements with other countries and regions will further promote RMB cross-border trade settlement and investment, as well as bilateral trade and investment and financial stability. These are important indicators of currency internationalization.

8.8.1 Overview of currency swap agreements

Since 2008, the PBOC has signed RMB currency swap agreements with almost 40 countries and regions, including Hong Kong, China, Malaysia, South Korea, Singapore, Australia, Brazil, the UK, the Eurozone, Switzerland, Russia, and Canada, with the amount exceeding RMB 3 trillion. Table 8-2 below outlines the dates and amounts of RMB.

Table 8-2   RMB Currency Swaps Signed between the PBC and Other Monetary Authorities

Unit: RMB billion, %

Date of Signing	Country/ Region	Contractual Amount	Date of Signing	Country / Region	Contractual Amount
25/11/2020	Hong Kong, China	500	30/03/2018	Australia	200
05/12/2019	Macau, China	30	22/12/2017	Thailand	70
23/11/2020	Russia	150	02/11/2017	Qatar	35
11/10/2020	Korea	400	21/07/2017	Switzerland	150
17/09/2020	Hungary	40	18/07/2017	Argentina	70
25/10/2019	Chile	50	06/07/2017	Mongolia	15
12/01/2020	Canada	200	19/05/2017	New Zealand	25
13/05/2019	European Central Bank	350	21/12/2016	Iceland	3.5
10/12/2018	Singapore	300	06/12/2016	Egypt	18
19/11/2018	Ukraine	15	17/06/2016	Serbia	1.5
12/11/2018	Indonesia	200	11/05/2016	Morocco	10
26/10/2018	Britain	350	14/12/2015	UAE	35
20/08/2018	Japan	200	26/09/2015	Turkey	12
28/05/2018	Malaysia	180	03/09/2015	Tajikistan	3
25/05/2018	Kazakhstan	7	15/05/2015	Ukraine	15
24/05/2018	Pakistan	30	25/03/2015	Armenia	1
03/05/2018	Nigeria	15	18/03/2015	Suriname	1
27/04/2018	Belarus	15	16/09/2014	Sri Lanka	10
11/04/2018	South Africa	30	26/03/2013	Brazil	190
03/04/2018	Albania	2	19/04/2011	Uzbekistan	0.7
Total		3,929.7			

(Continued)

Region	Asia-Pacific	2,267.7	Share	57.71%
	Europe	1,132		28.81%
	America	336		8.55%
	Others	194		4.94%
	Developed economies	2,708.5		68.92%
	Developing countries and regions	1221.2		31.08%

Source: Data from the PBC website.

8.8.2 Distribution features of RMB currency swaps

As shown in the table, most of the countries and regions that have signed RMB currency swap agreements with China are concentrated in the Asia-Pacific region, accounting for 57.71% of all agreements. Meanwhile, Europe and the Americas account for 28.81% and 8.55%, respectively. These figures appear to coincide with the activeness of offshore RMB centers and the acceptance of RMB in these regions.

8.8.3 Usage of RMB currency swap agreements

Most of the funds in the RMB swap agreements outlined in Table 8-2 were not actually used initially. Taking South Korea, for example, early on April 20, 2009, South Korea signed a nominal 180 billion RMB swap agreement with the PBC, with the amount being doubled on October 26, 2011. For quite some time, the Bank of Korea did not use the currency swap funds. In January 2013, the Bank of Korea used RMB in currency swaps for the first time when it granted a loan of RMB 62 million to the Korea Exchange Bank. On May 30, 2014, the PBC used KRW 400 million (about RMB 2.4 million) within the currency swap to support trade finance. It's the first time the PBC has used a counterpart's currency within currency swaps.

According to the data from the Monetary Policy Implementation Report issued by the PBC, the monetary authorities that had signed currency swap agreements with China had used RMB 22.149 billion by the end of 2016 and 22.15 billion by the end of 2017; the PBC had used USD 1.118 billion of foreign currencies in 2016 and USD 1.614 billion of foreign currencies in 2017. At the end of 2018, the monetary authorities that had signed currency swap agreements with China had used RMB 32.79 billion, and the balance of foreign currency used by the PBC was USD 471 million. In 2019, the balance of RMB used by foreign monetary authorities was RMB 32.92 billion, and the balance of foreign currency used by the PBC amounted to USD 323 million. In recent years, the amount of RMB currency swap agreements has trended upward, but the amount utilized as a proportion of the total contracted is still only slightly more than 1%. Therefore, there is still much potential room for these currency swap agreements to play a greater role.

8.9 Average Daily Turnover of the RMB Foreign Exchange Market

With the method to measure currency internationalization using data provided by the Bank for International Settlements, a calculation and comparison of inter-nationalization from 2007–19 of major currencies were made in the previous chapter. With the same method and updated data, this chapter will calculate the average daily turnover of domestic RMB since 2010, thus reflecting the situation in the domestic RMB foreign exchange market.

8.9.1 Turnover of RMB in the foreign exchange market

As shown in Table 8-3, the domestic foreign exchange market experienced significant growth from 2010H1 to 2016H1. The average daily transaction value in the domestic market increased 1.74 times from USD 27.3 billion to 74.8 billion, and the accumulated annual increase was 18.3%, which was more than three times higher than the 4.1% rate achieved by the global exchange market during the same period; growth continued from 2016 H1 to 2019 H1, with the average daily turnover increasing from 74.8 billion to 128.5 billion dollars – an accumulated annual increase rate of 19.8% (10.6% higher than the 9.2% rate achieved by the global exchange market during the same period). In addition, the 19.8% rate was 11.3% higher than the compound annual growth rate of 8.5%, notched by the average daily foreign exchange turnover of the world's top seven currencies in the world's nine major foreign exchange centers during the same period. This data indicates that the domestic RMB foreign exchange market grew rapidly from 2010 to 2019. However, it fell steadily from the second half of 2018 to the second half of 2019, with annual average turnover down 24.3%. This was largely due to US-China trade tensions during this period.

Table 8-3   Turnover RMB Foreign Exchange Market in Mainland China (2010 to 2021)

Unit: USD billion

Time/Markets	Spots		Forwards		Foreign Exchange Swaps	Currency Swaps	Foreign Exchange Options		Total Foreign Exchange Turnover	
Period	Inter Banks	Banks to Clients	Inter Banks	Banks to Clients	Inter Banks	Inter Banks	Inter Banks	Banks to Clients	Inter Banks	Banks to Clients
2010 H1	1,546.6	1,037.5	5.5	...	630.6	...	...	...	3,220.2	27.3
2010 H2	1,498.6	1,257.1	27.3	...	669.3	...	...	...	3,452.2	27.8
2011 H1	1,750.8	1,302.4	115.9	...	792.6	5.8	0.3	0.2	3,968.0	33.3
2011 H2	1,803.0	1,525.2	98.7	...	978.4	8.6	0.7	0.6	4,415.2	35.3
2012 H1	1,730.0	1,460.6	64.5	173.1	1,140.0	12.8	1.4	5.9	4,588.4	39.6
2012 H2	1,630.0	1,594.4	22.1	191.0	1,380.0	20.3	2.3	22.6	4,862.7	38.6
2013 H1	1,909.0	1,684.4	7.2	289.1	1,517.3	28.3	3.9	31.2	5,470.4	48.8
2013 H2	2,191.1	1,811.3	25.1	283.0	1,883.4	51.7	17.8	20.2	6,283.6	50.3
2014 H1	2,070.0	1,740.9	25.9	316.3	2,040.0	98.0	13.2	23.3	6,327.6	53.2
2014 H2	2,050.0	1,925.0	27.0	250.4	2450.0	128.8	135.5	39.6	7,006.2	56.1

(Continued)

2015 H1	2,062.9	1,567.6	17.3	251.1	3,100.0	170.2	120.8	65.0	7,354.9	61.8
2015 H2	2,799.4	1,830.2	19.9	206.7	5,251.4	81.7	168.0	50.9	10,408.2	84.6
2016 H1	2,531.8	1,459.5	44.2	108.4	4,426.8	62.8	183.7	84.2	8,901.3	74.8
2016 H2	3,395.1	1,449.0	108.8	117.1	5,578.2	61.7	563.4	123.7	11,396.9	91.9
2017 H1	2,902.5	1,492.4	40.4	129.1	5,560.1	203.0	159.3	121.4	10,486.3	88.1
2017 H2	3,495.5	1,599.0	63.0	193.5	7,856.6	69.4	211.9	109.4	13,598.2	112.4
2018 H1	3,253.0	1,654.5	38.4	289.4	7,550.6	58.3	246.1	109.7	13,200.1	105.2
2018 H2	4,380.2	1,776.9	49.1	165.0	8,911.7	96.5	365.0	126.5	15,871.0	137.7
2019 H1	4,002.4	1,640.3	42.8	150.3	8,900.6	81.8	318.4	133.7	15,270.2	128.5
2019 H2	3,935.0	1,778.5	33.2	154.4	7,477.8	72.6	262.8	135.2	13,849.5	104.2
2020 H1	3,430.6	1,676.9	51.3	170.4	7,353.2	129.8	227.0	133.4	13,172.5	104.7
2020 H2	4,947.7	1,940.8	53.1	289.6	9,017.9	85.3	339.6	141.2	16,814.9	130.7
2021 H1	4,953.8	1,994.5	52.3	414.3	9,301.4	87.9	424.8	176.3	17,405.3	139.1

Data source: Data from 2011–14 is based on the monetary policy implementation reports from the PBC and data from Chinamoney.com.cn; data for 2010 is calculated based on the data from the same period in 2011; data for 2015–2021 is based on the monthly foreign exchange data released by the SAFE. Since 2015, SAFE's foreign exchange data has only included the total amount of foreign exchange swaps and currency swaps, so the currency swap data since 2015 is calculated using the Monetary Policy Implementation Reports issued by the PBC. The currency swap data has been obtained by subtracting foreign exchange swaps from the total amount of foreign exchange swaps and currency swaps announced by the SAFE; the semi-annual turnover is the actual total semi-annual turnover, and the average daily turnover from 2015 to 2021 is the average daily turnover from April and October of that year, so as to be more comparable with international data.

Table 8-3 also shows that domestic RMB foreign exchange recovered significantly from the first half of 2020 to the same period in 2021, with an annual growth rate of 32.9% and an average daily turnover reaching a historic high of USD 139.1 billion in April 2021.

8.9.2 Product distribution turnover in the domestic RMB foreign exchange market

With the data provided in Table 8-3, we can calculate domestic spot exchange, forward exchange, swap, and option transactions as a proportion of the total transaction amount from 2010 to 2015; the results are given in Table 8-4. According to this table, the proportion of RMB foreign exchange spot transactions has continued to decline from more than 80% in 2010 H1 to 49.4% in 2015 H1, indicating that the domestic RMB market has shifted from traditional spot trading to the dominance of derivatives. In the first half of 2015, the proportion of spot transactions fell below 50% for the first time, and the proportion fell further to its lowest level of 37% in the first half of 2019. This trend aligns with the proportions of spot transactions in the global market; meanwhile, the proportion of foreign exchange swap transactions has continued to increase from merely 19.6% in 2010 H1 to the historical high of 58.3% in the first half of 2019. After experiencing fast growth in the initial stage of market development from 2012–16, the proportion of foreign exchange options trading began to decline from 2016 and has remained at about 3%, which is about half the international share of 6% of options turnover.

It is noticeable that the share of RMB forwards turnover reached its highest level of 5.4% in the first half of 2014, and it fell to below 3% after 2016, much lower than the international share of forwards turnover of over 10% since 2001.

Table 8-4   Distribution of Transactions of Main Products in the RMB Foreign Exchange Market (2010 to 2021)

Unit: %

Period	Spots	Forwards	Swaps	Currency Swaps	Options
2010 H1	80.2	0.2	19.6	…	…
2010 H2	79.8	0.8	19.4	…	…
2011 H1	76.9	2.9	20.0	0.1	0.0

(Continued)

Period	Spots	Forwards	Swaps	Currency Swaps	Options
2011 H2	75.4	2.2	22.2	0.2	0.0
2012 H1	69.5	5.2	24.8	0.3	0.2
2012 H2	66.3	4.4	28.4	0.4	0.5
2013 H1	65.7	5.4	27.7	0.5	0.6
2013 H2	63.7	4.9	30.0	0.8	0.6
2014 H1	60.2	5.4	32.2	1.5	0.6
2014 H2	56.7	4.0	35.0	1.8	2.5
2015 H1	49.4	3.6	42.1	2.3	2.5
2015 H2	44.5	2.2	50.5	0.8	2.1
2016 H1	44.8	1.7	49.7	0.7	3.0
2016 H2	42.5	2.0	48.9	0.5	6.0
2017 H1	41.9	1.6	53.0	1.9	2.7
2017 H2	37.5	1.9	57.8	0.5	2.4
2018 H1	37.2	2.5	57.2	0.4	2.7
2018 H2	38.8	1.3	56.2	0.6	3.1
2019 H1	37.0	1.3	58.3	0.5	3.0
2019 H2	41.3	1.4	54.0	0.5	2.9
2020 H1	38.8	1.7	55.8	1.0	2.7
2020 H2	41.0	2.0	53.6	0.5	2.9
2021 H1	39.9	2.7	53.4	0.5	3.5

Data source: Calculations based on data in Table 8-3.

8.10 Ranking Major World Currencies by Internationalization 2020–2021

The purpose of this section is to find shifts in internationalization or foreign exchange turnover of the top eight global currencies from 2019 to 2021.

8.10.1 Inconsistencies in the rankings from 2016 to 2019

Table 8-6 includes the average daily trading value of foreign exchange in major currencies from April 1998 to 2019, released by BIS in 2019. The data shows that the global share of RMB foreign exchange increased from 2.23% to 4.32% from April 2013 to April 2019. Meanwhile, during the same period, the average annual compound growth rate was 15.6%; this rate was three times higher than the 5.2% rate posted by the CAD over the same period. In addition, the average daily turnover of the RMB from 2013 to 2016 increased, and its global ranking rose from 9th to 8th from 2013 to 2016, maintaining this position until 2019.

In April 2016, the proportion of RMB cross-border settlements ranked 6th in the world, while its turnover proportion ranked 8th. In April 2019, the proportion of RMB cross-border payments ranked 5th, while foreign exchange turnover was ranked 8th. IMF COFER (Currency Composition of Official Foreign Exchange Reserves) data shows that the global share of RMB foreign exchange reserves increased from 1.1% (ranking 7th) in 2016 to 2.0% (ranking 5th) in the second quarter of 2019 and to 2.4% in the first quarter of 2021. These data show that both RMB cross-border payments and COFER had increased significantly by 2019 compared with 2016, yet it is surprising that no change occurred in the RMB foreign exchange turnover rankings from 2016 to 2019.

8.10.2 Differences in the data

According to the latest data from the Bank for International Settlements, the average daily turnover of the domestic RMB foreign exchange market in April 2019 amounted to only USD 101.23 billion, which was 27.3 billion lower than the average daily turnover of 128.5 in Table 8-3 for the same period. This difference is equivalent to a reduction of 21.2% of onshore average daily turnover, which has clearly reduced RMB's actual turnover share worldwide.

8.10.3 Comparing the data

According to data released by the Reserve Bank of Australia (www.rba.gov.au), the average daily turnover of the Australian dollar against all foreign currencies in Australia was USD 58.82 billion – exactly the same as the BIS figure from December 2019, yet the average daily turnover of the Canadian dollar against all foreign currencies in Canada was USD 55.30 in April 2019 (www.bankofcanada.ca), which was 5.74 billion lower than the daily average turnover of the Canadian dollar against all other currencies in April 2019 according to BIS data. These data discrepancies underline the potential errors in ranking these currencies.

8.10.4 Significant differences in data for the UK

Table 8-5 shows the average daily foreign exchange turnover of major currencies in the UK, comparing BIS data with data from the London Foreign Exchange Joint Standing Committee (FXJSC) under the Bank of England. As shown in the table, the average daily foreign exchange turnover of the 18 currencies from BIS data, not including the RMB, ranged from 5% to 38% higher than FXJSC data. Overall, the RMB amount calculated from BIS was 29% lower than the FXJSC. By observing the data in Table 8-5 carefully, we find the top eight currencies for which the BIS data is higher than the FXJSC data, including the Canadian dollar and the Australian dollar, which are 38% and 35% higher, respectively. While drastically decreasing RMB transactions, the BIS also substantially increases transactions involving the Canadian dollar and Australian dollar, causing the aforementioned two currencies to exceed RMB in foreign exchange transactions.

Table 8-5   Average Daily Turnover of Major Currencies in April 2019 according to BIS and the London Foreign Exchange Joint Standing Committee (FXJSC)

Unit: USD billion

	USD	EUR	JPY	GBP	AUD	CAD	CHF	RMB	Swedish Krona
BIS	3,201.53	1,286.93	552.32	592.68	232.80	162.05	174.37	56.67	82.83
FXJSC	2,557.91	1,060.32	408.69	477.29	171.48	117.18	142.90	80.02	68.59
BIS/ FXJSC	1.25	1.21	1.35	1.24	1.36	1.38	1.22	0.71	1.21

	NOK	NZD	KRW	SGD	ZAR	MXN	RUB	BRL	Polish Zloty
BIS	70.27	70.66	53.17	46.73	44.54	53.94	29.87	34.11	23.45
FXJSC	60.02	51.44	42.87	37.15	34.30	31.44	28.58	25.72	20.01
BIS/ FXJSC	1.17	1.37	1.24	1.26	1.30	1.72	1.05	1.33	1.17

Source: BIS website and FXJSC website.

8.10.5 Global ranking of RMB in 2019

Table 8-5 shows that only the daily turnover of RMB was suppressed in the BIS format, and turnovers of all other currencies were increased. It is natural to use the FXJSC RMB turnover of USD 80.02 billion as the actual turnover for RMB in the UK for April 2019, as it was neither suppressed nor increased. Then, the total

RMB average daily turnover would be 285.03 +80.02 +56.67 +27.30 = USD 335.7 billion. According to this figure, RMB would be 6th amongst global currencies in 2019, which is more consistent with its 5th place ranking in the proportion of global payments and foreign exchange reserves.

8.11 Global Rankings of Major World Currencies since 2019

8.11.1 Estimation of average daily turnover in the global foreign exchange market

Since the BIS only publishes data regarding average daily turnovers of the world foreign exchange market every three years, it is difficult to know the corresponding average daily foreign exchange turnover between these years; two methods are usually used to estimate the turnovers between two triennial data. One is to calculate the linear difference between two consecutive data points (every three years in this case), and the other is to calculate the compound annual growth rate between two consecutive data points (and assume this rate is the average annual growth rate of the next two years based on previously published data). Data for the two years between each rate are estimated using data from the starting year and the compound growth rate.

Guangping (Peter G.) Zhang and MA Jun (2015) used the average daily turnover in the two publication years, the number of foreign exchange derivatives in the first half of the year, and the number of foreign exchange derivatives in the first half of the non-announced year to estimate the average daily transaction amount for the first half of the non-announced year between the two publication years. Their results show that the average daily turnover in the global foreign exchange market in the first half of 2008 and 2009 was USD 4.43 trillion and 3.53 trillion, respectively. These results represent differences of 0.901 trillion and −0.213 trillion, respectively, compared to the estimates from the compound growth rate method, which were 3.527 trillion and 3.743 trillion, respectively. Zhang and MA's results are 25.5% higher and 5.7% lower than the results obtained under the compound growth rate method.

In the first half of 2008, the full effects of the financial crisis had not yet occurred, and the average daily transaction value at that time should have been higher than in 2007, while the average daily turnover in the first half of 2009 – after the outbreak of the financial crisis – should have been lower than the estimate provided by the average annual compound growth rate method. After using the data regarding derivatives in the international foreign exchange market for the first half of the year, the results of the new method are more accurate than our previous simple methods, and they are also more consistent with the intuitive logic of market changes. These global market estimates have made our judgments regarding the progress of RMB internationalization in different years more accurate.

8.11.2 Ranking of foreign exchange turnover of major international currencies

According to the data regarding the value of domestic RMB foreign exchange market transactions in Table 8-3, the average daily turnover of the overseas RMB foreign exchange market, we can calculate the market share of RMB foreign exchange transactions in recent years. Table 8-6 shows the results.

Table 8-6 Distribution of Daily Turnover of Major World Currencies (2007–2019)

Currency	2007	2010	2013	2014	2015	2016	2017	2018	2019
USD	85.60	84.86	87.04	80.70	76.30	87.58	87.28	92.35	88.30
EUR	37.04	39.05	33.41	32.90	32.30	31.39	31.67	34.21	32.28
JPY	17.25	18.99	23.05	17.90	17.40	21.62	18.11	17.42	16.81
GBP	14.87	12.88	11.82	12.40	12.30	12.80	12.71	12.99	12.79
AUD	6.62	7.59	8.64	8.10	7.50	6.88	6.84	6.81	6.77
CAD	4.29	5.28	4.56	3.70	3.80	5.14	5.08	4.85	5.03
CHF	6.82	6.31	5.16	5.20	4.90	4.80	5.09	4.96	4.96
RMB	0.45	0.86	2.23	2.80	3.40	3.99	4.10	4.21	4.32
SEK	2.70	2.19	1.76	1.90	2.10	2.22	2.16	2.09	2.03
MXN	1.31	1.26	2.53	2.40	2.30	1.92	1.85	1.79	1.72
NZD	1.90	1.59	1.96	2.00	2.00	2.05	2.06	2.07	2.07
SGD	1.17	1.42	1.40	1.50	1.70	1.81	1.81	1.81	1.81
HKD	2.70	2.37	1.45	1.50	1.60	1.73	2.33	2.93	3.53
NOK	2.10	1.32	1.44	1.50	1.60	1.67	1.71	1.76	1.80
KRW	1.16	1.52	1.20	1.30	1.50	1.65	1.77	1.88	2.00
TRY	0.18	0.74	1.32	1.30	1.40	1.44	1.32	1.20	1.08
INR	0.71	0.95	0.99	1.00	1.10	1.14	1.34	1.53	1.72

(Continued)

Currency	2007	2010	2013	2014	2015	2016	2017	2018	2019
RUB	0.75	0.90	1.60	1.40	1.30	1.15	1.13	1.11	1.09
BRL	0.39	0.69	1.10	1.10	1.00	1.00	1.02	1.05	1.07
ZAR	0.91	0.72	1.11	1.10	1.00	0.97	1.01	1.05	1.09
RMB*	0.45	0.86	2.23	2.80	3.40	3.99	4.36	4.72	5.09
RMB (domestic)	0.39	0.69	0.91	1.01	1.20	1.48	1.63	1.79	1.95
Ranking of RMB*	20	17	9	8	8	8	8	8	6
Ranking of RMB (domestic)	22	21	20	20	17	16	15	12	12
Foreign RMB*/ Domestic Transaction	0.15	0.25	1.45	1.77	1.83	1.70	1.67	1.64	1.61

Data source: Shares of major currencies in the global markets updated by the BIS in December 2019. For the years 2011, 2012, 2014, 2015, 2017, and 2018, the proportions of USD, EUR, JPY, GBP, CHF, and CAD were used; data for other currencies in the corresponding years are calculated using the linear interpolation method based on the proportions in 2010 and 2013, 2013 and 2016, and 2016 and 2019; the percentage of the global average daily turnover of domestic RMB* from 2017 to 2019 was calculated based on the total turnover of RMB foreign exchange in April of those years released by the SAFE.

According to the results in Table 8-6, RMB became the world's 6th rather than 8th largest trading currency in 2019, with its turnover share rising to 5.09%, higher than the corresponding shares of 5.03% and 4.98% of CAD and CHF.

8.12 Ranking Major World Currencies in 2020 and 2021

8.12.1 Semi-annual turnovers of the top eight currencies

The above data shows the changes in internationalization rankings of major world currencies from 2007 to 2019. However, since the next set of international foreign exchange data will not be released by the BIS until the second half of 2022, calculating data post-2019 requires using the aforementioned methods.

Average daily turnovers of major world currencies in the first half of 2020 can be estimated using global foreign exchange derivatives market data, which can also be used to rank turnover shares of the USD, Euro, Japanese yen, British pound, Swiss Franc, and Canadian Dollar, yet corresponding data is missing for the Australian Dollar and Chinese yuan. Therefore, difficulties will be encountered when judging shifts in internationalization rankings for this time period. However, semi-annual average daily foreign exchange turnovers of the world's top eight currencies in major foreign exchange markets provide us with extremely useful information to forecast trends after 2019.

London and Tokyo have published foreign exchange market data (including the RMB) for the months of April and October every year since 2008. In addition, the Monetary Authority of Singapore and the Federal Reserve Bank of America have also published the average daily turnovers of the foreign exchange markets (including the RMB) for the months of April and October every year since April 2016. Meanwhile, the Treasury Markets Association of Hong Kong (www.tma.org.hk) has released the average daily transaction data in the foreign exchange market (including the RMB) in April and October every year since October 2017. Furthermore, similar bi-annual data is released by the monetary authorities of Australia and Canada. SAFE (SAFE) of China has released monthly foreign exchange turnover for the mainland Chinese foreign exchange market since January 2015. Thus, we have the bi-annual foreign exchange turnovers of major world currencies in eight major world foreign exchange centers since 2017. These eight foreign exchange centers represent 81.54% to 83.83% of world foreign exchange turnover from April 2016 to April 2019. This share means they can represent the world foreign exchange market well enough, and this data can be used to judge internationalization changes of major currencies from 2020 to 2021. Table 8-7 shows the results below.

8.12.2 The top four world currencies

Table 8-7 shows that the world's top four currencies remained in their monopolistic positions from 2019 to 2021 without much change. The accumulated growth of average daily turnover for the American dollar was 7.1% from 2019 to 2020, only 1.4% lower than the accumulated change of the top eight currencies, indicating that the dollar's international position was not weakened much despite the COVID-19 epidemic and around USD 6 trillion of US national debt issuance from 2020 to the first half of 2021. The accumulated growth rates for the Euro, Japanese yen, and British pound were 6.4%, 3.1%, and 13.9%, respectively, from 2019 to 2020. Since the average rate across the eight major currencies was 8.5%, the Euro and yen weakened slightly, whilst the pound strengthened its internationalization.

Table 8-7   Average Turnovers of Major World Currencies (April 2019 to April 2021)

Unit: USD billion, %

Currency	Apr. 19	Apr. 20	Apr. 21	2019 to 2020	2020 to 2021	2019 to 2021
USD	5,110.3	4,586.6	5,473.6	−10.2	19.3	7.1
EUR	1,674.5	1,491.8	1782.3	−10.9	19.5	6.4
JPY	1,081.6	1,062.7	1,114.8	−1.8	4.9	3.1
GBP	696.4	596.3	793.4	−14.4	33.1	13.9
AUD	366.4	352.8	404.5	−3.7	14.7	10.4
CAD	290.0	284.9	369.3	−1.8	29.6	27.3
CHF	286.2	306.3	385.7	7.0	25.9	34.8
RMB	377.7	301.3	399.6	−20.2	32.6	5.8
Sum	9,883.1	8,982.7	10,723.2	−9.1	19.4	8.5

Data source: Summarized semi-annual foreign exchange turnovers from the London Foreign Exchange Joint Standing Committee (FXJSC) (www.bankofengland.com.uk), the New York Federal Reserve (www.forex.com), Monetary Authority of Singapore (www.mas.gov.sg), Hong Kong Treasury Market Association (www.tma.org.hk), Tokyo Foreign Exchange Market Committee (www.fxcomtky. com), the Australian Foreign Exchange Commission (afxc.rba.gov.au), Canadian Foreign Exchange Commission (www.cfec.ca), and SAFE (www.safe.org.cn) of China. The average daily turnovers of CHF in Switzerland in April 2020 and April 2021 are estimated using data from turnovers of major currencies in Switzerland in April 2019 and relating accumulated annual growth rates from April 2016 to April 2019.

8.12.3 RMB rankings in the nine major world foreign exchange markets

Table 8-7 shows that the average daily turnover of the RMB was USD 377.7 billion in April 2019, 11.3 billion higher than the corresponding average daily turnover of AUD (USD 366.4 billion) over the same period, and 87.7 billion and 91.6 billion higher, respectively than the corresponding average daily turnovers of the CAD and CHF. These results confirmed the sixth-place ranking of RMB in April 2019. Because the average daily turnover of RMB declined 20.2% over the next year – more than any other currency in Table 8-7 – RMB's ranking fell back to 7th in 2020.

Table 8-7 also shows that the average daily turnover of RMB increased 32.6% from April 2020 to 2021, the highest annual growth rate of all eight currencies, and its accumulated growth rate from April 2019 to 2021 was only 5.4%, lower than the corresponding rates of AUD, CD, and CHF (10.4%, 27.3%, and 34.8%, respectively). Therefore, it is reasonable to assert that RMB's ranking in April 2021 should be back in 6th place.

8.13 Conclusion

With the bi-annual turnover data of eight major world foreign exchange centers, we can find relatively reliable changes in the international positions of the top eight currencies from 2020 to 2021, even before the release of the next set of BIS world foreign exchange data in 2022. Our results show that the COVID-19 epidemic had a significant impact on global foreign exchange markets, and in turn, on the international positions of major world currencies.

The release of bi-annual turnovers from the Hong Kong Treasury Market Association since 2017 has given us a more reliable market basis for understanding internationalization changes, including RMB. This data also helps in conducting better forecasts for RMB's future trends. The data shows that from 2016 to 2019, RMB improved its world ranking from 8th to 6th, which is a remarkable result. Especially in recent years, the depreciation of RMB against the USD has led to the stagnation of indicators such as RMB cross-border payments, overseas RMB savings, and RMB international debt issuance. However, the domestic and offshore RMB foreign exchange markets have maintained considerable growth in spite of these challenges. The significant increase in RMB activity in global markets shows that its acceptance is still increasing. In recent years, the overseas environment for RMB internalization has improved significantly: in light of the favorable international environment and deepening domestic reforms, RMB internationalization is expected to return to the steady improvements it was making before 2015 and effectively promote the Belt and Road Initiative.

However, due to the vast impacts of US-China trade friction and the COVID-19 epidemic, turnover of the domestic foreign exchange market declined significantly. RMB's decrease of 20.2% was the highest amongst all major currencies. This steep decrease was a sign of the country's insufficiency in technological originality, which has led to trade restrictions, in turn resulting in a decline in RMB cross-border settlement and related derivatives product transactions. This ultimately led to a decline in the domestic RMB foreign exchange market.

Currency internationalization is a relatively long process. Although foreign experiences are useful references, it is still necessary to explore and move forward in many areas to steadily promote RMB internationalization based on

China's current situation. Exploration is indispensable and must be carried out in a planned or orderly manner; in other words, there should be a road map and timetable for promoting RMB internationalization. Efforts to promote RMB internationalization should mainly focus on domestic medium- and long-term strategic development and the steady and continuous improvement of national living standards. At the same time, the promotion of the RMB's internationalization should also be coordinated with the development of Asia's regional economy as well as the region's trade and financial markets. Ultimately, reform of the international monetary and financial system should be linked to the peaceful development of the world. Going forward, we should explore RMB internationalization and the corresponding implementation details based on the future development of China's and the world's economy, trade conditions, and science and technology while also making appropriate adjustments in accordance with changes in domestic and foreign economies, trade conditions, and markets. In the next few years, RMB internationalization is expected to achieve more significant results as China's technological originality capacity improves, gradually approaching and even reaching a status equivalent to the country's international economic and trade status.

CHAPTER NINE

Relationship between National Governance and Currency Internationalization

Since 2012, the CPC has attached great importance to the modernization of national governance and governance capacity. In 2018, President Xi set the goal to comprehensively deepen China's domestic reform, to improve and develop the socialist system with Chinese characteristics, and to advance the modernization of China's governing system and governing capabilities. Such goals refer to the fifth "Modernization," after industrial modernization, agricultural modernization, national defense modernization, and technological modernization. In recent years, there has been significant improvement in China's global influence, which is consistent with its growth in economic and trade status. Furthermore, China is also making its efforts in the modernization of national governance and governance capacity.

National governance is a broad concept, including not only metrics like judicial effectiveness, government effectiveness, government regulation, corruption control, and government stability, but also the soft power and the image of a nation.

This chapter discusses the empirical relationship between national governance and currency internationalization by introducing and assessing relevant empirical results from the World Bank.

9.1 Global Governance Index by the World Bank

The World Bank's "Global Governance Index" is the first index in the world with continuity and comparability that measures the national governance level. Since 1996, the World Bank has continuously recorded and compared the level of national governance in more than 200 countries or regions worldwide, covering six quantitative parameters: judicial effectiveness, regulatory quality, government effectiveness, corruption control, political stability and anti-violence, and discourse power and accountability. After more than 20 years of development and improvement, the Global Governance Index has become the most systematic quantitative index for measuring national governance. Interested readers can refer directly to the six indicators and related concepts of the World Bank's Global Governance Index by clicking on http://info.worldbank.org/governance/wgi or referring to Yu Keping (2009, 2014).

9.2 What Is "National Governance"?

"The issue of governance was first highlighted by the efforts of international organizations and transnational corporations to improve the socio-political environment in recipient or investment countries. Nevertheless, in recent years, the issue of governance has been given increased attention all over the world with more profound reasoning on government and market limitations in several fields (Yu Keping 2009). Firstly, the concept of governance has been widely used in globally listed companies, financial institutions, and the like for more than half a century, becoming an important part of regulatory practice for domestic and foreign authorities. However, the use of governance in the nation has come about much later. Not until the 1980s did national governance become the research focus of many scholars and international institutions – the earliest of which is the World Bank, which applied this concept to many policy tools in the late 1980s. In the 1990s, the United Nations and a number of international economic cooperation agencies also began to focus on this area and apply the relevant research results to international relations.

In the early 1990s, the World Bank defined national governance as "the way in which state power is used for national development to manage national economic and social resources." The United Nations Development Program defines national governance as a series of political system regulations that resolve conflicts among members of society and accept legal decisions. This definition is used by the UN Development Program to describe the proper function of social institutions, the extent to which they are accepted by the public, and government incentives to improve their efficiency. The Governance Analysis Framework (GAF) defines national governance as "the process of a social member's inter-action and decision-making to innovate, strengthen or regenerate social norms and institutions." Although the above definitions of national governance have different emphases, they all involve many aspects, such as the national legal system, the social structure, the rational exertion of the government function, and so on.

9.3 Comparison of National Governance in Major Countries or Regions

Due to many scholarships on national governance being theoretical, quantitative analysis is particularly important for understanding this concept at a deeper level. Using the results of the six main sub-indicators of global governance from 1996–2018, published by the World Bank in October 2019, we can calculate the results by using weighted averages of the six index evaluation results and their corresponding mean square difference for the first 64 economies with a global domestic production value of more than USD 100 billion in 2018 (see Table 9-1).

Table 9-1   Overall Governance Assessment Results and Cumulative Changes in the Top 64 Global Economies from 1996 to 2018

Country/ Region	1996	2012	2018	1996–2012	2012–2018
				Annual Change	
Major Developed Economies					
Australia	83.2	83.2	82	−0.1	−1.2
Austria	83.4	80.6	80.1	−2.8	−0.5
Belgium	79.1	77.9	75.4	−1.2	−2.5
Canada	83.8	82.8	82.7	−0.9	−0.1
Denmark	86.0	86.8	84.9	0.8	−1.9
Finland	85.5	87.6	86.5	2.1	−1.1

(Continued)

Country/ Region	1996	2012	2018	1996–2012	2012–2018
				Annual Change	
Major Developed Economies					
France	75.4	75.2	73.5	−0.1	−1.7
Germany	82.2	80.3	81.1	−1.9	0.7
Greece	65.6	56.3	55.9	−9.2	−0.5
Italy	67.6	60.7	60.1	−6.8	−0.6
Japan	71.7	76.0	76.6	4.3	0.6
Holland	86.3	85.3	84.6	−0.9	−0.7
New Zealand	86.2	86.9	86.8	0.6	−0.1
Norway	86.8	87.1	86.4	0.3	−0.7
Portugal	76.6	69.5	71.3	−7.0	1.8
Spain	76.3	69.3	66.5	−7.0	−2.7
Sweden	85.6	87.5	85.2	1.9	−2.3
Switzerland	84.7	85.8	86.0	1.1	0.2
UK	84.0	78.9	78.5	−5.1	−0.4
US	79.4	76.3	74.8	−3.1	−1.5
Average Level	80.5	78.7	77.9	−1.8	−0.8
Average Change Annually				−0.11	−0.13
Other Developed Economies					
Slovakia	58.7	63.2	62.9	4.4	−0.3
Czech	67.0	66.5	67.9	−0.5	1.5
Hong Kong, China	70.0	77.8	78.5	7.8	0.7
Ireland	81.1	79.0	78.1	−2.2	−0.9
Israel	67.8	63.9	63.6	−3.9	−0.3
South Korea	61.1	65.3	67.5	4.2	2.2
Puerto Rico	70.9	63.2	58.0	−7.7	−5.2
Singapore	80.3	77.7	79.5	−2.6	1.8

(Continued)

Country/ Region	1996	2012	2018	1996–2012	2012–2018
				Annual Change	
Taiwan, China	63.6	68.7	71.7	5.1	3.0
Average Level	69.0	69.5	69.7	0.5	0.3
Average Change Annually				0.03	0.05
Major Developing Economies					
Brazil	49.6	52.4	46.1	2.8	−6.2
Mainland China	39.5	35.1	41.2	−4.3	6.1
India	48.6	45.9	49.3	−2.7	3.4
Indonesia	36.1	43.2	47.6	7.0	4.5
Mexico	45.5	47.5	41.9	2.0	−5.7
Russia	37.4	33.7	34.9	−3.7	1.2
Saudi Arabia	41.9	37.2	42.9	−4.7	5.7
Turkey	46.8	49.8	40.5	3.0	−9.3
Average Level	43.2	43.1	43.0	−0.1	0.0
Average Change Annually				0.00	−0.01
Other Developing Economies					
Algeria	28.2	33.2	33.5	5.0	0.3
Angola	23.3	28.5	30.7	5.2	2.2
Argentina	53.6	44.5	50.7	−9.0	6.2
Bangladesh	36.9	34.4	34.1	−2.5	−0.3
Chile	73.5	75.3	70.8	1.8	−4.5
Columbia	38.6	45.4	47.0	6.8	1.5
Egypt	41.8	36.3	33.8	−5.6	−2.5
Hungary	67.5	62.7	57.8	−4.8	−4.8
Iran	34.3	26.6	29.4	−7.7	2.8
Iraq	12.4	24.5	21.2	12.1	−3.3
Kazakhstan	31.1	34.3	40.5	3.2	6.2

(Continued)

Country/ Region	1996	2012	2018	1996–2012	2012–2018
				Annual Change	
Kuwait	54.2	47.1	46.2	−7.1	−0.9
Malaysia	58.1	54.1	57.9	−4.0	3.9
Morocco	47.8	42.8	43.6	−4.9	0.7
Nigeria	26.5	29.8	31.5	3.3	1.7
Pakistan	35.6	29.8	32.6	−5.8	2.8
Peru	43.7	46.3	46.5	2.6	0.2
Philippine	47.5	43.5	43.8	−4.0	0.3
Ukraine	36.8	37.2	38.1	0.4	0.9
Ecuador	42.2	37.0	42.3	−5.2	5.4
Poland	65.6	67.0	62.7	1.4	−4.3
Katar	50.9	58.9	53.5	8.0	−5.4
Roumania	49.1	51.4	53.7	2.4	2.2
South Africa	62.3	55.0	53.4	−7.3	−1.6
Thailand	53.3	45.1	43.0	−8.1	−2.1
UAE	59.0	56.9	59.7	−2.1	2.8
Vietnam	38.5	35.4	39.8	−3.0	4.3
Average Level	44.9	43.8	44.4	−1.1	0.5
Average Change Annually				−0.07	0.09
Average Level of 35 Major Developing Countries	44.5	43.7	44.1	−0.8	0.4
Average Change Annually				−0.05	0.07
Average Level of 64 Economies	59.2	58.2	58.3	−0.9	0.0
Average Change Annually				−0.06	0.00

Data source: Based on results from the 1996–2018 model released by the World Bank in October 2019, the results in Table 9-1 convert the original assessment between −2.5 and 2.5 into a percentage system for intuitive comparison; 64 economies with a GDP over USD 100 billion in 2018 were updated by the IMF in October 2019.

Table 9-1 shows that the level of governance in major developed countries is generally high. From 1996–2012, the average level of governance in the 20 major developed countries was about 8%. However, from 1996 to 2012, the overall level of governance in these countries showed a downward trend, with an average decline of 1.8%. In particular, the level of governance in Greece declined by 9.2% from 1996–2012. Spain, Portugal, and Italy, respectively, recorded a cumulative decline of 70%, 7%, and 6.8% over the same period. In total, 13 developed countries, such as the US, Belgium, and Austria, have experienced varying levels of decline in governance. Only seven developed countries, including Japan, New Zealand, Finland, and Switzerland, experienced a slight improvement in governance level over the same period. From 2012 to 2018, 16 of the 20 developed countries still had varying levels of decline, and the average annual decline was above other developed and developing economies, underlining their relatively poor performance.

9.3.1 Other developed economies

Table 9-1 shows that Singapore, Hong Kong, China, and Ireland, among the nine other developed economies, are at the same level as the 20 major developed countries, while South Korea, Taiwan, China, the Czech Republic, Slovakia, Israel, and Puerto Rico are at a lower level of governance. From 1996 to 2012, the average governance level of the eight developed economies increased slightly by 0.5%, and even slowed slightly from 2012 to 2018, with a cumulative increase of only 0.3%.

9.3.2 The eight major developing countries

Table 9-1 shows that the average governance level of the eight developing countries declined very slightly from 43.2% to 43.1% between 1996 and 2012. This is not only a vast gap with the developed economies, but also slightly lower than the average governance level of the other 27 developing countries that were part of the world's top 64 economies in 2012. Between 1996 and 2012, four of the eight developing countries – Brazil, Mexico, Turkey, and Russia – experienced a marked decline in governance level, declining faster than the 20 developed countries. Although the overall level of governance is low in these countries, the cumulative average decline is the lowest at only 0.1%, indicating that the overall improvement in governance in the major developing countries over the past 23 years has been significantly higher than not only the developed economies, but also in the small and medium-sized developing countries. Last but not least, it is worth paying special attention to the level of governance in Indonesia, which increased by 11.5% from 1996 to 2018 – the highest of all 64 economies measured.

9.3.3 Other developing countries

Table 9-1 shows that of the 27 small and medium-sized developing countries, only 13 countries experienced a cumulative increase, while 14 countries experienced a cumulative decline. Overall, the level was comparable to that of major developing countries.

9.3.4 China's governance level

Table 9-1 shows that Mainland China ranked sixth among the eight developing countries in 2018, 51st among the 64 major economies, and 112th among the 182 economies with relevant assessment data from 1996 to 2018. This was significantly lower than China's 2018 ranking of 77th for GDP per capita, reflecting the fact that China's national governance needs improvement. However, despite China's national governance level only ranking 47th of the 64 major economies from 1996 to 2012, the cumulative increase from 2012 to 2018 reached 61%, the third fastest growth of all nations (just below Kazakhstan and Argentina). This underlines how China's national governance level has improved significantly since the 18th CPC National Congress.

9.4 Changes and Comparisons of Key Governance Indicators in Major Economies

Table 9-1 shows the overall assessment results and cumulative changes in governance level in major economies from 1996 to 2018. Table 9-2 presents the results and changes of the six governance indicators in these economies over the same period.

9.4.1 Key governance indicators for major developing countries

Table 9-2 shows that the average assessment result of judicial effectiveness and corruption control in the 20 major developed economies is slightly over 80%, with government and regulatory effectiveness close to 80%, and average discourse power and government stability are over 70% and 60%, respectively. The results show that major developed countries tend to do well in the first four governance areas, but not so well in discourse power and government stability.

9.4.2 Key governance indicators for other developed economies

Table 9-2 shows that the level of the first four governance indicators for the eight other developed economies, such as the Czech Republic and Hong Kong, China, is at 75% or so on average – slightly lower than the 20 developed countries. Besides, the average level of discourse power and government stability in these eight other developed economies is also lower than that of the 20 major developed economies.

Table 9-2   Six Governance Indicator Assessment Results of the Top 64 Economies

Unit: %

Country/ Region	Judicial Effectiveness	Government Effectiveness	Regulatory Effectiveness	Corruption Control	Government Stability	Discourse Power
Major Developed Economies						
Australia	84.3	81.9	88.6	86.1	69.5	78.6
Austria	87.5	79.1	80.9	81.9	68.4	77.6
Belgium	77.4	73.4	74.7	80.2	58.2	77.9
Canada	85.4	84.3	83.3	87.5	69.8	80.4
Denmark	86.7	87.4	83.5	93.0	69.2	82.2
Finland	90.9	89.7	85.7	94.2	68.5	82.2
France	78.8	79.6	73.5	76.3	52.2	73.6
Germany	82.6	82.4	85.0	88.9	62.1	78.4
Greece	53.1	56.8	55.9	48.7	51.9	67.1
Italy	54.9	58.3	63.4	54.7	56.2	70.9
Japan	80.7	83.5	76.6	78.5	71.2	70.5
Holland	86.3	87.0	90.4	90.2	67.4	81.9
New Zealand	87.5	83.4	89.6	93.5	80.8	82.5
Norway	89.3	87.7	85.2	91.8	73.1	84.7
Portugal	72.8	74.2	67.8	67.0	72.8	74.1
Spain	69.4	70.0	68.9	62.3	55.1	71.3
Sweden	87.9	86.6	86.0	92.8	68.3	82.2

(Continued)

Country/ Region	Judicial Effectiveness	Government Effectiveness	Regulatory Effectiveness	Corruption Control	Government Stability	Discourse Power
Switzerland	88.6	90.8	85.6	90.2	76.9	82.3
UK	82.8	76.8	85.2	86.5	51.0	77.7
US	79.1	81.5	81.6	76.5	59.5	70.8
Average Level	80.3	79.7	79.6	81.0	65.1	77.4
Other Developed Economies						
Slovakia	60.6	64.1	66.2	57.3	65.0	67.6
Czech	71.0	68.4	75.2	60.1	70.8	68.6
Hong Kong, China	85.4	88.1	94.1	83.5	65.9	59.4
Ireland	79.3	78.4	81.9	80.9	70.6	76.4
Israel	69.9	74.2	74.9	65.7	31.4	63.0
South Korea	74.7	73.7	71.9	62.1	60.9	65.9
Puerto Rico	61.7	46.9	68.6	50.8	58.0	59.8
Singapore	86.9	94.6	92.6	93.5	80.2	48.8
Taiwan, China	72.2	77.2	77.1	70.6	67.1	69.5
Average Level of Other Developed Economies	73.5	74.0	78.1	69.4	63.3	64.3
Average Level of Developed Economies	78.2	77.9	79.1	77.4	64.5	73.3
Major Developing Economies						
Brazil	44.4	41.1	43.7	41.6	42.9	57.8
Mainland China	46.0	59.5	47.3	44.6	44.8	21.0
India	50.5	55.7	46.3	46.3	30.9	57.6

(Continued)

Country/ Region	Judicial Effectiveness	Government Effectiveness	Regulatory Effectiveness	Corruption Control	Government Stability	Discourse Power
Indonesia	43.7	53.6	48.6	45.0	39.3	53.6
Mexico	36.5	46.9	53.0	32.7	38.6	49.9
Russia	33.7	48.8	39.2	33.1	39.9	28.8
Saudi Arabia	52.8	56.5	49.1	57.2	39.6	17.1
Turkey	43.6	50.1	49.1	43.3	23.4	33.3
Average Level of Major Developing Economies	43.9	51.5	47.0	43.0	37.4	39.9
Other Major Developing Economies						
Algeria	34.5	41.1	24.7	37.3	34.1	30.4
Angola	29.0	29.0	30.0	27.1	43.6	31.6
Argentina	45.2	50.5	45.1	48.3	50.4	61.3
Bangladesh	37.2	35.0	33.5	31.9	29.4	35.4
Chile	72.3	71.7	76.9	70.2	58.5	71.1
Columbia	41.8	48.3	56.6	44.0	33.7	53.8
Egypt	41.8	38.3	32.7	38.3	26.7	24.3
Hungary	61.1	59.7	62.0	51.1	65.1	56.4
Iran	36.1	41.4	24.1	30.8	23.9	23.6
Iraq	14.8	23.6	25.6	22.0	−1.1	30.3
Kazakhstan	41.4	50.4	52.8	40.0	50.0	26.6
Kuwait	54.2	48.2	49.3	44.2	52.2	38.2
Malaysia	62.5	71.5	63.6	56.3	54.7	48.3
Morocco	47.2	45.8	45.1	45.7	43.4	36.7
Nigeria	32.4	29.5	32.3	29.1	6.1	41.8
Pakistan	36.5	37.3	37.1	34.2	4.7	34.0
Peru	39.7	45.1	60.4	39.2	44.8	54.7

(Continued)

Country/ Region	Judicial Effectiveness	Government Effectiveness	Regulatory Effectiveness	Corruption Control	Government Stability	Discourse Power
Philippine	40.4	51.0	50.9	39.1	27.6	50.8
Ukraine	35.6	41.7	45.6	32.5	13.5	49.7
Ecuador	37.4	44.8	32.2	38.8	48.5	50.5
Poland	58.6	63.3	67.6	62.8	60.9	64.5
Qatar	64.7	62.6	60.3	64.5	63.6	26.1
Romania	56.5	44.9	58.9	47.6	51.2	59.2
South Africa	48.0	56.8	53.4	49.6	44.5	63.1
Thailand	50.5	57.0	52.2	42.0	35.3	29.9
UAE	66.1	78.6	68.6	73.0	64.9	27.8
Vietnam	49.9	49.9	42.3	40.3	54.1	21.1
Average Level of Other Major Developing Countries	45.8	48.8	47.6	43.7	40.2	42.3
Average Level of 35 Major Developing Countries	45.3	49.4	47.4	43.5	39.5	41.7
Average Level of 64 Economies	60.2	62.3	61.8	58.9	50.9	56.0

Data source: Based on the results of the 2018 Global Governance Assessment Model released by the World Bank in October 2019, the results in Table 9-2 convert the original assessment results between −2.5 and 2.5 into a percentage system for intuitive comparison; the conditions of the 64 economies is the same as Table 9-1.

9.4.3 Governance level in major developing countries

Table 9-2 shows that while the results from the eight major developing economies were significantly lower than in developed economies, government effectiveness was significantly higher, on average, than in the other five indicators. Regulatory effectiveness, judicial effectiveness, and corruption control were around 45% on average, with discourse power and government stability lower than 40%. These results indicate that major developing countries' governance indicators are still far behind the developed economies, on average.

9.4.4 Governance level of other developing countries
From Table 9-2, it is shown that the 27 small and medium-sized developing countries, on average, are left behind by the eight major developing countries in terms of government effectiveness and regulation quality, are comparable in judicial effectiveness, corruption control, and discourse power, and are slightly ahead in government stability.

9.5 National Governance, GDP, and GDP per Capita

In theory, the higher the level of national governance, the higher the level of national management and prosperity, and thus, the higher the GDP and per capita GDP. Countries or regions with higher GDP per capita tend to demand more from national governance, and these countries will accordingly attain a higher level of national governance. Above all, there should be a positive correlation between national governance and GDP per capita.

9.5.1 The relationship between national governance and GDP
Using the relevant data given in Table 9-1, we can measure the correlation between national governance indicators and GDP. The results show that the correlation coefficient between governance indicators and GDP in 167 well-documented major economies fell from 28.1% to 18.7% in 1996–2015, while it continued to rise to 19.2% in 2015–18. The positive correlation reflects the positive correlation between national governance and GDP, but the low coefficient is indicative of a weak correlation.

9.5.2 The relationship between national governance and GDP per capita
The positive correlation between national governance and GDP given above is weak – mostly because there are huge population and economic scale differences in different countries or regions, making it less comparable. Therefore, we use GDP per capita to measure the correlation with national governance. Using the data from Table 9-1 and GDP per capita data published by the IMF in October 2019, the correlation between national governance indicators and per capita GDP can be calculated. The results show that the correlation coefficient between

national governance indicators and per capita GDP for 166 countries or regions fell from 78.7% to 74.5% from 1996 to 2013, yet rose to 78.4% from 2013 to 2018, with an annual average of 89.0% from 1996 to 2018. The results show a strong positive correlation between national governance and GDP per capita.

9.6 The Relationship between Currency Internationalization and Governance

A comparison of the proportion of foreign exchange market transactions in major global currencies (that is, the currency internationalization) from 1998 to 2019 and the governance evaluation results of the corresponding countries given in Table 9-1 show the incidence relation between currency internationalization and governance level for a particular the country. This is discussed below in this section.

9.6.1 The relationship between currency internationalization and governance level

Using the data corresponding to Table 9-1, the correlation between currency internationalization and national governance for 2004, 2007, 2010, 2013, and 2016 can be calculated. The results show that the correlation coefficient between the average daily transaction amount of the first 38 currencies and their governance is 28.3%, 28.4%, 28.2%, 27.0%, and 26.0% annually; this works out as 27.6% on average, which is slightly higher than the average correlation coefficient of 23.4% between GDP and governance in 167 economies over the same period. It shows that the synergy effect between currency internationalization and national governance is slightly higher than that of GDP and national governance; it also shows that the results from the World Bank governance model are relatively reasonable.

9.6.2 National governance and per capita foreign exchange transactions

Since the variance between currencies and economic scale is so large, data from the 38 currencies published by the IMF from 2004–16 is used to calculate the correlation coefficient. As shown by the results, the correlation coefficient between these is high: 70.7%, 70.4%, 69.4%, 73.5%, and 77.5% in 2004, 2007, 2010, 2013, and 2016, respectively; the average across all years was 72.3%, slightly lower than the average correlation coefficient of 76.22% between per capita GDP and governance of the 167 economies of the same caliber given above. This proves that the internationalization of currency and national governance have a strong correlation.

9.7 National Governance and Other Relevant Indicators

In addition to the positive correlations between national governance and GDP, and per capita GDP and currency internationalization, governance level is also closely related to imports and exports, military expenditure, language and culture, learning intensity, patent quantity, sovereign credit rating, and other fields. The empirical results show that the positive correlation between national governance and sovereign credit rating of 118 major countries or regions is over 70%.

9.8 National Governance Impact

Gallup, a famous public opinion research institution in the US, publishes the latest public opinion research report on public perception of global leadership for China, the US, Germany, and Russia. According to the report, among the interviewees in 133 countries or regions, 34% recognized China's leadership – its highest recognition level since 2009 – while 31% recognized the global leadership of the US. It shows that the advantage of China over the US is enlarging, from which the latest changes in the soft power of the two can be observed. In Europe, Asia, and Africa, China is more recognized as a world leader than the US. China has the highest recognition in Africa at 53%, while the US has 52%. According to the relevant data, compared with China and the US, Germany has received wider acceptance in Asia and Europe. Besides, In Asia, Europe, and Africa, Germany is more recognized than China and the US on the whole, with net recognition over China and the US, too. Similar results were first shown in Gallup's 2017 survey report, indicating that China's international influence has increased significantly in recent years.

The results of global leadership in these major countries are obtained through sampling surveys of different countries or regions, showing representatives. However, in view of the limited sampling range and distribution, there are still limitations to the results. The concept of national leadership is actually close to the concept of National Governance Impact. This section uses the results of the World Bank's global governance assessment to calculate the influence of major economies on global governance on the basis of exploring a reasonable definition of governance influence between economies.

9.8.1 Definition of the national governance impact

The influence of one economy (X) over the governance impact of another (Y) can be defined as the effectiveness of X governance assessment results as an independent variable and Y governance assessment results as a dependent variable. We evaluate this effectiveness with simple linear regression. For instance, making the assessment results of US governance from 1996 to 2017 as an independent variable for the US governance impact over British governance, and British governance assessment results as a dependent variable, the validity of linear regression results is 79.8%, and the standard error of the regression is 4.62% at the same time. On the other side, when measuring the influence of British governance on the US with the results of the 1996–2017 British governance evaluation as an independent variable, and the results of the US governance evaluation as a dependent variable, we found that the effectiveness of the linear regression results is 79.8%, and the standard regression error is 4.94%. Therefore, the mutual influence of governance of the two economies can not be seen only by regression effectiveness, and the standard error based on regression effectiveness can better reflect the mutual influence. Thus, we define the influence of American governance at 17.3 (79.8%/4.62%) and the influence of British governance at 16.2 (79.8%/4.94%), showing that the US governance impact on Britain is 1.1 more than Britain's on the US. Therefore, the proportion of the aforesaid standard error can be used as a better indicator to assess the impact of national governance.

9.8.2 A more appropriate definition for national governance impact

The "regression validity/ standard error of regression validity" described above basically reflects the mutual influence between the two, but the definition does not make full use of the regression information between the two governance. For instance, the simple regression coefficient and its mean square difference of the effect of US governance on British governance described above are 0.8352 and 10.20%, respectively. It is shown that each change in the governance of the former will lead to a change of 0.8352%, while the change in the governance of the latter will lead to a change of 0.9549%. Although the latter has more influence on the former, the return coefficient of the latter is 11.66%, above 10.20% of the former's. Therefore, while the contribution of the regression coefficient and its mean square difference to mutual influence is considered, we divide the product of regression effectiveness and regression coefficient by the sum of regression standard error and regression coefficient as governance influence, finding that US governance impact on British governance is 4.49, while that of British governance on US governance is 4.59. In addition, from the mathematical analysis, the lower the simple linear total square sum of the influence of one economy governance on the governance of another economy, the better the regression effect of the former on the latter, and the worse the reverse. Therefore, we put the total square sum of influence regression into the denominator of influence above, so as to obtain a more appropriate and intuitive definition of governance influence. According to this definition, US governance impact on British governance was 2.03 from 1996–2017, while that of British governance was 2.05. This chapter uses this definition to calculate the mutual influence between the governance of any two economies.

9.8.3 Distribution of top 10 economies' governance impact on the overall governance of top 182 economies worldwide

Using the definition of governance impact above, We can calculate the total governance influence of the top 10 global economies on the top 182 global economies from 1996 to 2018. The calculation results are shown in Table 9-3, which shows that, as the world's largest economy, the US has the strongest overall influence on governance in the world's top 20 economies, at 7.752, followed by Italy's 7.418, and then the UK, Japan and Canada, with 6.438, 4.947, and 4.484, respectively. Also, as is shown in Table 9-3, China and France have total influence over the top 20 economies at 3.984 and 3.872, ranking 5 and 6, respectively. Italy's influence on the US is 0.872, similar to the US influence on Italy at 0.873, which seems unreasonable. The World Bank governance model needs to be further optimized, and the rationality of the original data used by the World Bank model also needs to be improved. The overall impact of governance in other major economies is largely comparable to the global impact of their economic trade.

The overall influence of the top 10 economies on 182 economies around the world is given in Table 9-3. The outcomes show the US has the greatest overall influence on governance economics globally, scoring 65.112, except for Italy, with a score of 67.896, which is hard to explain. The British, Japanese, French, and German scored 61.223, 58.195, 42.996, and 38.804, respectively, ranking from 3rd to 6th orderly. China scored 36.392, ranking No.7. These results are basically comparable to the intuitive perception of soft power in major countries, suggesting that the World Bank global governance model evaluation result is relatively objective and reasonable in this respect.

Table 9-3   The Influence of Global Top 10 Economies Governance on Global 182 Economies Governance (From 1996 to 2018)

Country	US	China	Japan	Germany	India	UK	France	Brazil	Italy	Canada
US	...	0.108	0.753	0.382	0.007	0.798	0.193	0.067	0.872	0.509
China	0.108	...	0.008	0.292	0.140	0.175	0.209	0.314	0.052	0.337
Japan	0.754	0.008	...	0.200	0.012	0.535	0.278	0.156	0.839	0.279
Germany	0.377	0.286	0.205	...	0.082	0.618	0.002	0.077	0.276	0.382
India	0.006	0.136	0.014	0.082	...	0.050	0.000	0.313	0.024	0.048
UK	0.798	0.174	0.535	0.623	0.052	...	0.087	0.000	0.732	0.566
France	0.190	0.213	0.281	0.002	0.000	0.086	...	0.190	0.278	0.014
Brazil	0.067	0.314	0.155	0.074	0.308	0.000	0.193	...	0.086	0.000
Italy	0.873	0.052	0.837	0.283	0.026	0.734	0.283	0.087	...	0.374
Canada	0.501	0.330	0.286	0.381	0.047	0.559	0.015	0.000	0.365	...
Russia	0.264	0.066	0.359	0.050	0.062	0.178	0.011	0.003	0.313	0.078
South Korea	0.432	0.142	0.197	0.426	0.048	0.683	0.016	0.000	0.386	0.585
Australia	0.277	0.041	0.246	0.008	0.092	0.111	0.589	0.247	.0301	0.000
Spain	0.885	0.031	0.852	0.217	0.000	0.629	0.311	0.158	0.922	0.306
Mexico	0.397	0.154	0.489	0.004	0.149	0.170	0.452	0.474	0.400	0.043
Indonesia	0.823	0.013	0.741	0.219	0.003	0.681	0.404	0.192	0.870	0.310
Turkey	0.008	0.631	0.065	0.100	0.156	0.008	0.606	0.429	0.032	0.159
Holland	0.681	0.269	0.341	0.462	0.001	0.609	0.041	0.025	0.550	0.432
Saudi Arabia	0.133	0.713	0.060	0.232	0.128	0.171	0.126	0.330	0.088	0.240
Switzerland	0.176	0.302	0.013	0.448	0.004	0.229	0.055	0.056	0.032	0.285
Total of Top 20 Economies	7.752	3.984	6.438	4.484	1.317	7.023	3.872	3.117	7.418	4.947
Total of 182 Economies	65.112	36.392	58.195	38.804	13.990	61.223	42.996	24.812	67.896	40.485

Data source: The linear regression results of the 1996–2018 governance assessment of the 182 economies released by the World Bank in October 2019.

9.9 Global Distribution of National Governance Impact

The total governance impact of the top 10 economies on the top 20 economies and on the world's 182 economies is described above, but its distribution in different regions of the world is difficult to see. The corresponding distribution results are shown in Table 9-4. Table 9-4 shows that China's overall governance influence in Southeast Asia, South Asia, and Central Asia has ranked first; China's overall governance influence in Western Asia is only slightly lower than that of the US, the UK, and Japan, ranking the fourth; China's influence in Europe and America is still weak, only slightly higher than that in India and Brazil. Last but not least, China's influence in Africa is comparable to that in France, showing China's influence in Africa has gradually increased in recent years under the "Belt and Road" Initiative.

Table 9-4 shows the total governance influence of different countries in different regions, which actually reflects the acceptance and development potential of the soft power of the country in the corresponding region. Therefore, the RMB has greater potential in Asia, particularly in Southeast Asia, Central Asia, and South Asia, and is relatively acceptable. In Europe, especially in the Eurozone, efforts are still needed to boost RMB internationalization. In addition, it is worth noting that the overall governance influence of the three countries (China, US, and Germany) in Asia, Europe, and especially in Africa in Table 9-4 is quite different from the results of the Gallup poll described above, which may be limited in the sampling range of the Gallup poll or a problem with the World Bank governance model and raw data.

Table 9-4 The Influence of Global Top 10 Economies Governance to Regions (From 1996 to 2018)

Region	US	China	Japan	Germany	India	UK	France	Brazil	Italy	Canada
Asia	16.86	12.44	14.09	11.63	3.60	16.70	12.01	7.75	17.69	11.64
Eastern Asia	3.24	1.22	1.78	2.50	0.53	3.32	1.22	0.76	3.22	2.80

(Continued)

Region	US	China	Japan	Germany	India	UK	France	Brazil	Italy	Canada
South-eastern Asia	2.75	2.97	2.25	2.23	0.54	2.57	2.78	1.68	2.69	1.65
Southern Asia	1.27	2.08	1.23	1.57	0.57	1.67	1.22	1.00	1.45	1.64
Central Asia	1.13	1.88	0.84	1.10	0.44	1.29	1.22	0.88	1.26	1.03
Western Asia	8.47	4.28	7.99	4.24	1.53	7.84	5.57	3.43	9.06	4.51
Oceania	0.40	1.48	0.53	0.74	0.64	0.45	1.83	1.50	0.51	0.57
Central and Eastern Europe	8.97	2.67	7.43	4.93	1.19	8.24	4.25	1.53	9.60	4.68
Eurozone	9.20	2.79	8.84	3.52	0.96	7.76	4.49	2.85	8.68	4.25
Western European Countries outside the Eurozone	8.50	2.74	7.81	3.39	1.56	6.16	4.68	2.75	7.33	3.71
Europe	17.47	5.41	15.24	8.31	2.75	14.41	8.92	4.28	16.93	8.39
Africa	17.96	11.05	15.98	11.53	3.43	16.67	11.09	5.92	18.83	11.92
America	12.42	6.01	12.35	6.59	3.56	12.01	9.14	5.37	13.94	6.96
South America	4.81	2.44	4.16	2.59	1.75	4.51	3.78	1.60	5.13	2.69
North America	7.61	3.57	8.19	4.00	1.81	7.50	5.36	3.77	8.81	4.28

Data source: Same as Table 9-3.

9.10 Promoting RMB Internationalization by Modernizing the National Governance System and Governance Capacity

9.10.1 Global ranking and problems of China's national governance in 2017 and 2018

Table 9-2 presents the evaluation results of six indicators in China's national governance in 2018: judicial effectiveness, government effectiveness, regulatory quality, corruption control, government stability, and discourse power, ranking 109th, 64th, 109th, 114th, 134th, and 186th of 182 countries or regions. The results of China's overall governance assessment weighted by six indicators ranked 112th globally. The six indicators were down 16, 7, 15, 24, 28, and 19 from 2017, but the weighted total results rose two places instead. These results show that the overall level of governance in China has improved significantly from 2017-2018, but the results of the sharp decline in the ranking of corruption control and government stability in China are obviously inconsistent with the fact that China has continued to fight corruption over the years, which means there are some problems in the data and calculation methods of the World Bank model, which are limited to the corruption cases found, but do not consider the strength of our country's continuous anti-corruption and clean government. In 2017 and 2018, the other five national governance indicators, except government efficiency, fell behind 77th and 79th of China's global ranking in per capita GDP, indicating that there were obvious problems in the global governance model and data, and there was some discrimination in the modernization of China's national governance system and governance capacity. After the weighted adjustment of uncertainty, the overall ranking improved by two places in 2018, which is more in line with the intuitive feelings and reflects the effectiveness and superiority of the model indirectly.

9.10.2 Global ranking of the global influence on China's national governance

Although China's overall ranking of national governance is much lower than the ranking of the per capita GDP, the results in Table 9-3 show that in 2017, China's national governance in the top 10 economies has reached or even exceeded the top major developed countries, significantly exceeding the overall ranking of national governance. From 1996 to 2018, China's national governance influence on the countries or regions along the "Belt and Road" and 165 countries and regions in Africa and South America ranks the front among the top 10 economies, significantly higher than that of the US, the UK, and Russia, and also significantly higher than China's overall ranking of national governance. Through economic and trade, investment, and currency internationalization, China's national governance has played an important role in the world.

9.11 Importance and Urgency of Establishing China's National Governance Monitoring and Evaluation System

After years of trial operation, the World Bank's global governance model can cover the historical data of most countries or regions in the world for nearly 20 years. Although there are still some problems with the model and data, especially some prejudice or even suppression against China, the model is the most authoritative in the world. Therefore, while strengthening communication and cooperation with international institutions such as the World Bank, China should publish the research results and related progress of the national governance in time and form a national governance evaluation model with Chinese characteristics.

Therefore, the establishment of the national governance model and monitoring system is of necessity and significance, which is beneficial to enhance the Chinese voice of national governance in the world, reflects the current situation of national governance timely, scientifically grasps the progress of reform in related fields in China, and coordinate the process of deepening reform in various fields. Similarly, Only by establishing national governance models and monitoring systems with Chinese characteristics, can China promote the overall goal of comprehensively deepening reform according to the established roadmap and timetable, improving China's national governance modernization level, and enhancing the national external image, RMB overseas acceptance, and RMB internationalization level. Only by making RMB internationalization similar to China's economic and trade international status, can China provide a stronger foundation for international local currency support for the "Belt and Road" initiative.

9.12 Create the World Miracle of National Governance in the New Era

National governance is an important part and the best reflection of a country's soft power, and the measurement of national governance reflects the real situation of national soft power. Since the reform and opening up, China has created a miracle of economic growth with a 10% average annual for the past three decades. In the future, China is expected to create a world miracle of national governance modernization in the next 30 years and make greater contributions to the construction of a community of human destiny.

The data show that in the 22 years from 1996 to 2018, only 86 of the world's 182 economies improved their governance levels to varying degrees, while the other 96 economies did not rise or fall, indicating that improving governance is hard work. Of the 86 economies with improving national governance levels, the overall governance levels of Georgia, Rwanda, Liberia, and Serbia have increased by 29.8%, 27.1%, 21.5%, and 20.4%, respectively; the national governance levels of Croatia, Sierra Leone, Albania, Macao, China, and Burma have increased by 13.7%, 12.8%, 12.6%, 12.1%, and 11.6%, respectively. In the same period, China's governance level has only increased by 3.5%. However, from 2012 to 2018, 98 of 182 economies experienced improved governance, and China had a cumulative increase of 5.1%, ranking first in the top 20 economies.

If China's national governance over the next 30 years is slightly higher than the average annual growth rate of 1.06% at 1.2% from 2012 to 2017, China's national governance is expected to reach the 2017 average of advanced economies in Table 9-1 around the middle of the 21st century. With an annual increase of 1.5%, China is expected to significantly exceed the average of advanced economies and will surpass the vast majority of advanced economies, ranking at the top in the world, by the middle of the 21st century.

9.13 RMB Internationalization Level Compatible with National Governance Situation

The rising level of RMB internationalization will be the best measure and manifestation of the great rejuvenation of the Chinese nation. In the next 30 years, in the middle of the 21st century, the process of China's national governance to create a world miracle will also gradually lay a more solid foundation for the internationalization of the RMB, which is also the improving process of RMB internationalization. The RMB is expected to surpass the Australian dollar, the yen, the pound and the Euro in 2030 or so, becoming the world's second-largest international currency. Improved national governance will keep providing the necessary support for the internationalization of RMB in this process.

9.14 Conclusion

National governance is an important embodiment of national soft power and an important part of national image. The content of this chapter shows a significant positive correlation between currency internationalization and currency parent governance level which means the higher the national governance level of a country, the higher the international acceptance of its currency, and then the higher the internationalization degree.

A country with its currency in a higher degree of internationalization would like to have more chances to influence and promote the governance level of other countries through various international activities such as international economy, trade, investment, science and technology, society, and culture. The correlation coefficient of more than 70% between the per capita monetary transaction amount and the monetary economy's parent governance level, shows a great influence of national governance on currency internationalization. Conversely, currency internationalization can also improve the level and influence of national governance.

CHAPTER TEN

The Role of AIIB in RMB Internationalization

THE ASIAN INFRASTRUCTURE INVESTMENT BANK (AIIB) and the New Development Bank were officially launched in the same year in 2015, marking the two major mileposts of the Belt and Road Initiative and the RMB internationalization. This chapter will give a brief introduction to both banks and further discuss their role in promoting RMB internationalization.

10.1 Historical Context of the AIIB and Its Member States

In recent years, Asia's economy has accounted for more than 30% of the global total, and its population accounts for more than 60% of the global total – it is arguably the region with the most economic vitality and growth potential in the world. However, due to limited construction funds, the construction of railways, highways, bridges, ports, airports, and telecommunications in some countries is seriously insufficient, which restricts economic development potential greatly. On October 2, 2013, President Xi held talks with President Susilo of Indonesia in Jakarta, saying that in order to promote connectivity and economic integration regionally, China would build the AIIB and provide financial support for infrastructure development in regional developing countries, including ASEAN members.

China's establishment of the AIIB has been widely supported in many parts of the world, and many countries have responded positively. Since the beginning of 2014, China has taken the lead in engaging with countries both inside and outside Asia. On October 24, 2014, finance ministers and authorized representatives of the founding member states signed a contract in Beijing to jointly set up the AIIB; the bank is headquartered in Beijing and has a legal capital of USD 100 billion. On June 29, 2015, the signing ceremony of the AIIB agreement (hereafter referred to Agreement) was held in Beijing.

10.2 Introduction and Distribution of AIIB's Signatories and Prospective Founding Members

By the end of 2016, there were 57 founding members of the AIIB, 37 of which are Asian countries; by July 28, 2020, the AIIB had 46 new members. As such, there are 103 prospective founding members. Table 10-1 elaborates on the global percentages of GDP and population from the AIIB's members. As Table 10-1 shows, these members made up 63.7% of the global GDP total, 73.1% of global purchasing power parity (PPP), and 78.9% of the global population. This underlines the importance of these 103 members and their support for China's initiative.

Table 10-1   Profile of Prospective Founding Members of the AIIB

Unit: USD million, %

Country	GDP	PPP	Pop.	Members	GDP	PPP	Pop.
Australia	13,762.6	13,648.4	25.6	Poland	5,658.5	12,869.2	38.0
Austria	4,477.2	4,793.6	9.0	Philippines	3,568.1	10,257.6	108.3
Azerbaijan	471.7	1,872.6	10.1	Denmark	3,471.8	3,128.4	5.8
Bangladesh	3,174.7	8,375.9	166.6	Kuwait	1,375.9	3,121.0	4.7
Brazil	18,470.2	34,563.6	210.0	South Africa	3,588.4	8,090.3	58.8
Cambodia	267.3	769.3	16.5	Lebanon	585.7	912.9	6.1
Brunei	124.6	359.2	0.4	Ghana	670.8	2,098.4	30.2
China	141,401.6	273,088.6	1,400.2	Algeria	1,727.8	6,814.0	43.4

(Continued)

Country	GDP	PPP	Pop.	Members	GDP	PPP	Pop.
Egypt	3,022.6	13,912.6	99.2	Togo	55.0	149.6	8.2
Finland	2,696.5	2,647.2	5.5	Hong Kong, China	3,729.9	4,908.8	7.6
France	27,070.7	30,611.4	64.8	Afghanistan	187.3	764.9	36.5
Georgia	159.3	454.0	3.7	Armenian	134.4	329.1	3.0
Germany	38,633.4	44,443.7	83.0	Fiji	57.1	108.7	0.9
Iceland	239.2	200.0	0.4	Timor-Leste	29.4	68.2	1.3
India	29,355.7	113,256.7	1351.8	Belgium	5,176.1	5,674.9	11.5
Indonesia	11,117.1	37,374.8	267.0	Canada	17,309.1	18,999.4	37.5
Iran	4,585.0	14,706.6	83.3	Ethiopia	911.7	2,401.7	95.6
Italy	19,886.4	24,427.7	60.4	Hungary	1,704.1	3,322.3	9.8
Israel	3,877.2	3,542.0	9.1	Ireland	3,849.4	4,128.0	5.0
Jordan	441.7	971.6	10.1	Peru	2,289.9	4,783.0	32.5
Kazakhstan	1,703.3	5,376.6	18.6	Sudan	308.7	1,759.9	43.2
South Korea	16,295.3	23,195.9	51.8	Venezuela	701.4	...	27.5
Kyrgyzstan	82.6	259.2	6.4	Chile	2,942.4	5,028.5	19.1
Laos	191.3	580.9	7.2	Greece	2,140.1	3,241.3	10.7
Luxemburg	694.5	668.5	0.6	Romania	2,437.0	5,465.9	19.5
Maldives	57.9	86.7	0.4	Bolivia	424.0	943.9	11.6
Malta	148.6	229.8	0.5	Cyprus	242.8	362.7	0.9
Mongolia	136.4	472.2	3.3	Bahrain	381.8	769.5	1.5
Myanmar	659.9	3,556.1	53.0	Samoa	9.1	12.4	0.2
Nipper	298.1	944.2	28.5	Argentina	4,454.7	9,035.4	45.1
Netherlands	9,023.6	10,052.7	17.2	Madagascar	125.5	459.7	27.1
New Zealand	2,046.7	2,062.3	5.0	Tonga	4.9	6.5	0.1
Norway	4,176.3	4,107.1	5.4	Cook Islands	...	...	...

(Continued)

Country	GDP	PPP	Pop.	Members	GDP	PPP	Pop.
Oman	766.1	2,039.6	4.3	Vanuatu	9.5	8.6	0.3
Pakistan	2,842.1	12,020.9	204.7	Belarus	625.7	1,956.0	9.5
Portugal	2,364.1	3,455.7	10.3	Ecuador	1,079.1	2,027.7	17.3
Qatar	1,918.5	3,658.4	2.8	Kenya	986.1	1,912.6	49.4
Russia	16,738.9	43,494.2	146.7	Papua new guinea	235.9	342.6	8.6
Saudi Arabia	7,792.9	18,985.1	34.1	Morocco	1,190.4	3,286.5	35.6
Singapore	3,628.2	5,850.6	5.7	Serbia	515.2	1,293.0	7.0
Spain	13,978.7	19,405.4	46.7	Libya	330.2	615.6	6.6
Sri Lanka	865.7	3,048.3	21.9	Cote d'Ivoire	444.4	1,171.1	26.3
Sweden	5,289.3	5,638.8	10.3	Guinea	133.7	332.7	13.6
Switzerland	7,153.6	5,656.5	10.3	Benin	143.7	407.2	11.8
Tajikistan	466.7	1,218.9	6.0	Rwanda	102.1	303.5	12.4
Malaysia	3,653.0	10,785.4	32.8	Tunisia	387.3	1,491.9	11.8
Turkey	7,437.1	23,465.8	83.0	Uruguay	599.2	829.7	3.5
The United Arab Emirates	4,057.7	7,463.5	10.7	Djibouti	31.7	60.0	1.1
UK	27,435.9	31,312.0	66.9	Croatia	607.0	1,125.9	4.1
Uzbekistan	604.9	2,972.2	33.0	Liberia	32.2	64.7	4.6
Vietnam	2,616.4	7,702.3	95.5	Senegal	239.4	646.0	16.8
Thailand	5,291.8	13,830.2	67.9	…	…	…	…
Total	551,236	1,035,506.2	5,957	Global	865,988.3	1,416,534.7	7,553.5
Global Percentage	63.7	73.1	78.9	…	…	…	…

Data source: www.aiib.org; the 57 prospective founding members; 103 members, www.imf.org.

Table 10-1 also shows that 41 of the 103 members are Asian countries, whose overall GDP and population account for 80% and 90% of Asia; 27 of the world's 39 nations categorized as developed are AIIB members, underlining its majority support amongst the developed world. Seventeen of the global top 20 economies (by size) are also members, with only the US, Japan, and Mexico not founding members.

10.3 Objectives, Capital Structure, and International Cooperation

The AIIB mainly invests in infrastructure construction in Asia, such as railways, roads, bridges, ports, airports, and telecommunications, so as to enhance support and promote development in Asia.

10.3.1 AIIB capital
The AIIB's authorized capital is 100 billion dollars, which is divided into 1 million shares with a par value of 100,000 dollars each. As of July 28, 2020, the total subscribed capital was 96.74 billion, with capital subscribed by Asian members accounting for 73.9 billion. China's subscribed capital amounted to 29.78 billion, 30.8% of the total (www.aiib.org).

10.3.2 Cooperation between the AIIB, World Bank, and IMF
Since the proposal for the establishment of the AIIB, the president of the World Bank, Mr. Kim Yong, the IMF president, Ms. Lagarde, and the president of the Asian Development Bank, Mr. Takehiko Nakao, have expressed their active support on several occasions. As the chief sponsor of the AIIB and an important shareholder of the World Bank and the ADB, China will actively promote cooperation between the AIIB and existing multilateral development banks such as the World Bank and the ADB in knowledge sharing, capacity building, personnel exchange, and project financing, etc.

10.3.3 Setting up the AIIB
From November 3–4, 2015, the eighth chief negotiator conference for preparation of the AIIB was held in Jakarta, Indonesia. According to the preparatory work plan, the AIIB will be formally established before the end of 2015 after the Agreement is approved by enough members with a sufficient share. (www.mof. gov.cn) On the morning of January 16, 2016, AIIB's opening ceremony was held in Beijing's Diaoyutai state hotel. President Xi attended and delivered a speech, emphasizing that through the joint efforts of all member states, the AIIB will become a professional, efficient, and clean new multilateral development bank of the 21st century.

10.4 Achievements

The AIIB ran started up business shortly after its establishment. "In the ten months of trial operation, AIIB has invested in six major projects, completed USD 809 million of investment, and is expected to complete USD 1.2 billion of project volume in 2016" (AIIB President Jin Liqun at the opening ceremony). Since its launch in January 2016, the AIIB has issued a total of USD 1.73 billion in loans to support nine infrastructure projects in seven countries: Pakistan, Bangladesh, Tajikistan, Indonesia, Myanmar, Azerbaijan, and Oman (*Daily Economic News*, January 17, 2017).

In addition to the significant expansion of AIIB membership as described above, its investment operation has also steadily expanded. According to Jin Liqun, president of the AIIB, up to now, independent projects account for about 40% of its total, with the rest co-financed with other multilateral development banks. The relevant data shows that since the establishment of the AIIB more than three years ago, the average loan total has been nearly USD 2.5 billion, and the average annual total loan volume has increased from 500 million in the previous two years to 1 billion.

10.5 Population and Economy amongst the BRICS

BRICS is an acronym that refers to Brazil, Russia, India, China, and South Africa, representing major emerging markets and developing economies in the world. Population, economy, and trade are the basis of finance and currency. This section briefly compares the differences in population, economy, and trade of the BRICS and their position in the world economy.

10.5.1 Population comparisons

The population is the basis of economic and social development. Table 10-2 shows a population comparison between the BRICS and other major countries and regions from 1000 to 2020. It shows that 1000 years ago, the total population of China and India made up nearly half of the world; in 1820, China's population exceeded one-third of the world's population; however, over the past 20 years, China's world population share has continued to decline, India's share has continued to rise slowly, Brazil's has also declined slightly, and Russia's population share has declined significantly as well. Despite this overall decline in the proportion of the global population, the BRICS still account for more than 40% of the world's population; in 2019, this figure was 41.93%.

Table 10-2 Historical Population Change between BRICS and Other Jurisdictions

Unit: %

Country/ Region	1000	1500	1820	1992	2002	2007	2011	2017	2019*	2020*
Brazil	...	...	...	2.9	2.9	2.9	2.9	2.8	2.8	2.8
Russia	2.7	3.9	5.3	2.8	2.4	2.2	2.1	2.0	1.9	1.9
India	28.0	25.1	20.1	16.8	17.3	17.5	17.7	17.8	17.9	17.9
China	22.0	23.5	36.6	22.3	20.9	20.1	19.6	18.8	18.5	18.4
South Africa	...	...	...	0.7	0.8	0.7	0.8	0.8	0.8	0.8
BRICS	52.6	52.5	61.9	45.5	44.2	43.4	43.0	42.2	41.9	41.8
BRICS ex China	30.6	29.0	25.3	23.2	23.3	23.3	23.4	23.4	23.4	23.4
Eurozone	...	...	...	5.7	5.2	5.0	4.8	4.6	4.5	4.5
US	...	0.5	1.0	4.9	4.7	4.6	4.5	4.4	4.4	4.3

Data source: "Development Centre Studies The World Economy A Millennial Perspective: A Millennial Perspective"; Russian data between 1000 and 1500 are data from the Soviet Union given by Professor Madison, and BRICS' data are those of the Soviet Union, India, and China; data after 1992 is estimated population data by IMF in October 2019; data in 2019 and 2020 are estimated data by IMF.

10.5.2 GDP comparison between BRICS and other jurisdictions and regions

Table 10-3 shows the GDP comparison of BRICS with other countries and regions from the year 1000 to 2020. The table shows that from 1000 to 1820, China and India accounted for 50% of the world's GDP. In 1820, China's GDP accounted for just under 1/3 of the world's GDP. In the past 20 years, China's GDP share has witnessed a significant increase. At the same time, the proportion of other BRICS countries also increased to varying degrees. The total proportion of GDP of the BRICS in 1992 was only 21.7% of the Euro area, whereas it surpassed the Euro area by 1.2% for the first time in 2011 and by 6.9% in 2015. According to forecast GDP data for the next few years released by IMF in October 2019, the proportion of BRICS' GDP in the world economy will exceed that of the US for the first time in 2020, and their role in the world economy will be further enhanced.

Table 10-3 Historical GDP Change between BRICS and Other Jurisdictions and Regions

Unit: %

Country/ Region	1000	1500	1820	1992	2002	2007	2011	2017	2019*	2020*
Brazil	...	...	...	1.5	1.5	2.4	3.6	2.6	2.1	2.1
Russia	2.4	3.4	5.4	0.4	1.1	2.4	2.8	2.0	1.9	1.8
India	28.9	24.5	16	1.2	1.5	2.1	2.5	3.3	3.4	3.5
China	22.7	25	32.9	2.0	4.3	6.1	10.3	15.0	16.3	16.9
South Africa	...	...	...	0.5	0.3	0.5	0.6	0.4	0.4	0.4
BRICS	54.1	52.9	54.4	5.5	8.6	13.6	19.7	23.3	24.2	24.8
BRICS ex China	31.3	27.9	21.5	3.6	4.4	7.4	9.4	8.3	7.8	7.9
Eurozone	...	...	...	26.6	20.7	22.1	18.6	15.7	15.4	15.2
US	...	...	...	10.8	11.7	14.8	16.9	16.3	16.1	16.0

Data source: Same as Table 10-2.

10.5.3 GDP per capita comparison

Using the data from Table 10-3, we can see the gap between the per capita GDP of the BRICS and other countries and regions. First of all, Table 10-3 shows that China's GDP in the world accounted for 16.3% in 2019, while Table 10-2 shows that China's population was 18.5% of the global total for the same year. China's per capita GDP of USD 10,100 was more than 80% of the world's per capita of USD 11,470, and the BRICS' GDP in the world accounted for 24.2% in 2019, while its population accounted for 41.9%. Per capita GDP in the BRICS is only 57.8% of the global per capita GDP, while the per capita GDP of the Eurozone and the US is 3.42 times and 5.68 times, respectively, that of the global average, underlying the still large gap between developing and developed economies.

10.6 Development and Cooperation amongst the BRICS

10.6.1 Early cooperation

In 2009, the leaders of China, Russia, India, and Brazil met in Yekaterinburg, Russia, and officially launched the cooperation mechanism. After several years of efforts and development, the BRIC mechanism has become important for cooperation between emerging market countries and developing countries. In 2010, the leaders of BRIC held their second meeting in Brazil. They mainly exchanged views on the world economic and financial situation and the reform of international financial institutions.

In 2011, the third BRIC leaders' meeting was held in Sanya, Hainan Province, China, and South Africa joined the BRIC cooperation mechanism as a full member. The "Sanya Declaration" adopted at the meeting made a detailed plan for the future cooperation of BRICS countries and reached a broad consensus on deepening exchange and cooperation in the fields of finance, industry and commerce, and energy. One of the important achievements of the Sanya summit was the five-member banks jointly signing the BRICS framework agreement on banking and financial cooperation, which proposed the steady expansion of local currency settlement and loan business, strengthening investment and capital raising cooperation in important projects, and carrying out capital market cooperation and information exchange.

10.6.2 New development in cooperation

BRICS leaders held their fourth meeting in India in 2012 and adopted the "Delhi Declaration," announcing the basic principles of the BRICS' integrated economy. During the meeting, the five development banks signed the "BRICS Banking Cooperation Mechanism in Multilateral Local Currency Master Facility Agreement" and "Multilateral Letter of Credit Confirmation Service Agreement," which strengthened their financial ties, underlined their new progress, and had epoch-making significance in promoting RMB application in major developing countries. According to the Agreement, China Development Bank, Brazil Development Bank, Russian Development and Foreign Economic Activities Bank, Export-Import Bank of India, and Southern African Development Bank of South Africa will steadily expand the scale of local currency settlement and loan business to serve the facilitation of trade and investment among BRICS' countries.

In 2013, BRICS leaders, at their fifth meeting in Durban, South Africa, designated the road map for the establishment of a development bank as an alternative to the World Bank. The meeting also proposed the establishment of a BRICS stability fund to play a preventive role in avoiding short-term capital flow pressure and strengthening global financial stability. The BRICS hope to launch their own platform in the world financial system (Xinhuanet July 14, 2014).

10.6.3 Implementation of cooperation

At the sixth summit held in Brazil in July 2020, the "Fortaleza Declaration" was jointly issued, launching the New Development Bank and establishing a BRICS emergency reserve fund. According to the plan, New Development Bank will begin operations in 2016, which will greatly simplify the mutual settlement and loan business between BRICS countries and reduce the dependence on the US dollar and Euro. Industry insiders generally believe that the bank will become an alternative to the International Monetary Fund and the World Bank. The establishment of the BRICS' emergency reserve fund (initially USD 100 billion) will also help create an emergency mechanism to deal with the international financial crisis.

10.6.4 The launch of the New Development Bank

In July 2015, the opening ceremony of the New Development Bank was held in Shanghai, with operations beginning in earnest in 2016. The bank will play its due role in the global market in the future.

10.6.5 Achievements of the bank

The New Development Bank has issued RMB 3 billion of green bonds in China's capital market. In terms of projects, seven projects were approved in 2016, all of which are sustainable development projects, with a total amount of USD 1.55 billion. In 2017, the BRICS bank also approved some new projects, and the total loan amount reached around USD 2.5 billion in 2017.

10.7 The AIIB Needs New Momentum

In just a few years from its inception to its formal establishment, the AIIB has gained the support of more than 80 countries and regions around the world, becoming the second-largest multilateral organization after the World Bank. However, despite the support of many countries and regions, the function of the AIIB needs to be supplemented by other complementary international institutions.

First of all, the AIIB is a multilateral international organization similar to the Asian Development Bank, the European Bank for Reconstruction and Development, the World Bank, and other international organizations. In fact, these organizations are policy-oriented financial institutions with the purpose of promoting regional development rather than making profits. The nature of the AIIB is actually similar to China Development Bank, Export-Import Bank of China, and Agricultural Development Bank of China, which is dedicated to the development of major domestic areas. Domestic policy banks are indispensable to national economic development, and international policy banks are also indispensable to regional development. Policy banks have their own policy advantages, but they also have their own limitations. Only by cooperating with other commercial banks can they effectively promote the development of the national economy, trade, science, and technology.

The same is true in the international market. The regional development banks use the strength of the main sponsor countries to promote the development of regional infrastructure and other fields, so as to promote the development of economy and trade. However, these development banks alone are far from enough – they must cooperate closely with other commercial banks. The AIIB is an effective complement to the ADB, working with it to promote infrastructure construction and development in Asia. However, the AIIB is a policy-oriented international institution; thus, it is difficult to directly mobilize domestic and foreign market forces to effectively promote this as well as the Belt and Road initiative. Therefore, creating an international commercial bank with RMB as the main capital, that is internationalized, commercialized, and market-oriented can form an effective supplement to the AIIB, and can also share the relevant investment risks. In turn, this promotes the development of the Asian economy more effectively with both policy and commercial aspects.

Finally, there are 27 developed economies in the 103 member states of the AIIB, accounting for 27.94% of the AIIB's equity. Developed economies have their own experience and advantages in banking and other international businesses, despite often making up a relatively low proportion. These developed economies cannot be effectively tied up through the equity of the AIIB, which makes it difficult to mobilize their enthusiasm. Chapter Eleven introduces the importance of close cooperation between China and Europe and further introduces the necessity of establishing international commercial banks complementary to the AIIB.

10.8 Promoting the Modernization of National Governance to the Successful Operation of the AIIB and the New Development Bank

From the perspective of shareholder range and global coverage, the New Development Bank has created a precedent for global south-south cooperation. The successful establishment of this and the AIIB will play an important role in reforming the global monetary system, the development of Asian trade and financial markets, and the implementation of the Belt and Road initiative.

However, the operation level of any institution completely depends on its governance, and the governance of the AIIB and the New Development Bank almost completely depends on the governance level of the main member states or shareholders. The existing major international institutions, such as the World Bank and the IMF, were initiated by major developed countries for many years and are mainly managed and operated by them. The political and legal systems and governance levels of these major developed countries are similar, so it is relatively easier to be cooperative and coordinated. However, there are great differences in the political and legal systems and national governance level among AIIB member states. Even among the five major developing countries of the New Development Bank, there are also great differences in national governance. There are institutional obstacles for these banks to reach their full potential.

10.9 Conclusion

In a short period of time, the AIIB has received a positive response and smooth launch from more than 80 countries and regions, which indicates support from many countries for China's strategic initiatives and, in fact, for RMB internationalization. The launch of the New Development Bank marks that the cooperation among the BRICS countries over the years has begun to blossom, and the results are just around the corner. The BRICS as a whole have more influence on the international stage than China alone, and they are more representative of global developing countries. China's Belt and Road initiative and the nationalization of the RMB will also be greatly promoted by making full use of the BRICS platform and further enhancing cooperation.

The results from this chapter show that although China's economic scale has exceeded that of the other four BRICS since 2009, there is still a certain gap between China and other BRICS in many aspects, especially in foreign exchange market reform and development. Therefore, strengthening cooperation with other BRICS will help promote RMB nationalization and China's financial reform and development, as well as the development of all BRICS nations and other emerging markets. In particular, it is worth noting that India, the largest country in South Asia, is a founding member of the AIIB and the New Development Bank. However, India has not yet signed an RMB currency swap agreement with China. Moreover, from 2008 to 2018, India's trade dependence on China dropped from 8.5% to 3.2%, ranking third from the bottom among China's 25 major Asian trading partners, showing that there is still great potential for more cooperation.

The New Development Bank has broad prospects and great potential, but its development will not be smooth sailing. Over the past year, Western media have pointed out many future challenges for the formal establishment and development of the New Development Bank. The biggest challenge is not internal strife but corruption in the recipient countries. The AIIB and the New Development Bank, which mainly serve emerging economies and developing countries, will indeed face relevant challenges in the future. Promoting the modernization of China's national governance will be important for the bank to realize its potential.

CHAPTER ELEVEN

The Mutual Relationship between the B&R Initiative and RMB Internationalization

Since president xi first put forward the Belt and Road (B&R) Initiative in 2013, the economic cooperation between China and countries along the B&R has been strengthened, which has encouraged RMB internationalization. On August 27, 2018, President Xi pointed out in his speech on the implementation of the B&R Initiative that it was necessary to improve financial security, speed up the formation of a policy system, promote RMB internationalization in an orderly manner, guide social funds to jointly invest in infrastructure and resource development projects in countries along the route, and provide foreign exchange fund support for outgoing enterprises. This speech pointed out the core relationship between the B&R Initiative and RMB internationalization. After RMB internationalization is raised to a higher level, the proportion of RMB that enterprises can use directly to support the B&R Initiative will increase, and the corresponding demand for foreign exchange funds will naturally decrease. This chapter briefly introduces the population, economic, and trade scale distribution of countries along the B&R and analyzes the significance of cooperation connecting China and Europe. This should help us to gain a clearer understanding of the impact of the B&R Initiative on global economic trade and its relationship with RMB internationalization.

11.1 Belt and Road (B&R) Initiative

In September and October 2013, President Xi proposed building a new Silk Road Economic Belt and the 21st Century Maritime Silk Road, respectively – together, they are referred to as the "B&R." The 21st Century Maritime Silk Road is proposed to further deepen cooperation between China and ASEAN and build a closer community with a shared future. The B&R spans Asia and Europe and involves more than 60 countries or regions along the route, including Southeast Asia, South Asia, Central Asia, West Asia, and Central and Eastern Europe. In fact, the broader "B&R" also connects Africa through West Asia and Europe. The B&R Initiative will become the longest-span economic corridor in the world, ending in China, running through Asia and even parts of Europe, and connecting Africa via West Asia and Europe. The B&R proposal is held in high esteem by Chinese, foreign media, and investment circles; its effective implementation will shift the dynamics of the global economy and trade.

11.2 Distribution of Population and Economic Scale in B&R Countries

Table 11-1 presents the distribution data of population, GDP, and per capita GDP in East Asia, Southeast Asia, South Asia, Central Asia, West Asia, and Central and Western Europe since 2003.

Table 11-1   Global Proportion of Population, GDP, and Per Capita GDP of B&R Related Regions

Unit: %

Global Proportion of Population	2003	2007	2010	2014	2015	2016	2017	2018	2019	2020
Eastern Asia	23.9	23.2	22.6	22.0	21.9	21.8	21.6	21.5	21.3	21.1
Mainland China	20.6	20.0	19.6	19.1	19.0	18.9	18.7	18.6	18.5	18.3
Southeastern Asia	8.6	8.6	8.6	8.7	8.7	8.7	8.7	8.7	8.7	8.7
Southern Asia	22.9	23.2	23.4	23.6	23.6	23.6	23.6	23.6	23.6	23.7
Central Asia	0.9	0.9	0.9	0.9	0.9	1.0	1.0	1.0	1.0	1.0
Western Asia	4.5	4.7	4.9	4.8	4.8	4.9	4.9	4.9	5.0	5.0

(Continued)

Global Proportion of Population	2003	2007	2010	2014	2015	2016	2017	2018	2019	2020
Asia	60.8	60.6	60.5	60.0	59.9	59.8	59.7	59.6	59.5	59.4
Asia Excluding Eastern Asia	37.0	37.5	37.8	38.0	38.0	38.1	38.1	38.2	38.2	38.3
Central and Eastern Europe	5.2	4.9	4.7	4.5	4.4	4.4	4.3	4.3	4.2	4.2
Countries along the B&R	42.2	42.4	42.5	42.4	42.4	42.4	42.4	42.4	42.4	42.5
Countries along the B&R plus China	62.8	62.4	62.1	61.5	61.4	61.3	61.2	61.1	60.9	60.8
Western Europe	6.3	6.1	6.0	5.8	5.7	5.7	5.7	5.6	5.6	5.5
Countries along the B&R plus China and Western Europe	69.0	68.5	68.0	67.3	67.2	67.0	66.8	66.7	66.5	66.3

GDP	2003	2007	2010	2014	2015	2016	2017	2018	2019	2020
Eastern Asia	18.7	17.0	20.5	22.5	23.9	24.4	24.5	25.2	25.7	27.2
Mainland China	4.2	6.1	9.1	13.3	14.9	14.8	15.2	16.2	16.8	18.2
Southeastern Asia	2.0	2.4	3.1	3.3	3.4	3.5	3.5	3.6	3.7	3.7
Southern Asia	2.0	2.6	3.1	3.2	3.6	3.8	4.1	4.0	4.1	3.6
Central Asia	0.1	0.3	0.3	0.5	0.4	0.4	0.3	0.3	0.3	0.3
Western Asia	2.9	4.1	4.5	4.8	4.5	4.4	4.4	4.3	4.4	4.1
Asia	25.8	26.4	31.6	34.3	35.7	36.5	36.8	37.4	38.2	39.0
Asia Excluding Eastern Asia	7.1	9.4	11.0	11.8	11.9	12.1	12.4	12.2	12.5	11.8
Central and Eastern Europe	3.1	5.0	4.9	4.8	3.9	3.7	4.1	4.2	4.2	4.1
Countries along the B&R	10.2	14.4	15.9	16.7	15.7	1538	16.5	16.4	16.7	15.8
Countries along the B&R plus China	14.4	20.5	25.1	30.0	30.6	30.6	31.7	32.6	33.6	34.0

(Continued)

Global Proportion of Population	2003	2007	2010	2014	2015	2016	2017	2018	2019	2020
Western Europe	30.6	30.0	25.3	23.3	21.7	21.5	21.1	21.4	20.4	20.4
Countries along the B&R plus China and Western Europe	45.0	50.5	50.3	53.3	52.3	52.0	52.8	54.0	54.0	54.4

Per Capita GDP	2003	2007	2010	2014	2015	2016	2017	2018	2019	2020
Eastern Asia	78.3	73.3	90.8	101.9	109.1	112.3	113.2	117.2	120.7	128.8
Mainland China	20.7	30.5	46.6	69.8	78.3	78.3	81.1	86.8	91.0	99.3
Southeastern Asia	23.4	28.3	35.4	37.9	38.8	40.1	40.7	41.1	42.6	42.9
Southern Asia	8.9	11.2	13.4	13.7	15.2	16.2	17.5	16.9	17.3	15.3
Central Asia	16.4	31.4	37.7	48.1	44.6	37.1	35.9	34.7	35.5	35.4
Western Asia	63.7	86.1	92.2	101.2	93.1	90.8	89.4	87.6	88.7	81.6
Asia	42.4	43.5	52.2	57.1	59.7	61.0	61.7	62.7	64.2	65.6
Asia excluding Eastern Asia	19.2	25.1	29.2	31.1	31.2	31.7	32.5	32.0	32.7	30.7
Central and Eastern Europe	58.6	102.5	104.0	108.1	87.1	85.3	94.9	98.9	100.4	97.7
Countries along the B&R	24.1	34.1	37.5	39.3	37.0	37.2	38.8	38.7	39.4	37.3
Countries along the B&R plus China	23.0	32.9	40.3	48.7	49.8	49.9	51.8	53.4	55.1	56.0
Western Europe	488.5	492.0	424.7	403.4	377.8	376.0	372.9	380.6	366.9	368.3
Countries along the B&R plus China and Western Europe	65.2	73.8	74.0	79.2	77.9	77.6	79.0	81.0	81.2	82.0

Data source: Population and GDP data was released by the IMF in October 2020, and the data of per capita GDP is calculated from GDP and population. The 2020 data was predicted by the IMF in October 2020.

11.2.1 Population distribution of the B&R related areas

Table 11-1 shows that the population proportion of countries along the B&R increased from 42.2% to 42.5% between 2003 and 2020. Moreover, when China was included, the population proportion decreased slightly from 62.8% to 60.8%. It is worth noting that from 2003 to 2020, the population of South Asia grew the fastest of these areas; in 2020, the total population of South Asia exceeded East Asia for the first time, becoming the most populous region in the world and accounting for nearly a quarter of the global population.

11.2.2 GDP of B&R countries

As shown in Table 11-1, the share of the Asian economy of the world rose from 25.8% to 39.0% between 2003 and 2020. It exceeded Europe's GDP share for the first time in 2010, becoming the world's largest economic region. However, Asia's economic development is quite uneven. With the exception of East Asia's GDP accounting for nearly a quarter of the global economy, West, South, and Southeast Asia each accounts for about 4% in the world, while Central Asia accounts for less than 1%. What's more, In recent years, the total economic scale of Central and Eastern European countries accounts for 4%, slightly higher than South Asia, and the total GDP of B&R countries accounts for only about 16% of the world. Since 2019, China's GDP has exceeded this.

11.2.3 GDP per capita distribution

Table 11-1 shows that in recent years, in addition to the relatively high per capita GDP in East and West Asia, which exceeds or approaches the global average level, the per capita GDP of Central and Eastern European countries has significantly decreased to 90% or so by 2014. The per capita GDP of Southeast Asia has continued to increase from 20% to more than 40% of the average, while the per capita GDP of Central Asia is slightly lower than that of South Asia, and the per capita GDP of South Asia has continued to rise from less than 10% to nearly 20% of the average, though remains the lowest in the entire B&R-related region. The average GDP per capita of all the countries along the B&R is only close to 40% of the global level, indicating that economic development in these countries or regions has great potential.

11.2.4 Trade distribution along the B&R and China

Although the countries or regions of East Asia remain China's most important trading partners, the proportion of China's trade with the countries or regions of East Asia has declined on the whole for more than a decade; at the same time, the proportion of China's trade with Southeast Asia, West Asia, South Asia, and Central Asia has continued to rise; many major countries in Southeast Asia, West

Asia, South Asia, and Central Asia still have low dependence on China's trade as well as a great room for growth. The B&R Initiative will further promote the development of the economy and trade between China and these countries or regions to attain mutual benefit.

11.3 International Influence and Significance of the B&R Initiative

With influence ranging across Eurasia, the Western Pacific, and Indian Ocean regions, the B&R Initiative will have a huge impact on economic trade and the financial markets of Asia, Eurasia, and even the world.

11.3.1 Medium-and long-term economic growth trends

Table 11-2 and the relevant data show that between 1700 and 1820, the sum of the GDP of China accounted for nearly half of the world, when Asia had been the center of the world economy for the majority of the past two thousand years. Table 11-2 shows a GDP comparison of the major economies from 1700 to 1980: due to factors such as the European Industrial Revolution, by the late 1880s, Europe had replaced Asia as the world's largest economy; however, Europe's position remained for only half a century, with the US replacing Europe as the world's largest economy by 1943, and by the end of WWII, the US had surpassed the whole of the European economy and accounted for 46.8% of the world's total.

Between 1820 and 1850, significant and sustained economic growth occurred in Europe and America. However, China's economic growth slowed significantly, being only 30% of the average annual growth rate between 1770 and 1820. From 1850 to 1880, Europe and the US continued to grow significantly, while China declined significantly. Owing to both external factors like aggression by the Great Powers and internal factors, such as failures from the Qing government to modernize science and technology, China fell badly behind Europe. With the industrial revolution and global plunder, Europe surpassed Asia for the first time around 1890. However, due to internal conflicts resulting in two world wars, the European economy suffered serious damage. By the end of WWII, America had become the largest economy, initiating the Bretton-Woods system and setting up various global institutions. Nowadays, the B&R Initiative will provide new opportunities for European economic recovery.

Table 11-2   Middle-and-Long Term Economic Scale, Annual Growth Rate, and Scale
Distribution of China, Asia, Europe, and the US from 1700 to 1980

Unit: 0.1 billion International Geary – Khamis dollars, %

Economic Scale	1700	1820	1850	1880	1913	1943	1945	1974	1980
China	828	2,286	2,472	1,897	2,414	2,705	2,632	7,519	10,411
Asia	2,015	3,866	4,105	3,898	6,121	8,050	6,628	64,870	87,247
Europe	812	1,599	2,613	3,771	9,022	13,400	11,200	41,851	48,492
Asia and Europe	2,827	5,465	6,718	7,669	15,143	21,450	17,828	106,721	135,739
US	5	125	426	984	5,174	15,811	16,448	35,267	42,306
Total	2,832	5,590	7,144	8,653	20,317	37,261	34,276	141,988	178,045

Compound Growth Rate	1700	1820	1850	1880	1913	1943	1945	1974	1980
China	...	0.85	0.26	−0.88	0.73	0.38	−1.35	3.69	5.57
Asia	...	0.54	0.20	−0.17	1.38	0.92	−9.26	8.18	5.06
Europe	...	0.57	1.65	1.23	2.68	1.33	−8.57	4.65	2.48
Asia and Europe	...	0.55	0.69	0.44	2.08	1.17	−8.83	6.36	4.09
US	...	2.68	4.16	2.83	5.16	3.79	1.99	2.79	3.08
Average	...	0.57	0.82	0.64	2.62	2.04	−4.09	5.02	3.84

Distribution of Economic Scale	1700	1820	1850	1880	1913	1943	1945	1974	1980
China	29.23	40.89	34.60	21.92	11.88	7.26	7.68	5.30	5.85
Asia	71.23	69.16	57.46	45.05	30.13	21.60	19.34	45.69	49.00
Europe	28.66	28.60	36.58	43.58	44.41	35.96	32.68	29.47	27.24
Asia and Europe	99.82	97.75	94.04	88.63	74.53	57.56	52.01	75.16	76.24
Total	100.00	100.00	100.00	100.00	100.00	100.00	100.00	100.00	100.00

Data source: The data from 1700 to 1820 comes from the paper, "Development Center Studies the World Economy a Millennial Perspective: A Millennial Perspective," written by Professor Maddison and released by the OECD.

11.4 International Recognition of the B&R Initiative

11.4.1 Response of relevant countries and international organizations

After President Xi proposed the B&R Initiative in 2013, it soon received many positive responses from relevant countries and regions. First, more than 70 countries and international organizations expressed their willingness to cooperate, and more than 30 countries signed a co-construction agreement with China. Second, financial support to the B&R Initiative was shown by the AIIB, and the Silk Road Fund was initiated by China. Third, the interconnection network was gradually formed. In the construction of the China-Pakistan, China-Mongolia, and China-Russia economic corridors, the partners have made preliminary achievements in infrastructure, finance, humanities, and other fields. The number of countries or regions that have signed B&R cooperation agreements with China is over 30 – over 50% of nations along the B&R.

The B&R Initiative is initiated by China but provides opportunities for the world. The proposal of this initiative conforms to the universal call of Eurasia to develop and cooperate and marks the rapid transition of China from a participant in the international system to a provider of public goods. The B&R initiated by China upholds the principle of co-negotiation, co-construction, and sharing instead of expansionism.

11.4.2 The United Nations' response to the B&R Initiative

On March 17, 2017, the United Nations Security Council unanimously adopted resolution 2344 on Afghanistan by 15 votes. It called on the international community to gather consensus on assistance to Afghanistan, strengthen regional economic cooperation through the B&R Initiative, and urge all parties to provide a safe and secure environment for the implementation, strengthen the docking of development policies, and promote practical cooperation in connectivity. The Council unanimously adopted resolution 2344, which, for the first time, enshrined the concept of "building a community of human destiny," embodied international consensus, and highlighted the framework proposed by China to promote global governance.

11.4.3 Updates on the B&R Initiative

On May 14, 2017, guests from more than 100 countries gathered in Beijing to participate in the B&R International Cooperation Summit Forum. On March 23, 2019, Italy became the first G7 member to join the B&R Initiative.

Between April 25–27, 2019, the second B&R International Cooperation Summit Forum was held in Beijing as scheduled. As of January 2020, China has signed 200 cooperation documents relevant to the B&R Initiative with 138 countries and 30 international organizations along the B&R.

11.4.4 Surveys on the five-year implementation of the B&R Initiative

Officially released at the International Financial Forum on June 21, 2018, the *B&R 5th Anniversary Report* consists of collected questionnaires from central banks of 26 representative countries or regions. It summarized the achievements, problems, and experiences in China's bilateral or multilateral cooperation with other countries under the B&R Initiative over the past five years. As is shown in the report, 63% of central banks consider the B&R Initiative of extreme importance and also one of the most important global initiatives of the past decade. In the report, 25% of the interviewees were even more optimistic, supposing annual economic growth brought by the initiative to be 2%–5%; 35% thought the B&R Initiative was more significant to their country than the IMF; 21% considered it more important than the World Bank; 14% thought it more important than the projects initiated by regional development agencies. As shown in the questionnaire, the biggest obstacles to the development of B&R projects are the legal framework, financing, government departments, and credit ratings (in that order).

11.5 Broad Cooperation Is Necessary

In order to strengthen financial support for the B&R Initiative, in addition to the establishment of the AIIB and the Silk Road Fund, China is also strengthening cooperation with other regional development banks. This section will briefly introduce this cooperation between China and other regional development banks.

11.5.1 Joining the African Development Bank in 1985

The African Development Bank was formally established in 1964, beginning operations on July 1, 1966, and headquartered in Abidjan, the economic center of Côte d'Ivoire. In 2002, due to political instability in Côte d'Ivoire, the headquarters were relocated to Tunisia. The African Development Bank is the largest intergovernmental development finance institution in Africa. With its goal to promote economic development and social progress in Africa, China became a member in May 1985. By the end of 2006, China held 24230 shares, accounting for 11.17% of the total of the African Development Bank (www.afdb.org).

11.5.2 Joining the Inter-American Development Bank in 2009

Established on December 30, 1959, the Inter-American Development Bank (IDB) is the first and largest regional and multilateral development bank headquartered in Washington. With 20 founding members (19 Latin American countries and the US), the membership of the IDB by the end of 2006 consisted of 28 countries in the Americas, including the US and Brazil, and 19 non-Americas members, including Japan, the UK, Germany, and South Korea. China formally applied for IDB admission in 1993 and again in 2004. After the international financial crisis of 2008, the IDB was eager for China to join, making China the 48th member of the Inter-American Development Bank in January 2009 and the fourth country in Asia to join (www.iadb.org).

11.5.3 Third-largest shareholder of the Asian Development Bank

Headquartered in Manila, the capital of the Philippines, the Asian Development Bank (ADB) was founded on November 24, 1966. On February 17, 1986, the ADB council adopted resolution 176, by which it agreed to admit the People's Republic of China as a member. By the end of June 2020, the ADB contained 68 members, 49 of which were from the Asia-Pacific. In respect of share size, China ranks third at 6.643%, while Japan and the US have an equal top share at 15.571% each and a one-vote veto power.

In the re-election of the board of directors in April 1987, China was elected as a member state and obtained a separate seat on the board. In 1986, the Chinese government designated the PBC as China's official contact with the ADB and its custodian bank in China, responsible for China's ties with ADB and the custody of its holdings of RMB and other assets in China. On June 16, 2000, the ADB Representative Office in China was established in Beijing.

11.5.4 Joining the European Bank for reconstruction and development

China's application to join the European Bank for Reconstruction and Development (EBRD) will not only help China expand its influence in international financial institutions, but also help Europe increase financing channels; it will also vigorously drive China-EU cooperation in infrastructure investment, regional development, and RMB internationalization. On January 15, 2016, the State Council of the PRC decided to join the EBRD Establishment Agreement and accepted the resolution on China's membership, becoming an official member.

11.6 Improving Economic and Trade Cooperation along the B&R

Full implementation of RMB internationalization depends on the wide acceptance of cross-border trade and investment and financing of RMB. With the
deepening implementation of the B&R Initiative, economic and trade development between China and countries along the B&R will continue to improve. In
2019, the gross import and export of Chinese goods were RMB 31.54 trillion, up
by 3.4% from 2018, while that of the EU, the US, and ASEAN increased by 8.0%,
10.7%, and 14.1%, respectively. Russia, Poland, and Kazakhstan increased by
7.9%, 18.4%, and 15.5%, respectively, all of which were higher than overall trade
growth. In RMB, China's imports and exports to countries along the B&R in
2019 total were 9.13 trillion yuan, an annual increase of 10.8%, 7.4% higher than
China's overall foreign trade growth rate, and accounting for 28.9% of China's
total foreign trade value. Of this, the export value was 5.17 trillion yuan – up by
13.2%; the import value of 3.96 trillion yuan was up by 8.1%. This indicates that
the cooperation between China and countries along the B&R has a significant
boost effect on both imports and exports.

11.7 The Importance of China-EU Cooperation for the B&R
Initiative

According to the data in Table 11-1, countries along the B&R account for over
40% of the global population, but for 1/6 of the global GDP, and their average per
capita GDP is only equivalent to 40% of the global average. Meanwhile, despite
only accounting for 6% of the global population, Western Europe makes up over
25% of global GDP, four times over the per capita average and nearly ten times
the average of countries along the B&R. Essentially, most countries along the
B&R are generally poor, and their social and political stability is relatively low.
Therefore, both the B&R Initiative and the realization of its effect on the economy
and trade take time. With most of the countries being developed countries,
Western Europe plays an important role in global finance and technology, so it is
beneficial for China to promote cooperation with this region.

The EU surpassed the US and Japan in 2003 and 2004, respectively, to
become China's largest trading partner, maintaining this position for more than
a decade. Despite the fact that the EU is China's largest trading partner and that
the economic, trade, and financial cooperation between major EU countries and
China has accelerated in recent years, the popularity of Euro-RMB clearing in

China-EU cross-border trade still needs to improve significantly. The proportion of RMB clearing in Germany and France is still low compared with the proportion of trade between both countries and China. Therefore, improving the popularity of RMB and Euro clearing can help RMB internationalization as well as the status of the Euro and pound in international clearing.

11.7.1 Increase the utilization rate

The UK and the Eurozone have signed 350 billion yuan foreign exchange swap agreements with China that have not yet been used. In recent years, China's trade with the Eurozone has exceeded six times its trade with the UK – yet the total amount of RMB foreign exchange swap agreements signed between the Eurozone and China is only the same as those signed with the UK, indicating that there is much more potential for financial cooperation between China and the Eurozone.

11.7.2 Increase financial cooperation with countries along the B&R

The introduction of strategic investors in China's banking industry more than a decade ago was actually aimed at creating successful listings – there was no real strategic cooperation with investors at that time. Ten years later, China's banking sector has made great achievements in its restructuring and development, and major Chinese banks have also made significant improvements in management and risk control, building a solid foundation. So far, China's major banks and some joint-stock banks have foreign partners holding part of their shares, while several large banks and joint-stock banks in China have successfully acquired the assets of some foreign banks abroad.

However, large banks and joint-stock banks in China still rarely hold shares of major foreign banks till now. In order to accelerate the B&R Initiative and promote RMB internationalization, especially in an environment where European finance has been affected by the European debt crisis in recent years, China can deepen its bond with Europe by holding some shares of listed companies that engage in banking, securities, insurance, and the like through the open market and other channels. This is helpful in providing international experiences for the operation of Chinese banks and other enterprise and allows both China and Europe to play to their strengths.

11.7.3 European Participation in the B&R Initiative

On September 17, 2018, the European Commission proposed a foreign policy plan to strengthen links to Asian infrastructure construction in the transportation, energy, and digital sectors. This was not intended to counter similar plans in China, according to the EU. Wildenfeld Yang, an expert on Europe-China relations at the German Mercato Center for China Research, said the EU's plan is largely in response to the B&R Initiative (Brussels September 19, 2018).

11.8 Interaction between the B&R Initiative and RMB Internationalization

Since reforming the RMB exchange rate in August 2005, the amplitude of the RMB exchange rate has been increasing, and enterprises and financial institutions engaging in cross-border trade, investment, and financing are facing increasingly greater exchange rate risks that can erode operating profits through exchange rate fluctuations. Increasing the use of RMB in cross-border trade, financing, and investment can not only effectively reduce the exchange risk, but also play a positive role in improving competitiveness in Chinese enterprises. Therefore, the higher the level of RMB internationalization, the more potential advantages for the B&R Initiative.

Supposing that the level of RMB internationalization stays the same or even falls, overseas investment, including B&R investment, will tend to create more overseas demand for the dollar. Only when the internationalization level of RMB continues to improve and the financing costs of all projects in the B&R region are controllable, can the foreign exchange risk be effectively reduced. Therefore, the continuous improvement of RMB internationalization is essential for the B&R Initiative.

On the other hand, only on the premise of improving RMB internationalization, will there be a positive relationship between the B&R Initiative and the effect of RMB internationalization. In other words, the promotion of RMB internationalization and the B&R Initiative are complementary.

Over the past six years since the B&R Initiative, China's economic and trade investment cooperation with the countries along the B&R has achieved remarkable results, and the cooperation has been expanding. The data show that China exports mainly mechanical and electrical products to the countries along the B&R. Among the imported products, the proportion of electrical equipment and fossil fuels is the highest. Private enterprises contributed 43% of the trade volume. Among countries along the B&R, South Korea, Vietnam, Malaysia, India, Russia, and other countries are the most important trading partners (*Big Data Report on B&R Initiative in 2018*).

From 2013 to 2018, the total volume of foreign trade between China and countries along the B&R reached USD 6469.2 billion. The overall growth rate of trade with these countries was higher than that of China's foreign trade, becoming an important force for the accelerated recovery of China's foreign trade. The implementation of the B&R has created 244,000 jobs for nations along the B&R; projects over USD 500 billion in combined value have been newly signed, 82 overseas economic and trade cooperation zones have been built, and FDI has exceeded USD 80 billion (Digital Transcripts on Achievements of the Five-Year Implementation of the B&R Initiative).

In 2019, Chinese investors made non-financial direct investments to 6,535 overseas enterprises in 167 countries or regions, with a total cumulative investment of 762.97 billion yuan, down by 4.3% year on year; the completed turnover of foreign contracted projects is 1192.75 billion yuan, up by 6.6% year on year; the newly contracted projects are worth 1795.33 billion yuan, up by 12.2% year on year; 487,000 workers of all kinds have been exported in foreign labor cooperation; there were still 992,000 workers staying abroad at the end of 2019. China's investment under the B&R Initiative has had steady progress, continuous optimization of investment structure, and a large number of foreign contracting projects, driving local development and realizing mutual benefits.

11.9 Obstacles to RMB along the B&R

The higher the level of RMB internationalization, the more frequent the use of RMB in the whole overseas market, and the greater the currency support of RMB to the B&R Initiative. Since the level of RMB internationalization still needs to be improved, there are still various obstacles to its popularization along the B&R. In 2019, China and B&R countries dealt with over RMB 273 trillion of cross-border receipts and payments, up by 32% year on year and more than double the figure from three years before. Companies along the B&R still use RMB most in clearing products, accounting for more than half of all RMB products, while financing products and deposit products account for 10% or so each, and fund and cash products account for less than 10% together.

Although RMB use along the B&R has increased significantly in recent years, there are still many obstacles – especially the gap between RMB and other major international currencies. These obstacles are mainly as follows: complex and changeable political environment of countries or regions along the B&R; the dual vulnerability of internal "high leveraged plus foreign capitalization" and external "high foreign debt plus deficit" caused by the less developed financial system of the countries along the B&R; strong control of foreign exchange and relying more on major currencies like the US dollar and Euro; the absence of a completed RMB use system. The overcoming of these obstacles will have a significant role in promoting RMB internationalization. In addition, the narrowing of the gap between RMB and major currencies will also reduce the dependence of countries along the B&R on the latter. These results actually demonstrate the need for accelerating RMB internationalization to provide higher international currency support for the B&R Initiative.

11.10 Conclusion

As one of the most promising projects of recent human history, the B&R Initiative provides an opportunity for global development and has received overwhelming support from China and countries along the B&R in the past five years, as well as being recognized by the United Nations.

In recent years, the B&R Initiative has been promoted and implemented in many fields and directions. However, any form of international trade, investment, commerce, technology, and culture needs to be supported by an international currency. In some ways, RMB internationalization is a necessary condition for the B&R Initiative.

The AIIB has set up a good platform for mutual benefit. However, the non-profit nature of the AIIB as an international multilateral platform and its equity calculation method based on GDP are difficult to mobilize and give full play to the international business experience of major countries in Western Europe, which are necessary and urgently needed to promote the B&R Initiative. Therefore, the establishment of the "Asia-Europe Bank" with the concept of internationalization, marketization, and commercialization can better tie the interests of China and Western Europe, thereby effectively promoting the B&R Initiative.

CHAPTER TWELVE

The Role of Capital Markets in Technological Innovation

THE STOCK MARKET IS NOT ONLY an important part of the global financial market, but also an important financing channel for science and technology companies; it plays an irreplaceable role in the global science and technology field as well as financial markets. The stock market is mainly traded within the borders of various countries, and the proportion of international exchange is relatively low. According to statistics, the average daily turnover of the global stock market is only USD 300 billion to 400 billion, far lower than the global foreign exchange market, which has an average daily turnover of several trillion dollars. Consequently, most research on currency internationalization pays less attention to the stock market. However, the stock market is of indescribable importance to the financing of science and technology enterprise and to the exit mechanism of various venture capital funds. Out of consideration for this, this chapter includes a targeted introduction and analysis of the relevant changes in the global stock market and its role in global technological innovation. At the same time, it also uses relevant enterprise data with the largest R&D investment in the world in recent years (released by the EU) to analyze the pursuit of scientific and technological dividends, the smoothness of R&D investment channels, and the investment heat in major scientific and technological innovation fields in major countries and regions.

12.1 Market Value Distribution of Global Stock Markets

12.1.1 Market value distribution in recent years

Table 12-1 shows that in recent years, the market capitalization of the two major US exchanges has taken the lead, ranking first and second in the world. The market capitalization of the Japan Exchange Group, Shanghai Stock Exchange (SSE), Hong Kong Stock Exchange (HKSE), Euronext, the London Stock Exchange Group, and Shenzhen Stock Exchange ranks 3rd to 8th in the global order. Compared with 2008, the total market capitalization of the top eight exchanges has increased significantly, from 55.7% to 69.0%. Over the same period, the proportion of the total market value of the top 16 exchanges has also increased from 72.5% to 85.3%, showing the continuous concentration of global stock markets after the international financial crisis. From 2008 to 2019, the market value growth of the Shenzhen Stock Exchange climbed to first place with a compound annual growth rate of 22.88%. The exchanges that ranked second to sixth in terms of growth rate during the same period were the NASDAQ Stock Exchange (US), Hong Kong Stock Exchange (HKSE), National Stock Exchange of India, Shanghai Stock Exchange (SSE), and Mumbai Stock Exchange. The corresponding annual compound growth rates were 17.29%, 12.59%, 12.36%, 12.30%, and 11.67%, respectively. In addition to NASDAQ, the five other exchanges with the fastest growth in market capitalization in the world belong to the two major developing countries, China and India, confirming how rapid growth of the stock market and rapid economic development often go hand-in-hand.

Table 12-1   Top 16 Stock Exchanges with a Global Market Value over One Trillion Dollars Distribution of the Year-End Market Value (2008–2019)

Unit: Trillion dollars, %

Stock Exchange	2008	2010	2011	2013	2015	2016	2018	2019	AAGR
New York Stock Exchange (NYSE)	9.21	13.39	11. 80	17.95	17.79	19.57	20.68	23. 33	8.82
NASDAQ (US)	2.25	3.89	3.85	6. 08	7. 28	7.78	9.76	13. 00	17.29
Japan Exchange Group	3.26	4.10	3. 54	4. 78	4.89	5.06.	5.30	6.19	5.99
Shanghai Stock Exchange (SSE)	1.43	2.72	2.36	2. 50	4.55	4. 10	3.92	5.11	12.30

(Continued)

Stock Exchange	2008	2010	2011	2013	2015	2016	2018	2019	AAGR
Hong Kong Stock Exchange (HKSE)	1.33	2.71	2.26	3.10	3.18	3. 19	3.82	4. 90	12.59
Euronext	2.10	2.93	2.45	3.58	3.31	3.46	3.73	4. 70	7.59
London Stock Exchange Group	0.00	3.61	3.27	4.43	3. 88	3.47	3.64	4.18	1. 64
Shenzhen Stock Exchange (SZSE)	0.35	1.31	1.05	1.45	3. 64	3.22	2.41	3.41	22.88
TMX Group	1.03	2.17	1. 91	2.11	1.59	2. 04	1.94	2.41	8.00
Bombay Stock Exchange	0.65	1.63	1.01	1.14	1.52	1.56	2.08	2. 18	11.67
National Stock Exchange of India (NSE)	0.60	1.60	0.99	1.11	1.49	1.53	2.06	2. 16	12.36
Deutsche Börse	1.11	1.43	1.18	1.94	1.72	1.72	1.76	2.10	5.95
Swiss Exchange (SWX)	0.88	1.23	1.09	1.54	1.52	1.41	1. 44	1.83	6.90
Korea Exchange (KRX)	0. 47	1.09	1.00	1.23	1.23	1.28	1.41	1.48	11.01
NASDAQ OMX Nordic	0. 56	1.04	0.84	1.27	1.27	1.25	1.32	1.61	10.04
Australian Securities Exchange (ASX)	0. 68	1.45	1. 20	1.37	1.19	1.32	1.26	1.49	7.32
Others	9. 85	18.27	16.75	19.34	16.76	27.89	10.25	13.80	3.11
Global	35.77	64.58	56.53	74. 93	76.80	89.87	76. 77	93.89	9.13

Data source: According to data compiled from the World Federation of Exchanges website, the average annual growth rate refers to the compound annual growth rate from 2008 to 2019 (Euronext is Europe's largest exchange, formed by a merger of the stock exchanges of five Eurozone countries: the Netherlands, France, Belgium, Portugal, and Ireland).

12.1.2 Distribution of stock market value in major countries and regions

Table 12-2 shows the distribution of the year-end market value among major countries and regions during 2008–2019. It shows that after the 2008 international financial crisis, the two major developing countries, China and India, have the highest average annual growth rate. The US ranks third with an average annual growth rate of 11.06%, surpassing any other developed countries and regions in

Table 12-2 and exceeding the total compound annual growth rate of 8.97%. This underlines the robustness and continued growth of the US stock market.

Table 12-2   Distribution of the Year-End Market Value among Major Countries and Regions (2008–2019)

Unit: Trillion dollars, %

Country/ Region	2018	2010	2011	2013	2015	2016	2018	2019	AAGR
US	11.46	17.28	15.64	24.03	25.07	27.35	30.44	36.33	11.06
Eurozone	5.61	7.15	5.95	8.20	7.31	7.45	7.80	8.79	4.17
Mainland China	1.78	4.03	3.41	3.95	8.19	7.32	6.32	8.52	15.30
Japan	3.26	4.10	3.54	4.78	4.89	5.06	5. 30	6.19	5.99
India	1.25	3.23	1.99	2.25	3.00	3.10	4.14	4.34	12.01
UK	2.72	3.10	2.80	3.80	3.33	2.98	3.12	3.59	2.55
Canada	1.03	2.17	1.91	2.11	1. 59	2.04	1.94.	2.41	8.00
Switzerland	0.88	1.23	1.09	1.54	1.52	1.41	1. 44	1.83	6.90
Australia	0.68	1.45	1.20	1.37	1.19	1.32	1. 26	1.49	7.32
Total	27.99	42.29	36.34	50.67	54.90	56.72	60.50	72.00	8.97
Others	7.78	22.29	20.19	24.26	21.90	33.15	16. 27	21.88	9.86
Global Share	78.3	65.5	64.3	67.6	71.5	63.1	78.8	76. 7	

Data source: Same as Table 12-1.

12.2 Distribution of Top 2,500 Companies in Research and Development

This section introduces the excellent performance of the global stock market over the past decade, especially the NASDAQ in the US, which to a large extent, helps us better understand the stock market's financing of science and technology enterprises, capital markets, and even global scientific and technological innovation. Through a specific analysis of the distribution of companies lacking profit data in the world's top 2,500 companies with the most research and development in major countries and regions, this section makes a preliminary judgment on the importance of science and innovation in this field.

A careful observation of the relevant data of the EU Enterprise R&D Investment Ranking Report in recent years shows that a certain number of enterprises with the largest research and development investment in the world lack profit data, or there is no profit data in the original table. Although the number of such enterprises and the corresponding proportion of R&D are not high, symbolically their performances to enter this list are particularly significant. Not only do these companies lack profitability data, but most of them also lack marketing data.

According to calculations from previous reports, the number of such enterprises in 2016–2019 was 246, 96, 67, and 78, respectively, of which 230, 49, 43, and 68 lacked marketing data, accounting for 93.5%, 51.0%, 64.2%, and 87.2% of the companies lacking profit data, respectively. The majority of the top 2,500 companies with the most R&D investment are listed companies. However, it should also be considered that unlisted companies often have difficulty in collecting marketing and profit data. Therefore, it should be noted that a number of unlisted companies, such as Huawei of China, are among those lacking profit data. Therefore, most enterprises without marketing data are actually newly established, or they have a long research and development cycle, or they are in the early stage of marketing, so even profits are difficult to calculate or reliable data is difficult to obtain. Other companies are unlisted; the data of such enterprises generally has problems that cannot be ignored. For example, in the 2018 EU report, Huawei has marketing data but no profit data; Huawei was not yet listed in 2019, but in the EU Enterprise R&D Investment Ranking Report in 2019, Huawei's profitability data is complete. Although the overall characteristics of such companies are highly complex, most of these enterprises are "junior" or have relatively long research and development cycles.

12.3 Industry Distribution and Enlightenment of R&D Investment in Companies Lacking Profit Data and Companies Enduring Loss

Table 12-4 shows the total number of companies lacking profit data, companies enduring loss and profitable companies and the distribution of their total R&D investment in pharmaceutical biotechnology and health, software and computer services, hardware, and equipment in 2019 in the US, EU, China, and other countries and regions.

Table 12-3 Distribution of Number and Total R&D Investment of Enterprises Lacking Profit Data, Enterprises with Negative Revenue, and Enterprises with Positive Income in the World's Top 2,500 Companies with the Most R&D Investment (2017–2019)

Unit: 100 million Euros, %

Country/Region	Companies Lacking Profit Data			Companies Enduring Loss			Profitable Companies			The Difference between Investments of the Former Two	Proportion of Total Investment of the Former Two
	Number	Investment	Global Share	Number	Investment	Global Share	Number	Investment	Global Share		
Year 2017											
US	76	40.6	77.7	242	286.0	52.5	504	2573.0	37.9	14.6	11.3
Mainland China	1	0.9	1.8	35	46.3	7.6	340	570.8	8.4	-0.8	7.6
UK	9	6.0	11.5	30	28.7	5.6	95	255.9	3.8	1.8	11.9
Canada	1	0.6	1.1	9	24.1	4.0	17	23.5	0.3	3.6	51.2
Taiwan, China	1	0.3	0.6	9	7.4	1.2	95	141.9	2.1	-0.9	5.1
Germany	1	0.5	0.9	14	24.4	4.0	119	726.1	10.7	-6.7	3.3
Ireland	0	0.0	0.0	7	36.0	5.8	6	62.0	0.9	4.9	36.8
Switzerland	0	0.0	0.0	2	0.9	0.1	50	283.1	4.2	-4.0	0.3
Japan	2	0.5	0.9	10	6.5	1.1	353	1030.7	15.2	-14.0	0.7

(Continued)

Country/Region	Companies Lacking Profit Data			Companies Enduring Loss			Profitable Companies			The Difference between Investments of the Former Two	Proportion of Total Investment of the Former Two
	Number	Investment	Global Share	Number	Investment	Global Share	Number	Investment	Global Share		
France	1	0.3	0.6	7	3.4	0.6	63	250.3	3.7	-3.1	1.4
Netherlands	0	0.0	0.0	7	3.0	0.5	32	181.1	2.7	-2.2	1.6
Korea	0	0.0	0.0	7	6.3	1.0	63	259.3	3.8	-2.8	2.4
Denmark	1	0.4	0.7	3	1.8	0.4	122	43.9	0.6	-0.3	4.8
Israel	1	0.3	0.5	5	4.2	0.7	16	29.3	0.4	0.3	13.3
Sweden	0	0.0	0.0	5	1.8	0.3	31	87.2	1.3	-1.0	2.0
Austria	1	1.0	1.8	2	0.7	0.3	13	10.0	0.1	0.1	14.0
India	0	0.0	0.0	1	0.4	0.1	24	41.7	0.6	-0.6	0.9
India	0	0.0	0.0	1	3.8	0.6	22	53.6	0.8	-0.2	6.6
Australia	1	0.9	1.7	2	0.8	0.3	12	29.5	0.4	-0.2	5.4
Others	0	0.0	0.0	0	83.6	13.4	12	204.0	3.0	10.4	29.1
European Union	13	8.2	15.6	13	103.5	17.9	503	1670.0	24.6	-6.6	6.3
Total	96	52.3	100.0	415	570.0	100.0	1989	6794.0	100.0	0.0	8.4

(Continued)

Country/Region	Companies Lacking Profit Data			Companies Enduring Loss			Profitable Companies			The Difference between Investments of the Former Two	Proportion of Total Investment of the Former Two
	Number	Investment	Global Share	Number	Investment	Global Share	Number	Investment	Global Share		
Year 2018											
US	40	21.8	33.3	266	352.9	51.8	472	2367.5	35.1	16.7	13.7
Mainland China	2	0.7	1.1	34	30.7	20.0	402	680.7	10.1	9.9	4.4
UK	3	1.6	2.5	33	21.4	3.2	99	262.2	3.9	−0.7	8.1
Canada	0	0.0	0.0	10	5.5	0.8	18	36.7	0.5	0.2	13.0
Taiwan, China	1	0.9	1.4	6	4.4	0.7	92	148.9	2.2	−1.5	3.5
Germany	11	18.9	28.9	21	12.1	4.3	103	1118.2	16.6	−12.3	2.7
Ireland	0	0.0	0.0	6	24.7	3.4	18	59.8	0.9	2.5	29.3
Switzerland	2	6.4	9.9	6	2.7	1.3	51	253.4	3.8	−2.5	3.5
Japan	0	0.0	0.0	11	13.4	1.9	328	985.2	14.6	−12.7	1.3
France	0	0.0	0.0	9	4.4	0.6	66	279.5	4.1	−3.5	1.5

(Continued)

Country/Region	Companies Lacking Profit Data			Companies Enduring Loss			Profitable Companies			The Difference between Investments of the Former Two	Proportion of Total Investment of the Former Two
	Number	Investment	Global Share	Number	Investment	Global Share	Number	Investment	Global Share		
Netherlands	0	0.0	0.0	2	1.1	0.1	38	10.5	0.2	0.0	9.3
Korea	0	0.0	0.0	3	2.0	0.3	67	286.1	4.2	−4.0	0.7
Denmark	0	0.0	0.0	5	2.4	0.3	25	49.3	0.7	−0.4	4.7
Israel	0	0.0	0.0	7	21.8	3.0	14	11.7	0.2	2.8	65.2
Sweden	0	0.0	0.0	4	34.5	4.8	32	55.2	0.8	3.9	38–4
Austria	3	2.2	3.4	2	1.2	0.5	11	10.3	0.2	0.3	24.9
India	0	0.0	0.0	2	0.7	0.1	29	48.6	0.7	−0.6	1.4
India	1	3.8	5.7	0	0.0	0.5	22	59.3	0.9	−0.4	6.0
Australia	1	1.2	1.9	1	0.4	0.2	12	27.8	0.4	−0.2	5.5
Others	2	7.7	11.8	0	0.0	1.1	102	3.3	0.0	1.0	70.3
European Union	18	26.5	40.6	82	101.7	17.7	414	1904.3	28.2	−10.5	6.3
Total	66	65.4	100.0	433	544.6	100.0	2000	6754.1	100.0	0.0	8.3

(Continued)

Country/Region	Companies Lacking Profit Data			Companies Enduring Loss			Profitable Companies			The Difference between Investments of the Former Two	Proportion of Total Investment of the Former Two
	Number	Investment	Global Share	Number	Investment	Global Share	Number	Investment	Global Share		
Year 2019											
US	56	39.8	59.3	266	351.4	53.8	447	2734.0	37.3	16.5	12.5
Mainland China	1	0.4	0.6	65	102.0	14.1	441	861.5	11.8	2.3	10.6
UK	3	2.8	4.2	34	39.5	5.8	90	250.7	3.4	2.4	14.4
Canada	0	0.0	0.0	12	10.3	1.4	16	35.9	0.5	0.9	22.4
Taiwan, China	0	0.0	0.0	11	7.5	1.0	83	157.9	2.2	-1.1	4.6
Germany	1	13.7	20.5	10	57.3	9.8	118	758.1	10.4	-0.6	8.6
Ireland	0	0.0	0.0	10	33.2	4.6	17	60.2	0.8	3.7	35.5
Switzerland	1	0.9	1.3	9	6.8	1.1	48	277.8	3.8	-2.7	2.7
Japan	1	0.3	0.5	7	6.7	1.0	310	1087.4	14.8	-13.9	0.6
France	0	0.0	0.0	7	3.7	0.5	61	304.9	4.2	-3.6	1.2
Netherlands	0	0.0	0.0	6	3.5	0.5	33	187.2	2.6	-2.1	1.8

(Continued)

Country/Region	Companies Lacking Profit Data			Companies Enduring Loss			Profitable Companies			The Difference between Investments of the Former Two	Proportion of Total Investment of the Former Two
	Number	Investment	Global Share	Number	Investment	Global Share	Number	Investment	Global Share		
Korea	0	0.0	0.0	5	8.0	1.1	65	304.6	4.2	-3.1	2.6
Denmark	0	0.0	0.0	5	3.6	0.5	25	54.8	0.7	-0.3	6.1
Israel	2	0.8	1.1	5	14.1	2.0	15	16.3	0.2	1.8	47.7
Sweden	2	1.1	1.6	4	2.2	0.4	27	92.9	1.3	-0.8	3.4
Austria	2	1.4	2.0	2	1.5	0.4	19	13.4	0.2	0.2	17.9
India	0	0.0	0.0	2	1.1	0.2	29	16.0	0.2	-0.1	6.4
India	1	3.8	5.7	0	0.0	0.5	25	52.9	0.7	-0.2	6.7
Australia	1	1.2	1.7	1	0.5	0.2	10	26.9	0.4	-0.1	5.9
Others	7	1.0	1.5	4	7.0	1.1	78	30.6	0.4	0.7	21.4
European Union	9	22.8	33.9	78	144.5	23.0	415	1775.1	24.2	-1.2	8.6
Total	78	67.1	100.0	465	660.3	100.0	1957	7324.1	100.0	0.0	9.0

Data source: Compiled and calculated based on the data published in the EU Enterprise R&D Investment Ranking Report from 2017 to 2019 (EU R&D Score Board: World-2,500 Companies Ranked by R&D), https://iri.jrc.Europa.eu/scoreboard18.htm.

12.3.1 Distribution of the number and the proportion of total R&D investment of companies lacking profit data and companies enduring loss

Table 12-4 shows that among the 328 companies lacking profit data and companies enduring losses in the US in 2019, as many as 201 companies engaged in the pharmaceutical, biotechnology, and health fields, accounting for 61.3%. The total R&D investment of these companies accounted for 37.8% of the total R&D investment of 328 US companies, more than any other field, highlighting that companies lacking profit data and companies enduring losses in the US are mainly concentrated in the pharmaceutical, biotechnology, and health sectors. Subsequently, among companies lacking profit data and companies enduring loss in the US, there were 70 companies engaged in software and computer services. The total R&D investment of these companies accounted for 21.8% of the total R&D investment of 328 companies in the US. Finally, there were 26 companies engaged in hardware equipment, and the total R&D investment of these companies only accounted for 7.3% of the 328 companies in the US. In conclusion, there were 297 enterprises in these three fields, accounting for 90.5% of the total 328 enterprises in the US and 66.9% of the total R&D investment.

In 2019, there were only 71 companies lacking profit data and companies enduring loss in the EU, slightly lower than China's 87, but their total investment of 17.20 billion Euros exceeded China's 87 total investments of 10.43 billion Euros. Moreover, of the total R&D investment of 17.2 billion Euros by 71 EU companies, 45 companies in the pharmaceutical, biotechnology, and health fields accounted for 66.9% of the total R&D investment, while the total investment in other sectors such as software and computer services, hardware and equipment in the EU accounted for only 33.1%. It can be concluded that although the EU has relatively few companies lacking profit data and companies enduring loss, they are mainly concentrated in key areas such as pharmaceuticals, biotechnology, and health.

There are a total of 87 companies lacking profit data and companies enduring losses in China, higher than 71 in the EU. However, there are only 8, 15, and 8 enterprises in the fields of pharmaceuticals, biotechnology and health, software and computer services, and hardware and equipment, respectively, with a total of 31 enterprises. According to statistics, the total R&D investment of the 31 companies accounted for only 48.5% of the total R&D investment of 87 companies. It can be concluded that the companies lacking profit data and companies enduring loss in China are mainly concentrated in traditional fields other than the three types of real "high-tech," such as automobiles and industry.

Table 12-4 The Total Number of Companies Lacking Profit Data, Companies Enduring Loss and Profitable Companies and the Distribution of Their Total R&D Investment in Pharmaceutical Biotechnology and Health, Software and Computer Services, Hardware, and Equipment in 2019 in the US, EU, China, and other Countries and Regions

Unit: 100 million Euros, %

Country/Region	Pharmaceutical Biotechnology and Health Companies	Software and Computer Service Companies	Technical Hardware and Equipment Companies	Others	Total	Investment in Pharmaceutical Biotechnology and Health Companies	Investment in Software and Computer Service Companies	Investment in Technical Hardware and Equipment Companies	Investment in Others	Total
America	201	70	26	24	321	164.3	94.4	31.6	143.7	434.0
European Union	45	11	7	31	94	115.1	14.7	3.5	38.7	172.0
China	8	15	8	36	67	7.6	14.0	29.0	52.3	102.9
Others	19	2	10	43	74	38.7	17.5	9.0	41.2	106.5
Total	273	98	51	134	556	325.7	140.6	73.2	275.9	815.3
America	62.6	21.8	8.1	7.5	100.0	37.8	21.8	7.3	33.1	100.0
European Union	47.9	11.7	7.4	33.0	100.0	66.9	8.5	2.1	22.5	100.0
China	11.9	22.4	11.9	53.7	100.0	7.4	13.6	28.2	50.8	100.0
Others	25.7	2.7	13.5	58.1	100.0	36.4	16.4	8.5	38.7	100.0
Total	49.1	17.6	9.2	24.1	100.0	39.9	17.2	9.0	33.8	100.0

Data source: Same as Table 12-3; EU data includes data from the UK.

The US and the European Union have a total of 246 companies in the pharmaceutical, biotechnology, and health fields, accounting for 87.5% of the 28 companies in this category, with corresponding total R&D investment accounting for 85.7%. In comparison, China has only eight companies in this field, and its total R&D investment is 760 million Euros, accounting for only 2.3% of the total R&D investment of 246 companies. It can be concluded that China is lagging behind in this field, and it needs to check the deficiencies in a timely manner to deal with the challenges that may arise in this field in the future.

12.3.2 Distribution of the number and the proportion of total R&D investment of profitable companies

Table 12-4 shows that although 229 of the 441 profitable companies in the US were outside the three types in 2019, the total R&D investment of these 229 enterprises only accounted for 22.0% of the total R&D investment of the 441 profitable companies in the US. In the US, there are only 69, 80, and 63 "high-tech" profitable companies, respectively, but the corresponding total R&D investment accounts for 25.0%, 27.5%, and 25.5% of the total R&D investment of 441 profitable companies, which is as high as 78.0% in total. The above-mentioned data shows that US companies with large R&D investment are mainly concentrated in three types of "high-tech" fields. Although the number of 480 profitable companies in the EU slightly exceeds 441 in the US, the total R&D investment of 191.15 billion Euros is only 71.0% of the 269.12 billion Euros in the US. Moreover, only 114 of the 480 positive-income companies are classified as three types of "high-tech" enterprises. The total R&D investment of these 114 "high-tech" companies accounts for only 30.6% of the total R&D investment of 480 companies, which is far lower than the corresponding share of 78.0% in the US. In comparison, only 126 of China's 420 profitable companies are classified as three types of "high-tech" enterprises, and the total R&D investment of these 126 "high-tech" enterprises accounts for only 41.2% of the total R&D investment of the 420 enterprises, slightly higher than the corresponding proportion of 30.6% in the EU. It can be clearly seen that the concentration of R&D investment by profitable companies in China and the EU in the three types of "high-tech" is significantly lower than that of the US.

12.3.3 Enlightenment from the number of companies and the distribution of total R&D investment in the fields of pharmaceuticals, biotechnology, and health

Table 12-4 shows that although the total R&D investment of 201 companies lacking profit data and companies enduring losses in pharmaceutical, biotechnology, and health sectors in the US was 16.43 billion Euros in 2019, accounting for only 19.6% of the total investment of 83.65 billion Euros of 270 companies in this sector in the US. However, it accounts for 74.4% of the total 270 such enterprises in the US. This data shows that profitable companies in the US pharmaceutical, biotechnology, and health fields are the main force leading the world in this field. However, 201 such enterprises, accounting for 74.4% of the total, are the reserve strength in this field in the coming years. Pharmaceutical, biotech, and health companies are the most numerous and have the highest proportion of total R&D investment among the 2,500 companies, but due to the relatively long development cycle of these companies, most of them still have no revenue or even marketing. However, a large number of such enterprises in the US have concentrated on increasing research and development in this field to accumulate such technological reserves for future development. Europe still has a big gap in this field, but it has always followed the US. Other countries and regions outside the US, Europe, and China also follow the European Union (the total number of companies in this field is 58, slightly lower than the EU's 110, but more than China's 49; Their total R&D investment of 36.80 billion Euros is slightly lower than the EU's total R&D investment of 45.35 billion Euros, but far exceeds China's total R&D investment of 4.59 billion Euros). In contrast, China not only lags behind the US and Europe in the number of enterprises and total R&D investment in this field, but also lags behind other countries and regions outside the US and Europe. Therefore, China needs to remedy this in time to meet the challenges that are likely to arise in this area in the future.

12.4 Research and Judgment on the Trend of Changes in the Total R&D Investment of Enterprises with the Most R&D in Major Countries and Regions

12.4.1 Research and judgment on the changing trend of the number of companies with the most R&D in major countries and regions

Table 12-3 shows that from 2017 to 2019, the number of enterprises in Mainland China, Austria, Ireland, India, Israel, and Denmark increased by 180, 8, 6, 6, 2, and 1, respectively. In addition, the US, Japan, Taiwan, China, France, Sweden, and the UK have lost 68, 38, 17, 15, 7, and 6 enterprises, respectively. The European Union and other countries and regions suffered even worse losses, with 18 and 20 enterprises, respectively. It can be seen that in recent years, the R&D efforts of enterprises in Mainland China have been significantly enhanced. Even if it is estimated by two-thirds of the average annual change of companies in different countries and regions from 2017 to 2019, by 2025, the number of Mainland China companies in the top 2,500 R&D companies in the world is expected to surpass that of the US, the country with the largest number of R&D companies in the world, by around 2025.

12.4.2 Research and judgment on the trend of changes in the total R&D invest-ment of enterprises with the most R&D in major countries and regions

Table 12-3 shows that since the average R&D investment amount of enterprises in Mainland China is significantly lower than that of the US, Europe, and Japan, even if the total number of enterprises in Mainland China surpasses Japan and the EU in 2019, the total R&D investment amount is still lower than that of Japan and the EU. According to the data in Table 12-3, from 2017 to 2019, the average annual compound growth rate of total R&D investment of enterprises in Mainland China, which invest the most in global R&D, is as high as 25.5%, only slightly lower than the average annual compound growth rate of 29.2% in Austria during the same period. At the same time, it is more than twice as high as the 11.2% compound annual growth rate of the Netherlands, which ranks third in terms of compound annual growth rate. Even if it is estimated to be lower than the average annual compound growth rate of 25.5% of the total R&D investment of enterprises in Mainland China from 2017 to 2019, shown in Table 12-3, the annual compound growth rate of Japan's 6.7% during the same period, the total R&D investment of enterprises in Mainland China is still expected to surpass that of Japan for the first time in 2020. Moreover, assuming half of China's compound annual growth rate between 2017 and 2019, and that the EU and the US maintain the same growth rate over the same period, the total R&D investment of China's leading companies is also expected to exceed that of the EU and the US by 2025 and around 2035, respectively. In summary, China's scientific and technological innovation capabilities will be significantly improved.

12.5 Research and Judgment on the Number of Companies with the Largest R&D of Major Currency Issuers and the Trend of Total R&D Investment

Although the relevant data given in Table 12-3 and Table 12-4 help us have a clear understanding of the R&D efforts of major countries and regions, the R&D efforts of major currency issuers have not been clearly visible. Table 12-5 shows the relevant results of the number of R&D enterprises in the top eight currency issuers and other currency issuers in the world and the distribution of their total R&D investment.

12.5.1 The leading role played by the US

Table 12-5 shows that although the proportion of US enterprises and their total R&D investment among the top 2,500 enterprises with the largest R&D investment in the world in 2019 accounted for 30.8% and 38.0%, respectively, ranking the first in the world, it can be found through comparison that these two proportions are significantly lower than the proportion of 44.2% of the transaction amount of USD in the global foreign exchange market in 2019. In 2019, the proportion of US profitable companies and their total R&D investment among the top 2,500 enterprises with the largest R&D investment in the world accounted for 23.0% and 36.3%, respectively, and remained the first place in the world. However, through comparison, it can be found that these two proportions are significantly lower than the proportion of 44.2% of the transaction amount of USD in the global foreign exchange market in 2019. In contrast, the proportion of US companies lacking profit data and companies enduring loss and their total R&D investment among the top 2,500 enterprises with the largest R&D investment in the world in 2019 accounted for 57.7% and 53.2%, respectively. Not only does it maintain the first place in the world, but also the two proportions are significantly higher than the proportion of 44.2% of the transaction amount of USD in the global foreign exchange market in 2019. It can be concluded that the pursuit of technological dividends by US profitable companies is significantly higher than that of other currency issuers. It is particularly noteworthy that in 2019, 201 US companies lacking profit data and companies enduring loss focusing on the fields of pharmacy, biotechnology, and health entered the top 2,500 R&D investment enterprises in the world, not only the global share is as high as 73.6%, the corresponding total R&D investment is also as high as 50.4%. The rankings of R&D investment and total R&D investment of US companies lacking profit

Table 12-5   Distribution of Number and Total R&D Investment of Companies Lacking Profit Data, Companies Enduring Loss, and Profitable Companies that Have Entered the List of the World's Top 2,500 Companies with the Most R&D Investment among the World's Top Eight International Currency Issuers (2019)

Unit: 100 million Euros, %

Distribution of the Number and Proportion of Companies Lacking Profit Data and Companies Enduring Loss

Country/Region	Pharmaceutical Biotechnology and Health Companies	Software and Computer Service Companies	Technical Hardware and Equipment Companies	Others	Total
US	201	70	26	24	321
Eurozone	26	4	2	15	47
Japan	1	0	0	7	8
UK	15	3	4	14	36
Australia	1	0	0	1	2
Canada	6	2	2	1	11
Switzerland	8	0	0	3	11
China	8	15	8	36	67
Others	15	4	8	26	53
Total	281	98	50	127	556

The Total R&D Investment Amount and Proportion Distribution of Companies Lacking Profit Data and Companies Enduring Loss

Country/Region	Pharmaceutical Biotechnology and Health Companies	Software and Computer Service Companies	Technical Hardware and Equipment Companies	Others	Total
US	164.3	94.4	31.6	143.7	434.0
Eurozone	100.3	9.0	1.1	14.0	124.4
Japan	0.8	0.0	0.0	6.2	7.0
UK	11.7	4.6	2.0	22.5	40.8
Australia	0.5	0.0	0.0	1.2	1.7
Canada	5.7	2.6	1.3	0.4	10.0
Switzerland	7.0	0.0	0.0	1.2	8.1
China	7.6	14.0	29.0	52.3	102.9
Others	27.8	15.9	8.2	34.5	86.5
Total	325.7	140.6	73.2	275.9	815.3

(Continued)

Country/Region	Distribution of the Number and Proportion of Profitable Companies					R&D Investment and Proportion Distribution of Profitable Companies				
	Pharmaceutical Biotechnology and Health Companies	Software and Computer Service Companies	Technical Hardware and Equipment Companies	Others	Total	Pharmaceutical Biotechnology and Health Companies	Software and Computer Service Companies	Technical Hardware and Equipment Companies	Others	Total
US	64	79	61	244	448	659.7	552.9	684.8	793.8	2,691.2
Eurozone	35	18	13	247	313	201.9	72.0	107.7	1,128.5	1,510.2
Japan	35	9	0	266	310	131.3	49.0	0.0	907.1	1,087.4
UK	17	11	3	60	91	99.2	17.3	9.2	126.4	252.1
Australia	2	2	1	5	10	8.4	1.0	6.7	10.8	26.9
Canada	14.3	17.6	13.6	54.5	100.0	0.3	7.1	2.3	26.4	36.2
Switzerland	11.2	5.8	4.2	78.9	100.0	180.8	2.5	1.8	92.3	277.4
China	41	45	40	314	440	38.3	147.1	168.8	506.8	861.0
Others	18.7	12.1	3.3	65.9	100.0	58.2	187.6	223.7	206.9	676.5
Total	20.0	20.0	10.0	50.0	100.0	1,378.2	1,036.5	1,205.1	3,799.2	7,418.9

(Continued)

Country/Region	Pharmaceutical Biotechnology and Health Companies	Software and Computer Service Companies	Technical Hardware and Equipment Companies	Others	Total	Pharmaceutical Biotechnology and Health Companies	Software and Computer Service Companies	Technical Hardware and Equipment Companies	Others	Total
	Distribution of the Number and Proportion of All Listed Enterprises					R&D Investment Amount and Proportion Distribution of All Listed Enterprises				
US	265	149	87	268	769	824.0	647.3	716.4	937.5	3125.2
Eurozone	61	22	15	262	360	302.2	81.1	108.8	1,142.5	1,634.6
	Distribution of the Number and Proportion of All Listed Enterprises					R&D Investment Amount and Proportion Distribution of All Listed				
Japan	36	9	0	273	318	132.1	49.0	0.0	913.4	1,094.4
UK	32	14	7	74	127	110.9	21.9	11.2	149.0	292.9
Australia	3	2	1	6	12	8.9	1.0	6.7	12.0	28.6
Canada	7	5	4	84	10	6.0	9.7	3.6	26.8	46.2
Switzerland	13	23	2	20	58	187.8	2.5	1.8	93.5	285.5
China	49	60	48	350	507	45.9	161.1	197.8	559.1	963.9
Others	49	1	86	113	249	86.0	203.6	232.0	241.4	762.9
Total	515	285	250	1,450	2,500	1,703.8	1,177.1	1,278.3	4,075.1	8,234.2

Data source: Same as Table 12-3.

data and companies enduring loss are at the forefront of the world, which not only reflects the high degree of the pursuit of US-funded companies in terms of technology dividends and the high degree of smooth financing channels, but also serves as the reserve army of US science and technology in pharmaceutical, biotechnology and health fields in the future. It will play a positive role in US science and technology to continue to lead the world and provide effective support for the USD in the future.

12.5.2 Proportion of total R&D investment of different types of enterprises in Eurozone, Japan, and the UK

Table 12-5 shows that in 2019, the number and proportion of enterprises from the three major currency issuers of the Eurozone, Japan, and the UK, entering the world's 2,500 enterprises with the largest R&D investment were 32.2% and 36.7%, respectively, slightly higher and slightly lower than the corresponding proportion of the US. According to statistics, it can be found that the number of profitable companies in the three major currency issuers and their total R&D investment accounted for 36.7% and 38.4%, both slightly higher than the corresponding proportions in the US. However, the number of companies lacking profit data and companies enduring loss in the three major currency issuers and their total R&D investment accounted for 16.4% and 21.1%, respectively, which are far below the corresponding half of the US. Therefore, it can be concluded that the technological reserve of these currency issuers is much lower than that of the US, resulting in the sustainability of technological innovation.

12.5.3 The proportion of other currency issuers' total R&D investment and its impact on currency internationalization

Table 12-5 shows that in 2019, the total number of Australian and Canadian enterprises that entered the world's top 2,500 R&D companies and their total R&D investment ranked the last two in the eight major currency issuers. In addition, the total number of Swiss and British enterprises that entered the world's top 2,500 R&D companies and their total R&D investments are only higher than Australia and Canada among the eight major currency issuers, while significantly lower than the US, the Eurozone, Japan, and China. Moreover, the total R&D investment of major enterprises in Switzerland and the UK also has a considerable share of US capital. It can be seen that the scientific and technological support of the Swiss franc and the British pound is relatively low among the eight major currencies. In the next few years, the international ranking of the British pound is expected to be replaced by the RMB.

12.6 The Dependence of Major International Currency Issuers on the US in Terms of Technology

According to relevant data on R&D investment by US-funded enterprises in major countries and regions from 2007 to 2016 published on https://www.bea. gov by the US Bureau of Economic Analysis, in 2016, the R&D investment of US funded enterprises in the UK, Japan, Canada, China, and Australia was USD 8.275 billion, USD 7.899 billion, USD 1,095 million, USD 775 million and USD 172 million respectively, equivalent to 27.8%, 7.5%, 21.9%, 1.5%, and 5.9% of the total R&D investment of enterprises with the largest R&D investment in the world in these countries in the same year (calculated based on the Euro-US exchange rate 1.0555 at the end of 2016). The US Bureau of Economic Analysis website did not publish data on R&D investment by US-funded enterprises in major Eurozone countries such as Switzerland, France, Germany, and Ireland in 2016. From 2007 to 2011, according to the R&D investment data of US enterprises in Switzerland, it can be calculated that the average annual compound growth rate of US enterprises' R&D investment in Switzerland in the four years was 7.54%. Based on half of the compound annual growth rate, which is 3.27%, and the 2011 R&D investment amount of US-funded enterprises in Switzerland is 9.821 billion US dollars, it can be estimated that the US-funded enterprises' R&D investment in Switzerland in 2016 is 11.82 billion US dollars, which is equivalent to 40.0% of the total R&D investment of 27.98 billion Euros by the 58 Swiss companies with the largest global R&D investment in the same year. According to the data published on the website of the US Bureau of Economic Analysis, the total R&D investment of US-funded enterprises in Europe was USD 44.64 billion in 2016, minus the R&D investment in Britain, Denmark, Sweden, and other non-Eurozone countries in the same year, and minus the R&D investment in Switzerland estimated above, it can be immediately estimated that the R&D investment of US-funded enterprises in the Euro area in the same year was USD 23.43 billion.

The above results show that Switzerland has the highest dependence on the US in terms of R&D investment, as high as 40%; the UK and Canada rely on the US for R&D investment at around 25%; the Eurozone and Japan's dependence on the US for R&D investment is relatively low, only about 10%; while among the major US allies, the dependence on the US for R&D investment is the lowest, indicating that Australia is not a place for US R&D. In addition, China is basically only a production place and market for US enterprises. The R&D investment of US-funded enterprises in China, the world's second-largest economy, is only slightly higher than that of Australia, indicating the huge space for rational cooperation between the two countries. The dependence of the above major currency issuers on the R&D investment of US-funded enterprises is not only consistent with the correlation between the scientific and technological autonomy of the US and the scientific and technological autonomy of these currency issuers, but also more consistent with the relationship between the number of bonds held between the US and major currency issuers.

12.7 The Acceleration of Global Profitable Companies Has Led to an Increase in the Market Value of the Science and Technology Sector and the Subsequent Enlightenment of China

12.7.1 Global stock markets have been severely hit by the Coronavirus

Since the beginning of 2020, the global Coronavirus has continued to spread, which will undoubtedly have an influence and impact on the global economy, trade, and capital markets rarely seen in years. Table 12-6 shows the total market value change rate, the Coronavirus diagnosis rate, the cure rate, and the ratio of cure rate to the diagnosis rate of countries and regions with a global stock market value of more than 30 billion US dollars from the end of 2019 to the end of June 2020. Table 12-6 shows that at the end of the first half of 2019–2020, the global stock market value dropped by 6.92%. Except for China and Iran, the market value of the stock markets of all other countries and regions has declined to varying degrees. Among them, the stock markets of the US, Japan, pan Europe, and Germany decreased by 4.80%, 8.51%, 8.48%, and 7.84%, respectively; meanwhile, it is worth noting that the stock markets of India, the UK, South Africa, Brazil, Russia, and Spain fell by 15.50%, 22.78%, 21.84%, 38.43%, 22.22%, and 22.14%, respectively. It can be seen that the Coronavirus has a greater impact on the stock markets of these countries.

Table 12-6   The Total Stock Market Value, Half-Year Change Rate, Coronavirus
Diagnosis Rate, Cure Rate, and the Ratio of Cure Rate to the Diagnosis Rate of Countries
and Regions with a Global Stock Market Value of More than 30 Billion US Dollars (from
the End of 2019 to the End of June 2020)

Unit: 100 million US dollars, %

Country/ Region	Market Value at the End of 2019	Market Value in June 2020	Half-Year Market Value Change Rate	Diagnosis Rate	Cure Rate	Diagnosis Rate/Cure Rate
US	374,822.3	356,820.0	−4.80	81.01	41.66	194.47
Mainland China	85,155.0	91,816.4	7.82	0.60	93.94	0.63
Japan	61,910.7	56,640.5	−8.51	1.47	88.50	1.66
Hong Kong, China	48,992.3	48,904.2	−0.18	1.60	91.85	1.74
Netherlands, France, Portugal, Belgium, Ireland	47,017.1	42,860.1	−8.84	35.17	41.32	85.1
India	43,424.8	36,693.7	−15.50	4.06	58.67	6.91
UK	41,828.7	32,298.1	−22.78	46.90	0.61	7,687.71
Saudi Arabia	24,068.2	21,957.9	−8.77	55.35	68.18	81.17
Canada	24,091.0	20,980.5	−12.91	28.25	64.91	43.51
Germany	20,981.7	19,337.0	−7.84	23.53	91.22	25.79
Switzerland	18,344.5	17,607.8	−4.02	36.62	91.94	39.83
Korea	14,848.4	14,092.0	−5.09	2.46	89.59	2.74
Taiwan, China	13,320.5	13,289.3	−0.23	0.19	97.32	0.19
Australia	14,876.0	13,239.5	−11.00	3.04	90.17	3.37
South Africa	10,563.4	8,256.6	−21.84	24.73	48.95	50.53
Brazil	11,873.6	7,310.4	−38.43	64.94	55.15	117.76
Russia	8,086.4	6,290.0	−22.22	44.49	62.91	70.73
Iran	1,496.5	6,308.4	321.55	27.05	82.67	32.71

(Continued)

Country/ Region	Market Value at the End of 2019	Market Value in June 2020	Half-Year Market Value Change Rate	Diagnosis Rate	Cure Rate	Diagnosis Rate/Cure Rate
Spain	7,972.9	6,207.9	−22.14	64.08	66.53	96.32
Singapore	6,972.7	5,859.2	−15.97	76.46	85.91	89.01
Thailand	5,692.3	4,725.2	−16.99	0.46	96.55	0.47
Indonesia	5,233.2	3,983.4	−23.88	2.05	43.20	4.75
Malaysia	4,039.6	3,550.2	−12.11	2.63	96.49	2.72
Mexico	4,136.2	3,019.9	−26.99	17.52	77.11	22.72
Philippines	2,753.0	2,210.5	−19.71	3.33	27.32	12.17
Israel	2,373.7	1,963.4	−17.29	27.03	70.45	38.37
Turkey	1,849.7	1,786.2	−3.43	23.96	86.50	27.70
Qatar	1,600.5	1,427.9	−10.79	338.34	84.30	401.37
UAE (United Arab Emirates)	2,468.2	2,147.6	−12.99	44.88	76. 85	58.41
Vietnam	1,498.2	1,326.5	−11.46	0.04	92.96	0.04
New Zealand	1,078.8	1,015.7	−5.85	3.02	97.50	3.09
Kuwait	1,181.4	949.2	−19.66	97.80	79.77	122.60
Peru	989.6	843.5	−14.77	86.82	60.62	143.23
Colombia	1,320.4	808.2	−38.79	18.26	41.68	43.81
Morocco	654.2	538.5	−17.68	3.45	71.87	4.81
Greece	536.5	392.7	−26.81	3.16	40.70	7.77
Kazakhstan	406.4	386.8	−4.83	11.38	60.64	18.77
Egypt	442.0	365.3	−17.35	6.73	26. 89	25.02
Argentina	393.9	319.9	−18.80	13.82	33.95	40.71
Luxembourg	442.3	311.3	−29.62	68.64	93.78	73.20
Others	28,599.9	23,827.7	−16.69	15.91	53.87	29.52
Total	948,337.0	882,669.1	−6.92	21.82	54.17	40.28

Data source: The stock market value data is the same as Table 12-1.

According to the data of stock market value decline and Coronavirus diagnosis rate, cure rate, and the ratio of diagnosis rate to cure rate of exchanges in different countries or regions in Table 12-6, it can be calculated that the correlation between the change rate of the stock market value and the Coronavirus diagnosis rate and cure rate is −3.36% and 2.57%, respectively. Although the two correlations are in the right direction (the higher the diagnosis rate is, the more serious the Coronavirus is and the greater the negative impact on the stock market, while the higher the cure rate is, the better the response to the Coronavirus is and the better the stock market performance), both correlations are too low, indicating that there should be serious problems in the statistics of Coronavirus data all over the world.

12.7.2 The accelerated growth of the US science and innovation sector leads the development of the global technology stock market

Table 12-4 shows that between the end of 2019 and the end of June 2020, affected by the continuous spread of the Coronavirus, although the total market value of the two US stock markets fell by 4.80%, the US NASDAQ market grew against the trend during the same period 12. 64% or an increase of USD 1.64 trillion (the market value of the New York stock market in the US dropped by 14.07% or USD 3.44 trillion in the same period), accounting for 56.82% of the total market value increase of USD 2.89 trillion on the world's nine defying market capitalization exchanges during the same period (Besides the two exchanges in the US NASDAQ and Mainland China, the market capitalization of the six exchanges, including the Cayman stock exchange, the Hanoi exchange, the Taipei exchange, the Rwanda exchange, the Iran Farah exchange and the Tehran exchange, has increased to a certain degree. Among them, the total value-added of the two Iranian exchanges accounted for 19.71%, and the total market value of the other four exchanges accounted for only 0.44% of the total value-added of the nine exchanges). The proportion of the market value of the NASDAQ stock market in the total market value of the US stock market increased from 34.69% at the end of 2019 to 41.05%, with an increase of 6.36% in the first half of 2020, exceeding the cumulative increase of 5.64% in the four years from 2015 to 2019. This not only shows the positive impact of the Coronavirus on listed technology companies, but also reflects the accelerating accumulation of technology stock bubbles during the Coronavirus. If estimated based on the growth rate in the first half of 2020, around the end of 2020 or the end of the first quarter of 2021, the market value of the NASDAQ stock market is expected to exceed half of that of the US stock market for the first time. Meanwhile, the support of the capital market for scientific and technological innovation and the development of scientific and technological enterprises will also be further improved.

12.7.3 The huge potential of Mainland China in the stock market and technology sector

Inspired by the achievements of Mainland China in fighting the Coronavirus and the results of resuming work and production, as of the end of June 2020, the market value of the Shenzhen Stock Exchange, the second largest domestic stock market, has increased by 14.87% from the end of 2019, which is higher than the US NASDAQ's increase of 12.64% over the same period. At the same time, the total market value of the Shanghai Stock Exchange also increased by 3.11% during the same period. At the end of June 2020, the total market value of the two major domestic stock markets increased by 7.82% or USD 0.67 trillion over the end of 2019, accounting for 23.03% of the total increase of USD 2.89 trillion of the nine global stock exchanges in the same period, second only to NASDAQ in the US, accounting for 56.82%, highlighting China's achievements in fighting the Coronavirus and the effectiveness of resuming work and production.

China's Science and Technology Innovation Board was launched in July 2019. By the end of 2019, there were 70 listed companies with a total market value of 863.69 billion yuan, accounting for 1.48% of the total market value of the domestic stock market during the same period. By the end of June 2020, there were 116 companies listed on the Growth Enterprise Market with a total market value of 2006.404 billion yuan, accounting for 3.09% of the total market value of 64.88 trillion yuan of China's stock market during the same period, equivalent to one-thirteenth of the market value of NASDAQ in the total market value of the US stock market 41.05%. There are also a certain number of technology companies in the domestic companies that have been listed on the Shanghai Stock Exchange, Shenzhen Stock Exchange, and Hong Kong Stock Exchange. Therefore, the market value of China's technology companies should be a certain margin higher than the market value of the technology board. It can be concluded that the gap between the proportion of China's science and technology stock market value in the whole stock market value and the US should be smaller than the one-thirteenth mentioned earlier. However, even if the value of China's science and technology stock market, which is not included in the science and technology sector, is equivalent to the total market value of the science and technology sector, the total market value of listed companies in China's science and technology enterprises at the end of June 2020 is about 4 trillion yuan, accounting for only about 15% of the total market value of China's stock market in the same period, only slightly higher than one-third of the 41.05% of the US. It is equivalent to the proportion of 5.25% of China's science and technology internationalization level in 2019 and 12.81% of the US' science and technology internationalization level of 44.47%, which shows that the support of China's capital market for science and innovation enterprises is similar to that of China's science and technology internationalization level, and still has great potential.

12.8 Conclusion

This chapter mainly introduces the market value of global stock markets, major stock exchanges in the world, and the market value distribution and securitization degree of major countries and regions in the past ten years. As can be seen from the results of this chapter, the NASDAQ stock market of the US has grown at a rate nearly twice the market value of the traditional large stock market of the US in the past ten years, and its annual growth rate has exceeded the compound annual growth rate of the two major developing countries, China and India. US technology stocks have grown rapidly in the past ten years, providing technology companies with rare effective channels for financing, R&D investment, mergers and acquisitions, and the exit of venture capital funds. It not only shows the benign cycle of US technological innovation and capital market, but also shows its unique trend of leading global development.

It is undeniable that the capital market is an important channel for the development of various funds and the financing of science and technology enterprises, but the scale of the capital market itself cannot accurately reflect the smoothness of financing channels for science and technology enterprises in different countries and regions. In recent years, the number of companies lacking profit data and companies enduring loss among the 2,500 companies with the most R&D in the world published by the European Commission and their total R&D investment-related data can better reflect the pursuit of science and technology dividends and the smoothness of R&D investment channels. The total number of enterprises that have entered the 2,500 companies with the most R&D in the world and the distribution of the corresponding total R&D investment in major countries and regions can not only clearly show the importance of the corresponding countries or regions to R&D, but also show the pursuit of scientific and technological dividends and the smoothness of R&D

financing channels. In addition, the horizontal comparison between the number of enterprises that have entered the 2,500 companies with the most R&D in the world and the total R&D investment amount in different years also reflects the importance of science and technology innovation in various regions. The number of companies lacking profit data or even marketing data that have entered the 2,500 companies with the most R&D in the world and the regional distribution and industry distribution of the total R&D investment amount can more clearly and in-depth reflect the intensity of the pursuit of R&D dividends in various regions. At the same time, it also shows other problems in various regions, such as financing channels, financing environment, and investment priorities. In recent years, the number of US enterprises that have entered the 2,500 companies with the most R&D in the world and the corresponding total R&D amount accounted for more than half of the world, far exceeding the relative monopoly of the USD in the world. The number of US companies lacking profit data or even marketing data that have been listed in the global 2,500 enterprises is also the largest in the world, while the vast majority of these enterprises are engaged in the fields of pharmacy, biotechnology, and health with a long R&D cycle. Facts show that these enterprises are the reserve force of US science and technology. In the next few years, such enterprises will gradually enter negative profit, and then enter the list of positive profit enterprises, and play a greater support and driving force for the US to lead the global science and technology innovation and the stable position of the USD.

In recent years, not only the number of Chinese enterprises that have entered the 2,500 companies with the most R&D in the world and their total R&D amount has continued to grow rapidly, but the number of companies enduring loss and their total R&D investment has also increased to a position second only to the US. Through research, it can be found that the vast majority of Chinese enterprises that have been listed in the global 2,500 enterprises are mainly engaged in traditional fields other than the three "high-tech" fields of pharmacy, biotechnology, and health, software and computer services, and hardware equipment; the R&D investment of Chinese enterprises in the three key areas of pharmacy, biotechnology and health is only 2.8%, which is relatively low. In addition, only a few Chinese companies lack profit data that have been listed in the global 2,500 enterprises, which is not only a very poor number but also not continuous enough. It clearly points out the shortcomings of China's long-term research and development cycle of science and technology reserve forces that need to be significantly improved.

CHAPTER THIRTEEN

The Relationship between Sci-Tech Internationalization and Currency Internationalization

TECHNOLOGICAL INNOVATION CAPABILITY IS THE DRIVING force of economic and trade development, while the economy and trade are the foundation of currency internationalization. Therefore, the technological innovation capability or level of technological internationalization of any currency issuer should be highly correlated with currency internationalization. This chapter uses the sci-tech internationalization results of Table 4-6 of major international currency issuers and the currency internationalization results of major currencies given in previous chapters to explore the relationship between the two internationalization measures, to find problems with the association in noticeable years, and then to obtain an optimal currency internationalization measure through overcoming correlation problems between sci-tech internationalization measure and traditional currency internationalization measure.

13.1 Sci-Tech Internationalization of Major Currency Issuers

Table 4-6 gives the sci-tech internationalization of five major blocs and other countries and regions, yet we still do not know about the sci-tech internationalization of the Euro, GBP, and other major international currency issuers since

IP5 reports do not have patent family data for these. However, as exports of charges for the use of intellectual properties (IP) are highly correlated with the number of international patents or sci-tech internationalization, costs of exports for IP use in the Eurozone, UK, and Switzerland of EPC States total exports of charges for use of IP to multiple the EPC States internationalization in Table 4-6 to estimate the corresponding sci-tech internationalization of Eurozone, UK, and Switzerland; similarly, we can estimate sci-tech internationalization of Australia and Canada by multiplying weights of exports of charges for the use of IP of these two countries of total exports of charges for the use of IP with sci-tech internationalization of "others" in Table 4-6. The results of sci-tech internationalization of all eight major international currency issuers are given in Table 13-1 from 2000 to 2019.

Table 13-1   Comparison of Sci-Tech Internationalization of Major Currency Issuers with Currency Internationalization (2000 to 2019)

Unit: %

Sci-Tech Internationalization of Major Currency Issuers								
Year	US	Eurozone	Japan	UK	Australia	Canada	Switzerland	China	Others
2000	42.98	11.51	28.10	4.68	0.36	1.81	1.17	1.03	8.36
2001	42.68	11.34	27.94	4.27	0.36	1.60	1.22	0.94	9.66
2002	42.51	11.66	27.24	4.06	0.44	1.76	1.32	0.76	10.26
2003	42.03	11.08	27.92	3.56	0.39	1.40	1.33	0.55	11.74
2004	42.79	10.71	26.82	3.18	0.41	1.32	1.35	0.94	12.48
2005	44.74	11.90	25.81	3.27	0.26	1.32	1.59	0.54	10.58
2006	45.52	11.09	26.74	2.90	0.27	1.41	1.29	0.56	10.22
2007	47.20	11.39	26.21	2.75	0.26	1.40	1.28	0.77	8.72
2008	48.88	11.52	24.10	2.21	0.22	1.26	1.41	1.02	9.38
2009	48.17	11.50	23.83	2.26	0.25	1.15	1.98	0.79	10.07
2010	47.57	10.99	25.83	2.12	0.27	0.77	1.99	1.30	9.13
2011	47.02	10.70	24.34	1.89	0.22	0.77	2.00	1.04	12.03
2012	47.21	10.87	24.56	1.81	0.18	0.81	2.39	1.25	10.92
2013	49.9	10.73	23.43	2.13	0.15	0.87	2.30	0.93	10.33

(Continued)

Year	US	Eurozone	Japan	UK	Australia	Canada	Switzerland	China	Others
2014	47.07	10.82	24.19	2.19	0.16	0.87	2.06	0.71	11.93
2015	45.07	10.49	24.67	2.25	0.14	0.75	1.89	1.19	13.54
2016*	45.63	11.60	21.52	2.16	0.16	0.89	2.48	1.29	14.28
2017*	45.04	12.03	18.55	2.36	0.17	0.89	2.38	4.14	14.45
2018*	45.76	12.59	17.00	2.50	0.17	0.94	2.45	4.25	14.35
2019*	46.38	12.97	14.75	2.38	0.16	0.93	2.25	5.61	14.57
Avg.	45.67	11.37	24.18	2.75	0.25	1.15	1.81	1.48	11.35

Currency Internationalization of Major Currencies

Year	USD	Euro	JPY	GBP	AUD	CAD	CHF	RMB	Others
2001	44.93	18.96	11.77	6.52	2.16	2.24	2.99	0.00	10.42
2004	44.00	18.70	10.42	8.25	3.01	2.10	3.01	0.05	10.45
2007	42.80	18.52	8.62	7.43	3.31	2.14	3.41	0.23	13.53
2010	42.43	19.52	9.49	6.44	3.79	2.64	3.15	0.43	12.10
2013	43.52	16.70	11.52	5.91	4.32	2.28	2.58	1.12	12.05
2016	43.79	15.70	10.81	6.40	3.44	2.57	2.40	1.99	12.89
2019	44.15	16.14	8.40	6.40	3.38	2.52	2.48	2.16	14.37
Avg.	43.66	17.75	10.15	6.76	3.35	2.36	2.86	0.85	12.26

Sci-Tech Internationalization of Currency Issuers – Currency Internationalization

Year	USD	EUR	JPY	GBP	AUD	CAD	CHF	RMB	Others
2001	−2.26	−7.62	16.18	−2.26	−1.81	−0.65	−1.77	0.94	−0.76
2004	−1.21	−8.00	16.41	−5.07	−2.60	−0.78	−1.66	0.90	2.03
2007	4.40	−7.13	17.59	−4.69	−3.05	−0.74	−2.13	0.55	−4.81
2010	5.14	−8.54	16.33	−4.32	−3.53	−1.87	−1.16	0.87	−2.93
2013	5.60	−5.98	11.91	−3.78	−4.16	−1.41	−0.28	−0.18	−1.72
2016	1.84	−4.10	10.71	−4.24	−3.28	−1.68	0.08	−0.71	1.39
2019	2.23	−3.17	6.35	−4.02	−3.22	−1.59	−0.23	3.44	0.21
Avg.	2.25	−6.36	13.64	−4.05	−3.09	−1.25	−1.02	0.63	−0.91

Sci–Tech Internationalization of Currency Issuers/Currency Internationalization

(Continued)

Year	USD	EUR	JPY	GBP	AUD	CAD	CHF	RMB	Others
2001	0.95	0.60	2.37	0.65	0.16	0.71	0.41	245.46	0.93
2004	0.97	0.57	2.58	0.39	0.14	0.63	0.45	19.70	1.19
2007	1.10	0.62	3.04	0.37	0.08	0.65	0.38	3.42	0.64
2010	1.12	0.56	2.72	0.33	0.07	0.29	0.63	3.02	0.76
2013	1.13	0.64	2.03	0.36	0.04	0.38	0.89	0.84	0.86
2016	1.04	0.74	1.99	0.34	0.05	0.35	1.03	0.65	1.11
2019	1.05	0.80	1.76	0.37	0.05	0.37	0.91	2.59	1.01
Avg.	1.05	0.65	2.36	0.40	0.08	0.48	0.67	38.28	0.93

Data source: Sci-tech internationalization of the US, Japan, and China is from Table 4-6; Sci-tech internationalization of Eurozone, the UK, and Switzerland is estimated by multiplying the IP exports of these three regions by total IP exports and sci-tech internationalization of EPC States in Table 4-6, respectively; Sci-tech internationalization of Australia and Canada is estimated by multiplying the weights of IP exports of charges for the use of IP of total exports of charges for the use of IP of "others" and Sci-tech internationalization of "others" in Table 4-6.

13.1.1 Comparing sci-tech internationalization of major currency issuers

Table 13-1 shows that the US sci-tech was not only by far the highest of all eight major currency issuers from 2000 to 2019, but it was also higher than the total internationalization of the other seven major world currency issuers on average (45.67% compared to 42.98%, respectively). This further underlines its near monopolistic role; although Japan was ranked 3rd, the average annual Japanese sci-tech internationalization of 24.18% was more than twice the corresponding sci-tech internationalization of the Eurozone (11.37%); the average yearly Sci-tech in the UK was 2.75% over the same period, consistent with the pound's 4th place global ranking. Although AUD and CAD were ranked 5th and 6th, the average annual sci-tech internationalization figures for Australia and Canada were only 0.25% and 1.15%, lower than that of Switzerland and China.

13.1.2 Comparing sci-tech internationalization and currency internationalization

Table 13-1 shows that US sci-tech internationalization was on average higher than the corresponding USD internationalization, indicating the US has enough sci-tech to support USD; Japanese sci-tech was on average more than twice the internationalization of JPY, indicating that JPY internationalization has been insufficient compared to Japanese sci-tech, or JPY should have played a greater role in the international foreign exchange market; Eurozone sci-tech was not in line with the Euro's position as the world's second currency, with its sci-tech value than two-thirds of the Euro internationalization value. However, the Euro's ratio of 0.64 was more than 50% higher than the corresponding ratio of 0.41 for the British pound, indicating that GBP internationalization was less supportive of British sci-tech than the Euro; the ratio of CHF was 0.63 – very similar to that of the Euro.

It is noticeable that the 0.07 ratio of average annual Australian sci-tech internationalization compared to the internationalization of AUD was the lowest of all eight major international currencies; the second lowest was the Canadian dollar at 0.49, indicating that Canadian sci-tech support for the Canadian dollar was also the weakest. Of the eight major currencies, only the USD, JPY, and RMB had more than enough support from sci-tech for currency internationalization.

13.2 Correlation Coefficients between Sci-Tech and Currency Internationalization

Based on the results given in Table 13-1, we can calculate the correlation coefficients between the internationalization of the eight major currencies and the internationalization of the corresponding currency issuers from 2000 to 2019. Table 13-2 shows the results.

Table 13-2   Distribution of Correlation Coefficients between Sci-Tech Internationalization of Major Currency Issuers and Currency Internationalization (2000 to 2019)

Unit: %

Year	2001	2004	2007	2010	2013	2016	2019
2000	89.88	88.15	85.43	86.45	89.96	89.39	85.96
2001	89.89	88.13	85.70	86.61	90.14	89.62	86.32
2002	90.57	88.82	86.59	87.45	90.85	90.35	87.18
2003	89.47	87.63	85.66	86.40	89.97	89.52	86.37
2004	90.33	88.55	86.87	87.48	91.02	90.71	87.80
2005	92.47	90.84	88.92	89.68	92.84	92.43	89.59

(Continued)

Year	2001	2004	2007	2010	2013	2016	2019
2006	91.64	89.94	87.90	88.69	92.10	91.69	88.74
2007	92.48	90.86	88.63	89.52	92.82	92.39	89.46
2008	94.08	92.60	90.75	91.49	94.56	94.27	91.73
2009	94.15	92.67	90.96	91.63	94.66	94.38	91.90
2010	92.51	90.86	88.80	89.62	92.98	92.61	89.78
2011	93.13	91.55	90.16	90.66	93.91	93.73	91.30
2012	93.11	91.50	89.88	90.50	93.75	93.51	90.97
2013	94.14	92.70	91.10	91.65	94.77	94.59	92.20
2014	93.39	91.84	90.44	90.93	94.11	93.93	91.50
2015	92.19	90.56	89.39	89.77	93.10	92.99	90.56
2016*	94.49	93.07	92.39	92.61	95.39	95.39	93.51
2017*	95.34	94.08	93.73	93.82	96.35	96.63	95.22
2018*	96.21	95.10	94.90	94.94	97.17	97.50	96.34
2019*	96.40	95.46	95.54	95.48	97.45	97.96	97.20
Avg.	92.79	91.24	89.69	90.27	93.40	93.18	90.68

Data source: The horizontal axis corresponds to the data on the internationalization level of the world's top eight currencies every three years from 2000 to 2019; the vertical axis corresponds to the level of sci-tech internationalization of the eight major international currency issuers over the same time span.

Table 13-2 shows the correlations have been over 90% on average, indicating very high mutual dependence and support; this is consistent with our intuition that Sci-tech and currency support each other.

13.3 Problematic Correlation Coefficients

13.3.1 Problematic correlation coefficients

The high correlation coefficients in Table 13-2 are intuitively correct, yet it is difficult to see the direct relationship between currency internationalization and technological internationalization over different years from such similar data. Figure 13-1 shows the relationship between the two more intuitively.

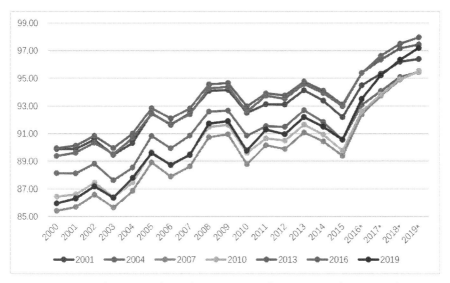

Figure 13-1   Correlation Coefficient between Sci-Tech Internationalization and Currency Internationalization (2000 to 2019) (Unit: %)

Data source: Same as Table 13-2.

Figure 13-1 shows that correlation coefficients between sci-tech internationalization and currency internationalization in 2010 were mainly higher than those of 2007, as evidenced by the higher average annual correlation coefficient of 93.4% compared to 89.7%. These results are somewhat counterintuitive since 2007 occurred before the global financial crisis the following year.

2010 was the second year of quantitative easing in the US, following the financial crisis; the daily average of USD was 82.2, and the USD internationalization index (the proportion of USD in global foreign exchange transactions shown in Table 4-1) was 42.43%, the lowest since 1998, indicating that in 2010 when USD index was the lowest, the support of currency to sci-tech should be lower than that of 2007 before the financial crisis, but Figure 14-1 shows that the correlation between technology and currency in 2010 was generally higher than the corresponding correlation in 2007, indicating that the relevant results in Figure 13-1 or Table 13-2 are with questionable.

13.3.2 Reasons for the problematic correlation coefficients

The complex correlation coefficients in Figure 13-1 are the results of overall foreign exchange derivatives trading in total foreign exchange daily turnover. Statistics from BIS show that foreign exchange derivatives as a proportion of the total increased from 68.85% in 2001 to 69.77% in 2007, indicating steady growth in this area before the financial crisis; it decreased significantly to 62.53% in 2010 and further to 61.72% in 2013; it recovered to 67.49% and 69.87% in 2016 and 2019, respectively – back to the pre-crisis levels. The correspondence of the lowest ratio of foreign exchange derivatives daily turnover was 61.72% in 2013, and the highest average annual correlation coefficient of 93.40% in Table 13-2 gives us an indication of the source of the problematic correlation coefficient in Figure 13-1, since the figures in Table 4-1 are not based on actual money-changing hands, but on the nominal trading value of foreign exchange derivatives: about two-thirds of foreign exchange daily average turnover is not real money changing hands; thus, the correlation coefficients between sci-tech internationalization and currency internationalization is also exaggerated.

13.4 Reassessing the Coefficient with Actual Foreign Exchange Turnover

13.4.1 Currency internationalization with actual foreign exchange turnover

The relationship between sci-tech internationalization and currency internationalization used data from Table 4-1 based on the average daily transaction value of traditional foreign exchange. However, Table 4-1 data is based on the nominal amount of foreign exchange daily turnover, which exaggerates the actual foreign exchange daily turnover. This section uses the negligible daily turnover of foreign exchange in major international currencies released by BIS to estimate the actual average daily transaction value of foreign exchange data. The corresponding results of the relationship between technology and currency internationalization are different from those given in Table 13-3.

Comparing currency internationalization results in Table 13-3 and in Table 13-1, we find that average annual USD internationalization and GBP internationalization declined 1.96% and 0.32%, and for the Euro and JPY it increased 1.58% and 1.08%, indicating the exaggerated contribution of high foreign exchange derivatives trading of USD and GBP. By contrast, the Euro and JPY were restored to reasonable levels because of relatively low foreign exchange derivatives trading.

Table 13-3 Comparison of Sci-Tech Internationalization of Major Currency Issuers with Currency Internationalization (2000 to 2019) Unit: %

Year	USD	EUR	JPY	GBP	AUD	CAD	CHF	RMB	Others
2001	42.61	21.17	12.85	5.59	1.84	2.06	3.42	0.00	10.47
2004	42.81	21.34	10.43	6.94	2.63	1.92	3.22	0.07	10.64
2007	39.84	20.55	10.01	7.46	2.73	1.95	4.24	0.41	12.83
2010	40.17	22.72	10.00	7.06	3.74	2.62	3.09	0.29	10.32
2013	41.59	18.22	14.54	5.58	4.73	2.28	2.12	0.86	10.06
2016	42.18	15.71	11.79	6.39	4.20	3.08	1.83	2.04	12.77
2019	42.70	15.58	8.96	6.09	4.14	2.98	2.20	2.40	14.94
Avg.	41.70	19.33	11.23	6.44	3.43	2.41	2.87	0.87	11.72
Sci-Tech Internationalization of Currency Issuers – Currency Internationalization									
2001	0.07	−9.83	15.10	−1.32	−1.48	−0.46	−2.20	0.94	−0.81
2004	−0.02	−10.63	16.39	−3.76	−2.23	−0.60	−1.87	0.88	1.84
2007	7.36	−9.15	16.21	−4.71	−2.46	−0.55	−2.95	0.36	−4.11
2010	7.40	−11.74	15.83	−4.94	−3.47	−1.85	−1.10	1.01	−1.15
2013	7.53	−7.49	8.89	−3.46	−4.58	−1.41	0.17	0.07	0.28
2016	3.45	−4.12	9.73	−4.23	−4.04	−2.19	0.65	−0.75	1.51
2019	3.68	−2.61	5.79	−3.71	−3.98	−2.05	0.04	3.21	−0.37
Avg.	4.21	−7.94	12.56	−3.73	−3.18	−1.30	−1.04	0.82	−0.40
Sci-Tech Internationalization of Currency Issuers/Currency Internationalization									
2001	1.00	0.54	2.18	0.76	0.19	0.78	0.36	193.05	0.92
2004	1.00	0.50	2.57	0.46	0.15	0.69	0.42	13.95	1.17
2007	1.18	0.55	2.62	0.37	0.10	0.72	0.30	1.86	0.68
2010	1.18	0.48	2.58	0.30	0.07	0.29	0.65	4.45	0.89
2013	1.18	0.59	1.61	0.38	0.03	0.38	1.08	1.08	1.03
2016	1.08	0.74	1.82	0.34	0.04	0.29	1.36	0.63	1.12
2019	1.09	0.83	1.65	0.39	0.04	0.31	1.02	2.34	0.98
Avg.	1.10	0.60	2.15	0.43	0.09	0.49	0.74	31.05	0.97

Data source: Sci-tech internationalization is the same as in Table 13-1; currency internationalization is calculated on the assumption that 5% of foreign exchange derivative nominal turnover is the actual daily turnover plus the actual daily turnover of spot foreign exchange.

13.4.2 Currency internationalization with actual foreign exchange turnover

Using the sci-tech internationalization results in Table 13-1 and currency internationalization data given in Table 13-3, we can calculate the internationalization level of the top eight major currencies and the internationalization of currency issuers from 2001–2019. Table 13-4 and Figure 13-2 give the corresponding results.

Table 13-4   Distribution of Correlation Coefficients between Sci-Tech Internationalization of Major Currency Issuers and Currency Internationalization (2000–2019)

Unit: %

Year	2001	2004	2007	2010	2013	2016	2019
2000	89.83	87.03	85.86	85.02	92.64	90.41	86.35
2001	89.86	87.04	86.08	85.00	92.66	90.64	86.78
2002	90.57	87.82	86.96	85.82	93.23	91.34	87.66
2003	89.51	86.62	86.00	84.53	92.28	90.55	86.97
2004	90.20	87.48	86.96	85.30	92.91	91.64	88.41
2005	92.32	89.85	89.07	87.85	94.73	93.25	90.01
2006	91.39	88.82	87.94	86.73	94.05	92.55	89.19
2007	92.13	89.71	88.60	87.66	94.73	93.18	89.81
2008	93.54	91.44	90.45	89.40	95.89	94.88	92.03
2009	93.64	91.54	90.68	89.47	95.90	94.97	92.22
2010	92.10	89.69	88.67	87.55	94.66	93.30	90.12
2011	92.64	90.40	89.82	88.19	95.02	94.35	91.75
2012	92.65	90.36	89.62	88.17	95.02	94.12	91.35
2013	93.45	91.43	90.62	89.24	95.74	95.09	92.50
2014	92.89	90.69	90.11	88.50	95.21	94.54	91.93
2015	91.81	89.44	89.12	87.19	94.22	93.67	91.12
2016*	94.02	92.11	91.97	89.99	95.85	95.85	93.96
2017*	94.67	93.16	93.06	91.07	96.19	96.87	95.57
2018*	95.45	94.22	94.13	92.22	96.71	97.63	96.62
2019*	95.48	94.61	94.55	92.67	96.47	97.91	97.40
Avg.	92.41	90.17	89.51	88.08	94.70	93.84	91.09

Data source: Calculated using sci-tech internationalization data in Table 13-1 and currency internationalization data (others are the same as in Table 13-1).

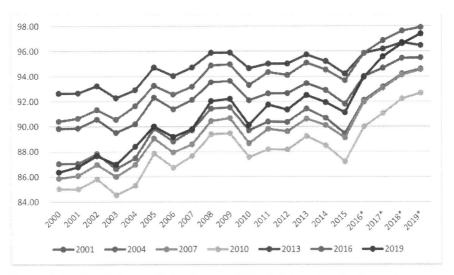

Figure 13-2   Correlation Coefficient between Sci-Tech Internationalization and Currency Internationalization (2000 to 2019) (Unit: %)

Data source: Same as Table 13-3.

Figure 13-2 clearly shows that correlation coefficients between sci-tech internationalization and currency internationalization were significantly lower in 2013 than 2007, and Table 13-4 shows the average annual correlation coefficients with 2010 currency internationalization of 88.08% was 1.43% lower than the yearly average of 89.61%. Apart from these two years before and after 2008, the average annual correlation coefficients between currency internationalization and sci-tech internationalization in Table 13-4 increased by 1.31%, 0.66%, and 0.41%, respectively, from the corresponding annual average correlation coefficients in Table 13-1.

The lowest average annual correlation coefficient with 2010 – the first full year of quantitative easing in the US – was consistent with very weak financial support for sci-tech in 2010 right after the 2008 global financial crisis. Results in Table 13-4 compared to those in Table 13-2 show that the USD's support for sci-tech steadily rebounded from 2013 to 2019, which is consistent with American financial recovery. The results in Table 13-4 show the rationality of using actual foreign exchange derivatives turnover rather than the nominal value.

13.5 The Best Measure of Currency Internationalization

The results shown in Figure 13-2 are significantly better than those shown in Figure 13-1, i.e., the nominal daily trading value given in Table 4-1 is regarded as the trading value is not a good measure of currency internationalization. Essentially, this is because nominal foreign exchange derivatives do not represent actual transfer transactions. The results in Table 13-4 are significantly better than those in Table 13-1, underlining the effectiveness of "discounting" the nominal transaction amount. Yet a new problem arises: is a 95% "discount" of foreign exchange derivatives or foreign exchange derivatives' nominal amount of 5% the best result? This section attempts to find the best measurement method of currency internationalization through the correlation between currency internationalization and technology internationalization corresponding to different discounts on the nominal transaction amount of foreign exchange derivatives.

13.5.1 Searching for optimum currency internationalization measurement

The mutual support of sci-tech internationalization and currency internationalization is logical, and we have found evidence in this chapter. Currency internationalization results from the average daily transaction amount of foreign exchange turnover calculated according to different "discount rates are different, leading to different correlation coefficients. However, the criterion for judging which discount method is best should be that the overall average correlation coefficients pre-2008 (financial crisis) and after 2014 (end of quantitative easing) are reasonable, and the corresponding overall average correlation is the highest in all years.

Using the same method to calculate the coefficient with different "discount" rates for foreign exchange derivatives turnover in other years, and then calculating the correlation between sci-tech internationalization and currency internationalization, Table 13-5 gives the corresponding results.

Table 13-5 shows that correlation coefficients between sci-tech internationalization and 2010 currency internationalization surpass correlation coefficients with 2007 currency internationalization. At least 50% of foreign exchange derivative turnover is considered as actual foreign exchange turnover, indicating that too much weight given to foreign exchange derivatives turnover leads to incorrect results. Overall average correlation coefficients with 2007–2019 currency internationalization increases when the percentage of foreign exchange derivatives turnover as actual foreign exchange derivative turnover reaches

30.6%, with the highest overall average correlation coefficients of 91.526576; the overall correlation coefficients decline when the percentage of foreign exchange derivatives turnover as actual foreign exchange derivative turnover is over 30.6%.

It is noticeable that the overall average correlation coefficient between sci-tech internalization and currency internationalization reaches the peak of 91.526567% when 30.6% of nominal foreign exchange derivatives turnover is regarded as the actual foreign exchange turnover.

Table 13-5   Comparison of Average Correlations between Different Measurement Results for Currency and Technology Internationalization (2000–2019)

Unit: %

"Discount" Rate	2007	2010	2013	2016	2019	Correlation Coefficient
2.00%	89.45	87.84	94.75	93.89	91.12	91.411904
3.00%	89.47	87.92	94.74	93.87	91.11	91.423699
4.00%	89.49	88.00	94.72	93.86	91.10	91.434454
5.00%	89.51	88.08	94.70	93.84	91.09	91.444258
6.00%	89.53	88.15	94.69	93.82	91.08	91.453191
7.00%	89.55	88.22	94.67	93.80	91.07	91.461327
8.00%	89.56	88.29	94.65	93.79	91.06	91.468731
9.00%	89.58	88.35	94.63	93.77	91.05	91.475463
10.00%	89.59	88.41	94.61	93.76	91.04	91.481578
15.00%	89.64	88.69	94.52	93.69	90.99	91.504463
20.00%	89.67	88.92	94.43	93.62	90.95	91.517705
25.00%	89.69	89.11	94.33	93.57	90.92	91.524387
28.00%	89.70	89.21	94.28	93.54	90.90	91.526127
30.00%	89.70	89.27	94.25	93.52	90.89	91.526549
30.50%	89.70	89.28	94.24	93.52	90.89	91.526575
30.60%	89.70	89.29	94.24	93.52	90.89	91.526576
31.00%	89.71	89.30	94.23	93.51	90.88	91.526570
31.50%	89.71	89.31	94.22	93.51	90.88	91.526536
32.00%	89.71	89.33	94.21	93.51	90.88	91.526475

(Continued)

"Discount" Rate	2007	2010	2013	2016	2019	Correlation Coefficient
35.00%	89.71	89.41	94.16	93.48	90.86	91.525575
45.00%	89.72	89.64	94.01	93.41	90.82	91.517752
48.00%	89.72	89.69	93.96	93.39	90.81	91.514431
49.00%	89.72	89.71	93.95	93.38	90.80	91.513255
50.00%	89.72	89.73	93.93	93.38	90.80	91.512050
60.00%	89.71	89.89	93.80	93.32	90.77	91.498812
80.00%	89.70	90.11	93.58	93.24	90.72	91.469927
100.00%	89.69	90.27	93.40	93.18	90.68	91.442045

Data source: Calculated using foreign exchange derivatives turnovers of eight major international currencies released by BIS from 2007 to 2019 and various "discount" rates of foreign exchange derivatives.

13.5.2 Optimum currency internationalization

Using the optimum currency internationalization point of 30.6% in Table 13-5, we can find results for the eight major currencies, which are given in Table 13-6. Table 13-6 shows that support of US sci-tech internationalization to USD internationalization becomes stronger as the difference between the two increases from 2.01% in Table 13-1 to 2.98% in Table 13-6, resulting from using actual rather than nominal derivatives turnover and lower USD internationalization in Table 13-5. We will discuss related issues further in Section 13.7.

Table 13-6   Comparison of Sci-Tech Internationalization of Major Currency Issuers with Currency Internationalization (2000 to 2019)

Unit: %

Currency Internationalization of Major Currencies								
Year	USD	EUR	JPY	GBP	AUD	CAD	CHF	RMB	Others
2001	43.81	20.03	12.29	6.07	2.00	2.15	3.20	0.00	10.45
2004	43.41	20.01	10.42	7.60	2.82	2.01	3.12	0.06	10.55
2007	41.38	19.49	9.29	7.44	3.03	2.05	3.81	0.32	13.20

(Continued)

Currency Internationalization of Major Currencies									
Year	USD	EUR	JPY	GBP	AUD	CAD	CHF	RMB	Others
2010	41.25	21.20	9.76	6.76	3.76	2.63	3.12	0.36	11.16
2013	42.50	17.50	13.12	5.74	4.54	2.28	2.34	0.98	11.00
2016	43.00	15.70	11.30	6.40	3.82	2.82	2.12	2.02	12.84
2019	43.46	15.87	8.67	6.25	3.75	2.74	2.35	2.27	14.64
Avg.	42.69	18.54	10.69	6.61	3.39	2.38	2.86	0.86	11.97
Sci-Tech Internationalization of Currency Issuers – Currency Internationalization									
2001	−1.13	−8.69	15.66	−1.80	−1.65	−0.56	−1.98	0.94	−0.79
2004	−0.62	−9.30	16.40	−4.42	−2.42	−0.69	−1.76	0.89	1.94
2007	5.82	−8.09	16.93	−4.70	−2.77	−0.65	−2.52	0.46	−4.47
2010	6.33	−10.21	16.07	−4.65	−3.50	−1.86	−1.13	0.94	−1.99
2013	6.62	−6.78	10.31	−3.61	−4.38	−1.41	−0.04	−0.05	−0.66
2016	2.63	−4.11	10.22	−4.24	−3.66	−1.93	0.36	−0.73	1.45
2019	2.92	−2.90	6.08	−3.87	−3.58	−1.81	−0.10	3.33	−0.07
Avg.	3.22	−7.16	13.10	−3.90	−3.14	−1.27	−1.02	0.83	−0.66
Sci-Tech Internationalization of Currency Issuers/Currency Internationalization									
2001	0.97	0.57	2.27	0.70	0.18	0.74	0.38	216.96	0.92
2004	0.99	0.54	2.57	0.42	0.14	0.65	0.43	16.37	1.18
2007	1.14	0.58	2.82	0.37	0.09	0.68	0.34	2.44	0.66
2010	1.15	0.52	2.65	0.31	0.07	0.29	0.64	3.63	0.82
2013	1.16	0.61	1.79	0.37	0.03	0.38	0.98	0.95	0.94
2016	1.06	0.74	1.90	0.34	0.04	0.32	1.17	0.64	1.11
2019	1.07	0.82	1.70	0.38	0.04	0.34	0.96	2.47	1.00
Avg.	1.08	0.62	2.24	0.41	0.09	0.49	0.70	34.78	0.95

Data source: Sci-tech internationalization is the same as in Table 13-1; currency internationalization is calculated using 30.6% of foreign exchange derivative nominal turnover as the actual daily turnover, plus daily turnover of spot foreign exchange.

13.6 Function of Foreign Exchange Derivatives Trading Implied in the Best Measure of Currency Internationalization

Since most of the notional amounts involved in foreign exchange derivatives transactions actually have less than 5% of this figure in actual trading, the best currency internationalization point should occur lower than 5%. Yet, Table 13-5 shows the result of the best currency internationalization point of 30.6%, which is not only puzzling but even a little strange. However, after careful analysis of the relevant results, the answer can be found in the functions of foreign exchange derivatives trading. Foreign exchange derivatives transactions are not only cash that changes hands, but more importantly, they provide traders with the necessary exchange rate "safe haven," which reduces the risk of corporate investment or cross-border R&D investment, thereby promoting the internationalization of technology development. Therefore, the best point of currency internationalization is 30.6%, which clearly exceeds 5.0%. The result reflects the investment function of currency as well as the hedging function of foreign exchange derivative transactions. If the overall average correlation of 5%, corresponding to 91.444258%, is regarded as the investment function of currency, then the corresponding increase from 5% to 30.6% or 25.6% should reflect the degree of support of the currency's hedging function to technology.

This section aims to deepen the understanding of the trading functions of foreign exchange derivatives by analyzing the best measurement of currency internationalization.

13.7 Overestimations and Underestimations

13.7.1 Internationalization of three major currencies

The high correlation coefficient between currency internationalization and sci-tech internationalization indicates that the interaction between the two is considerable. Table 13-1 shows that the internationalization level of US sci-tech is significantly higher than that of the USD, indicating that US sci-tech has sufficient support for the dollar. The sci-tech of Japan is 136%, higher than JPY internationalization on average from 2000 to 2019, and the sci-tech internationalization/JPY internationalization ratio is the highest among the eight major international currencies.

Results from Table 13-6 show that the ratio of US sci-tech internationalization/ internationalization of USD increases from 1.05 in Table 13-1 to 1.08 with the optimum currency internationalization, indicating that USD is more under measured internationally; the ratio of Japanese sci-tech internationalization/ internationalization of JPY decreases from 2.36 in Table 13-1 to 2.24 with the optimum currency internationalization, indicating the reverse of USD.

13.7.2 Over-Measuring the internationalization of five major currencies

Table 13-1 shows that the ratios of average annual sci-tech internationalization/ average annual currency internationalization of the Eurozone, UK, Australia, Canada, and Switzerland are 65%, 40%, 8%, 48%, and 67%, respectively; or internationalization of the Eurozone, UK, Australia, Canada, and Switzerland is 35%, 60%, 92%, 52%, and 33% lower than their currency internationalization rates, respectively. In other words, their sci-tech internationalization rate is not sufficient to support the internationalization of their currencies, which are mainly funded (indirectly) by Japanese and US sci-tech internationalization.

Similar ratios in Table 13-6 show that the proportion of average annual sci-tech internationalization/average annual currency internationalization of the Eurozone decreases from 65% to 62% with the best measure of currency internationalization. The ratios of average annual sci-tech internationalization/average annual currency internationalization of the UK, Australia, Canada, and Switzerland increase from 40%, 8%, 49%, and 70% slightly to 41%, 9%, 49%, and 70% respectively with the best measure of currency internationalization, indicating that expect Euro, GBP, AUD, Canadian dollar and CHF are slightly less over-measured internationally with the best measure of currency internationalization.

13.7.3 Under-Measurement of Chinese Yuan internationalization

Table 13-1 and Table 13-6 show that the ratios of sci-tech internationalization/ yuan internationalization were very high due to the extremely low Chinese yuan foreign exchange turnover in 2000 and 2004; regardless of the extremely high ratios of these two years, the ratios decrease slightly from 2.10 in Table 13-1 from 2007 to 2019 to 2.03 for the same time period. This indicates that the yuan was under-measured internationally from 2007 to 2019, and the degree of under-measurement was second only to the Japanese yen.

Data for Korean sci-tech internationalization and Korean won internationalization shows that the won has been under-measured internationally; the degree of under-measurement is between the JPY and RMB, indicating that all three major Asian currencies are under-measured internationally compared to the over-measured three major European currencies.

13.8 Conclusion

We have found high correlation coefficients between currency internationalization and sci-tech internationalization for the eight major currency issuers,
indicating a mutually supporting relationship. The unusually higher
correlation coefficients between sci-tech internationalization and currency
internationalization of 2010 compared to 2007 help shed light on the problem
of using nominal foreign exchange derivative turnovers. By stripping off most
of the nominal turnover, the corresponding currency internationalization
results are more reasonable. This helps us to understand the functionality of
foreign exchange derivatives trading – the hedging function of foreign exchange
derivatives is much more critical than their cash function.

Relationship between Monetary Autonomy and Currency Internationalization, Technological Autonomy and Technology Internationalization

SCI-TECH IS THE BASIS FOR ECONOMIC development; thus, Sci-Tech originality capacity determines economic progress. Furthermore, economy and trade development is the basis for currency usage; thus, economy and trade originating capacity determine the monetary originating capacity. Based on data of trade settlements of major world currencies, we define monetary autonomy first in this chapter in line with sci-tech originating capacity discussed and analyzed in the previous chapter. We explore the relationship between monetary autonomy and sci-tech originating capacity in this chapter, and then find empirical evidence among monetary autonomy, sci-tech originating capacity, and currency internationalization. Empirical evidence on the mutual relationships among sci-tech originating capacity, monetary autonomy, technology internationalization, and currency internationalization will help us to understand better the relationship between technology internationalization and currency internationalization.

14.1 Interest Rate Determination

As the interest rate is the most critical factor affecting and determining the price of all assets, the interest rate is not only the critical factor of the whole financial market and the whole economy, but also the source of all risks, as well as the most significant factor affecting monetary autonomy. All monetary authorities have the power as to what extent to raise and lower interest rates in their economic domains, yet different monetary authorities have different degrees of freedom to raise or lower their interests depending on their concerns for cross-border capital flows, foreign exchange rates, and so on. Taking US dollar for example, the rise and fall of USD interest rates are determined mainly by the economic conditions of the US, with little regard for changes in current accounts, foreign currency reserves, or capital flows. Changes in US interest rate under the Federal Reserve Board before the international financial crisis in 2008 and after withdrawal from the quantitative easing policies in 2014, fully reflected the independence of the USD from 2007 to 2020. Other monetary authorities, including those of the Eurozone, Japan, the UK, Switzerland, and other countries, often need to consider capital flow and other issues to adjust their interest rates according to the interest rate of USD. Under similar circumstances, the interest rate policy of the People's Bank of China (PBC) must take factors such as the stability of RMB exchange rate and cross-border capital flows into consideration. Thus, the lower the degree of monetary autonomy, the more restrictive factors of interest rate policy, and the lower the degree of freedom.

14.1.1 Currency issuance

The right of currency issuance is the connotation within the scope of national sovereign rights, but currency issuance with a low degree of monetary autonomy must be subject to changes in the current account and other factors, and the constraints of foreign factors often exceed the domestic economic factors. Studies show that trade surplus as a share of money supply change (M1 change) averaged around 20.4% from 2002 to 2004, yet it jumped to 75.5% from 2005 to 2007; the share jumped to 152.3% in 2008 because of the world financial crisis; the average share returned to 77.4% from 2009 to 2012, slightly higher than the pre-crisis average share 75.5% from 2005 to 2007 (Zhang 2021). Although the share fell steadily to below 50% from 2013 to 2020, it is still significantly higher than most other major economies in the world. These data indicate that RMB issuance has been primarily determined by commodity exports that have been significantly affected by foreign-funded enterprises in China over the years. As currency issuance is affected by external factors, the excess deposit margin ratio in China is a passive way to re-draw the excess currency back to the monetary authority, which is a clear sign of low monetary autonomy.

14.1.2 Gold reserves

The share of gold reserves in foreign exchange reserves of various monetary authorities also reflects their degrees of financial freedom to a certain degree. Although the economic function of gold has weakened significantly, the steady amount of gold reserves of the US and the Eurozone indicates that the monetary role of gold has not been eliminated. A lower share of gold reserve in foreign exchange reserve means a higher percentage of foreign currency reserve in foreign exchange reserve, or higher dependence on the foreign currency of a monetary authority.

14.1.3 Currency pricing power

In addition to interest rates and economic growth rates, the most critical factor in determining the currency price is the change in the current account balance, which is mainly affected by trade in goods and services. Therefore, when an economy's export trade is mainly determined by foreign enterprises, its currency pricing power falls into the hands of foreign investors. Currencies without enough independent pricing power are in fact only dependent currencies or derivative currencies, and derivative currencies cannot become real international currencies.

14.1.4 Overseas listing

Overseas listing is another reflection of the enterprises' reliance on overseas capital markets or technology, as well as the currencies of the object listing country. Overseas listing brings dividends of the listed company to overseas investors. As a result, overseas listing increases the financial wealth of the investors in the overseas country, thus increasing consumption and investments and ultimately supporting the currency of the object listing country or region. Therefore, the more companies listed abroad, the higher the reliance of the listed company on the target listed country. Since the US is the country with the most significant number of listed foreign enterprises and the largest number of listed foreign companies, the US dollar is the most independent currency in the world capital market.

14.2 Concept of Currency Originality Capacity

The ability or degree of monetary autonomy involves various aspects such as currency issuance, circulation, pricing, reserve, etc. The higher the monetary autonomy, the lower the degree of influence of other currencies on essential decisions such as currency issuance, circulation, and pricing, except for the domestic economic and trade factors. Conversely, the lower the ability of monetary autonomy, the higher the degree of influence of other currencies on currency issuance due to factors such as current account balance and foreign exchange reserve changes. In other words, the higher the degree of monetary autonomy, the more flexible the monetary policy is. Otherwise, the lower the ability for financial independence, the higher the degree of reliance on other economic policies. Therefore, a currency with low autonomy is an appendage or derivative of currencies with high autonomy and does not have necessary qualifications to become an international currency.

Zhang (2021) also shows that the proportion of China's commodity trade surplus in China's currency issuance (M1) increased from 22.8% in 2002 to 151.2% in 2008. Affected by the 2008 world financial crisis, China's commodity trade surplus accounted for 24.3% of China's currency issuance in 2009, yet it continued to increase to an average of 77.5% from 2009 to 2012. The ratio dropped slightly to 56.2% in 2013 and surged to a historical high of 218.2% in 2014, accounting for 74.5% of the total from 2009 to 2014. The average ratio declined slightly to 72.3% from 2015 to 2020, and it rose to 128.7% in the first half of 2021. The high proportions of commodity trade surpluses over money issuances imply a high dependence of money supply on foreign capital through foreign trade.

The exchange rate of RMB against the USD is mainly affected by the current account balance, which is dominated by the commodity trade, while the balance of trade in goods and trade in services is also primarily affected by foreign enterprises, so the initiative of RMB exchange rate pricing is also heavily influenced by foreign enterprises. In this way, due to the low monetary autonomy, the RMB issuing right and pricing power, which originally belonged to the scope of the national sovereign, cannot be controlled independently to some extent.

14.3 Definition and Measurement of Currency Originality Capacity

Corresponding to the sci-tech originality capacity (OC) measure defined, measured, and analyzed in the previous chapters, monetary autonomy or originality capacity (COC) refers to a currency's global foreign exchange transactions as a percentage of the currency's international transactions plus the currency's trade and capital account transactions using foreign currency. The higher the proportion, the lower the dependence of the currency issuer on other currencies, and the higher the originality capacity or autonomy of the currency. Conversely, the higher the reliance of the currency issuer on foreign currencies, the lower the independence.

14.3.1　Rationality of negligence of capital market daily turnover

Data from the world federation of exchanges show that the average daily turnover of the world stock market was USD 27.8 billion, 22.4 billion, 28.9 billion, and 34.2 billion in April 2010, April 2013, April 2016, and April 2019, respectively, representing merely 1.40%, 0.84%, 1.14%, and 1.04% of the corresponding average daily turnover of global foreign exchange market given in Table 4-1 respectively. What is more, most of the world stock turnover is domestic rather than international. There, the average daily turnover of the world stock market can be neglected compared to the average daily turnover of the global foreign exchange market. The similar scale of the world bond market average daily turnover to the world stock market turnover and the majority domestic trading nature of the world bond market make similar negligence of world bond market turnover of not much influence on currency originality capacity.

14.3.2　Calculation of currency originality of RMB and USD

Table 4-1 shows that the average daily turnover of RMB in the global foreign exchange market accounted for 4.32% of the world's total average daily turnover, or USD 285.03 billion in 2019. The average daily commodity and service trade was USD 20.491 billion in China at the same time. The proportion of RMB trade settlement was 19.1% in 2019. Therefore, China's trade settlement was dependent on $20.491 \times (1-0.191) =$ USD 16.577 billion in foreign currencies. The average daily turnover of world foreign exchange cannot be directly compared with daily world trade value because the former was 28.49 times, 30.05 times, and 33.58 times of the latter in 2013, 2016, and 2019, respectively, and different currencies have different similar ratios. For simplicity, we use the world ratio of 33.58 to convert the daily average trade of USD 16.577 billion in China in 2019, or USD 556.726 as China's dependence on foreign currencies for her trade settlement in 2019. Therefore, RMB originality capacity was $0.285 / (0.285 + 556.726) = 33.86\%$ in 2019. Using the same method, we can obtain RMB originality capacity of

1.00%, 2.31%, 8.04%, 12.15%, 22.21%, 34.09%, and 33.86% in 2001, 2007, 2010, and 2016, respectively.

Similarly, we can obtain USD originality capacity from 2001 to 2019 using the above definition and the proportion of US dollar exports and imports in US dollar settlement in corresponding years given in Sato (1998). As ratios of US exports settled in US dollars in 1980, 1988, 1992–1996 were 97%, 96%, and 98%, with accumulated change of merely 1% from 1980 to 1996; and US imports settled in US dollars in 1980, 1988, 1992–1996 were 85%, 85% and 88.8% the same time, with accumulated change merely 3.8% to 1980 to 1996. Thus, the USD settlement of US exports and imports reached stable levels up to 1996. Therefore, we assume that the ratio of US dollar exports and imports settled in USD remains at the average annual growth rate of 1% / 16 = 0.06% and 3.8% / 16 = 0.24% from 1980 to 1996. Then, we can estimate US exports and imports settled in USD from 2001 to 2019 with ratios of 98.0% and 88.8% in 1996 and the assumed average increase accordingly. Therefore, we can obtain USD originality capacity in 2001, 2004, 2007, 2010, 2013, 2016, and 2019 following the same procedure above to find RMB originality capacity. The results are shown in Table 14-1.

14.3.3 Calculation assumptions to obtain originality capacities of other major world currencies

Using exports and imports data of goods and services of Japan, the average annual changes in Japanese exports and imports settled in Japanese yen from 1988 to 1996 were 0.32% and 1.64% (calculated using Table 3 of Sato 1998). Assuming the average annual change remains the same from 1996 to 2019, we can obtain Japanese exports and imports settled in Japanese yen and then find yen originating capacity in Table 14-1. Similarly, we can obtain results for the British pound using British exports and imports of both goods and services from World Development Indicators of the World Bank, and the average annual changes of British exports and imports settled in the British pound from 1980 to 1996 were −0.88% and 0.86% (calculated using Table 3 of Sato 1998). Assuming the average annual change remains the same from 1996 to 2019, we can obtain British exports and imports settled in pound and then find pound originating capacity in Table 14-1.

As Sato (1998) did not have export and import settlement data for Euro, we use the arithmetic average export and import settlements ratios of Germany, France, and Italy to stand for corresponding settlement ratios for Euro. The average annual changes of Euro exports and imports settled in Euro from 1980 to

1996 were −0.33% and 0.90% (calculated using Table 3 of Sato 1998). Following the same procedures as to calculate yen and pound originality capacity above, we can obtain Euro originality capacity in Table 14-1. The Euro results in Table 14-1 are not directly comparable with others because exports and imports of the Euro Zone released by WTO include intra-Euro trading; thus, Euro exports and import values are significantly larger than those of other currency issuers. We use Intra-EU exports and imports ratios to exclude the intra-Euro exports and imports, estimate comparable exports and imports data for Euro Zone, and find corresponding Euro originality capacity results in Table 14-1 as Euro 2.

As relating comparable settlement ratios of exports and imports of Switzerland, Australia, and Canada with the Swiss franc, Australian dollar, and Canadian dollar were absent in Sato (1998), we must use exports and imports data of charges for the use of IP of these three countries compared with the UK and US. According to preliminary statistics, the average ratio of exports of costs for use of IP in Switzerland over exports of charges for the use of IP in UK was 94.80% from 2008 to 2019, and the average ratio of imports of charges for the use of IP in Switzerland over imports of charges for the use of IP in UK was 98.57% the same period. Both average ratios were close to 100%, implying that the technology internationalization of the two countries was similar. Thus, we assume that the proportion of Swiss exports and imports settled with the Swiss franc was 94.80% of the proportions of British exports settled with the British pound and 98.57% of British imports paid with the British pound from 2001 to 2019, and similarly obtain Swiss franc originality capacity from 2001 to 2019 given in Table 14-1.

We use average ratios of Australian exports and import of charges for the use of IP over US exports and imports of charges for the use of IP 1.13% and 9.48% from 2008 to 2019 and assume Australian proportions of exports and imports settled in the Australian dollar as the multiplications of the corresponding US proportions with average ratios of exports and imports 1.13% and 9.48%. Australian originality capacity from 2001 to 2019 can be obtained accordingly following similar procedures above, and the results are given in Table 14-1. Canadian dollar originality capacity from 2001 to 2019 can be similarly calculated in Table 14-1.

14.3.4 Distribution of currency originality of major world currencies

Table 14-1 shows that USD had the highest originality capacity (OC) of all eight currencies, with OC over 99% from 2001 to 2019. Euro, JPY, and GBP, the three second-tier world currencies, had a currency originality capacity about 10% lower than the USD OC; their OC was close to 90%; AUD and CHF had originality capacity slightly lower than the three second-tier currencies Euro, JPY, and GBP; and CAD and RMB were ranked 7th and 8th in OC, respectively.

Table 14-1   Distribution of Monetary Autonomy of Major International Currencies (2001–2019)

Unit: %

Currency	2001	2004	2007	2010	2013	2016	2019
USD	99.21	99.28	99.39	99.46	99.47	99.48	99.56
EUR	79.14	76.89	77.66	80.29	76.43	75.20	74.42
JPY	88.62	87.55	87.40	88.49	90.38	90.36	88.64
GBP	88.58	90.22	90.20	90.40	88.46	89.00	89.13
AUD	89.04	88.19	88.20	87.65	87.24	85.56	84.37
CAD	66.09	66.08	68.89	74.44	68.94	72.19	71.64
CHF	91.47	91.17	92.30	90.10	85.28	84.38	85.74
RMB	0.32	2.31	8.04	12.15	22.21	34.09	33.86
EUR	87.94	84.95	91.28	91.91	89.59	89.47	88.88
Others	44.72	28.90	52.53	47.74	42.51	44.51	54.97

It is noticeable that RMB OC increased over 100 times from 0.32% in 2001 to 33.86% in 2019, yet RMB OC as a percentage of USD OC was from 0.3% in 2001 to 34.0% in 2019, indicating much to catch in years or decades to come.

14.4 Currency Originality with Better Currency Internationalization Measures

Currency originality measures in Table 14-1 were based on the currency internationalization data corresponding to the nominal turnovers of global foreign exchange markets. The results in Chapter 13 show that the currency internationalization corresponding to the nominal foreign exchange turnovers is not accurate because most of the nominal amount of foreign exchange derivatives is not actual cash transactions or cash exchanged. Thus, the corresponding currency internationalization results are not accurate enough. We measure the currency originality capacity of major world currencies using the corresponding daily average turnovers corresponding to better currency internationalization in Chapter 13, and the results are shown in Table 14-2.

Table 14-2   Distribution of Currency Originality of Major International Currencies Corresponding to the Better Currency Internationalization Measures (2001–2019)

Unit: %

Currency	2001	2004	2007	2010	2013	2016	2019
USD	98.46	98.64	93.58	99.02	99.05	99.01	99.10
EUR	67.67	65.45	65.36	71.47	65.99	61.76	59.58
JPY	80.94	78.94	79.38	81.74	85.93	83.90	80.58
GBP	79.03	81.91	82.62	84.84	80.95	81.14	80.56
AUD	73.99	78.84	77.94	79.94	80.40	77.77	75.48
CAD	49.42	49.81	52.20	62.12	55.92	60.28	58.61
CHF	85.69	85.04	87.34	83.60	75.00	71.71	74.58
RMB	0.19	1.49	5.93	6.11	12.56	17.93	21.72
EUR	86.64	85.23	85.03	87.48	83.74	81.90	80.20
Others	29.75	17.92	35.76	32.31	27.82	44.51	39.05

Changes from Table 14-1

Currency	2001	2004	2007	2010	2013	2016	2019
USD	−0.75	−0.64	−5.81	−0.44	−0.42	−0.47	−0.43
EUR	−11.47	−11.44	−12.30	−8.83	−10.44	−13.44	−14.84
JPY	−7.68	−8.61	−8.01	−6.76	−4.45	−6.46	−8.06
GBP	−9.55	−8.31	−7.58	−5.55	−7.50	−7.86	−8.61
AUD	−15.05	−9.35	−10.26	−7.71	−6.84	−7.78	−8.89
CAD	−16.66	−16.26	−16.68	−12.32	−13.02	−11.91	−13.03
CHF	−5.78	−6.13	−4.96	−6.50	−10.28	−12.67	−11.16
RMB	−0.13	−0.82	−2.11	−6.04	−9.65	−16.16	−12.14
EUR	−1.31	0.28	−6.25	−4.43	−5.85	−7.57	−8.68
Others	−14.97	−10.98	−16.77	−15.43	−14.69	0.00	−15.91

Data source: Using the currency internationalization data in Table 13-5 and the same method in Table 14-1.

Currency originality results in Table 14-2 are all lower than Table 14-1 because many foreign exchange derivatives turnovers are eliminated. Table 14-2 shows that the originality capacity USD remained at the level of around 90% from 2001 to 2019 with the slightest changes, which are still significantly higher than the originality capacities of any other currencies, indicating that the US dollar is still far ahead of other currencies in originality capacity. Originality capacities of Euro 2, Japanese yen, British pound, and Australian dollar were 8% to 9% lower with the better currency internationalization measures than with nominal currency internationalization measures in Table 14-1; and those of Canadian dollar, Swiss franc, and Chinese yuan were 11% to 13% lower than those in Table 14-1. The ratio of Chinese yuan originality capacity over that of USD increased over 100 times from 0.2% in 2001 to 21.72%, showing a more significant gap between the two currencies.

14.5 The Relationship between Currency Originality Capacity and Sci-Tech Originality Capacity

With the above estimation results of major currency originality capacity (COC) and the corresponding sci-tech originality capacity (STOC) measures of major currency issuers given in Table 7-1, we can easily calculate the relationship between principal monetary autonomy and its issuers' technological autonomy. The results are shown in Table 14-3.

Table 14-3 Distribution of Correlation Coefficients between Currency Originality Capacity and Sci-Tech Originality Capacity of Major Currency Issuers (2001–2019)

Unit: %

Results Corresponding to COC Measures in Table 14-1								
Year	2001	2004	2007	2010	2013	2016	2019	Average
2000	36.35	34.12	36.33	36.33	41.54	43.48	45.82	39.14
2001	36.90	34.50	36.87	36.83	41.93	43.76	46.17	39.56
2002	37.98	35.35	37.98	37.86	42.77	44.44	47.00	40.48
2003	39.07	36.42	38.93	38.83	43.76	45.34	47.81	41.45
2004	36.81	34.32	36.59	36.55	41.74	43.45	45.71	39.31

(Continued)

Results Corresponding to COC Measures in Table 14-1							
Year	2001	2004	2007	2010	2013	2016	2019	Average
2005	40.19	37.49	40.12	40.04	44.98	46.54	48.92	42.61
2006	39.60	37.16	39.39	39.48	44.56	46.24	48.40	42.12
2007	38.33	35.92	38.10	38.18	43.37	45.08	47.19	40.88
2008	36.44	33.99	36.19	36.22	41.50	43.23	45.29	38.98
2009	37.67	34.75	37.58	37.28	42.14	43.59	46.16	39.88
2010	36.00	33.55	35.74	35.52	41.00	42.69	44.81	38.47
2011	36.74	33.98	36.53	36.18	41.40	42.90	45.27	39.00
2012	36.41	33.81	36.11	35.84	41.19	42.76	44.93	38.72
2013	38.12	35.50	37.77	37.53	42.80	44.29	46.47	40.36
2014	37.42	34.10	37.18	36.60	41.41	42.52	45.30	39.22
2015	34.34	30.68	34.05	33.22	38.03	38.97	41.94	35.89
2016	34.13	30.16	33.96	33.02	37.55	38.35	41.54	35.53
2017	24.84	21.61	24.54	23.82	29.39	30.80	33.20	26.89
2018	26.19	23.02	25.83	25.20	30.79	32.20	34.50	28.25
2019	23.14	20.22	22.84	22.28	28.14	29.79	31.91	25.47
Average	35.33	32.53	35.13	34.84	40.00	41.52	43.92	37.61

Results Corresponding to COC Measures in Table 14-2							
Year	2001	2004	2007	2010	2013	2016	2019	Average
2000	44.65	39.82	38.53	40.95	48.08	54.35	52.93	45.61
2001	45.04	40.07	38.93	41.28	48.35	54.66	53.11	45.92
2002	45.89	40.73	39.83	42.09	49.03	55.42	53.7	46.67
2003	46.66	41.46	40.65	42.84	49.88	56.12	54.25	47.41
2004	44.7	39.56	38.58	40.73	48.06	54.08	52.32	45.43
2005	48.08	42.79	42.02	44.09	51.07	57.08	55.22	48.62

(Continued)

2006	47.39	42.31	41.29	43.57	50.73	56.6	54.84	48.1
2007	46.24	41.17	40.09	42.34	49.62	55.44	53.7	46.94
2008	44.58	39.42	38.34	40.44	47.85	53.56	51.85	45.15

Results Corresponding to COC Measures in Table 14-2

Year	2001	2004	2007	2010	2013	2016	2019	Average
2009	45.62	40.09	39.5	41.27	48.26	54.32	52.47	45.93
2010	44.55	39.3	38.35	39.94	47.45	52.93	51.4	44.85
2011	45	39.53	38.87	40.35	47.67	53.36	51.63	45.2
2012	44.77	39.35	38.6	40.04	47.48	52.89	51.25	44.91
2013	46.08	40.67	40.02	41.52	48.94	54.39	52.6	46.32
2014	44.7	38.85	38.79	40.1	47.31	53.43	51.13	44.9
2015	41.27	35.19	35.44	36.48	43.95	50.29	47.66	41.47
2016	41.07	34.7	35.22	36.11	43.31	49.78	47.05	41.03
2017	33.08	27.17	26.86	27.79	36.01	41.85	39.61	33.2
2018	34.31	28.45	28.12	29.8	37.34	43.07	40.8	34.46
2019	31.86	26.2	25.5	26.62	35.03	40.68	38.68	32.08
Average	43.28	37.84	37.18	38.88	46.27	52.22	50.31	43.71

Data source: Calculated with sci-tech originality capacity results in Table 7-1, and currency originality capacity results in Table 14-1 and Table 14-2, respectively.

Table 14-3 shows that the average correlations coefficient between currency originality capacity using traditional nominal foreign exchange turnovers and sci-tech originality capacity is 37.61% from 2000 to 2019, indicating a relatively mutual supporting relationship between sci-tech originality capacity and currency originality capacity. The average correlations coefficients between currency originality capacity using better currency internationalization and sci-tech originality capacity are 43.71% from 2000 to 2019, indicating a higher mutual supportive relationship between sci-tech originality capacity and currency originality capacity.

14.6 Mutual Influence between Currency Originality Capacity and Sci-Tech Originality Capacity

The relatively high degree of correlation between currency originality capacity and sci-tech originality capacity indicates that the two originality capacity measures are mutually supportive of each other, but we do not know the degree of mutual influence between the two. We use the same method in the previous chapter to analyze the difference in the degree of mutual leverage between the two.

14.6.1 Sci-tech originality capacity to influence currency originality capacity

Since we have continuous annual data on sci-tech originality capacity from 2001 to 2019, and only data on currency originality capacity are triennial data every three years during the same period, it is difficult for us to match sci-tech originality capacity and currency originality capacity. For the annual impact results, we can only obtain the regression results of the impact of currency originality capacity on sci-tech originality capacity, as shown in Table 14-4.

Table 14-4   Regression Results of the Influence of Currency Originality on Sci-Tech Originality Capacity with Currency Originality in Table 14-1 (2001–2019)

Sci-Tech OC 2001 to 2010 as Independent Variables and COC of 2010 as Dependent Variable				
−434.069	2,306.151	−2,097.14	82.149768	77.5502
689.6401	1,259.611	1,879.011	714.98125	14.6699
0.541809	27.03124	N/A	N/A	N/A
1.182498	4	N/A	N/A	N/A
3,456.149	2,922.753	N/A	N/A	N/A
Sci-Tech OC 2001 to 2010 as Independent Variables and COC of 2013 as Dependent Variable				
−305.666	2,078.934	−2,009.7	107.77883	75.6148
622.0903	1,136.233	1,694.963	644.94934	13.233
0.556607	24.38355	N/A	N/A	N/A
1.255336	4	N/A	N/A	N/A
2,985.478	2,378.23	N/A	N/A	N/A

(Continued)

Sci-Tech OC 2001 to 2010 as Independent Variables and COC of 2016 as Dependent Variable				
−250.4	1,820.534	−1,810.6	128.73119	76.9118
525.421	959.6688	1,431.576	544.72781	11.1767
0.578931	20.59448	N/A	N/A	N/A
1.374906	4	N/A	N/A	N/A
2,332.57	1,696.531	N/A	N/A	N/A
Sci-Tech OC 2001 to 2010 as Independent Variables and COC of 2019 as Dependent Variable				
−235.569	1,548.034	−1,532.64	132.63104	76.4235
503.8583	920.285	1,372.825	522.37278	10.718
0.546219	19.74931	N/A	N/A	N/A
1.203708	4	N/A	N/A	N/A
1,877.953	1,560.141	N/A	N/A	N/A
Sci-Tech OC 2004 to 2013 as Independent Variables and COC of 2013 as Dependent Variable				
399.7946	−819.318	1,857.342	−1556.435	74.1435
560.3643	806.0734	1,100.452	1,229.9468	12.6434
0.603915	23.04606	N/A	N/A	N/A
1.524711	4	N/A	N/A	N/A
3,239.225	2,124.484	N/A	N/A	N/A
Sci-Tech OC 2004 to 2013 as Independent Variables and COC of 2016 as Dependent Variable				
286.4368	−645.803	1,650.186	−1,393.78	75.8121
483.4711	695.464	949.4482	1,061.1735	10.9085
0.607495	19.88368	N/A	N/A	N/A
1.547737	4	N/A	N/A	N/A
2,447.658	1,581.443	N/A	N/A	N/A
Sci-Tech OC 2004 to 2013 as Independent Variables and COC of 2019 as Dependent Variable				
305.7299	−655.067	1,367.285	−1,096.277	75.2538
459.2868	660.6754	901.9547	1,008.0913	10.3628

(Continued)

0.58489	18.88906	N/A	N/A	N/A
1.409002	4	N/A	N/A	N/A
2,010.908	1,427.186	N/A	N/A	N/A
Sci-Tech OC 2007 to 2016 as Independent Variables and COC of 2016 as Dependent Variable				
−496.628	1,284.069	−1,062.59	265.05082	74.5543
206.7931	488.2678	494.9561	329.5717	7.43749
0.769939	15.22285	N/A	N/A	N/A
3.346666	4	N/A	N/A	N/A
3,102.161	926.9406	N/A	N/A	N/A
Sci-Tech OC 2007 to 2016 as Independent Variables and COC of 2019 as Dependent Variable				
−376.295	1,067.076	−980.707	285.26304	74.0648
223.4021	527.484	534.7094	356.04191	8.03484
0.685344	16.4455	N/A	N/A	N/A
2.17807	4	N/A	N/A	N/A
2,356.276	1,081.818	N/A	N/A	N/A
Sci-Tech OC 2010 to 2019 as Independent Variables and COC of 2019 as Dependent Variable				
−405.315	12.88745	390.6593	11.372957	83.3515
98.60101	147.5197	305.872	267.61304	4.18433
0.930106	7.750856	N/A	N/A	N/A
13.30733	4	N/A	N/A	N/A
3,197.791	240.303	N/A	N/A	N/A
Average Regression Effectiveness (R-Square)	64.05%			
1/(1-Average R-Square)		2.78		

Data source: Standard multiple regressions with currency originality capacity data in Table 14-1 as independent variables and sci-tech originality capacity in Table 7-1 as dependent variables.

Table 14-4 shows that in the first four regressions of the influence of sci-tech originality capacity of the three years of 2001, 2004, 2007, and 2010 on currency originality capacity of the three years of 2010, 2013, 2016, and 2019 all had the regression effectiveness (R-Square) over 54%; five of the other six standard multiple regressions all had regression effectiveness more significant than 60%, and the average regression effectiveness of all ten regressions is 64.05%, implying that sci-tech originality capacity has a considerable influence on currency originality capacity.

14.6.2 Currency monetary autonomy in technological autonomy

Table 14-5 shows the regression results of the influence of currency originality capacity on sci-tech originality capacity from 2001 to 2019. Table 14-5 indicates that currency originality capacity has a positive impact on sci-tech originality like that of Table 14-4, while the influence of currency originality capacity on sci-tech originality capacity is lower than that of the latter on the former.

Table 14-5   Regression Results of Influence of Currency Originality Capacity on Sci-Tech Originality Capacity with Currency Originality in Table 14-1 (2001–2019)

Currency OC 2001 to 2010 as Independent Variables and Sci-Tech OC of 2010 as Dependent Variable				
0.019172	−0.05232	−0.021579	0.0559321	0.171826336
0.064493	0.115437	0.0413223	0.1141868	0.876528516
0.187267	0.3429	N/A	N/A	N/A
0.230417	4	N/A	N/A	N/A
0.10837	0.470321	N/A	N/A	N/A
Currency OC 2001 to 2010 as Independent Variables and Sci-Tech OC of 2013 As Dependent Variable				
0.021407	−0.06239	−0.024943	0.0668961	0.209434126
0.065891	0.117939	0.042218	0.1166621	0.895529936
0.217982	0.350333	N/A	N/A	N/A
0.278743	4	N/A	N/A	N/A
0.136844	0.490934	N/A	N/A	N/A
Currency OC 2001 to 2010 as Independent Variables and Sci-Tech OC of 2016 as Dependent Variable				
0.020711	−0.06861	−0.030524	0.078521	0.286866131
0.064258	0.115016	0.0411717	0.1137706	0.873334038

(Continued)

0.233288	0.34165	N/A	N/A	N/A
0.304271	4	N/A	N/A	N/A
0.142064	0.4669	N/A	N/A	N/A
Currency OC 2001 to 2010 as Independent Variables and Sci-Tech OC of 2019 as Dependent Variable				
0.018063	−0.06143	−0.025219	0.0678456	0.361676854
0.065663	0.117532	0.0420724	0.1162596	0.892440208
0.139496	0.349125	N/A	N/A	N/A
0.16211	4	N/A	N/A	N/A
0.079037	0.487552	N/A	N/A	N/A
Currency OC 2004 to 2013 as Independent Variables and Sci-Tech OC of 2013 as Dependent Variable				
0.071463	−0.02068	0.0148852	−0.047642	−1.288461152
0.032337	0.046431	0.0312394	0.0266739	0.672577842
0.618946	0.244549	N/A	N/A	N/A
1.624298	4	N/A	N/A	N/A
0.388561	0.239218	N/A	N/A	N/A
Currency OC 2004 to 2013 as Independent Variables and Sci-Tech OC of 2016 as Dependent Variable				
0.070331	−0.0227	0.0193493	−0.049368	−1.256973811
0.032364	0.046469	0.0312649	0.0266956	0.673126473
0.606532	0.244749	N/A	N/A	N/A
1.5415	4	N/A	N/A	N/A
0.369356	0.239608	N/A	N/A	N/A
Currency OC 2004 to 2013 as Independent Variables and Sci-Tech OC of 2019 as Dependent Variable				
0.073585	−0.02511	0.0171593	−0.048877	−1.174993898
0.030968	0.044465	0.0299168	0.0255445	0.644101971
0.612788	0.234196	N/A	N/A	N/A
1.582564	4	N/A	N/A	N/A
0.347199	0.21939	N/A	N/A	N/A

(Continued)

Currency OC 2007 to 2016 as Independent Variables and Sci-Tech OC of 2016 as Dependent Variable				
0.045695	−0.02206	−0.056847	0.0437216	−0.587329292
0.139034	0.157163	0.0657821	0.0717077	1.455596481
0.289313	0.328931	N/A	N/A	N/A
0.40709	4	N/A	N/A	N/A
0.176181	0.432782	N/A	N/A	N/A
Currency OC 2007 to 2016 as Independent Variables and Sci-Tech OC of 2019 as Dependent Variable				
0.054218	−0.02783	−0.060694	0.0450488	−0.602802646
0.134288	0.151798	0.0635365	0.0692598	1.405906645
0.287422	0.317702	N/A	N/A	N/A
0.403356	4	N/A	N/A	N/A
0.16285	0.403739	N/A	N/A	N/A
Currency OC 2010 to 2019 as Independent Variables and Sci-Tech OC of 2019 as Dependent Variable				
0.090849	−0.01739	−0.006245	−0.044792	−1.581803651
0.047114	0.059324	0.0805493	0.0293267	1.102623514
0.591653	0.240502	N/A	N/A	N/A
1.448898	4	N/A	N/A	N/A
0.335224	0.231365	N/A	N/A	N/A
Average Regression Effectiveness (R-Square)	37.85%			
1/ (1-Average R-Square)		1.61		

Data source: Same as Table 14-4.

14.6.3 Mutual influence of sci-tech originality capacity and currency originality capacity on each other

Table 14-5 shows that the average regression effectiveness of ten regressions of currency originality capacity influencing sci-tech originality capacity is merely 37.85%, 26.21% lower than the corresponding average ten regressions of sci-tech originality capacity influencing currency originality capacity 64.05% in Table 14-4. The share of the average regression effectiveness of sci-tech originality 65.05%

in Table 14-4 over the sum of two average regression effectiveness 65.05% and 37.85%, or 64.05%/ (65.05% +37.85%) = 62.86%, is 25.72% higher than the share of the average regression effectiveness 37.85% in Table 14-5 over the sum of two moderate regression effectiveness 37.14%. The higher percentage of sci-tech originality capacity implies it has a greater influence on currency originality capacity.

It is noticeable that the results in Table 14-4 and 14-5 are results corresponding to currency originality capacity in Table 14-1 with nominal foreign exchange turnover. The mutual influence of sci-tech originality capacity and currency originality capacity is quite different from the corresponding currency originality capacity in Table 14-2. Regression results show that the average regression R-Square of sci-tech originality capacity influencing currency originality capacity with currency originality capacity in Table 14-2 is 65.07%, and the average regression R-Square of currency originality capacity influencing sci-tech originality capacity with currency originality capacity in Table 14-2 is 70.66%, much higher than the corresponding average regression R-Square 37.85% in Table 14-5. The share of the average regression effectiveness of sci-tech originality is 65.07% in Table 14-4 over the sum of two average regression effectiveness 65.05% and 37.85%, or 64.07% / (65.07% +70.66%) = 47.94%, is 4.12% lower than the share of the average regression effectiveness 70.66% in Table 14-5 over the sum of two moderate regression effectiveness 52.06%. The slightly lower percentage of sci-tech originality capacity implies that sci-tech originality capacity has a lower influence on currency originality capacity.

14.7 Relationship between Currency Originality Capacity and Currency Internationalization

The positive correlation between currency originality capacity and currency internationalization is obvious. This section briefly discusses the degree of mutual influence between these two.

14.7.1 Correlation between currency originality capacity and currency internationalization

Using the data of currency internationalization of the world's top eight international currencies from 2007 to 2019 given in Table 4-1 (the currency internationalization measured by the corresponding daily average foreign exchange turnover based on the nominal foreign exchange turnover) and Table

14-1 of corresponding currency originality capacity, we can calculate that correlation coefficients between currency internationalization and currency originality capacity in Table 14-1 are 43.0%, 41.4%, 42.2%, 42.2%, 43.4%, 41.0%, and 42.4% from 2001 to 2019, respectively; and correlation coefficients between currency internationalization and currency originality capacity in Table 14-2 are 52.8%, 48.9%, 45.3%, 49.2%, 52.0%, 63.7%, and 49.3% from 2001 to 2019, respectively. These results indicate currency internationalization and currency originality capacity have a greater mutual influence, each with better currency internationalization measures.

14.7.2 Mutual influence between currency originality capacity and currency internationalization with nominal foreign exchange turnover

Following the procedures to find mutual influence between technology internationalization and currency internationalization, we can find mutual influencing results between currency originality capacity and currency internationalization. Regression results show that the average regression R-Square of currency originality capacity influencing currency internationalization (currency originality capacity in Table 14-1 and currency internationalization in Table 4-1) is 39.88%; and the average regression R-Square of currency internationalization influencing currency originality capacity (Table 14-1) 56.95%. The share of the average regression R-Square of currency originality 39.88% over the sum of two moderate regression effectiveness 39.88% and 56.95%, or 39.88% / (39.88% + 56.95%) = 41.18%, is 17.63% lower than the share of the average regression effectiveness 56.95% over the sum of two average regression effectiveness 58.82%. The lower percentage of currency originality capacity implies currency originality capacity has a lower influence on currency internationalization.

14.7.3 Mutual influence between currency originality capacity and currency internationalization with better currency internationalization measures

Similarly, we can find mutual influencing results between currency originality capacity and currency internationalization. Regression results show that the average regression R-Square of currency originality capacity influencing currency internationalization (currency originality capacity in Table 14-2 and currency internationalization in Table 13-6) is 56.40%; and the average regression R-Square of currency internationalization influencing currency originality capacity (Table 14-2) 55.11%. The share of the average regression R-Square of currency originality 56.40% over the sum of two average regression effectiveness 56.40% and 55.11%, or 56.40%/ (56.40% +55.11%) = 50.58%, is 1.16% higher than the share of the average regression effectiveness 55.11% over the sum of two average regression effectiveness 49.42%. The higher percentage of currency originality capacity implies currency originality capacity has a lower influence on better currency internationalization.

14.7.4 Reasonable results of mutual influence between currency originality capacity and currency internationalization

The above results of mutual influence between currency originality capacity and currency internationalization appear conflicting, yet they are in fact not conflicting at all. The higher impact of currency internationalization on currency originality corresponding to nominal foreign exchange turnover clearly means the over-valued nominal foreign exchange turnover exaggerates the function of currency internationalization. The influence of better currency internationalization on relating currency originality is greater because better currency internationalization eliminates the majority (69.4%) of foreign exchange nominal derivatives turnover; thus, a greater influence of currency originality capacity corresponding to better currency internationalization is reasonable.

14.8 Mutual Influence between Sci-Tech Originality Capacity and Technology Internationalization

We have studied mutual influencing relationships between technology internationalization and currency internationalization, relationships between currency originality capacity and sci-tech originality capacity in Section 14.6, and relationships between currency originality capacity and currency internationalization in Section 14.7. Only the relationships between sci-tech originality and technology internationalization need further exploring before we can know the relationships between two internationalization measures of sci-tech and currency and two originality capacity measures of sci-tech and money.

14.8.1 Influence of sci-tech originality capacity and technology internationalization on each other

Using the same procedures to find the mutual influence of technology internationalization and currency internationalization, we can find the mutual impact of sci-tech originality capacity and technology internationalization. Regression results show that the average regression R-Square of sci-tech originality capacity influencing technology internationalization is 97.42%, and the average regression R-Square of technology internationalization influencing sci-tech originality capacity is 98.90%. The share of the average regression R-Square of sci-tech originality capacity 97.42% over the sum of two moderate regression effectiveness 97.42% and 98.90%, or 97.42%/ (97.42% +98.90%) = 49.62%, is 0.75% lower than the share of the average regression effectiveness R-Square 98.90% over the sum of two average regression effectiveness 50.38%. The lower percentage of sci-tech originality capacity implies that sci-tech originality capacity has a lower influence on technology internationalization.

14.8.2 More evidence of the mutual influence of sci-tech originality capacity and technology internationalization

The above results of mutual influence between sci-tech originality and technology internationalization are obtained using the same method to find the mutual influence of technology internationalization and currency internationalization using four consecutive currency internationalization data and corresponding technology internationalization data. To a high degree, the results are reasonable because we have made the best use of existing data on currency internationalization based on the triennial foreign exchange turnover data from 2001 to 2019.

However, the situation is different when we study the relationships between sci-tech originality and technology internationalization as we have continuous annual data of both sci-tech originality capacity and technology internationalization from 2000 to 2019; thus, we can have more regressions of mutual influence of sci-tech originality capacity and technology internationalization without considering triennial data of currency internationalization.

Results of 15 standard multiple regressions of 5-continuous annual sci-tech originality data from 2001 to 2019 as independent variables and relating technology internationalization as dependent variables show that the average regression R-Square of these 15 regressions is 98.38%; the average regression R-Square of corresponding 15 standard multiple regressions of 5-continuous annual technology internationalization data from 2001 to 2019 as independent variables and relating sci-tech originality capacity as dependent variables is 98.66%. The share of the former average R-Square 98.38% of the two average R-Squares is 49.93%, and the percentage of the later average R-Square, 98.66% of the two average R-Squares, is 50.07%, indicating that technology internationalization has greater influence on sci-tech originality capacity as in Section 15.8.1.

Similarly, results of 14 standard multiple regressions of 6-continuous annual sci-tech originality data from 2001 to 2019 as independent variables and relating technology internationalization as dependent variables show that the average regression R-Square of these 14 regressions is 98.55%; the average regression R-Square of corresponding 14 standard multiple regressions of 6-continuous annual technology internationalization data from 2001 to 2019 as independent variables and relating sci-tech originality capacity as dependent variables is 98.64%. The share of the former average R-Square 98.55% of the two average R-Squares is 49.98%, and the share of the later average R-Square, 98.64% of the two average R-Squares, is 50.02%, also indicating that technology internationalization has a greater influence on sci-tech originality capacity as in Section 15.8.1. Therefore, technology internationalization has a greater influence on sci-tech originality with continuous annual data as with consecutive triennial data.

14.8.3 Rationality of greater influence of technology internationalization on sci-tech originality capacity

The additional evidence of the greater influence of technology internationalization on sci-tech originality capacity with 5 to 6 continuous annual data is consistent with the same result with four consecutive triennial data. The rationality of greater influence of technology internationalization on sci-tech originality lies in the fact that the former reflects the accumulation of weighted international patents, or more specifically accumulation of weighted patent families as shown in the previous chapter, and sci-tech originality capacity is the measure of annual exports and imports of charges for the use of IP. Thus, the accumulated measure of patent families in the previous years should possess inertia of sci-tech innovation to influence the current measure of sci-tech originality capacity.

14.9 Summary of Mutual Influence of Sci-Tech USD Currency Originality Capacity and Sci-Tech & Currency Internationalization

Mutual influencing relationships between technology internationalization and currency internationalization, relationships between currency originality capacity and sci-tech originality capacity in Section 15.6, relationships between currency originality capacity and currency internationalization in Section 15.7, and relationships between sci-tech originality and technology internationalization in Section 15.8 are interactive and somewhat complicated. We summarize the relationships of mutual influence of the above four symmetric concepts of sci-tech originality capacity, currency originality capacity, technology internationalization, and currency internationalization. In addition, currency internationalization and currency originality capacity have two related concepts: traditional currency internationalization and better currency internationalization are related to conventional currency originality capacity and better currency originality capacity using the different ways of currency internationalization. Thus, it is difficult to grasp the results of the interaction between the concepts and metrics. Figure 14-1 shows the mutual relationships among sci-tech originality capacity, technology internationalization, currency originality capacity, and currency internationalization.

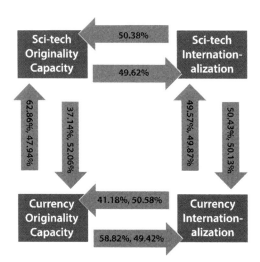

Figure 14-1   Summary of the Mutual Influence between Sci-Tech Originality Capacity, Technology Internationalization, Currency Originality Capacity, and Currency Internationalization (2001–2019)

Data source: Table 14-4, Table 14-5, and results from Sections 14.7 and 14.8. The first number following each arrow represents the result of traditional currency internationalization using nominal foreign exchange average daily turnovers, and the second number following each arrow represents the result of better currency internationalization using 30.6% of foreign exchange derivatives average daily turnovers. The results between sci-tech originality capacity and technology internationalization correspond to Section 14.8.1 for consistency.

Figure 14-1 shows that the influence of technology internationalization has more impact on currency internationalization. Whatever currency internationalization measures are used, technology internationalization also has more influence on sci-tech originality capacity, implying the importance of technology internationalization. Currency internationalization has more impact on currency originality with better currency internationalization measures as it is more reasonable with discounted foreign exchange derivatives turnovers; sci-tech originality capacity has more influence on currency originality capacity with better currency internationalization measures. All the above results show the importance of technology internationalization and sci-tech originality capacity.

14.10 Conclusion

We define and measure currency originality capacity flowing the sci-tech originality definition. With the definition and measurements of the currency originality capacity of major international currencies, we find the mutual influence of currency originality capacity and sci-tech originality capacity using the same method, and the mutual impact of currency originality capacity and currency internationalization using the same process. With the mutual influence of sci-tech originality capacity and technology internationalization using the same method, we find mutual influences among two pairs of originality capacity of sci-tech and currency, two pairs of internationalization of sci-tech and currency. The importance of technology internationalization lies in the fact it represents accumulated qualified patent families, or it contains inertia of sci-tech innovation.

Results of this chapter show that technology internationalization has more influence on both currency internationalization and sci-tech originality capacity, indicating the critical roles of technology internationalization; currency originality is influenced by both sci-tech originality and currency internationalization, implying the influence of technology internationalization on currency originality through both currency internationalization and sci-tech originality, which implies the importance of technology internationalization.

Attention should be paid to the importance of better currency internationalization, for our understanding of mutual influence between currency internationalization and currency originality capacity can be missleading without it, and our understanding of mutual influence between sci-tech originality capacity and currency originality capacity can also be miss leading without it.

Bibliography

Sato, Kiyotaka. 1998. "The International Use of the Japanese Yen: The Case of Japan's Trade with East Asia." *ICSEAD Working Paper Series*, no. 16 (August).

CHAPTER FIFTEEN

The Development and Future of RMB Internationalization

15.1 Anticipation of Future Technological Autonomy for Major Currency Issuers

15.1.1 Anticipation of US technological autonomy

Technology is the main driving force affecting economy and trade, and naturally, one of the main factors affecting currency internationalization. Thus, in order to have a better forecast for future internationalization trends of major currencies, it is necessary to first make a more accurate prediction of its technological autonomy. From 1992 to 1994, US technological autonomy increased from 81.15% to 82.03%, the highest point in history, and then continued to decline to 72.25% in 2002, an average annual decrease of 1.47%; in 2011, it continued to rise to 76.49%, with an average annual increase of 0.69%; from 2011 to 2017, it dropped to 72.68%, with an average annual decrease of 0.63%; and from 2017 to 2019, it rebounded slightly to 73.31%, with an average annual increase of 0.32%. These results show that from 1994 to 2017, three cycles of American technological autonomy occurred, with each cycle lasting nearly eight years; the annual average decline of 0.63% in the latter cycle is significantly lower than the previous decline of 1.47%; the average annual rate of decrease in the next year was 43.0% of the previous rate of decrease; judging from this, in the eight years beginning in 2017, US technological autonomy should enter the next recovery cycle. From 2017 to

2019, the average annual growth rate of US technological autonomy was 0.32%, which was 45.6% of the average annual growth rate of 0.69% in the previous recovery cycle. In order to reflect the unique advantages of the global monopoly of US technology (the US intellectual property royalties surplus still accounted for nearly 60% of the global surplus in 2018), we assume that the average annual decline in the future will be 35.0% of the average annual decline from the previous cycle. Overall, the decline in US technological autonomy is more moderate compared to the previous 30 years. Table 15-1 shows the relevant results.

15.1.2 Anticipation of Japan's technological autonomy

From 1979 to 2003, Japan's technological autonomy increased from 20.13% to 52.72%, an average annual growth rate of 1.30%; from 2003 to 2015, it continued to increase to a historical high of 68.17%. The increase of 1.19% shows that Japan's technological autonomy has almost risen in a straight line during the 36-year period from 1979 to 2015; however, it dropped to 64.09% from 2015 to 2019, an average annual decrease of 1.02%. It is worth noticing that in 2019, the degree of technological autonomy dropped by 3.60% from 2018, the highest annual decline in 42 years. It shows that Japan's technological autonomy peaked at nearly 70%, and its growth is weak, indicating that the intensity of US suppression increases when it approaches American technological autonomy. As Japan's technological autonomy continued to increase significantly for more than 30 years before 2016, but has only declined for four years since 2015, it will be difficult to judge changes in its technological autonomy over the next 20 years. However, based on the average annual growth rate of 0.49% from 2007 to 2019, Japan's technological autonomy is expected to surpass that of the US for the first time. The relevant results are shown in Table 15-1.

15.1.3 Anticipation of technological autonomy in the Eurozone

Although the Euro area includes Germany – a major technological nation with an IP royalties surplus in recent years – France, the second largest Euro country, only has a surplus of about USD 2 billion, which is only one-tenth of Germany; the degree of technological autonomy is limited, and technological autonomy in three major Eurozone countries – Italy, Spain, and the Netherlands – is still less than 50%. While these nations have IP royalty deficits, Ireland has the largest IP deficit in the world, even surpassing China. Overall, technological autonomy for the entire Eurozone has only been around 40%.

In addition, Germany's technological autonomy reached a historic peak of 68.64% in 2014. However, it then experienced a rare decline (like Japan), indicating that its technological autonomy also encountered growth resistance similar to the US; from 2006 to 2017, French technological autonomy fell by an average annual rate of 1.16%. From 2007 to 2016, Italian technological autonomy fell by 0.41% annually. From 2006 to 2018, Dutch technological autonomy fell by an average annual rate of 0.99%, and the average annual growth rate of Spanish technological autonomy from 2006 to 2017 was only 0.4%. Taking all these negative growth rates into account, it can be assumed that the overall technological autonomy of the Eurozone only increased at an average annual rate of 0.06% from 2006 to 2015. Table 15-1 shows the relevant forecast results.

15.1.4 Anticipation of China's technological autonomy

According to Table 4-1, from 2008 to 2019, China's technological autonomy began to increase sharply since 2016. However, this three-year period from 2016 to 2019 is too short for making predictions on China's scientific and technological autonomy in the years to come. China's technology autonomy faces many challenges, and exceeding Germany's average growth in this department of 1.82% from 2000 to 2009 will be very difficult.

The report from the 19th National Congress of the CPC clearly stated that "from 2020 to 2035, the scientific and technological strength will be greatly improved, and China will join the forefront of innovative countries." That means China's scientific and technological autonomy capability must reach a relative autonomy level of 50%; that is, IP royalties will turn from a deficit to a surplus. A qualitative change requires an average annual increase of at least 2% from 2020 to 2035 to truly enter the forefront of global innovation; then by 2035, the surplus of China's IP royalties must reach 20 billion dollars – the surplus value of Japan and Germany. To even approach this level, annual average growth over the next 15 years will need to be at least 3%.

In the next 15–30 years, the construction of China's scientific and technological autonomous capacity will continue, and the annual increase in technological independence will be around 2.00% (an average annual increase of 2.7% to 3.0% in the 30 years from 2020 to 2050 is not likely). It will take 15 years to increase China's technological autonomy from 20% to about 50%. Table 15-1 shows the corresponding results of 6 possible scenarios where China's technological autonomy will increase by 1.5% to 3.0% annually over the next 30 years.

15.1.5 Prediction of changes in Chinese technological autonomy

Based on the technological autonomy of the major currency issuers described above and future trends, we can estimate changes in their technological autonomy. Table 15-1 shows the corresponding results: Japan's technological autonomy is expected to surpass the US for the first time around 2035, and is expected to exceed 80% for the first time by 2050, with the highest technological autonomy in the world; if the average annual growth rate of China's technological autonomy in the next 30 years is 1.50%, 1.75%, 2.00%, 2.25%, 2.50%, and 3.0%, then, by 2040, 2037, 2035, 2033, 2032, and 2030, respectively, China's science and technology is expected to reach 50% for the first time; and by 2051, 2046, 2043, 2040, 2038, and 2035, respectively, China's science and technology autonomy is expected to reach about 66%, the level of the of Japan and Germany in recent years. If China's average annual growth rate in the next 30 years reaches 1.50%, 1.75%, 2.00%, and 2.25%, by 2050, China's scientific and technological autonomy is expected to reach 65.0%, 72.5%, 80.0%, and 87.5%, respectively. In the next 30 years, it will be difficult to increase the autonomy of science and technology by 2.00% per year, and a figure of around 1.5% is more likely.

Table 15-1   Changes in the Science and Technology Autonomy of the World's Top Eight Currencies (2019–2050)

Unit: %

Currency Issuer	2019	2020	2025	2030	2035	2040	2045	2050
US	73.31	73.55	74.79	73.69	74.57	74.93	74.54	75.02
Eurozone	41.40	41.50	42.20	42.70	43.20	43.70	44.20	44.70
Japan	67.69	68.18	69.95	72.40	74.86	77.31	79.76	82.22
UK	65.45	65.74	66.89	68.32	69.75	71.18	72.60	74.03
Australia	21.10	20.91	20.64	19.69	18.74	17.78	16.83	15.88
Canada	29.04	28.74	28.12	26.60	25.08	23.56	22.04	20.52
Switzerland	64.53	64.80	65.89	67.22	68.54	69.87	71.20	72.52
China 1	16.22	20.00	27.50	35.00	38.75	45.00	51.25	57.50
China 2	16.22	20.00	28.75	37.50	46.25	55.00	63.75	72.50
China 3	16.22	20.00	30.00	40.00	50.00	60.00	70.00	80.00

(Continued)

Currency Issuer	2019	2020	2025	2030	2035	2040	2045	2050
China 4	16.22	20.00	31.25	42.50	53.75	65.00	76.25	87.50
China 5	16.22	20.00	32.50	45.00	57.50	70.00	82.50	95.00
China 6	16.22	20.00	35.00	50.00	65.00	80.00	95.00	110.00

Data source: The estimated annual changes in autonomy of major currency issuers are estimated, including China 1, China 2, China 3, China 4, China 5, and China 6, respectively, corresponding to the estimation results of various growth rates; the figure corresponding to an annual average of 3.00% in the year 2050 exceeds 100%, which is obviously impossible.

15.2 New Method to Forecast Currency Internationalization

15.2.1 Limitations of science and technology influence

Technology is indeed an important factor in affecting trade, foreign exchange transactions, and currency pricing, but it is not the only factor. The relevant IP data shows that although Germany's technological autonomy has been comparable to Japan and Switzerland over the past decade (and slightly higher than the UK), the technological autonomy of the entire Eurozone has been significantly lower than Japan, Switzerland, and the UK (less than 40% annually); nevertheless, the Euro far surpasses the yen and the British pound as the world's second-largest currency. The main reason for this is simply because the economic and trade scale of the Eurozone far exceeds Japan and the UK. Therefore, while considering the importance of technological autonomy, the economic and trade scale of currency issuers is also a key factor in determining currency internationalization.

15.2.2 Introduction to the new method

The results in Chapter 14 show that trade is the main force in the global foreign exchange market, and therefore, the decisive force in the global foreign exchange market and currency internationalization; the results in previous chapters show that technological autonomy is the decisive factor in the choice of settlement currency for imports and exports; thus, technological autonomy actually represents trade exports; the main import force is the main reflection of the purchasing power of a country or region. Imports and exports are inseparable, so we measure the autonomy of import and export trade by the product of the technological autonomy of different currency issuers and the global proportion of domestic output (the two together cannot better reflect the high dependence of imports and exports). The autonomy of currency in the global foreign exchange market is the autonomy of currency internationalization; this indicator should be a better way to predict currency internationalization. Table 15-2 shows the internationalization levels of major currencies estimated by this method in 2013, 2016, 2019, and 2020. Comparison of the results is measured by the global proportion of foreign exchange transactions.

Table 15-2   Comparison of the Product of the Global Share of Technological Autonomy and Output Value of Major International Currency Issuers and the Share of Average Daily Transactions in the Foreign Exchange Market (2013–2020)

Unit: %

Data Type	The Product of the Proportion of Domestic Output Value and Degree of Autonomy				The Product Accounts for the Proportion of the Total Score of Eight Currencies				
Currency	2013	2016	2019	2020	2013	2016	2019	2020	Average Annually
USD	1,667.3	1,799.6	1,794.8	1,825.4	52.2	54.3	52.2	51.3	52.5
EUR	644.3	656.8	631.9	629.3	20.2	19.8	18.4	17.7	19.0
JPY	428.9	428.2	392.8	399.3	13.4	12.9	11.4	11.2	12.2
GBP	228.3	207.1	211.6	206.9	7.1	6.3	6.2	5.8	6.3
AUD	34.0	33.1	33.4	33.3	1.1	1.0	1.0	0.9	1.0
CAD	89.8	61.4	57.6	54.9	2.8	1.9	1.7	1.5	2.0
CHF	51.1	56.9	51.9	54.7	1.6	1.7	1.5	1.5	1.6
RMB	50.7	68.3	266.7	354.5	1.6	2.1	7.8	10.0	5.3
Total	3,194.4	3,311.5	3,440.8	3,558.1	100.0	100.0	100.0	100.0	100.0
Currency	Percentage of Average Daily Foreign Exchange Turnover in the World				Percentage of Daily Average Transaction Value in Total of Eight Currencies				
USD	43.52	43.79	44.15	43.88	49.5	50.3	51.6	50.2	50.4
EUR	16.70	15.70	16.14	14.10	19.0	18.0	18.8	16.1	18.0
JPY	11.52	10.81	8.40	10.51	13.1	12.4	9.8	12.0	11.8
GBP	5.91	6.40	6.40	5.90	6.7	7.3	7.5	6.8	7.1

(Continued)

	2013	2016	2019	2020	2013	2016	2019	2020	Average Annually
AUD	4.32	3.44	3.38	3.45	4.9	3.9	4.0	4.1	4.2
CAD	2.28	2.57	2.52	2.82	2.6	3.0	2.9	3.2	2.9
CHF	2.58	2.40	2.48	3.59	2.9	2.8	2.9	3.9	3.2
RMB	1.12	1.99	2.16	3.15	1.3	2.3	2.5	3.6	2.4
Total	87.95	87.10	85.63	87.39	100.0	100.0	100.0	100.0	100.0

Currency					Ratio of Proportion of Product and Proportion of Average Daily Transaction				
USD					105.5	108.1	101.2	102.2	104.2
EUR					106.2	110.1	97.4	109.6	105.8
JPY					102.5	104.2	116.3	93.3	104.1
GBP					106.4	85.1	82.3	86.1	90.0
AUD					21.7	25.3	24.6	23.7	23.6
CAD					108.4	62.8	57.0	47.8	69.0
CHF					54.6	62.3	52.2	37.5	52.0
RMB					125.1	90.1	307.2	276.6	199.8
Total					100.0	100.0	100.0	100.0	100.0
Correlation between the Product of Eight Currencies and the Average Daily Transaction Amount of Foreign Exchange	99.65%	99.85%	98.91%	98.40%					

Data source: The proportion of domestic output value is the same as in Table 15-1, and the degree of currency autonomy is calculated based on this data; data for the proportion of daily average currency turnover is the same as in Table 1-1; the average daily transaction value of the eight major currencies from 2007 to 2019 given in Table 1-1 of the Bank for International Settlements, which accounted for 86.47 in the world. It is estimated that the eight major currencies will account for 85.56% of the world in 2020.

Table 15-2 shows that the global share of the output of the three major currencies (USD, EUR, and JPY) is very close to the ratio of technological autonomy to the average daily foreign exchange turnover. The former is only 4.2%, 5.8%, and 4.1% higher than the latter. (The ratio of the product of the Euro and the yen to the currency's turnover in the foreign exchange market is slightly higher, which can be understood as part of the import capacity, such as crude oil, which has to be settled in US dollars due to the domination of the USD), indicating that the output value of the currency matrix and the performance of technological autonomy are very good substitute parameters for the average daily transaction value of the currency; the ratio of the sterling, CAD and CHF's output to the average daily transaction value of the foreign exchange is less than 100% to varying degrees.

The AUD's output to the average daily foreign exchange turnover is 23.6% per year, which is less than a quarter of the level, indicating that the import and export capacity is not enough to support the international status of their currencies. The reason these currencies have excessive internationalization statuses is due to the support of the US dollar (US holdings of net long-term bonds issued by the UK, Canada, Australia, and Switzerland give a similar basis for US support); the ratio of the output of technological autonomy to US global output value share and the average daily foreign exchange transaction share being slightly higher than 100% can be understood as US support for the other "Five Eyes Alliance" countries. In addition, Table 15-2 shows a high correlation of over 99% between the global share of output value and technological autonomy of the eight major currencies and their average daily foreign exchange turnover share in 2013, 2016, 2019, and 2020.

15.3 Anticipation of Future Changes

15.3.1 The proportion of domestic output value and technological autonomy

Table 15-2 shows that although the global share of the domestic output value of different currencies and the share of technological autonomy has a high correlation with the currency internationalization of the corresponding year, the two dimensions are very different. Therefore, it is necessary to adjust the dimensions: the adjustment method involves multiplying the results of currency internationalization from the previous year by the global proportion of domestic output and the product of technological autonomy in the total score of eight currencies and then dividing by two in 2020, which is given in Table 15-2.

15.3.2 Forecast results for internationalization changes of major global currencies

Using the forecast results of the global proportion of domestic output of the major currency economies and the forecast results of their technological autonomy given in Table 15-1, the results are consistent with previous currency internationalization results. We can use the product method of the proportion of domestic output and technological autonomy given in Table 15-2 to predict real changes in the nationalization of major currencies in the future, as shown in Table 15-3.

Table 15-3   Forecast of the Proportion of Transactions in Major International Currency and US Government Debt to Domestic Output Foreign Exchange Markets (2020–2050)

Unit: %

Currency	2019	2020	2021	2022	2025	2030	2035	2040	2045	2050
USD	44.15	43.88	43.65	43.14	40.77	36.98	34.60	32.24	29.97	28.27
EUR	16.14	14.10	13.39	13.86	13.38	13.96	13.47	13.04	12.71	12.43
JPY	8.40	10.51	10.65	10.45	9.74	9.15	7.90	6.83	5.94	5.18
GBP	6.40	5.90	5.86	5.82	5.63	5.23	4.80	4.42	4.09	3.80
AUD	3.38	3.59	3.50	3.39	3.43	3.14	2.78	2.45	2.18	1.93
CAD	2.52	2.82	3.02	2.65	2.78	2.53	2.25	2.00	1.78	1.59
CHF	2.48	3.45	3.34	3.40	3.45	3.55	3.74	3.95	4.21	4.49
RMB (1)	2.61	3.15	3.47	3.61	4.95	6.49	8.17	9.74	11.13	12.23
RMB (2)	2.61	3.15	3.51	3.69	5.17	6.95	8.89	10.71	12.34	13.64
RMB (3)	2.61	3.15	3.55	3.77	5.39	7.65	10.09	12.42	14.52	16.23
RMB (4)	2.61	3.15	3.59	3.85	5.62	7.88	10.33	12.66	14.76	16.46
RMB (5)	2.61	3.15	3.63	3.92	5.84	8.35	11.06	13.63	15.97	17.87
RMB (6)	2.61	3.15	3.71	4.08	6.29	9.27	12.50	15.58	18.39	20.70

Data source: The proportion of the average daily transaction amount of each major currency in April 2019 was updated by the BIS in December 2019. The proportion of RMB in 2019 is from RMB*; for the eight major currencies in 2020, the proportion of daily average transaction value is estimated from the data; the proportion of foreign exchange transactions in various currencies from 2021 to 2050 is based on the global proportion of domestic output value in the corresponding year given in Table 15-1. The monetary autonomy performance of the corresponding year is estimated; the six different scenarios of the global average daily turnover of RMB and foreign exchange accounted for the global proportion and the assumption in Table 15-1. China's scientific and technological autonomy will increase by 1.50% and 1.75% each year from 2020 to 2050, 2.00%, 2.25%, 2.50%, and 3.00% correspond to the same scenarios.

15.3.3 The gap between RMB and the US dollar internationalization in 2050

Table 15-3 shows that even if China's technological autonomy increased annually by 3.00% in the 30 years after 2020, the average daily turnover of RMB and foreign exchange accounts for 20.70% of the world, only slightly over 70% of US dollar's 28.27%. However, China's technological autonomy from 2020–2050 will not be able to maintain an average annual growth rate of 3.00%); the hypothesis given in Table 15-1 is that China's technological autonomy will increase by 2.25% to 2.50% annually from 2020 to 2050. By 2050, China's technological autonomy will reach 87.50% to 95.00%, which is also high; therefore, it is reasonable to assume that China's technological autonomy will increase by an amount closer to 2.00% annually over the next 30 years. The average daily turnover of RMB and foreign exchange at that time will account for 16.23%, which is only slightly more than half of USD (28.27%).

15.4 Historical Review of Major Global Currency Shifts

By current forecasts, China's economy, as measured by GDP, is expected to surpass the US around 2030. Yet, 20 years later in 2050, RMB internationalization will still be quite far behind dollar internationalization, and may even still rank third after the Euro. If the average annual growth rate of China's technological autonomy from 2020 to 2050 is less than 1.59%, then RMB internationalization will almost certainly remain behind the Euro by 2050). Such things may be hard to accurately predict. However, the global history of change in the status of the world's major international currencies relative to their economies over the past 100 years can give us relevant answers.

"Reserve currencies have come and gone. In the past 2,500 years, there have been more than a dozen reserve currencies in the world, and they have all withdrawn from the stage of history. The pound lost its reserve status in the first half of the 20th century, and the US dollar will lose in the first half of the 21st century. The loss of reserve status will lead to a series of economic and political crises in the US (Persaud 2004)." The history of many reserve currencies should enlighten us when analyzing the international finance of today. However, due to the lack of data and information available, most sources on international currencies before the nineteenth century are difficult to corroborate and are beyond the scope of this book.

15.4.1 Changes in the international status of the pound sterling

As the UK led the global industrial revolution and British maritime hegemony made it the world's largest trading nation, it also made the pound sterling a well-deserved major global currency of the nineteenth century. Statistics show that in 1860, the UK absorbed 30% of global exports. By 1890, the proportion had dropped to 20% (Imla 1958). At the same time, the UK was the world's largest exporter of processed goods and services, as well as a global consumer of food and raw materials. A large number of imports, exports, and re-exports have naturally made London the origin and concentration of global commodity trading and forward/futures exchanges, and the discovery center of major commodity spot and forward prices. These prices are naturally denominated in British pounds. From 1860 to 1914, about 60% of world trade was settled in British pounds (Williams 1968). This large amount of trade made the UK the world's largest credit country; London also became the world's long-term investment and financing center, and then became the world's largest financial center. In addition, the British Empire began to encourage the use of pound sterling throughout the empire by the early 18th century to simplify and standardize various transactions. The global monopoly of the British pound declined before the beginning of World War I. In 1913, the share of British pounds in global reserves fell to 48%, below 50% for the first time (Table 1, Eichengreen 2005); the overall decline began before the war, but it took nearly half a century until the end of the 1950s when the British pound's status as the world's number one international currency was officially replaced by the US dollar.

15.4.2 Pound sterling spillover effect

With the rise of Western European nations such as France and Germany, Britain's monopoly on global trade and currency gradually declined. Historical data shows (the output value priced in 1990 International Geary-Khamis dollars) that in the second year following German reunification – in 1873 – the German output value of 79.98 billion surpassed France for the first time. By 1899, German output value surpassed France by 31.9%. In 1899, Deutsche Mark reserves of 15% were still slightly lower than French francs of 16% (Table 1, Eichengreen 2005), the same below); in 1908, Germany's output value surpassed Britain by 1.4% for the first time; by 1913, Germany's output value surpassed Britain and France, respectively, by 5.7% and 64.3%, while the mark's reserve ratio remained unchanged at 15% in 1899, 33%, and 18% lower than the British pound and French franc, respectively. These results show that the size of the currency's economy and trade is not the only determinant of the currency's international status, which could lack behind the economic status for many years or even decades.

15.4.3 The rise and predicament of the US dollar

The dominance or monopoly of the US dollar in the global financial system is proven by the fact that its status has risen instead of falling for more than a decade after the global financial crisis, despite the crisis originating in the US in 2007. In 2008, the US dollar accounted for 63.8% of global reserves – almost the same as its 63.9% before the crisis. From 2008 to 2013, the year before the US government stopped its quantitative easing policy, the US dollar share of the global total fell slightly to a new low of 60.9%. However, it rose to 65.7% in 2015 – higher than 65.1% and 63.9% in 2006 and 2007 before the crisis; yet after the crisis, only the US dollar was traded in the global foreign exchange market in 2010. The US dollar's proportion of global reserves (42.43%) was slightly lower than its 42.8% in 2007, while the proportions of 43.52%, 43.79%, and 44.15% in 2013, 2016, and 2019, respectively, not only exceeded the 2007 proportion but also continued to grow.

Although the US dollar's international status seems difficult to shake, as early as 2005, the US was at the peak of a growth cycle before the financial crisis hit (its nominal domestic product increased by 6.74% in 2005, the highest since 1990). The scholar Eichengreen (2005) raised doubts and concerns about the long-term attractiveness of US dollar reserves. Mr. Eichengreen expressed concerns that US global debts make up more than 25% of US domestic output, and its current account deficit is 6% of its domestic output. Ultimately, he accused the US authorities of allowing high inflation in order to increase its debt-to-domestic output ratio; in some ways, this is a repeat of the British pound's loss of international reserves. The article published by Mr. Eichengreen in 2005 was based on the relevant data from 2004. The ratio of US government debt to domestic product and the ratio of US debt to the global total were only 66.1% and 6.2%, respectively. However, the ratio of US government debt to domestic output was only 65.4%, and while the ratio of its current account deficit to domestic output fell back to just over 4.0% in 2019, its share of global debt increased to 31.9%.

The ratio of US government debt to domestic product increased to 108.7%, while the average annual growth rate of US nominal domestic products was 5.25% from 1990–2004, but fell to 3.62% from 2005–2019. The current account deficit remained stable at more than 4% of the nominal domestic product. A drop in the growth rate of below 4% will inevitably lead to a significant increase in the proportion of foreign holdings of US bonds in US domestic output that exceeds the steady rate (Mussa 2004). According to updated IMF data from October 2020, the ratio of US government debt to domestic output in 2020 increased by 22.5% to 131.2% compared with 2019; this is nearly twice the 2004 level of 65.4%. Japan's corresponding maximum growth rate of 17.6% in 2009 was 4.9% lower. At the end of November 2020, the ratio of US global debt to domestic output increased to 33.9%; based on estimates of the USD 1.9 trillion stimulus package in response to the Covid pandemic by US President Joe Biden, the ratio of US government debt (USD 28.7 trillion) to domestic output (USD 23 trillion) in 2021 exceeds 120%. Eichengreen (2005) worries that the US owes a quarter of global debt and domestic output, and this ratio exceeded one-third in 2020. However, the rapid growth of US government debt is unlikely to have an impact on foreign attitudes towards US debt: from July to November 2020, US government bonds held abroad did indeed fall for four consecutive months, but the cumulative amount was only USD 43.4 billion, and the cumulative decline was only 0.61% of the USD 7.1 trillion held in July 2020. We need to pay close attention to changes in global attitudes towards US debt, as shown by relevant market data.

15.4.4 Judging future trends of international currencies

Eichengreen (2005) took into account the economic and trade scale of the Eurozone and other factors and pointed out that in the future, only the Euro could approach reserve currency status alongside the US dollar; the conditions for the RMB to share the global reserve function are not yet mature. Mr. Eichengreen's article was published in 2005. In 2004, China's domestic output value was only 19.2% of the Euro area's output value, and trade was only equivalent to the same proportion. However, in 2018, China's domestic output value surpassed the Euro area for the first time, and the ratio of China's trade to the Eurozone was also close to half at that time. In 2014, China's domestic output was only 16.0% of the US. In 2019 and 2020, China's domestic output increased to 68.7% and 73.2% of the US, respectively. In 2019, the ratio of China's domestic output value compared to the US increased to 68.7%. Since 2014, China's trade has exceeded the total US trade on average. This data shows that RMB should be much closer to being a major reserve currency than it really is now.

The results above show how the US dollar replaced the British pound as the world's dominant international currency almost 90 years after US output value surpassed that of the UK for the first time in 1872. Even after deducting the 42 years before the establishment of the Federal Reserve in 1914, USD took nearly half a century to replace the British pound as the main international currency; in addition, although Germany surpassed France and the UK in output value in 1873 and 1908, respectively, the international reserve status of the German mark in 1913 was still less than that of the French franc and the British pound; it is a gigantic difference. This is highly suggestive of a sizeable lag time between a nation's economic status internationally and its currency internationalization. As shown in Table 15-3, in 2050 – when the Chinese economy is projected to have surpassed the Eurozone for 32 years and the US economy for 20 years – RMB internationalization may still be lower than the Euro and probably still some way off the US dollar level. Of course, the development of modern technology has made the development of the global financial market much faster than before, and changes in currency internationalization rankings may also occur faster. At the same time, economic, trade, and technological aspects, such as currency use inertia, and factors, such as regulation, also impact currency internationalization. The relevant historical data given in this section is a useful guidepost for assessing international changes in major currencies in the future.

15.5 The Future Development of the Domestic Foreign Exchange Market

The forecast results given in Table 15-3 show that by 2025, 2035, and 2045, the RMB will become the fourth, third, and second largest international currency in the world, and its global share of the global foreign exchange market will reach, respectively, around 5.39%, 8.89%, and 14.52%; according to Table 1-1, the global average daily foreign exchange turnover growth rate from 1998 to 2019 was estimated at 7.22%. By 2025, 2035, and 2045, this value will be as high as 9.34 trillion, 18.76 trillion, and 37.66 trillion dollars, of which the average daily turnover of RMB foreign exchange will be as high as 0.53 trillion, 1.94 trillion, and 7.01 trillion dollars, respectively. Such a high average daily RMB turnover will bring huge business opportunities to domestic and foreign financial institutions. As the domestic and foreign RMB and foreign exchange markets will maintain a coordinated and rapid growth in the future, even if the ratio of the overseas to domestic average RMB turnover in 2025, 2035, and 2045 is 2 times, 2.5 times, and 3 times higher than proportionally estimated, by 2025, 2035, and 2045. Both domestic and foreign financial institutions should prepare for the sustained and significant growth of the domestic foreign exchange market in the future.

15.6 Monitoring Cross-Border Capital Flows

Although an important condition of RMB internationalization is that RMB can be used freely, the capital account is closely related to free use. One more capital account is opened, and there is one more channel for cross-border capital flow. Therefore, effective monitoring and supervision of cross-border funds is a major challenge trend in RMB capital account convertibility. I have been paying attention to and researching this issue since my first book on RMB derivatives more than ten years ago. According to data released by the People's Bank of China, due to the US government stopping quantitative easing, China's foreign exchange reserves fell in 24 the 29 months from July 2014 to November 2016. From the third quarter of 2014 to the third quarter of 2016, in 9 quarters of the year, China's foreign exchange reserves declined in 8 quarters; it is particularly noteworthy that from the third quarter of 2014 to the first quarter of 2015, the decline in China's foreign exchange reserves accounted for 47.1% of the global total. In the second quarter of 2015, global foreign exchange reserves increased by 29 billion dollars, while China's foreign exchange reserves fell by 36.2 billion dollars. In the third and fourth quarters, China's foreign exchange reserves accounted for the global decline. The proportions were as high as 66.1% and 69.4%, respectively; in the first quarter of 2016, global foreign exchange reserves increased by USD 87.8 billion, while China's foreign exchange reserves fell by USD 117.78 billion; in the second half of 2016, China's foreign exchange reserves fell by USD 292.66 billion – 90.53% of the 323.28 billion global total. This data shows how the withdrawal of quantitative easing by the US government had a colossal impact on China's cross-border capital flows and foreign exchange reserves. Although since 2017, the direction of change in China's foreign exchange reserves has mostly been in line with total international foreign exchange reserves, and the proportion of China's changes in the world has also fallen to a more reasonable level of below 30%, the withdrawal of cross-border funds has become a serious problem. How to effectively manage and control cross-border capital flows while minimizing the negative impact of relevant measures on RMB internationalization has become a major task at present and for the foreseeable future.

The cross-border RMB settlement business pilot is an inevitable consequence of RMB internationalization as well as the area where the most progress has been made in more than six years. However, the gradual implementation of cross-border RMB settlements has indirectly opened up new channels for the inflow and outflow of international hot money. The fact that the average annual growth rate of China's trade surplus from 2004 to 2007 exceeded 100% has made more scholars and experts realize that, without policies promoting RMB cross-border settlement, funds flowing into China's open trade projects and China's domestic fixed asset investment level would not achieve such an increase in corresponding years (Li Dongping 2008). However, since the first quarter of 2009 and the second half of 2014, the capital account has turned to withdrawal, and China's economy has been affected to a certain extent. After the launch of RMB cross-border settlement and overseas direct investment business, new channels for cross-border capital flow have been added. Therefore, in the process of steadily advancing the RMB settlement business, it is necessary to continuously improve the RMB management system. Also, the establishment of a monitoring system and prevention mechanism for cross-border capital flows will be a several-year task. Even if the RMB capital account is fully opened in the next few years, the monitoring system for cross-border capital flows will be an indispensable permanent mechanism to ensure the smooth operation of China's economy.

15.7 IMF Monitoring of Cross-Border Capital Flows

15.7.1 Changes in the regulatory attitudes of international organizations

The traditional international financial theory believes that the control of cross-border capital flows will distort the efficiency of capital allocation on a global scale. Therefore, it should not only be encouraged, but also prohibited. However, many emerging economies suffered from the impact of the Asian financial crisis in the late 1990s, underlining how capital account liberalization has not provided economic and financial stability; it is also difficult to find a close relationship between capital account liberalization and economic growth in empirical research. Until recently, traditional financial theories still dominated the international financial supervision system. Any control measures of developing countries on capital flows (even very small ones) are often criticized as unnecessary and labeled as financial protectionism. The IMF is tasked with financial responsibility: before and after the outbreak of the Asian financial crisis, the prerequisite that the IMF often attaches to the rescue of various member states is to require the rescued countries to liberalize capital controls, promote the free flow of capital, and carry out system reforms to promote trade freedom. These practices have been widely criticized over the years. Despite this, the IMF's attitude and practices have not changed significantly: since the outbreak of the global financial crisis in 2008, the international community pointed out that the

IMF did not give any early warning of the outbreak, which raised many questions about its function. Therefore, the IMF has organized a series of related studies and has published related research results since the end of 2010, which support the later introduction of cross-border capital flow control practices. On April 5, 2011, the IMF officially announced the organization's change in attitude towards managing capital flows and put forward recommendations for the application of policy tools in different countries and regions. This will play a role in the stability of the international economy, trade, and finance.

15.7.2 Content and policy recommendations from the IMF

In 2011, the IMF studied the impact of cross-border capital flows in several major global emerging countries or regions on economic and financial markets of the past two decades (China wasn't included). The main ideas and policy recommendations were for management and control: inflow of cross-border funds will first promote investment and economic growth of the inflowing country or region, and then promote the growth of foreign exchange reserves, currency appreciation, and prices of the inflowing country. Simultaneously, the withdrawal of cross-border funds will stabilize the economy and financial system of the inflowing country. Bringing impacts of varying degrees, serious ones will have the consequences of crises.

The report "Managing Cross-Border Capital Flows-Which Tools to Use," published by the IMF, provides two types of policy measures, namely prudential supervision and capital control for controlling cross-border capital flows. The purpose of prudential supervision measures is to improve the ability of financial institutions to bear greater risks, or to set an upper limit for financial institutions to bear additional risks. Prudent supervision measures can be divided into foreign exchange-related and other measures; the former is mainly aimed at the domestic banking industry. Foreign exchange prudential supervision measures are mainly for treating different currencies differently, not to take measures in which country the parties involved are. A common practice is to impose limits on the proportion of a bank's foreign currency investment net positions in total capital. Others include restrictions on a bank's foreign currency loans. The main purpose of other prudential regulatory measures is to reduce systemic risks. These measures include controlling the loan growth rate of the domestic financial system, setting a ceiling on the loan/market value ratio, setting a ceiling on areas where the concentration of assets and industry loans is too high, and countercyclical capital requirements. The report also involves many other measures, which will not be introduced here. Interested readers can refer to Guangping (Peter G.) Zhang (2015).

15.7.3 The relationship between implementation measures and capital account convertibility

The IMF's guidelines on cross-border speculative capital management and control, announced on April 5, 2011, are the first such guidelines since World War II and are of epoch-making significance. For the first time, the need to manage and control cross-border speculative funds and propose management and control guidelines and specific policy recommendations laid out, marking the organization's acceptance of the prudent management and control of cross-border speculative funds. Since many detailed issues need to be further discussed, the implementation of the guidelines will take some time, and many issues will become clearer in the future.

15.7.4 Establishing an Early Warning and Monitoring System

Before the outbreak of the international financial crisis in May 2008, then-Vice Premier Wang Qishan clearly pointed out that we should "improve foreign exchange management methods, improve foreign exchange management laws and regulations, and strengthen the supervision of cross-border capital flows" (2008 Keynote speech at Lujiazui Forum). During the international financial crisis, the impact of capital outflows on China's economy demonstrated the importance of monitoring to maintain the steady development of the economy and financial system. "Preventing the occurrence of systemic regional financial risks" is an important task for China's financial industry, as proposed in the 13th Five-Year Plan. With the further advancement of the RMB cross-border business, China's cross-border fund monitoring will face more new tasks and requirements.

15.8 The Contribution of Technology and Currency in the Global Surplus IP Royalties

Import and export data for intellectual property royalties – including all major quantitative information on IP rights, patents, copyrights, and royalties – can be directly compared in currency. Therefore, IP royalty data is more comprehensive than international patents when analyzing science and technology autonomy. The previous chapter used the relevant data to define technological autonomy and optimized technological internationalization parameters based on the data. Technological autonomy and technological internationalization are good indicators to compare the technological levels of different countries, and technological autonomy is directly related to the surplus and deficit of IP royalties. Technological autonomy reflects the level of technological levels of different countries and regions. However, it fails to accurately reflect the contribution of different countries and regions to the net science and technology exports of IP royalties. Due to the importance of technology to the entire economy, its contribution to the net export value of IP royalties of major currency issuers will be analyzed.

15.8.1　Distribution of global IP royalties surplus

As introduced in the previous chapter, only ten countries in the world have technological autonomy of more than 50%. All other developed countries and all developing countries have a deficit or have a technological autonomy of less than 50%. The US IP royalties surplus has remained far greater than any other nation. Table 15-4 shows the distribution of IP royalty surpluses from 2007 to 2019.

Table 15-4　Comparing the Surplus Distribution of IP and Related Growth Rates (2007–2019)

Unit: USD million

Year	US	Japan	Germany	Switzerland	UK	Sweden	France	Denmark	Israel	Finland	Total
2007	598.8	65.5	−23.8	104.3	94.7	50.7	44.4	7.2	−0.1	−1.8	940.0
2008	619.1	73.9	−18.3	98.6	100.5	44.6	53.7	9.7	0.5	−5.9	976.4
2009	563.1	48.6	2.2	149.9	86.9	47.5	52.5	12.0	1.4	4.2	968.4
2010	638.5	79.1	11.5	167.5	96.8	57.9	36.1	7.0	−0.7	10.2	1,103.9
2011	741.4	98.2	33.3	206.7	110.9	66.4	48.3	10.7	3.2	17.2	1,336.1
2012	728.1	119.9	39.0	162.1	92.8	75.5	39.7	8.7	4.1	17.1	1,287.1
2013	785.3	137.6	164.6	117.6	98.8	78.3	21.0	5.7	9.8	16.2	1,434.8
2014	788.2	163.9	225.2	116.7	104.1	91.9	18.2	8.3	9.8	14.9	1,541.3
2015	759.7	194.4	171.8	121.2	129.4	88.5	6.9	2.8	10.6	16.2	1,501.6
2016	710.1	188.9	213.4	111.0	119.5	71.3	23.2	6.1	11.6	19.1	1,474.2
2017	737.4	203.4	213.8	102.7	120.4	75.2	16.2	23.9	12.8	23.1	1,528.9

(Continued)

Year	US	Japan	Germany	Switzerland	UK	Sweden	France	Denmark	Israel	Finland	Total
2018	749.4	237.9	210.2	98.4	126.3	70.3	4.5	34.0	16.1	26.7	1,503.0
2019	746.7	206.8	206.6	94.3	132.6	65.7	4.3	48.4	17.6	30.9	1,554.0

Data source: Belgium posted a deficit in IP royalties for 6 of the 11 years from 2007 to 2017, and the average annual surplus is less than 200 million dollars. Therefore, we did not include this country in the table.

Table 15-4 shows that the US is not only the country with the largest surplus in IP royalties, but also accounted for more than 70% of the global surplus in 2007 and 2008; from 2009 to 2013, the proportion dropped slightly, yet remained above 60%; from 2014 to 2017, the US IP royalties surplus continued to drop slightly, but still accounted for more than 56% of the total surplus; from 2014 to 2017, Germany, with an average annual surplus of royalties exceeding USD 20 billion, became the second largest exporter of IP rights after the US. From 2015 to 2017, Japan's royalty surplus was close to 20 billion, making it the third-largest exporter of IP rights in the world;

From 2007 to 2017, Switzerland's annual IP royalty surplus was USD 13.26 billion, exceeding the average annual level of Japan and Germany. However, in recent years, the annual average surplus of Swiss IP royalties was only about half of Germany and Japan. Therefore, Switzerland should be ranked as the fourth largest IP exporter globally; from 2007 to 2017, the UK had an annual surplus of more than USD 10 billion in IP royalties, which is slightly lower than Switzerland. In recent years, the UK's surplus has also been comparable to Switzerland. Therefore, the UK should rank fifth in the world; from 2007 to 2017, Sweden's annual average IP surplus was USD 6.80 billion, ranking sixth; from 2007 to 2009, the average annual IP surplus in France was equivalent to that of Sweden, but since 2010, there has been a clear downward trend. In 2017, the surplus of French IP royalties dropped below that of Denmark and Finland. However, since its average annual surplus from 2007 to 2017 was USD 3.27 billion, overall, it was significantly higher than Denmark and Finland. Thus, France should rank as the seventh largest IP exporter, with Denmark, Israel, and Finland ranked eighth to tenth intellectual, respectively.

Corresponding to the total surplus of the world's top ten IP royalties given in Table 15-4, which continued to exceed USD 120 billion, is the IP royalties deficit of all other developed economies and all other countries and regions. Statistics show that since 2013, the Eurozone and Mainland China have maintained a deficit of over USD 20 billion, ranking as the top two respectively, followed by India, Canada, Singapore, Australia, and Thailand – whose total deficits are from 5-8 billion. Table 15-1 shows that between 2020 and 2040, as China's technological autonomy continues to increase and eventually surpass 50% of relative autonomy for the first time, China will become a net exporter of IP royalties. This will help the nation to assume a leading position in global innovation.

15.8.2 The impact of quantitative easing on the surplus of IP royalties

Table 15-4 shows that in 2006–2008, 2008–2014, and 2014–2019, the compound annual growth rate of the US IP royalties surplus was 13.66%, 4.11%, and −1.08%, respectively, indicating that before the 2008 global financial crisis it increased rapidly, but the growth rate decreased significantly afterwards, and even decreased post-2014, when the US government reigned in its quantitative easing policy. US monetary policy clearly has a significant impact on the surplus of US IP royalties, or this surplus not only reflects IP itself, but is closely related to monetary policy or currency internationalization.

15.8.3 Unknown competition among major IP royalty surplus countries

A careful study of the data in Table 15-4 shows that from 2006 to 2008, the total net export surplus of the top ten nations increased by 12.42% annually, slightly lower than the 13.66% growth rate of the US over the same period. From 2008 to 2014, the total net exports of the top ten countries increased by 12.42%. The compound annual growth rate was as high as 7.91%, almost double the US growth rate of 4.11%. Moreover, the average annual growth rate of the total surplus from 2014 to 2019 was 0.16%, which is also significantly higher than its annual growth rate of −1.08%. In addition, as shown in Table 15-4 of the above three time periods, the average annual compound growth rates of the total surplus of the other top nine nations are 10.36%, 13.23%, and 1.40%, respectively. The average annual growth rates of the first two time periods were 0.76 times and 3.22 times that of the US over the same period. In the last period, it exceeded the US average annual growth rate by 2.48%.

These results show that while the 2008 global financial crisis had a significant impact on the US IP surplus, it also gave other countries outside the US a rare opportunity to increase their surpluses significantly. After the crisis, the combined IP surplus growth rate of the top nine nations (excluding the US) was significantly higher than the growth rate of the US. It also shows that the US, the global technology hegemon, has also faced this problem for more than a decade.

Due to the huge overall pressure of competition from other net exporters of IP, this competition has little to do with countries other than these nations. (All other developed countries and developing countries in Table 15-4 maintain deficits in intellectual property royalties.)

15.9 Conclusion

The results show that the US dollar contributes slightly more to the surplus of US intellectual property royalties than US science and technology. The technological contribution to the surplus still exceeds the total contribution of other major international currencies, such as the Euro, Japanese Yen, British Pound, and Swiss-Franc. Also, US technology has a monopolistic effect in the world. These results actually explain, to a certain extent, that during the US three consecutive interest rate cuts in 2019, the US dollar index not only did not decline, but rose slightly instead. At the same time, the outstanding balance of US government bonds increased by more than 4 trillion in 2020, while the US dollar index fell by only 1%. The resilience of the US dollar in the global market is largely due to US's control of the global economy and the entire financial market with the help of its technology.

The continuous improvement of RMB internationalization not only places higher requirements on the development of domestic and foreign RMB markets, but also on the depth and breadth of domestic and foreign capital markets. Its internationalization requires the marketization of RMB interest rates and exchange rates to gradually reach a higher degree. At the same time, in order to make the RMB more accepted globally, it also proposes higher requirements for the opening of the RMB capital account, and the further opening of the capital account links the domestic and foreign RMB market tightly. Further marketization of RMB interest and exchange rates helps to significantly release interest rate and exchange rate market risks. The demand for domestic and foreign RMB interest rate and exchange rate market risk management will also increase significantly, leading to a more active domestic and foreign market for RMB FX and interest rate derivatives.

In addition, the level of science and technology and the scale of economy and trade under its influence are indeed the main factors that determine the internationalization of currencies. However, historical experience shows that the internationalization of currencies is also determined by many other factors, such as inertia and currency convertibility. Examples like the US and Germany achieving economic dominance in scale (over Britain and France) yet not achieving the same currency dominance till much later showcase this long time lag. The final result depends on the speed at which China's technological autonomy continues to increase and progress in the deepening of reforms. I believe that with the continuous improvement of China's technological independence, national governance, and business environment, as well as the continuous reform of the financial market and science and technology, RMB internationalization will also continue to improve. The "One Belt One Road" construction and the construction of a community with a shared future for mankind will also have more solid support through currency internationalization.

Bibliography

Chan, Norman T. L. 2014. "Opening Remarks at the Second Hong Kong, China-Australia RMB Trade and Investment Dialogue," Hong Kong Monetary Authority, May 22.

Eichengreen, Barry. 2000. "From Benign Neglect to Malignant Preoccupation: US Balance of Payments Policy in the 1960s." In *Economic Events, Ideas and Policies: The 1960s and After*. Edited by George L. Perry and James Tobin. Washington, D.C.: The Brookings Institution, 185–242.

———. 2005. "Sterling's Past, Dollar's Future: Historical Perspectives on Reserve Currency Competition." *National Bureau of Economic Research*.

Federal Reserve Bank of New York. "The Foreign Exchange and Interest Rate Derivatives Markets: Turnover in the US," April 2001 to April 2013.

Inlah, Albert. 1958. *Economic Elements in the Pax Britannica*. Cambridge, Mass.: Harvard University Press.

Mussa, Michael. 2004. "Exchange Rate Adjustments Needed to Reduce Global Payments Imbalances," In *Dollar Adjustment: How Far? Against What?* Edited by C. Fred Bergsten and John Williamson. Washington, D.C.: Institute for International Economics, 113–138.

Perasud, Avinash. n.d. "When Currency Empires Fall." www.321gold.com/editorials.

Triffin, Robert. 1964. "The Evolution of the International Monetary System: Historical Reappraisal and Future Perspectives." *Princeton Studies in International Finance*, no. 12.

Williams, David. n.d. "The Evolution of the Sterling System." In *Essays in Money and Banking*. Edited by C. R. Whittlesey and J. S. G Wilson. Oxford: Oxford University Press, 266–297.

Xu, Jiangshan. 2011. "Looking at China's Interest Rate Marketization from Foreign Experience." *Futures Daily*, March 10.

Zhang, Guangping. 2019. *RMB Internationalization and Product Innovation*. 9th ed. Beijing: China Finance Press.

Zhang, Guangping, Ma Xiaojuan, et al., trans. 2014. *Exotic Options*. Beijing: Machinery Industry Press.

CHAPTER SIXTEEN

Future Studies

AFTER THIS BOOK MANUSCRIPT WAS HANDED over to the publisher over half a year ago, I thought of applying exchange options from my earlier book, *Exotic Options: A Guide to Second Generation Options* (first published in 1997), into the analysis of science & technology change. This idea has brought a series of new research papers with many new results relating to the major results of this book. However, as most of these research papers are highly mathematical, I felt it better not to include the details here. Yet, it is useful to introduce them briefly in the last chapter of this book.

16.1 Introduction to Exotic Options

Exotic options are a special type of options trade in the over-the-counter market (OTC) of major world financial centers over three decades ago. Guangping (Peter G.) Zhang (1997) introduced and priced over thirty types of OTC options. Of the many types of exotic options, correlation options are those with more than one underlying asset, and the underlying assets are correlated to each other. Correlation options have great potential to be used for analyzing sci-tech originality capability and comparative advantages of sci-tech from one economy to another.

16.2 Using Exotic Options to Study Science and Technology

Using the same assumptions and following the same methods used in Guangping (Peter G.) Zhang (1997), Guangping (Peter G.) Zhang (2021a) used IP export and imports of one economy as assets and found the impact of IP imports on IP exports, or the stimulus of imports on exports for IP use in major economies. Zhang (2021b) found comparative advantages of sci-tech or exports of charges for the use of IP of one economy over another.

These working papers contained evidence that some of the exotic option parameters, such as price sensitivities of exotic options, can reflect sci-tech progress better than sci-tech originality capability. We need to do more research using exotic options to find more sophisticated parameters for measuring science and technology.

16.3 Other Applications

The theoretical results of Zhang (2021a) can be extended to analyze the comparative values of the gross national product (GDP) of one economy compared to another. More importantly, GDP sensitivity of one economy with respect to GDP of another economy can be obtained accordingly. I also found similar results considering commodity trade, service trade, foreign exchange, international reserves, and market capitalization of various stock exchanges as assets. Essentially, we can use this new method to find relative values of one asset compared to another for most economic and financial variables, and the results using this method can be more accurate and intuitive than those obtained using traditional regressions.

Bibliography

Zhang, Guangping (Peter G.). 1998. *Exotic Options: Guide to Second-generation Options*. 2nd ed. World Scientific Publishing Co Pte Ltd.

———. 2001. "Science & Technology Originality Capability Implied in Prices of Exchange Options to Exchange Export and Import of Charges for the Use of Intellectual Properties for One Another." Unpublished Working paper.

———. 2001. "Comparative Advantages of Science & Technology of Major Exporters and Importers of Charges for the Use of IP." Unpublished working paper.

Zhang, Guangping (Peter G.), and Ken Lin. 2021. "Empirical Evidence of Impacts of Science & Technology on Gross Domestic Products and Their Major Components Including Total Factor Productivity." Unpublished working paper.

Dr. Guangping (Peter G.) Zhang obtained his BS and MS in Computer Science in Mainland China before he was sent to study in the US in 1987. He has served as Manager, Senior Associate, or Vice-President in various financial institutions, including MMS International (Standard & Poor's Group), the Union Bank of Switzerland (New York Branch), and the Chemical Bank (head office) in New York City. After working for the Chase Manhattan Bank (Tokyo Branch) as a Vice-President for about three years, he broadened his expertise in financial law at Harvard Law School. He joined Shanghai Futures Exchange in 2003 as Chief Financial Engineering Advisor and Senior Director of the Research & Development Center of the Exchange. He joined the newly established Supervisory Cooperation Department for Banking Innovation of China Banking Regulatory Commission (CBRC) in November 2005 as Deputy Director General. He was re-allocated to CBRC Shanghai Bureau as Deputy Director General in October 2007. As an experienced financial expert, he published many articles and books in English and Chinese. His representative books include *Exotic Options: A Guide to Second-Generation Options* (Second Edition, 1998), *Chinese Yuan (RMB) Derivative Products* (English Edition, 2004), and *Chinese Yuan Internationalization and Product Innovation* (First Edition in 2010 and 10th Edition in 2021). He has completed a series of research papers on the impacts of science and technology on international trade, foreign exchange trading, and currency internationalization based on quantitative measures of science and technology originality capability and science and technology internationalization in the past two years.

ABOUT THE TRANSLATOR

Mr. Chen Wei graduated from UIBE with a master's degree in law. He now works at Fangda Partners and once served in the PBOC Head Office. His research interests lie primarily in asset management and FinTech. He has published many articles in CSSCI journals, *Financial News*, *China Banking and Insurance News*, and other national academic journals.